The Media and Political Process

This book is due for retu

The Media and Political Process

The Media and Political Process

P. Eric Louw

⑤ SAGE Publications
London ● Thousand Oaks ● New Delhi

First published 2005

SAGE Publications Ltd
1 Oliver's Yard
55 City Road
London EC1Y 1SP

SAGE Publications Inc.
2455 Teller Road
Thousand Oaks, California 91320

SAGE Publications India Pvt Ltd
B-42, Panchsheel Enclave
Post Box 4109
New Delhi 110 017

British Library Cataloguing in Publication data

A catalogue record for this book is available
from the British Library

ISBN 0-7619-4083-9
ISBN 0-7619-4084-7 (pbk)

Library of Congress Control Number available

Typeset by C&M Digitals (P) Ltd., Chennai, India
Printed in Great Britain by Athenaeum Press, Gateshead

Contents

vi Contents

List of abbreviations

ANC – African National Congress (South Africa)
BBC – British Broadcasting Corporation
CNN – Cable News Network (USA)
Coin-ops – Counter Insurgency Operations
EU – European Union
FARC – Revolutionary Armed Force of Columbia
FLN – National Liberation Front (Algeria)
FRELIMO – Front for the Liberation of Mozambique
FRETELIN – Revolutionary Front for an Independent East Timor
GATT – General Agreement on Tariffs and Trade
IMF – International Monetary Fund
IRA – Irish Republican Army
IT – Information Technology
ITN – Independent Television News (UK)
MPLA – Popular Movement for the Liberation of Angola
NATO – North Atlantic Treaty Organization
NGO – Non Governmental Organization
NWO – New World Order
OECD – Organization for Economic Cooperation and Development
PACs- Political Action Committees (USA)
PLO – Palestine Liberation Organization
PR – Public Relations
PRC – People's Republic of China
Psy-ops – Psychological Operations
SA – South Africa
SABC – South African Broadcasting Corporation
SWAPO – South West African People's Organization (Namibia)
UN – United Nations
UNITA – United National Army for the Total Independence of Angola
USA – United States of America
USSR – Union of Soviet Socialist Republics
UK – United Kingdom
WHAM – Win Hearts and Minds
WTO – World Trade Organization
ZANU-PF – Zimbabwe African National Union – Patriotic Front
ZAPU – Zimbabwe African People's Union

1 Introduction

A core question for anyone interested in political studies, media studies or journalism studies is: 'what is the relationship between the media and politics in contemporary Western democracies?' Attempts to answer this question have given rise to the expanding field of Political Communication. This book aims to introduce students to some core themes and questions in Political Communication. Doing so will involve examining the following:

- The argument that there has been a substantial media-ization of Western politics;
- The growth of spin-doctors and public relations-ized politics;
- The relationship between media-coverage and policy making;
- The evolution of political journalism;
- The way politicians have learned to use different media forms;
- How television has changed the nature of politics.

The Media and Political Process aims to introduce undergraduates to a range of themes associated with the notion that since the arrival of mass communication, a particular kind of *image making* has grown into a central feature of the political processes of Western democracies. The book will argue that a core feature of mass democratic politics is *'hype* making'. Just as magicians use smoke-and-mirrors to distract their audiences and conjure up illusions, so too does the political machine and its media staffers. In today's Western democracies, television is the primary (but not exclusive) vehicle for this smoke-and-mirrors show. This show involves four sets of players: politicians-as-performers; the **spin industry**; media workers (journalists, presenters/hosts and researchers); and their audiences. A fifth set of players are policy makers – but they tend to remain back stage; shielded from as much scrutiny as possible by the smoke-and-mirrors show. A core aim of this book is to unravel the *symbiotic relationships* between journalists, spin-doctors and politicians within contemporary *televisualized politics*.

The book will argue that **demagoguery** has become a core feature of twentieth-century Western politics, with politics now characterized by a range of demagogic arts geared to *steering mass public opinion*. These demagogic arts will be described and analyzed.

The book is also about describing how contemporary mass audiences increasingly experience 'steered' politics as a set of *secondhand media images*, projected into their lives by the media, especially television. Nimmo and Combs (1990: 18) liken this contemporary secondhand experience of **media-ized** politics to Plato's prisoners in a cave (see Box 1.1).

Box 1.1 Plato's prisoners in a cave

In his *Republic*, Plato relates the tale of prisoners in an underground den, bound so they cannot turn their heads. They can see nothing that goes on around them, only the shadows of those things that the fire throws on the cave wall. When they converse, they give names to and talk about the shadows of things, thinking they are naming the real things and not shadows. Suddenly one prisoner is released. The objects that produced the shadows are passed before his eyes. He is perplexed. He thinks the shadows he formerly saw are truer than the objects shown to him. Compelled to look at the piercing light of the fire, he turns away from the objects to the images on the wall. The shadows are clearer than the objects, again more real. Finally, hauled out to the sunlight, slowly the prisoner adjusts to seeing the objects for what they are. Yet pushed back into the cave, blinded by the sudden darkness, he sees even less than his fellow prisoners who were not released. The prisoners conclude it is better not to ascend to the light and vow to kill anyone forcing them to do so.

In this regard, the book is about exploring the following questions, namely – is the televisualization of politics transforming politics into a set of dancing 'shadows' which flicker through our lives, and which possibly hide more than they reveal? Have we perhaps become prisoners of an electronic cave? Are the secondhand televisualized images of politics we now receive:

- An accurate 'reflection of reality' (a mirror)?
- A blurred and skewed reflection (Plato's shadows)?
- The result of demagoguery which carefully crafts the images we get to see?

- The result of a complex media-ized 'construction process' involving journalists, spin-doctors, politicians, public opinion pollsters and audiences.

1.1 The media as 'a mirror'

In liberal democracies mainstream journalists are trained to be 'objective'. Objective journalism is solidly grounded in an empiricist understanding of the world (see Box 1.2), i.e. journalists have been taught to believe that:

- News exists 'out there' in the 'real world';
- This news exists *independently* of media organizations and journalists;
- The journalist's job is to *find* this news;
- Having found the news the journalist must record it *objectively* – i.e. ensure there is *correspondence* between what is described in the story and the world 'out there';
- Journalists are expected to eliminate their own *subjectivity* by applying routinized journalistic formulas (see chapter 4).

Box 1.2 Empiricist understanding of the world

(This worldview also underpins 'objective journalism')

- A real objective world exists 'out there' *independent* of thinking subjects;
- Humans get access to this real world through their *senses*. Senses connect the 'inner world (of thinking) to the 'outer world' of empirical reality;
- Knowledge of the world is achieved by carefully *recording* empirical regularities;
- *Subjectivism* must be *eliminated* from knowledge. This is achieved by building in 'controls';
- 'Good' empirical knowledge results from ensuring there is *correspondence* between what is described and the world 'out there'. This correspondence must be verifiable.

This mainstream model of liberal journalism believes that its practices result in stories that are an accurate reflection of reality – i.e. journalists believe they simply hold a mirror up to society, and describe it 'the way it is'. This notion of 'journalism as a mirror' has been disputed by **constructivists** (see Box 1.3) who have analyzed the media, e.g. Tuchman (1978). Tuchman argued that journalists actually *construct the news*, rather than reflect the news (see 4.3 on p. 72). This constructivist view of journalism will strongly inform the arguments developed in this book (see 1.4 on p. 7).

Box 1.3 Constructivist understanding of the world

- Humans cannot passively receive inputs from the world 'out there' in the way cameras record images, because all incoming sense-data is processed by humans as thinking beings;
- All observation of the world is *subjectively guided.* Existing ideas (e.g. theory) knowledge, and experience (coded in our language-systems) structure the way we receive and interpret incoming data-inputs;
- *Paradigms* already in our head guide how we look at the world (e.g. the questions we ask and what we focus our senses upon) and how we process and interpret incoming sensory inputs. Hence people using different paradigms are effectively living in different worlds;
- Knowledge is the result of an *internal* (subjective) cognitive process – i.e. what we choose to think about; and how we choose to think about it (i.e. knowledge is guided by theories, ideas and experience already in our heads);
- So knowledge comes from where we choose to point the camera rather than a mechanical process of recording and it is our existing thoughts that guide what we choose to focus on. A significant determinant of our 'existing thinking' is how we have been socialized, and what we have already been exposed to via education and previously received media images.

However, the mainstream model of liberal journalism does acknowledge that an accurate portrayal of 'reality' (a mirror) is not always achieved. Although journalists strive to create an accurate *correspondence* between what is described in their story and the world 'out there', they do not always succeed. When it comes to political reporting this is blamed on the work of **spin-doctors** – i.e. demagogues who work to prevent journalists from finding all the 'facts'. Spin-doctors have become a convenient scapegoat. They are viewed as practitioners of the **dark arts** who work to obstruct objective journalists doing their job. And there is some validity in this portrayal. However, this portrayal is only half the story. The other half of the story is the role journalists themselves play in *constructing* a view of the world more akin to the shadows in Plato's cave than a mirror.

This book will argue that political reporting has indeed been PR-ized – i.e. spin-doctors have learned to 'steer' the portrayal of news. However, PR-ization involves a symbiotic relationship between a range of people including spin-doctors, public opinion pollsters, politicians *and journalists*. The practices of objective journalism are implicated in the process of obscuration because spin-doctors have learned to use the practices of mainstream liberal-journalism to help them *construct* the view of the world they are trying to portray. The shadows in Plato's cave are constructed – and it is spin-doctors and journalists working symbiotically who construct them.

Journalists have every right to criticize the way spin-doctors try to alter the shadows projected onto the cave wall. Journalists are correct to be skeptical. The problem is that journalists are not skeptical enough – they only focus their skepticism on others, never on themselves. This book will suggest that skepticism needs to be focused on journalistic practices themselves, and journalists need to focus more on their own roles in constructing images that are so often obscurations.

1.2 Being skeptical

This book will deliberately examine the processes of political communication with a skeptical and jaundiced eye. Its focus will be liberal democracies and the media practices associated with liberal democratic political systems. This focus should not be taken to mean that liberal democracy is viewed as a form of governance especially deserving of criticism. *The Media and Political Process'* critical approach can just as easily be applied to other forms of governance. Liberal democracy has simply been focused on because it has arguably become the most important form of contemporary governance. (For anyone interested in reading a deconstruction of Soviet-communist governance from a critical and skeptical perspective paralleling in many ways this author's approach, see Bahro (1981).

The Media and Political Process proposes we increasingly inhabit a world of secondhand televisual images that increasingly naturalize 'the way things are' Skepticism demands that we pay serious attention to *how televisual images are constructed* so that we 'de-naturalize' them. In this regard, it is important to constantly ask ourselves what the cameras are pointed at;

what they are not pointed at; and why? In essence, this book can be seen as an attempt to point the cameras in new directions. As Kuhn (1970) has noted, asking different questions produces different knowledge (see 1.4 on p. 7). In the same way, shifting the camera angle changes the view of the world we are presented with. This book is deliberately geared to provoking critical thinking about televisualized politics in liberal democracies. Consequently, the book will be deliberately provocative as a way of metaphorically shifting camera angles that we increasingly take for granted. In adopting a critical approach, this book is not attempting to construct 'a truth'; rather it is attempting to provoke discussion through a series of expositions grounded in *critical theory* and *constructivist* thinking. The book hopes to create skeptical readers of the media by revealing something of the symbiosis that has grown up between spin-doctors, journalists and politicians. In this regard, it was noted earlier that journalism is a skeptical profession. But it was suggested that journalists are not skeptical enough, because they focus their skepticism on others, but never on themselves. With this in mind, it is hoped that readers of this book not only will develop skepticism of media-ized politics, but also will be skeptical of this book itself. It too has been *constructed*.

1.3 Towards a critical constructivist approach to political communication

Plato's shadows in a cave are helpful when thinking about political communication. However, in our contemporary era we need to revise the picture of the cave. Today it is not shadows that are the problem. Instead, there is a television screen attached to the back wall of the cave that receives highly constructed and mediated images of the world beamed in from outside. The pictures are not fuzzy and shadowy; indeed they are crisp and clear and colorful. But that does not necessarily make them accurate reflections of any 'reality' outside the cave. They are just as problematic as the shadowy images in Plato's cave; perhaps more problematic because they now look so 'real'.

This book will propose that we should be highly skeptical about televised pictures, and skeptical about the people and organizations that make them. We must ask critical questions like:

- Who constructs these televised images?
- What are the interests, biases, worldviews and agendas of those who make these images?
- Do the work practices of all those involved in making these images in any way skew the pictures we receive? If so, how?

In essence, we must not accept these televisual representations at face value. Rather we must be clear about how and why they were made, and how they almost certainly portray a partial and skewed view of the world. Instead of uncritically looking at the picture on the screen, we should be thinking about the camera, the cameraman, the cameraman's boss, the journalist's bias, the journalist's boss, and the spin-doctors who seek to influence all of this. We must start to critically think about what the camera is pointed at. Why has it been pointed at this? What is behind the camera that we are not getting to see? What is being edited out? By whom? And how does the journalist's or continuity announcer's voice-over change how we see the pictures? To what extent, and under what circumstance, do spin-doctors successfully 'steer' people? Why do so many people fall for the 'hype' and scripted 'faces' of manufactured celebrity?

What is being proposed is the deployment of a particular methodological approach, namely constructivism. With this in mind, we'll now take a brief digression to examine the constructivist approach.

1.4 The constructivist approach

Although constructivism is a theory of knowledge, it is especially well suited to understanding the processes of media-ized communication. Constructivism is a way of seeing and understanding the world based on the premise that as human beings we experience the world mentally – i.e. we relate to the world *through our minds*. Hence 'knowing' becomes an 'internal' (cognitive) process. For constructivists, it is our minds that structure the world for us by *actively engaging* in a process of '*construction*'. This stands in contradistinction to **empiricism** because empiricists argue that we know the world because our senses give us 'access' to the world 'out there'. For empiricists, we simply come to understand what is 'out there' by examining and studying it – hence, objectivists/empiricists seek to construct knowledge as corresponding to, or reflecting, reality (as in a mirror) (see Box 1.2). Constructivists, however, argue that we do not (and cannot) simply passively receive information from the world 'out there'. Instead, our knowledge of the world is actively built up (constructed) by a thinking subject (inside of our heads). This means our knowledge of the world is effectively *separated* from the world 'out there' – because it is based on an 'internal world' that is part of how the knower *experiences* his/her environment. Hence the human knowledge of the world is inherently 'subjective', not 'objective' – i.e. we arrive at our understanding of the world by *interpreting* the world (see Box 1.3). Von Glaserfeld (1995) has gone as far as to propose that each human being constructs his/her knowledge of the world based upon his/her own selfish need to 'control' perception so as to make it conform to his/her own needs and end goals.

Constructivism can be traced back to two core thinkers – Thomas Kuhn and Lev Vygotsky. Kuhn (1970) saw knowledge as growing out of 'language communities' – i.e. *paradigms* (ways of seeing/knowing the world) arose from the questions that were routinely asked about the world. Because, for Kuhn, knowledge was the result of the questions one asked, if one changed the questions the knowledge base necessarily shifted. Hence knowledge/understanding was effectively constructed by a language community (framed by what questions it was deemed acceptable to ask, and the rules that guided how questions could be answered). Similarly, Vygotsky (1978) saw our minds as developing through language acquisition, which structured our access to the world. During the 1970s and 1980s, this constructivist thinking merged into cultural studies (which blended semiological analysis, neo-Marxist conceptions of ideology and structuralist anthropology) to produce a 'linguistic turn' in the humanities and social sciences. From this grew the post-structural turn, which views human knowledge as an ever-shifting series of contextually bound mental constructions (i.e. interpretations of the environment), rather than as any reflection of an external 'real' and 'knowable' world.

One danger inherent in constructivist thinking is that it can lapse into pure relativism. To correct for this, it is necessary that each paradigm develops a coherent set of criteria in terms of which it can 'justify' the world-view it constructs. Each paradigm needs to be able to justify its approach. This necessitates developing a self-reflexivity, an internal coherence, plus a consensus about the linguistic rules that apply within that paradigm. This provides some basis for selecting between different worldviews-as-constructions, i.e. not all constructions are equally good – some have more coherence and explanatory value than others.

1.5 A brief outline of the book

The Media and Political Process is divided into three parts. *Part 1* is an introduction to the (ever-evolving) role played by *the media* within liberal democracies. Specifically, this section will focus on how politics has been *media-ized* and *public relations-ized*, and how the appearance and performance of politicians has become scripted to fit the televisualization of Western politics during the second half of the twentieth century. Effectively Part 1 is concerned with examining the extent to which politics has become a *media construct*. The role of journalists within this media-ization of politics will be specifically examined. *Part 2* focuses on how political identities are *communicatively constructed* and how 'political identity' functions as a kind of 'conceptual glue' to hold political systems together. The book examines the importance of this 'glue' and how this is 'produced'. *Part 3* looks at different parts of the political system with a view to examining the extent to which various elements of the political process have been media-ized, plus the role of various media-players (spin-doctors, journalists and politicians) within this media-ized political process. A number of themes are discussed – the nature of spin-doctoring; the way in which political-celebrities are constructed; how political belief-systems are sold to voters; how war is sold to voters; how terrorists use the media; and how the media impacts on the making and execution of foreign policy.

PART 1 ● ● ●

An Introduction to Political Processes and the Mass Media

Part 1 of this book is an introduction to the role played by the media within liberal democracies. Just as the political processes of liberal democracy have mutated, so too has the relationship between politicians and the media. Chapter 2 examines how politics has been media-ized as professional communicators have come to script the performances and appearance of politicians. It will be argued that the televisualization of Western politics has significantly altered:

- The political process;
- The nature of being a politician; and
- The way journalists now relate to the political process.

Chapter 3 will examine the evolution of liberal democracy and argue that political public relations and spin-doctoring have emerged as a direct response to the mass enfranchisement of citizens. Chapter 4 will examine the role of the **mass media** and journalists within liberal democratic systems and explore some implications of a growing symbiotic relationship between journalists, politicians and spin-doctors.

2 Politics: Image Versus Substance

Chapter 2 introduces some core *themes* and *concepts* upon which this book's approach to political communication will be built. It will argue that the political processes of contemporary liberal democracies have been substantively media-ized, i.e. a significant amount of the time and energy of politicians and their professional support-staff is now focused on *impression management* and *media relations*. Further, it will be argued that the political machinery of liberal democracies consists of two functions, namely a *policy-making* dimension and a 'hype' dimension.

The *'hype'* dimension will be the core focus of this book. Chapter 2 begins by examining some definitions of politics and liberal democracy; the players in the political process; and the notion of 'hype'. Thereafter, the relationships between the *policy-making* dimension and *'hype'* dimension will be spelled out. Finally, the way the game of political impression management and media-ized politics is played will be discussed.

Politics is a phenomenon intimately bound up with the process of communicating because being a politician is an intensely social (communicative) occupation, engaged in by those who organize and regulate social power-relationships and make decisions governing the allocation and distribution of scarce social resources. Carrying out these roles necessarily involves communicating (about choices). This communication may involve direct face-to-face discussions, or it may be mediated through intermediaries like emissaries, soldiers or journalists. Political communication is a multi-dimensional multi-form phenomenon, e.g. speech, body-language, memoranda, media releases and political violence. The spectrum of communicative possibilities is endless – including one-on-one deal making with colleagues/allies; negotiating with opponents; making promises to win support; making threats (often only implicit) that rule breaking will incur sanctions (e.g. imprisonment); and threatening, or unleashing, coercion and violence. To be successful, politicians must master this repertoire of communicative possibilities and learn to deploy the communicative form appropriate to the challenge being faced.

Politics may always have been a communicative art. The question is – did twentieth-century mass communication alter the nature of political communication?

2.1 What is politics?

Resource scarcity has always characterized human existence, with no society (to date) able to satisfy the demands of all its members. This necessitates resource-allocation decision making – i.e. deciding who gets what; how resources and people are organized; and who is licensed to take these decisions. Because such decisions produce winners and losers, mechanisms are also required to persuade people to accept the decisions (and the decision-making process itself), and/or enforce the decisions (on the losers). Further, since decisions affect people's life-chances (by impacting on who emerge as winners and losers), struggles ensue over who occupies key decision-making positions. Struggle also emerges over the values underpinning the organization-and-allocation of resources. So at its most elemental, politics is:

- A decision-making process;
- A struggle over gaining access to the decision-making positions;
- The processes of legitimating and/or enforcing decisions.

Legitimation is the dimension of the process most obviously involving the media. However, in contemporary liberal democracies, the media's impact on political processes has become much wider than simply a legitimation mechanism.

Considering the above processes of decision making, resource allocation, enforcement and legitimation has led to the building of five theories of 'what constitutes politics'. Each emphasizes a particular aspect of the overall process. Each has value.

Pluralist theory is probably the most important of the five because it has become so hegemonic and 'commonsensical' in **Anglo** political thinking that pluralism's core ideals are now simply assumed to underpin the very nature of liberal democratic governance. An influential pluralist theorist is Dahl (1967). Pluralists argue that power and influence are dispersed among a wide array of society's interest groups. These interest groups (as well as individuals) all actively promote their own interests. The sum total of this pressure group activity drives democratic political systems, and prevents one group from becoming a dominant ruling **elite**. Pluralism incorporates two assumptions:

- That an active citizenry exists, with all interest groups being equally active in promoting their positions. In reality this does not occur. Bennett and Manheim (2001) have suggested that the 'death' of this aspect of pluralism is a recent phenomenon – a 'death' brought about by the growth of 'strategic political communication campaigns' geared to manipulation. They suggest that strategic communication has produced a shift from pluralism to neopluralism (2001: 284). It is a moot point whether this is a recent phenomenon or not;
- That a wide array of pressure groups competes. In competition they cancel 'each other out', so no one group can become dominant. However, situations exist where demographics favour one group, leading to, for example, one-party dominant democracies (Giliomee and Simkins, 1999).

A second understanding of governance is *public choice theory*, advocated by Downs (1957). This is closely related to pluralism. Downs argues that the two primary drivers of the political process are the desire of politicians to stay in power and the self-interest of voters. This compels politicians to try and maximize 'good publicity' (push 'popular' themes) and minimize 'bad publicity' (hide or disguise 'unpopular' themes).

A third approach is elite *theory*. A well-known advocate of this was Mills (1959), who argued (in contradistinction to pluralist theorists) that the USA's political system was run by a minority of the population who functioned as a ruling elite. Theorists like Pareto (1968) and Mosca (1939), have gone as far as to suggest that the division of society into dominant elites and subordinate masses is a universal and unalterable fact of human organization. Others have argued that elites arise contextually. Dahl, for example, has suggested that a recent contextual 'obstacle' to pluralist democracy is the emergence of the 'control of information' by policy elites in contemporary Western societies (Entman and Bennett, 2001: 468–9).

A fourth approach is the *class conflict model*, advocated by Marxists like Lenin (1969). Marxists argue that conflict between capitalists and the working class is inevitable. Capitalists (the 'bourgeoisie') use 'the state' to advance their interests, repress working-class interests, and promote ideologies serving to 'disguise' class domination. The working classes engage in a struggle to end class domination and capture the state. A more recent theory of social conflict, with some parallels to the Marxist approach, has been developed by feminists arguing that males use the political system to advance their gender interests and repress women.

Women engage in a gender struggle to overthrow the dominance of male patriarchy.

A fifth theory is the *state-centered approach* to governance developed by Nordlinger (1981). For Nordlinger, 'the state' is as much a political actor as any other interest group within the (pluralist) political process. Hence the state-as-actor (and bureaucrats, as state functionaries) will significantly impact on policy formulation.

Each of the above has explanatory power, but none individually provides a comprehensive understanding of the political process. Liberal-pluralists, public choice and state-centered theorists have focused on decision making and legitimation but have been less inclined to consider struggle and enforcement issues. Struggle and enforcement have dominated the class conflict approach. A comprehensive understanding of politics requires attention be paid to decision making, struggle, legitimation and enforcement.

Humans have, over time, devised a range of different mechanisms for staffing and organizing political decision making, enforcement and legitimation. This resulted in a diversity of political systems including tribal governance, monarchies, aristocracies, oligarchies, dictatorships and democracies. This book will focus on the Western liberal democratic forms, especially the varieties that evolved in the Anglo world.

2.1.1 Liberal democracy

Liberal democracy is not a neat or static model of governance; rather it is an ever-evolving set of practices and processes. At heart, the process involves a rule-governed competition over gaining access to power, holding on to it and using it to achieve social outcomes. Power is sought because power holders can ensure (through policy formulation) that resource distribution occurs in accordance with their interests and those of their supporters. Within liberal democracies one gains access to power by winning elections. This requires politicians persuading large numbers of people to vote for them, which means engaging in a game of impression management. For many decades this has involved impression management via the mass media – politicians and the political organizations underwriting them have to grab the attention of potential voters (in an increasingly cluttered media environment); hold their attention; and deliver effective messages in ever-shrinking time-frames (now often limited to five-second sound bites). This dimension of politics is concerned with image making, **myth** making and **hype**, directed at a mass audience who are frequently only marginally interested in politics and often, passive citizens. If the active political players are successful at impression management and hype, they can cajole sufficient numbers of their passive mass-citizenry to vote for them and thereby gain access to the sites where substantive politics happens – i.e. policy-making sites and the levers of power for executing policy.

So, successful politicians must learn to work simultaneously within two parallel political environments (each governed by their own practices and **discourses**) – one involves hype making, imagery and mythology; the other involves substantive policy making. But because these two political 'worlds' (of policy and hype) have to be coordinated, politicians must also learn to work within a third dimension of the political process, namely a 'meta-world' where the political game itself is planned and managed (see Table 2.1, p. 21).

2.1.2 Insiders, semi-insiders and outsiders

People can relate to the liberal democratic process in three ways – as insiders, semi-insiders or outsiders. The distinction is crucial for understanding the relationship between political processes and the media.

- *Insiders* are politically active, privy to policy debates, and engaged in both the 'policy' and 'hype' dimensions of the political game. Political insiders are always a small minority of the population. They play both 'elite politics' (i.e. strategizing, planning and policy, and organizing power) and 'mass politics' (i.e. impression management). However, because liberal democracy promotes the belief that mass citizens (voters) control the political system, the 'insider' elites must constantly deflect attention away from the existence of a two-tiered system of insiders (the ruling elite) and outsiders (the ruled). The existence of insiders is not equivalent to a conspiracy, because, firstly, intense competition for limited numbers of insider positions militates against conspiracy. Secondly, the political game has become a large industry, and the sheer size militates against conspiracy, Becoming an insider does not require 'conspiring', it requires choosing to become politically active, and then mastering the rules of the game (e.g. learning the practices and discourses of insider-engagement, and how to 'manage' outsiders and semi-insiders). Thirdly, the policy elite is divided into factions who, though they collaborate on some issues, are in competition with each other on other issues;
- *Semi-insiders* are aware of 'the game' political elites play, and aware of policy issues on the agenda, but are not privy to insider discussions of policy or strategy. Semi-insiders are involved in 'mass politics' as *informed* spectators of the game. Political insiders include parliamentarians,

policy-staffers, senior bureaucrats, senior intelligence advisors, senior members of the judiciary, political party insiders, spin-doctors and insider-intellectuals (advisors). Semi-insiders include (some) journalists, public opinion pollsters, political party 'outsiders' (rank-and-file party members), and analysts and **pundits** (intellectuals);

- *Political outsiders* are the citizens/electorate who are passive consumers of the myths, hype and images disseminated by the mass media. They consume what semi-insiders (such as journalists) and insiders (such as spin-doctors) construct and disseminate to them. The majority of citizens appear content to be passive outsiders – their participation in the political process being limited to voting occasionally for those candidates pre-selected and pre-packaged by political parties. (Many are choosing to not even engage in such limited 'participation' as ever-growing numbers are opting not to vote.) A minority of citizens and organized interest groups who become politically active may become semi-insiders due to their engagement with the political process. And, in some contexts, organized interest groups may become semi-insiders or even (temporary) insiders – for example, Trade Union leaders may become insiders when labor parties are in power. Interest groups trying to influence the policy process will often employ lobbyists because they know how to access insiders.

Ultimately, liberal democracy involves interplay between:

- A political elite of (active) 'insiders' who divide their time between politically 'substantive' work (e.g. policy formulation, and service and infrastructure delivery) and political 'hype' (e.g. impression management);
- Politically active 'semi-insiders' acting as 'stage-hands' or as a communicative bridge between the elite and masses;
- A (passive) mass of 'outsiders' who consume the work of insiders and semi-insiders.

Hence, liberal democracy requires considerable energy be expended in perception management geared towards the 'outsider' masses. So expertise in the use of mass communication (and hype) has become a key function of political management. In fact, a precondition for gaining (and retaining) access to the sites of 'substantive' politics is mastery of the arts of manufacturing-and-delivering successful 'hype'.

2.1.3 Hype

Hype is a colloquialism widely used within the media industry. 'Hype' involves stimulating an atmosphere of excitement or enthusiasm. This activity is carried out by politicians (trying to whip-up support for themselves); sports coaches (trying to activate teams); choreographers of mass-entertainment (scripting mass sports events, pop concerts and so on); and publicists/advertisers (trying to make some product fashionable/ popular). Hype has come to encode the notion that hype makers are aware they are creating publicity that is somehow 'false', a 'bluff', or a 'con-job'. Hence, professional hype makers (e.g. spin-doctors) are regarded as 'confidence tricksters' engaged in deliberately deceiving audiences to advantage themselves or their employers. The end result is seen as some sort of 'false' belief. In politics, such 'false belief' might be myth and **ideology**; celebrity (a manufactured 'face'); or it could be simply 'fluff' and distraction (aimed at setting the agendas of journalists and the public). The **Frankfurt School** (Adorno and Horkheimer, 1979) suggests that the **culture industry** professionalizes and industrializes hype making, and that manufactured hype is a core feature of commercial mass media production.

2.2 Politics: hype and substance

Gaining and retaining political power involves engaging in the complex business of **hegemony** building. Gramsci (1971) proposes that hegemony building involves three tasks:

- Building consent and **legitimacy** for society's dominant group/s, and building support for the interests and goals of the dominant. Getting the masses to accept as 'natural' the leadership, moral codes, practices and discourses of the dominant group/s. This legitimacy-making work is at its most obvious in the media and education systems;
- Organizing alliances and compromises between society's interest groups. This work is most visible within parliaments, where bargains are struck, deals are done and compromises identified;
- The deployment of coercion. For Gramsci, violence underpins all hege-monies. It may not be necessary to use violence against most citizens, but the threat of coercion is necessarily omnipresent – e.g. law enforce-ment (by the police and judicial system). Understanding the conse-quences of breaking the law is enough to deter most citizens from doing so. A successful hegemony also legitimates its deterrent 'forces' (police, courts and prisons).

Gramsci's notion of hegemony is useful for understanding governance but does not go far enough. Although Gramsci addresses the mix of hype and coercion, he fails to address the issue of 'substantive' delivery. Politicians would be unlikely to retain power if they relied exclusively on hype and/or violence – i.e. they must also deliver services and infrastructure; law and order (a 'safe' environment); social organization (facilitating economic activity); and defence from external threats. Successful 'substantive delivery' necessarily boosts legitimacy. So Gramsci's hegemony-building model needs modification to include four inter-related components: legitimacy-and-hype; politicking deals-and-alliances; substantive delivery; and coercion.

Hype and legitimacy are the central concerns of this book, but these are not seen as more important than other components. Instead, the work of impression management, plus building consent, legitimacy, beliefs and identities, and (when necessary) 'distraction', is necessarily enmeshed within the wider political game of policy work and managing the political process itself. The inter-relationship between all these dimensions of the political process can be shown diagrammatically (see Table 2.1). Actions taken in the 'hype-zone' (column 3) necessarily impact upon both policy and management decisions in columns 1 and 2. By the same token, front-stage performances within the hype-zone are related to back stage performances within the management-arena, as well as related to front and back stage performances in the policy-arena.

Table 2.1 encodes four proposals about the nature of the political process. Each has implications for how we understand the relationship between the mass media and politics.

2.2.1 Two outputs of the political process

Proposal one   The political process is geared towards two core outputs – policy and impression management. Policy work is deemed to be the political process' 'substantive' dimension, wherein interests are aggregated and deals struck, and decisions (and laws) made concerning resource allocation, service and infrastructure delivery, and war and peace (Dye, 1998). The substantive dimension also involves executing decisions (e.g. resource allocation, service delivery, and enforcing and adjudicating laws). Although some policy formulation is performed off-stage, most policy output is in the public realm and hence attracts media attention. Much policy work is not done by politicians, but rather carried out by civil servants and policy staffers. The political process' other core output involves image making (including selling politicians; propagating beliefs, myths, ideologies and identities; and legitimating the system). This hype output has been substantially media-ized and is consequently intimately enmeshed with relationships between journalists and spin-doctors, and journalists and politicians. To some extent, the arrival of televisualized politics saw many politicians become more closely associated

Table 2.1 *The three dimensions of the political process*

The Three dimensions of politics:	(1) Policy	(2) Process Management	(3) Hype
	'Elite' politics (geared to delivery)	'Elite' politics (geared to planning delivery and performance)	'Mass' politics (geared to image and myth making to be consumed by voters)
Driven by:	• Cabinet • Policy staff • Bureaucrats • Judiciary • Intellectuals • Lobbyists • Diplomats	• Political party 'insiders' • Spin-doctors • Negotiators • Intelligence community • 'Insider' intellectuals	• Journalists • Culture industry • Pollsters • Pundits and media commentators
Output:	*Output as 'substantive'* • Resource allocation • Laws • Violence (internal) • Foreign policy (war and peace) • Service delivery • Deal making (between interest groups) • Aggregating interests	*Output as 'planning and coordination'* • Inventing beliefs and ideology • Inventing identity • Selecting politicians and staffers • Strategizing about 'Policy' 'Hype'; and the 'policy–hype' relationship	*Output as 'image making'* • Politician as celebrity • Identities to consume • Belief and ideology propagation • Articulating interests • Legitimacy • 'distraction' (if needed)
Site (located in):	• Parliament • Bureaucracy • Courts • Violence-making machinery	Political elite 'back-rooms' and 'elite' media	The culture industry and 'mass' media
	Front-stage and back stage performances	*Back stage performance (hidden from political outsiders)*	*Front-stage performance (to be consumed by political outsiders)*

with 'image making' than 'policy making' – partly because the televisualized politics appears to have increasingly pushed politicians into the role of (on-stage) 'performance' or 'fronting' for the political machine, while policy staffers and bureaucrats get on with the (back room) job of making the machine work. As a result of taking on this 'fronting' or 'façade' role, politicians assume the role of popular culture celebrities (see chapter 8), which means that 'these days a politician's taste in music can assume as much importance as do their policies or their values' (Street, 2001: 273). In this regard, there is value in deploying Ervin Goffman's (1971) ideas on impression management; 'team-work' involved in maintaining suitable impressions; and front-stage and back stage performances. Goffman provides helpful analytical tools for unpacking the behaviour of political actors. Especially useful is the idea of how waiters learn different behaviours for deployment (off-stage) in the kitchen as opposed to (on-stage) in the dinning-area (1971: 118–21). The same holds true for those staffing the political machine.

2.2.2 Coordinating policy and hype

Proposal two   Policy and hype work, and the relationship between them, have to be coordinated, planned and strategized. This involves a third dimension of meta-level work, namely, managing the political process. Such management may not appear to be an output, but is vital for enabling the policy and hype outputs. Teams of back stage political insiders, which now include communication professionals (see chapter 7), perform this work. Western journalists (as semi-insiders) are fascinated with trying to either expose or double-guess this insider work. Some, such as Kathleen Hall Jamieson (1992), suggest that this has produced a form of political journalism focusing on 'politics as a competitive game' (see 4.2 on p. 76), which she argues has negatively impacted on how politics is now conducted (1992: chapter 7).

2.2.3 Two types of political practice

Proposal three   There are two types of political practice – elite politics and mass politics. Elite politics is geared towards policy making. Mass politics involves practices geared towards addressing, **steering** and cajoling voters. Mass politics conceptualizes citizens as politically passive – i.e. as a mass audience who can be manipulated, directed, and (if need be) pacified and distracted. Mass politics does not take 'the masses' seriously, i.e. as people whose ideas need to be incorporated into policy making. Rather, it treats them as semi-involved outsiders who, instead of being consulted, are at most 'polled' as a mass 'public', and thereafter addressed through carefully crafted messages aimed at influencing their voting behaviors. Walter Lippmann saw '**public opinion**' as the outcome of the deliberate self-conscious art of persuasion (1965: 158). For Lippmann, the notion that public opinion emanated spontaneously within democracies was false (1965: 163). Instead, public opinion was the outcome of leaders cultivating symbols and stereotypes, designed to organize and lead the 'rank and file' (1965: 150). Lippmann argued that the USA's 'masses' (outsiders) were led by carefully crafted communication (designed by insiders). The result – discussed by a number of contributors to Bennett and Entman (2001) – is to 'manipulate' and 'shut' citizens out of policy processes. Successful strategic communication results in the rank and file (the led) acting in accordance with 'pictures' put into their heads (by leaders), i.e. 'public opinion' is manufactured into existence by a communicatively skilled elite. Insider politics takes two forms. One is the work of framing and executing policy. A second form involves strategic planning; staffing-and-organizing the political machine; and drafting the hype it is hoped the media will pick up and disseminate.

When disputes arise among policy makers the policy elite sometimes turn to their PRs/spin-doctors who will be required to influence media content (i.e. 'steer' journalists) in order to mobilize public opinion. The faction of policy makers most successful at 'steering' public opinion in their direction will then use this mobilized public as leverage in their negotiations. Mobilizing/steering mass publics (through hype) during inter-fractional struggles between policy insiders is an important tool of policy elites. The masses (and journalists) are 'used' much as a chess player uses pawns.

2.2.4 Two types of media

Proposal four   Just as there are two types of political practice, so there two types of media; one used by the 'information rich', the other by the 'information poor':

- Political elites (of 'active' insiders) are information rich – they seek information from a diversity of elite-specialist (niche) media. However, political elites also pay attention to the mass media to monitor what coverage they (and their opponents) receive, and issues that journalists place onto the public agenda;
- Politicians deploy the mass media to communicate with voters. Most voters are information poor, passive 'outsiders' whose only engagement in the political process is to vote every few years for candidates presented to them by political parties. Most voters are now almost entirely dependent upon the mass media for information about the political process, candidates and issues. Given their reliance on mass media for political information, they become passive consumers of what journalists (semi-insiders) choose to report. For this reason, politicians and spin-doctors invest considerable energy trying to influence mass media agendas to generate stories useful to their cause.

The above distinctions are important when analyzing the relationship between politics and the media. They focus on three issues important for understanding political communication:

- Although 'media-hype' is an integral part of the political process, politics is not reducible to 'hype';
- There is a relationship between the substantive and hype dimensions of politics such that successful politicians must learn to juggle both;
- Although 'hype' and image-and-myth making are only one dimension of the political process, it is an important dimension, centrally implicated in the process of building and managing power.

This raises the question: what is the relationship between power and the media-hype? To answer this, one needs to consider where power comes from (see 2.3 on p. 24).

2.2.5 Sometimes spin-doctoring fails

Proposal five   The machinery of hype making is not seamless and does not always deliver the results intended by spin-doctors. Public relations professionals and spin-doctors would clearly prefer that their plans always work, but in reality the hype machinery is itself a complex patchwork of human relationships, differential abilities and struggles – it is staffed by people who sometimes make mistakes, betray their teams (e.g. leak information to the opposition), or who lose control of the symbiotic relationship they have with journalists. Further, spin-doctors have no control over how their products will be decoded – their audiences are not routinely steered because aberrant **decoding** is always a possibility. In addition, since every politician has a spin machine (which competes with every other spin machine), they cannot all win all the time. Within this competition, some spin operations succeed and some fail.

2.3 The media as a power resource

Power is a slippery phenomenon with numerous definitions. For the purposes of this book, power will be seen as the capacity to get one's own way when interacting with other human beings. Weber (1978) expressed this best when saying that those with power are able 'to realize their own will even against the resistance of others'. Lukes added an interesting rider to this Weberian notion. Lukes (1974) noted that having power not only grants one the ability to have one's interests prevail over others, but is also the ability to stop conflicts from emerging by preventing oppositional agendas from even being raised. Broadly speaking, power emerges from three sources:

- Access to resources (to implement one's will and buy others);
- The occupation of certain social positions (which enhance one's capacity to get one's will complied with, and/or constrain the capacity of others to act);
- Language as a relation-structuring agent.

Politics involves a struggle to gain access to certain key social positions. Occupying such positions then grants access to a range of resources which can be used to further one's interests, and those of one's constituency. Gaining (and retaining) access to these positions (and resources) involves possessing two skills, namely an ability to manipulate the machinery of language making (e.g. the media) and/or the machinery of coercion. In some contexts coercive-skills are fundamental for hegemony building. However, in Western liberal democracies, language-manipulation skills have become equally crucial for hegemonic success. In fact, it could be argued, the sites of institutionalized communication (e.g. mass media) have become absolutely crucial for building political power in Western liberal democracies.

A number of sites of institutionalized communication have been 'licensed' to manufacture and circulate dominant Western social discourses including:

- The media;
- Educational institutions;
- Parliaments;
- Courts of law.

For politicians, these sites are key cultural resources, and mechanisms for linguistically structuring social relationships. Consequently, access to these sites of institutionalized communication is struggled over. But access to such sites is controlled and limited, and often regulated by credentialism.

Arguably, the media became the most important cultural resource during the twentieth century because it was the central site for impression management and defining social position and status (e.g. 'publicity' has become a resource politicians must battle over). The media also became important agents for positioning people (through discourse). Media discourses are struggled over because they legitimate (or delegitimate) particular hierarchies of positions and the incumbents of such positions.

Given the importance the media assumed as sites of impression management, they became key 'king makers' and legitimators/de-legitimators from the second half of the twentieth century. Not surprisingly, media institutions became prized possessions for those seeking power, or seeking to influence those with power. Owning or controlling a media institution empowers the owner to hire and fire meaning makers. From this can emerge a secondary power – power derivative of the capacity to make or break political leaders, and circulate, or suppress, information and ideas. Whether the ownership/control of media actually confers power will depend on the individuals concerned, the context they operate within, and other struggles taking place within that context. Power is not automatic, it is the outcome of struggle. However, such struggles are not fought on level playing fields, because certain players are advantaged (or disadvantaged) by having more (or less) access to the sources of power at the start of play. Pre-existent access to power or key social positions is necessarily an advantage in the next round of the struggle over power.

At heart, Table 2.1 suggests that those seeking to gain, and maintain, power within liberal democracies will (among other skills) need to master the ability to generate media hype. This is because successful (mass-) impression management, image making and myth making have become prerequisites for gaining access to those sites (and social positions) where policy formulation and implementation occur. Not surprisingly, this has led to the growth of institutionalized political impression management – i.e. the growth of an industry of professional agenda setters, impression managers, celebrity makers and myth makers. Nimmo and Combs (1990: 66) say this industry exists to construct fantasies. It is this spin industry which concerns this book.

2.4 The game of political impression management

Goffman (1971) argues that humans encounter each other through symbolic interactions, and these interactions are stage-managed. We manage the impressions ('faces') we present to others, just as others manage their presentations to us. We also collaborate in jointly managing the rules governing both our self-presentations, and the interactions between the various stage-managed 'selves'. For Goffman, impression management lies at the heart of being 'social'. The game of collectively stage-managing interactions between the different 'faces' (generated by impression management) is what makes a society possible. Essentially, rule-governed impression management constitutes the governing mechanism of 'polite' and 'ordered' society.

Becoming a politician means adopting a particular (rule-governed) 'face'. If this face bears little resemblance to the politicians' own inner convictions it could be said to constitute a 'mask'. To be a successful politician one has to project a mask deemed appropriate by the constituency one is trying to attract as supporters. In the **OECD** this face (or mask) increasingly has to suit the medium of television. The features of this face are governed, in the first instance, by the 'profile' of the political party to which the politician belongs. There was a time when decisions about the party's 'profile', and the 'faces' the party wished to project, were taken by party bosses. However, increasingly such decision making is shifting to teams of employed communication professionals. Teams of communication and 'image' consultants, spin-doctors, pollsters and advisors now 'guide' the impression management politicians engage in (see chapters 7 and 8). They specialize in scripting Goffmanesque front-stage performances. And in a world where people increasingly prefer visual communication, these communication professionals now often specialize in televisually 'inventing', scripting and 'projecting' the 'politician-as-face'. In the hands of these communication professionals, the (successful) politician-as-face becomes a manufactured celebrity – the carrier of an appropriate 'appearance', as carefully crafted as a pop star or fashion model.

Whether contemporary politics involves more impression management than in earlier times is a moot point. But even if no more impression management is now required, what has changed is the growth of a professionalized industry of impression managers who:

- Research the political environment to decide what sort of political face will be most popular;
- 'Invent' such a face;
- Groom and coach candidates to perform this role.

Significantly, professional communicators have thereby joined the ranks of party insiders, where they help to pre-select candidates based on judging how well aspirants can function in the role of politician-as-media-performer. Hence communication professionals have become part of the crucial process of deciding how the political machine is staffed. This necessarily impacts on the 'substantive' policy dimension of the political process because, although originally selected for their performance (hype) abilities, once elected, 'performers' get to impact on policy making. In this regard, the USA's governance model has advantages over the British model because the US President can construct his Cabinet from specialists who do not have to be selected for their ability to be elected (i.e. their media-performance abilities). However, the British system requires Cabinets be constructed from the ranks of those pre-selected and elected for their performance abilities (which are not necessarily the same abilities required for 'back stage' policy work).

But political impression management involves more than building 'faces', scripting individual political performances and constructing celebrities (see chapters 7 and 8). Managing political communication also involves scripting and disseminating principles, ideas, sentiments and beliefs (see chapter 9) fostering the emergence of adherents (followers) for the mythologies and political identities thereby constructed (see chapter 6). These mythologies and identities serve as lighthouses or touchstones for the masses (political outsiders), helping them to navigate and orientate themselves in relation to the various political players. Skillful impression managers personalize messages by attaching them to politicians. Today's highly scripted political performances (which increasingly take the form of short sound bites and photo opportunities) are the basis for simultaneously constructing celebrity-politicians and the belief systems they embody. Professional communicators, in a sense, also construct the followers, because followers effectively build their 'political identities' from meanings supplied by the texts and performances crafted by impression managers. The process of disseminating beliefs and myths, and constructing political identities lies at the heart of what Almond (1965) called 'political socialization'.

Making political followers is consequently an exercise in second hand construction – the beliefs and identities of political outsiders are generally acquired by internalizing media messages produced by impression managers (insiders) and journalists (semi-insiders). Internalizing these messages necessarily involves voters reading and interpreting texts. This in turn involves a form of 'active' engagement with the political environment. However, it is a strangely passive 'activity' because it involves a dependence on texts produced by others, and agendas set by others. Most importantly it is 'passive' because the masses are positioned in a marginal relationship to society's core political decision making, knowledge making and information-producing centers.

For most people, this positioning is acceptable because politics is not an especially important concern in their lives. The majority of people appear content to be 'passive' – it is, after all, easier to allow others to construct ready-made 'explanations of the world' for one. So significantly, within liberal democracy, policy elites can safely conceptualize the masses as being 'passive' – they acquire their political identities by being followers. The only political action expected of them is to vote every few years when elections are called (by politically active insiders). And because they are not required to action their political beliefs or identities in any other way, there is no need to construct deep belief systems among political outsiders. In fact, shallow and fluid beliefs among the masses are more functional for pluralist-liberal democracies because they make the 'steering' job of political managers easier. So constructing liberal democracy's mass voters necessarily positions them as outsiders and passive, and is, as Habermas (1976: 142–3) noted, contemptuous of them.

Within this system of impression management, political journalists are semi-insiders. This creates a number of tensions and even contradiction for journalists. For one thing mainstream liberal journalists generally see themselves as members of a **Fourth Estate** (Schultz, 1998: chapter 2), whose job it is to act as 'watchdogs' over politicians. The Fourth Estate notion places journalists 'inside' the democratic political process – as active participants tasked with making sure the legislative, executive and judicial players do not abuse their power or become corrupt. The Fourth Estate idea is premised on three notions:

- Journalists are political insiders (or at least can gain access to the political system's inner-workings);
- The electorate are active political players;
- The media are able to operate autonomously of the government.

Journalist training inculcates the assumption that the Fourth Estate functions as the eyes and ears of a politically active electorate, and thereby ensures that electors control the elected, rather than the other way around. This Fourth Estate notion sits uncomfortably with the realities of 'insider/outsider' politics; the passivity of the mass of voters; the game of political impression management; and the way in which journalists and political players become mutually dependent upon each other. Journalists do not like to see themselves as susceptible to the impression management of spin-doctors, as the vehicles for selling stage-managed celebrity, or to convey scripted beliefs and identities to passive outsiders.

But when working as political journalists, those occupying these roles discover that:

- Political journalists are only semi-insiders;
- Political journalists need to work in a *de facto* symbiotic relationship with politicians because there is a mutual dependency between them (Negrine, 1994: 16);
- Political journalists need to work with the spin-doctors and political minders crafting the performances and 'faces' of politicians. These professional impression managers effectively become the interface between political insiders and journalists (as semi-insiders);
- Far from being Fourth Estate watchdogs, journalists are accomplices in the impression management game.

Perceptive journalists discover that they are simply part of the political system's hype machinery, and that the people they work with most closely – indeed symbiotically – are impression managers (who are insiders). These impression managers function *not* to inform journalists (semi-insiders) or voters (outsiders) of the real inner workings of the political machine, or of substantive policy issues. Habermas, in fact, suggested that those running liberal democracies necessarily try to obfuscate and disguise core policy-making processes in order to ensure that the steering and managing of the socio-economic system is carried out efficiently, and not interfered with by the demands of outsiders (1976: 111–24) – i.e. political outsiders (mass voters) are 'distracted' in the interests of 'rational' governance (1976: 122–43). Habermas suggested that the most serious challenge liberal governance could face would be if these 'passive masses' were to become active (and demanded to actually be involved in policy making). It is a moot point whether the masses are passive because:

- They are inherently disinclined to be active;
- They are content with what liberal democracy delivers (and hence have no spur to political activism);
- They are 'made' passive through socialization, education and media constructions;
- They are 'distracted' by the media;
- They are steered by an agenda-setting process.

It seems most likely that a mixture of all the above is involved. However, this book is primarily concerned with the issue of 'distraction'. Distracting the masses is achieved through the media by impression managers who use what they call 'puffery' and 'fluff' to try and 'catch' journalists. If they succeed (which is not always the case), the media become complicit in the process of managing political perceptions. This has bred a cynicism among many journalists. Hence, in places like the USA, UK, Canada and Australia, an interesting new genre of political journalism has emerged – cynical journalism, where journalists now focus on reporting 'the game' of politics. This, as Jamieson (1992: chapter 7) has argued, could be seen as a cause of the (dysfunctional) spiral of cynicism currently infecting Anglo (and other) liberal democracies (see 13.4 on p. 276).

Impression management is an inescapable feature of politics. But is it merely a 'superstructural overlay' – a 'secondary game' politicians must play to attract voters during the elections and then distract them the rest of the time (so they do not get in the way of policy work)? Marxists tend to see 'ideology' (image making and myth making) in this way – i.e. as merely a superstructural overlay on top of the 'real' work of political/economic management. A more useful framework, however, is to recognize that although differences exist between the practices of 'substantive' and 'hype' of politics, this does not mean that 'substantive' politics is more important than 'hype' politics. Rather, Table 2.1 (p. 21) proposes that both are equally 'necessary', differentiated merely by division of labour requirements. Further, the two dimensions are not autonomous of each other – hype work necessarily impacts on the policy work and vice versa.

Hence, those staffing one dimension must necessarily pay attention to what is being done in the other dimension.

However, even if impression management has always been a feature of politics, some suggest that the arrival of televised politics added a new dimension to the game, by deepening the impact of institutionalized mass communication on political processes. This led some – e.g. Entman (1989); Nimmo and Combs (1990); and Riddell (1998) – to suggest contemporary Western democratic politics has been media-ized.

2.5 What is media-ized politics?

Nimmo and Combs (1990: 18) propose that politics has become a second-hand reality for most Americans because they do not encounter politics in a direct (firsthand) manner, involving active participation. Instead, passive mass audiences encounter mediated politics via the media. This US media-ized form of politics is equally true of other OECD countries. Nimmo and Combs (1990: 18) go further, likening the contemporary experience of politics to Plato's prisoners in a cave (see Box 1.1) who acquiesce to their fate of being deprived from real-world experiences.

Nimmo and Combs propose that the majority of Americans now accept as normal the fact that they are confined to encountering politics as a set of secondhand (manipulated and distorted) media images, projected onto their cave walls by television (see chapter 1). In fact, it might be suggested they are comfortable with being passive 'publics', led by elites who manufacture the images, stereotypes and mythologies they consume. The same could be said of most Britons, Canadians and Australians.

At heart, contemporary politics in Anglo liberal democracies is about creating 'a public'. Publics are assembled by professional 'public builders' from individuals who are isolated and atomized by the practices and discourses of Western individualism and competition. The mass media assemble these publics. So the media functions as a form of social glue, constructing and holding together public opinion. But these publics (containing millions of individuals) do not involve actual human interaction or communication between those incorporated into these 'publics'. The members of these publics do not know each other, or communicate with each other. They will never know each other, or communicate with each other. Yet publics can be 'brought together' by the mass media and can even be 'guided' (by the media) to carry out the same action (e.g. mourning the death of a celebrity they do not personally know, e.g. Princess Diana). Such 'publics' and 'public opinion' are the ultimate artificial 'hyper' construct. These publics have no real 'presence' because they are assembled in the ether of media representations. One cannot find 'a public', because it does not 'exist'. But one can find 'public opinion' by constructing it as an intellectual exercise (i.e. conducting public opinion surveys). Publics are assembled in, and through the media, by the demagoguery of the professional hype makers who know how to use the media to shift perceptions. The process involves **agenda setting** – i.e. creating the perceptual frameworks through which 'publics' experience the world from one perspective only. Entman (1989: 77–8) argues that the key means to predispose people to thinking in a certain way is to influence what they think about by providing them with ready-made 'schematas' or frameworks. Such frameworks serve to guide the subsequent behavior of media audiences and so turn them into publics (who behave 'collectively', despite being isolated individuals). Such demagogic power derives from the widespread atomization (and hence isolation) of individuals in Western society. Instead of interacting with other human beings, isolated individuals now experience a form of manufactured substitute 'pseudo-interaction' received through mass media messages – i.e. they receive media-ted experience. For political 'outsiders' few possibilities exist for crosschecking and sharing alternative opinions because these 'outsider' individuals have been atomized and the media turned into their primary vehicle for 'interacting'. The result is a dramatic media-ization of experience wherein individuals become 'a public' of passive followers, 'guided' by the limited agendas presented to them by the media. The result is (passive) publics, instead of (actively engaged) citizens. The possibilities for manipulating such mediated (passive) outsiders are countless. Building this media-ted public opinion has fostered a symbiotic relationship between different interests – i.e. the public opinion industry is good for:

- Policy elites (insiders) who wish to make policy with as little interference from the (outsider) masses as possible;
- Media workers because it provides them with employment;
- Media proprietors because it has generated a profitable industry.

Public opinion-driven politics is at heart media-ized politics – where the media machine, and the demagogue's arts of manipulating mass media output, have become central to governance. Entman (1989) argues that this manipulation has produced democracy without citizens. In place of active citizens we have publics – 'publics' who are 'herded' and 'steered' by skilled media operators. This steering process 'delivers' voters; and provides policy makers with as much freedom as possible from 'outsider' pressures. Riddell (1998: 8) contends that this has seen the focus of political debate shift away from Parliaments to television studios. He argues that British politicians now invest more energy into their televisual performances outside the Houses of Parliament on College Green ('sound bite heaven') or at Millbank (BBC, ITN and Sky) studios than into working within the House of Commons (1998: 9). Seaton (1998: 117) agrees with Riddell. Both Riddell and Seaton suggest that media performance has 'become' politics – i.e. media-ized politics. However, what Riddell and Seaton overlook is that television studios are still only one part of the political process (albeit, an important one). The media-ization of political performance may have reduced the importance of Parliamentary performances, but media-ization has not absorbed the policy-making process. Instead, it appears, policy making has been largely shifted out of Parliament in order that, as far as possible, policy is not corrupted by media attention. Policy has been located back stage as a function of executives (Cabinets, Prime Ministers' Departments, the White House and so on). So policy is now an activity carried out by political behind-the-sceners, not political performers. A division of labor exists: politicians-as-performers work on stage (in television studios, and to a lesser extent in Parliament); while politicians-as-policy makers work back stage (with their policy staff, bureaucrats, advisors and lobbyists). Riddell and Seaton do a good job examining the 'on-screen' politicians-as-performers, but fail to consider the 'off-screen' policy dimension.

It seems fair to say that media performance has become a core feature of contemporary political processes, so that even policy workers must pay attention to the media. But does media-ization necessarily translate into a new political genre, transformed by the workings of the hype-machine? This would seem to be the case for four reasons.

Firstly, a spin industry of professional impression managers has been integrated into the political machine (see chapter 7). They have impacted on the political process by seeking out the most cost-effective ways of delivering success to their employers. This drove politics to becoming televisualized (see 8.2 on p. 179). Television is a hype-maker's dream medium because its visualness, and the medium's preference for movement and sensation produce an urgency, immediacy and persuasiveness that other media lack. Television also encourages easily digestible simplifications, stereotypes and clichés. In societies where television has become the dominant medium, culture itself has been visualized, with other media forms increasingly adopting visualized styles. The spin industry quickly recognized the persuasive possibilities visualized culture held when trying to manipulate the masses through hype. The result has been a visualization of political performance, with US politicians leading the way. This produced a 'hype industry' of televisualized spin-doctoring and agenda setting.

Secondly, the televisualization of politics altered the sort of people selected to be performance-politicians (see chapter 8). What is now required is an ability to wear whatever 'face' ('mask') one's minders require; to perform in front of television cameras; to look attractive and/or 'leader-like' on screen; to speak in sound bites; and preferably say nothing substantive when journalists are around. To be pre-selected as a politician now requires displaying an understanding of, and willingness to behave in accordance with, the requirements of hyped politics, and to stick to the script provided by impression managers. This has impacted on the political machine's staffing profile, so that it can be argued, televisualization impacts not only upon the hype dimension, but also upon the policy dimension of the political process.

Thirdly, the growth of a spin industry generated (an institutionalized) symbiotic relationship between spin-doctors and journalists. But because such a symbiosis clashes with journalism's (Fourth Estate) professional ideology (see chapter 4), political journalists experienced dissonance between the reality of their daily work (as semi-insiders within a hype machine) and the mythology of themselves as 'truth-finders'. To resolve this dissonance cynical journalists 'expose' the nature of the political 'game' and its 'hype' to their audiences. This appears to be generating a political malaise in some Western societies because, instead of being part of a communication process legitimating the political process, cynical journalists have become de-legitimators of the system (see 13.4 on p. 276). This is dysfunctional for liberal democracy. How liberal democracy will resolve this problem, born of media-ization gone wrong, is as yet unclear.

Fourthly, media-izing politics generated a re-alignment in the way power was distributed within the political machine. Liberal democracy was born at the turn of the nineteenth century as an **oligarchy**, with power residing in the hands of a bourgeois/burgher (middle class) elite. This elite organized its decision making in Parliaments. By the late nineteenth century, a widened franchise created a potential danger for the middle classes that they might lose political control. Ewen (1996) contends that this danger stimulated the creation of public relations (PR) in the USA. Ewen argues that the American middle classes created PR as a mechanism to try and manipulate the masses. This PR mechanism (designed to 'steer' and control the masses and avoid the use of violence), grew during the twentieth century into a large spin industry. By the turn of the century the spin-doctors were insiders within the political machine. Furthermore, the growing importance of political spin-doctoring produced an observable bifurcation in the machinery of governance – with part of the political machine specializing in agenda-setting impression management-and-hype, and the other half specializing in policy formulation. This bifurcation saw a decision-making move into those back rooms inhabited by Cabinet Ministers and their policy staffers, and out of 'public spaces' (such as televised Parliaments). The shift of real decision making away from Parliaments disenfranchised not only the masses, but also the middle classes, because power has increasingly moved into the hands of a political technocrat elite – i.e. policy technocrats and communication technocrats.

Summary

You should now be familiar with the following key concepts: impression management; hype; myth making; image making; spin-doctors; politicians-as-performers; politician-as-face; information poor; information rich; ruling elite; public opinion; as well as the nature of the symbiotic role between politicians, spin-doctors and journalists.

For further consideration

1 Do you think that viewing politics as a game of 'impression management' over-emphasizes the importance of communication and media in the political process?
2 Is it reasonable to say: 'in politics perception is everything'?
3 Can one conceive of politics without hype?
4 The notion of a ruling elite lends itself to conspiratorial thinking. Does this invalidate the notion of elites?
5 See if you can identify the way in which a recent political issue was handled by the two varieties of media: (a) the media geared to the information rich; and (b) the media geared to the information poor.
6 What role can a journalist play in building or undermining a politician's power?
7 Do you think the notion of a passive public is justified or exaggerated?
8 Is it an exaggeration to see mass publics as being routinely manipulated? While pondering this question, consider the following:

- Do the masses opt to be passive? (i.e. Are they voluntarily in Plato's cave, perhaps because it is comfortable?)
- Are the masses 'constructed' as passive? (i.e. Are they involuntarily imprisoned in Plato's cave?)

(Continued)

For further consideration   Continued

- Are the masses 'steered' by a process of agenda setting? (i.e. Is it more correct to think in terms of 'constructed' television images, rather than 'unconstructed' shadows in a cave?)
- Are most people able to 'see through' media constructions? (i.e. Is 'manipulation' impossible to achieve and sustain?)

9   Is cynicism a good or bad thing in journalists?
10 Do you think the proposal of a division between 'policy' and 'hype' is exaggerated?

3 Western Political Development: An Evolving Symbiosis of Media and Politics

Chapter 2 argued that contemporary politics has been substantially media-ized. Chapter 3 sketches out the context within which this took place – i.e. media-ization emerged due to a series of historical developments which culminated in the sort of political system operative today. It focuses on the emergence and growth of liberal democracy and the way in which a liberal media system has been intimately bound up with the evolution of the liberal democratic system. The chapter argues that encoded into today's liberal democracies are residues of the way in which this form of governance evolved – i.e. bourgeois/burgher struggles against feudalism produced liberal oligarchies which were then reformed into democracies. It is argued that these reform processes produced a *massification* of the political process which necessitated that the middle classes develop mechanisms to 'steer', 'communicatively manage' and 'tame' the masses. The function of 'steering' the masses led to the growth of public relations, spin-doctoring and a mass (popular) media system – themes that will be developed in more detail in chapters 4 and 7. Chapter 3 focuses in particular on the evolution of British and US democracy, unraveling the roles played by John Locke, J.S. Mill and the Glorious Revolution and the American Revolution in the emergence of Westminster and US democracy. The chapter then moves on to explore the role of the Northcliffe and Pulitzer Presses, as well as Walter Lippmann and the growth of US public relations, in today's media-ized democracies.

Over time humans have arranged and organized the political process in many different ways. This book focuses on one of these, namely the Western liberal democratic form. This does not imply that liberal democracy is deemed a universal or superior model of governance. Rather, the focus derives from liberal democracy having become hegemonic over large swathes of the globe, including the world's economic heartland, the OECD (thanks to the military prowess of first Britain, then the USA).

Within the OECD, liberal democracy is so naturalized it is now virtually taken-for-granted that this should be the model for governance globally. This view slides easily into teleological thinking, which confers upon liberal democracy the status of an idealized end-point of political evolution. An extreme version of such thinking was Fukuyama's (1989) 'end of history' thesis, which (prematurely) proposed that liberal democracy would necessarily come to dominate the globe. In a less extreme form, mainstream Western journalists often uncritically and unconsciously propagate a teleological view of liberal democracy's 'superiority' and evolutionary advantage over other systems of governance. Liberal democracy grew to such dominance through a series of historical accidents. In particular, this form of governance is strongly associated with the evolution of Anglo political processes over the last three and a half centuries. Unpacking this evolution helps to explain both how the media and politicians have become symbiotically intertwined within contemporary liberal democracy, and the origins of beliefs still informing the professional self-image of liberal journalists.

3.1 The origins of liberal democracy

Liberal democracy arose from the European **bourgeoisie/burghers** struggle to free themselves from the control of absolutist monarchies and aristocracies, i.e. overlord remnants of the **feudal system**. During the first half of the sixteenth century the burgher estate (middle classes) of northwestern Europe built a merchant capitalist trading network. Antwerp was its center. Amsterdam's stock exchange and insurance houses organized the network's financial transfers (a role later transferred to London). The Augsburg Fuggers were the network's main bankers. The Fuggers were also Charles V's financial backers and were (through Charles V) responsible for establishing the Habsburg hegemony over Europe and the New World. Under Charles V the Habsburg dynasty came to rule Spain (and its vast American empire), Austria (and its East European empire), Germany, southern Italy, plus the Netherlands and Belgium. This Habsburg empire was the superpower of the sixteenth century. Under Habsburg suzerainty, the bourgeois/burgher merchant network organized the early transatlantic trading system and colonization of South America, and used the wealth extracted from the Habsburg's Spanish-American empire to build Western European capitalism. Within this mercantilist system, the English and Dutch dominated shipping and trading. The burgher merchants driving this system also gave rise to an early form of 'international journalism' in the shape of *The Fugger News-Letters* (Von Klarwill, 1924), because they needed to keep themselves informed about global political and economic issues.

These burghers soon found the feudal system constrained their interests – because nobles monopolized the political process. This often produced policies unhelpful for profit-seeking merchants. The accumulation of economic and social power was not evenly dispersed in all parts of this merchant network. Power ultimately aggregated in two places where the burgher estate managed to successfully build territorial bases, namely Holland and England. The first successful burgher-driven revolutions were the Dutch Republic (1566–1609) and Cromwell's English Republic (1642–1660). Significantly, in both cases the burghers were forced to build political systems based upon compromises with their local aristocracy, because these aristocrats continued to be politically powerful. (In England, for example, the gentry remained politically dominant until at least the 1780s.) In both Holland and England the result was a ruling oligarchy – an alliance of the propertied burghers, nobles and gentry (Birn, 1977: 40–54). This alliance was institutionalized within Parliaments at London and The Hague, where the oligarchy's governing deals were worked out.

Although Cromwell's Republic was ultimately defeated, his rule ended absolutist monarchy in England. Consequently, although England's monarchy was restored, it was restored as a constitutional monarchy – i.e. a political system effectively dominated by burgher interests. In England, the landed gentry and (urban) burghers ultimately struck a landmark 'compromise deal' ('the Glorious Revolution' of 1688) to share power under a constitutional monarch. This political deal generated socio-economic convergence between the burghers (who imbibed the gentry's aristocratic practices and discourses) and the gentry (who adopted the burgher's economic practices and became agrarian capitalists) (Barrington-Moore, 1973: 32–9). This Anglo-oligarchic alliance thereafter used its Parliamentary power-base to destroy England's peasantry through the enclosure of land (1740s onwards). By driving the peasants off the land and into cities, they built a working class to service Britain's capitalist industrialization. The deal effectively laid the foundations for Anglo liberal democracy and what became the **Westminster Parliamentary system**, because the various parties to the deal had to learn to work together within a proto-pluralist framework of negotiations and power sharing. This political system proved to be incredibly resilient and politically successful, creating the basis for Anglo-capitalist colonization of not only the rest of the British Isles, but also eventually the whole of North America and the British Empire. By successfully building

Europe's first stable political process for generating policies favourable to capital accumulation, the English burghers created a secure power-base from which to ultimately accumulate wealth and power on a global scale.

Although English liberal democracy proved the most successful model for building capitalism, the first bourgeois/burgher power-base was actually in Holland. However, Holland's political revolution proved less successful than its English equivalent, and the weakness of the Dutch model facilitated English burghers grabbing from the Dutch dominance of the mercantilists trading network. As a result London (the Bank of England) replaced Amsterdam as Europe's core financial center. Control of global trade also shifted – the mercantilist trading network, originally launched under the Spanish-Habsburg hegemony and taken over by Holland, was eventually inherited by England. From this grew the British Empire and later the **Pax Americana**. Both Britain and the USA have exported Anglo liberal democratic clones and mutations to various sites around the globe.

But what was the original Anglo model from which emerged the various forms of contemporary liberal democracy?

3.2 The early Anglo model

Anglo liberal democracy's roots lie in the Glorious Revolution's (1688) compromise deal, which tamed the monarchy through an alliance of urban merchants, the county gentry, armed forces and civil servants, who together constituted England's new ruling oligarchy. Both political parties – the Whigs (who advocated limiting royal authority and increasing Parliamentary power) and Tories (who adopted a more conservative position) – represented the same English oligarchic interests. Significantly, this ruling alliance exercised its power through Parliament. The monarchy's ability to wage war was circumscribed by Parliament's monopoly over raising taxes and by a Bill of Rights. The judiciary was independent of the monarch, and the King's right to operate a censorship system abolished. Within this model, Parliament became the fulcrum of governance – where the new ruling alliance solved its problems of socio-economic management (and thereby created conditions for accumulating capital). So having captured power, the English alliance built the Westminster Parliamentary model for reaching (compromise) decisions and an electoral mechanism for choosing which of their number would go to Parliament to make these governing decisions. This Parliament emerged as a governance mechanism for promoting capitalism.

The key intellectual source for this Westminster model was John Locke's *Second Treatise of Government* (1966), wherein he developed his vision for rational liberalism. Locke (1632–1704) was born into a burgher Puritan family and became a key Whig intellectual just as Anglo burghers constructed their ruling alliance with England's landed gentry. As with many liberal thinkers of his age, Locke's ideas were influenced by his years of exile in Holland – which, as the first burgher power-base, became a political hotbed of liberal thinking; Europe's center for refugees (from feudal absolutism and religious persecution); and an early bourgeois/burgher publishing center. Locke's ideas on liberalism and governance argued for a political order serving the interests of the burgher estate trying to assert its dominance over Europe. Echoes of these early formulations of rational liberalism can still be heard in the discourses used by contemporary Western journalism.

Locke advocated the following:

- Government-by-legislature (Parliament);
- Where no one (e.g. nobles) was above the law; and
- Wherein the executive was subordinate to the legislature;
- Those elected to Parliament were deemed to be trustees – i.e. entrusted to make good laws to secure the lives, liberties and property of those electing them;
- People had a right to overthrow governments that failed to promote their basic rights to life, liberty and property;
- People also had a right to know what their government was doing (i.e. freedom of information), so they could decide if it was acting as a good trustee.

In this sense Locke's ideas created the basic premises upon which England's liberal democracy was built. He argued for a government guaranteeing the burghers freedom from governance in which they played no part (i.e. freedom from being governed by absolutist monarchies). Further, Locke proposed that (liberal) governments be obligated to protect property rights and to promote conditions within which individuals could most effectively accumulate capital. For Locke, good governance meant creating policy frameworks maximizing what the burghers needed, namely, conditions favourable to creating wealth and property. The American Declaration of Independence was constructed upon these same Lockean notions of the rights of individuals to life, liberty and property. This is not surprising given that its drafters were (overseas) members of the same Anglo oligarchy which had created England's Parliament.

So the early Anglo (English and American) liberal system was built upon the following Lockean-derived notions:

- Governments were obliged to build secure environments wherein individuals could compete to improve their lot;
- Individuals had the right to expect the state to protect their property, and the right to be treated as equal before the law (i.e. hereditary nobles and monarchs were no longer to be regarded as superior);

- The latter did not mean that all individuals were regarded as equal in early liberal systems, given that these societies were premised upon class differences and slaves were regarded as property to be protected. But it did mean the *Rule of Law* applied – i.e. no one was subject to arbitrary laws; laws/policies now emerged from a prescribed legislative process (not the capricious will of nobles); and all laws were equally applicable to everyone (including law makers).

Locke wanted to develop a form of government to free burghers from laws that did not benefit the creation of wealth – i.e. the sort of laws European monarchs and nobles had imposed on the emergent burger estate. He believed that the best guarantee for securing the rights to life, liberty and property was a liberal democratic government wherein legislators were elected to represent the interests of the electors. Importantly, Locke developed two other rights, echoes of which can still be heard in the discourses of contemporary Western journalism: first, the right to overthrow governments failing to maximize the above conditions. Locke had in mind those European monarchs, aristocrats and ecclesiastical rulers whose feudal-derived social hierarchies limited opportunities for burgher progress; and second, the right to a free-flow of information so people could monitor their government's performance. In this regard Locke challenged the censorship imposed by Europe's hereditary rulers. This free-flow of information principle eventually led to the notion of the Fourth Estate media (see chapter 4). These Lockean principles grew into a discourse still informing the professional self-image of liberal journalism.

3.2.1 Liberal oligarchies

Significantly, these early liberal systems were not democracies. They were oligarchies because only a small minority of people was enfranchised. Only property owners elected parliamentarians in early liberal systems. Only a quarter of England's population had the vote in 1720; and the USA's post-revolutionary 1787 constitution only gave the vote to approximately six percent of the population (i.e. wealthy white males). So early liberal Parliaments operated like exclusive clubs, where only those within the burgher oligarchy had access to the political process and to information about it. Within these early liberal political processes there was no need to develop 'hype' machinery (alongside/parallel to policy machinery) to manage and steer public opinion, because a direct relationship existed between policy making and the ruling elite. Since only the ruling oligarchy had access to the political machine, there was no need for image making/performances geared towards preventing the derailment of (elite) policy making by the unfulfillable demands and dislocating interventions of the (non-elite) masses. Instead of a hype-making mass media, early liberal oligarchies were serviced by low circulation media catering to the needs of the propertied elite, e.g. Benjamin Franklin's *Pennsylvania Gazette*. The earliest struggles for a (liberal) 'press freedom' were associated with journalists working on these small oligarchy-serving media, such as the 'Cato doctrine' of free speech formulated in 1720s' London (Emery, 1962: 23) and New York's Zenger libel case in 1734 (1962: 76–83).

3.2.2 New policy-making practices

The early Parliaments (serving liberal oligarchies) developed policy-making practices substantively different from the feudal ones that had preceded them. These parliamentary practices became central to later liberal democratic systems. Most significantly, policy making was no longer conducted away from all public scrutiny. Feudal policy making was inherently out of sight because the nobility made decisions behind closed doors. Effectively, feudal political decision making resembled family decision making – noble family members took decisions in private. The shift to a bourgeois/burgher public sphere, meant decision making became more 'open' due to the nature of Parliaments as debating forums. However, although more open than the feudal system, early liberal Parliaments were not fully open to scrutiny, as demonstrated by John Wilkes' struggle for the Press' right to report on Parliamentary debates (Williams, 1984: chapter 3). In fact, it is important to note that the media was not a significant feature of early liberal parliamentary processes. The early Parliament served an oligarchy working to establish its (still fragile) hegemony and put into place policy frameworks servicing the needs of early capitalism. The print media, such as it existed at this stage, simply serviced the needs of nobles, ecclesiastics, and the (still numerically small) oligarchy of gentry, merchants and civil servants. There was as yet no mass media, no mass public and no **mass democracy**. Parliamentary debate was only 'open' to some – the oligarchy. This meant presses were small-scale affairs. Many newspapers were effectively just propaganda sheets for individual politicians, with the latter paying to have information published or suppressed. Even John Wilkes, the man credited with winning the right of journalists to report Parliamentary proceedings in 1771, ran a propaganda sheet serving the interests of London merchants.

A second change was that early Parliaments institutionalized a form of pluralist decision making because the propertied classes were not a homogeneous group. So, although early Parliament represented only limited interests – the country gentry and urban merchants – this, nonetheless, led to the emergence of what became a basic function of liberal Parliaments, namely, brokering deals between different social sectors. This generated a policy-making style quite different from that associated with feudalism. As the franchise was extended, so the number of social sectors increased, as did the complexity of brokering deals. This, in turn, required ever more complex mechanisms of political communication through which information could flow between the parties engaged in the bargaining processes. Hence, managing communication flows became a feature of engaging in politics.

A third change initiated by Parliamentary government was the phenomenon of institutionalized representatives. Although early liberal parliaments represented only a minority of the population, the numbers involved in the political process were considerably larger than feudalism's familial networks. Consequently, it was not possible to have everyone within the oligarchy actually participate in policy-making debates. The only practical solution was to develop mechanisms through which the many could select a few of their number to represent their interests in Parliament. Hence was born representative government and the notion of electing representatives.

The arrival of representative government generated a series of issues concerned with organizing the political process, some of which became enmeshed in the issue/s of the relationship between Parliament and the media. A core issue raised by representative politics was who should be represented. Without representative politics it was impossible to give a voice to everyone in societies whose memberships numbered in the millions. Representative politics created a mechanism through which everyone could potentially be given an indirect voice in Parliament via the election of someone to represent their interests. The question of who could vote had implications for the meaning of citizenship. By creating a mechanism for mass representative Parliamentary government, a pathway was ironically opened for challenging (minority) rule by the very burgher oligarchies that created liberal Parliaments in the first place.

Another set of issues involved how to control representatives. Should representatives obey every wish of their constituents, or exercise independent judgment? Further, how could representatives be:

- Made accountable to those electing them;
- Prevented from becoming corrupt;
- Prevented from abusing their power.

John Stuart Mill (1986) tried to devise solutions to such issues. J.S. Mill (1806–73) concluded that 'liberty of the press' was a fundamental part of the solution – because free-flowing information was the best guarantee against corruption and power abuse. From this grew the media-as-watchdog notion – i.e. the media kept voters informed, thereby ensuring bad representatives were removed at the next elections. A related set of issues involved how the media could serve as a vehicle for informing voters (so they could make good choices), and informing representatives about community feelings (so they made better decisions). Journalists latched onto Mills' ideas, and systematically promoted the view that the media was ideally positioned to fulfill the role of an independent information broker within this system of representative government. Hybridizing Mill's and Locke's principles produced the professional discourse now underpinning liberal journalistic thinking about their role in society.

Ultimately, solving the problems of representative government led to the notion (advocated by journalists and media proprietors from the early nineteenth century onwards) that the media be regarded as an integral part of liberal governance, because it improved the circulation of ideas and information in society, making government more transparent, and improving the level of debate. It is a moot point whether the media has actually successfully fulfilled these functions – especially after mass-enfranchisement changed the nature of liberal democracy and spawned the growth of an array of techniques to manipulate mass public opinion.

3.3 The massification of liberal democracy

At the start of the nineteenth century, Anglo liberal parliamentary systems were closed shop oligarchies of the propertied classes (landed gentry and wealthy urban merchants). Mass liberal democracy was gradually born through reforming the electoral systems of the USA, Britain and Britain's colonies. These reforms came in four waves.

Firstly, male franchise was gradually extended by removing property qualifications. The USA led the way, removing most property requirements for white males by 1820 (replacing them with tax requirements). By 1830 most white US males could vote after taxpaying qualification was removed. In Britain, three Reform Acts extended the vote to males: in 1832 small property owners in urban areas got the vote; in 1867 urban workmen were enfranchised; and in 1884–5 agricultural workers were enfranchised. Australia removed property tests for white male voters in the 1850s (following the 1854 Eureka armed rebellion of gold miners protesting about a lack of political representation, land tenure laws, and Chinese migration). Canada removed property tests for white male voters between 1898 and 1911, and New Zealand did so in 1879. However, South Africa's Cape Colony actually increased (tripled) property qualifications in 1892 to remove many black people from the voters role. (Blacks were enfranchised, if they met property qualifications in 1854.) During a second wave of electoral reforms, requirements that Parliamentary candidates

Table 3.1   *Reforming Anglo liberal oligarchies in liberal democracies*

	Stage 1	Stage 2	Stage 3	Stage 4	Stage 5
Evolutionary steps in building liberal democracy	Liberal oligarchy	Male suffrage reforms	Property restriction for Parliamentary candidates abolished	Female suffrage reforms	Non-white suffrage reforms
Who had the vote	Propertied classes (males)	All white males	All white males	All whites	All citizens
Who could stand for Parliament	Propertied classes (males)	Propertied classes (males)	All white males	All whites	All citizens

needed to own substantial amounts of property were abolished, with Australian states, for example, removing these requirements at the close of the nineteenth century. During a third phase of reforms, white women were given the vote – New Zealand (1893); Australia (1902); USA, Britain and Canada (1918); and South Africa (1930). During a fourth phase of reforms, non-white people were given the vote. Canada lifted voting restrictions on Asians in 1948 and gave native-Americans the vote in 1960; the USA removed restrictions preventing black people from voting in 1964–6; and Australia enfranchised Aboriginals in 1967. In Southern Africa, two political systems tried to avoid this fourth phase of electoral reform – in apartheid South Africa, blacks were given a vote in 'black homelands', but denied a vote for the central Parliament (Louw, 2004); while in Rhodesia, an electoral system based on property, income and educational qualifications restricted the franchise to the (mostly white) middle classes (Wood, 1983). The fourth reform wave reached South Africa in 1994 when black people were enfranchised. These waves of reform are represented in Table 3.1.

This gradual widening of the franchise ultimately produced universal adult suffrage within Western liberal democracies. Effectively, liberal oligarchies reformed themselves until they became liberal democracies. This changed the political process and the media reporting that process. But the question is: did this gradual widening of the franchise undermine the position of the original (propertied) oligarchs? Or was the reform designed to preserve the basic outlines of Locke's rational liberalism? For Locke, good governance meant creating policy frameworks serving burgher/middle-class interests by maximizing conditions favourable to wealth creation and property accumulation. Ultimately, a reform served the propertied classes and preserved their hegemony – they admitted new groups into their (liberal) political process, but simultaneously learned to manage this ever-growing mass of voters such that massification of liberal political processes did not undermine the *de facto* control that the propertied classes continued to exercise. Essentially, reformers within the liberal oligarchies of the USA and UK adopted a gradual approach to widening the franchise – different blocks of voters were let into the political process incrementally, as those inside the existing hegemony identified leaders of different social sectors they could either co-opt or form alliances with. An example was the way sections of England's liberal oligarchy established free trade by using an 1840s' alliance with (formerly disenfranchised) small property owners to repeal the Corn Laws.

Massifying the voting-system was a conservative strategy designed to preserve Locke's liberal good governance. Examining developments in the USA, the first liberal state to reform itself, helps reveal how massifying the franchise was a conservative strategy. The US liberal oligarchy reformed itself during the presidency of the USA's seventh President, Andrew Jackson (1767–1845). During the Jacksonian era (1816–40), the USA was transformed into a liberal democracy because the vote was granted to almost all white males. However, although the Americans massified their voting system under Jackson, the US propertied elite retained control of both Federal and State policy making. (The USA's federal system made it possible for each state's elite to devise their own methods for reforming their system while retaining effective control.) As Pessen notes, although Jackson spoke in ringing tones of the common man's right to high office, he staffed his cabinet and civil service with men of wealth and social eminence; maintained a government of the propertied for the propertied; and built a system rendering ordinary persons politically impotent, although they had been given the vote (1978: 97–8). What the Jacksonian system pioneered was a political process in which cliques continued to control policy making. They learned to manage political parties able to appeal to voters without having to deliver on voter demands that threatened the oligarchy's core interests (1978: 227). The Jacksonian elite also learned, while inventing early American democracy, how to mobilize demagogic speech making and showmanship to appeal to, flatter and manage the common man (1978: 158–60). As soon as the USA turned to mass democracy, party managers invented the art of political hype so that 'common men' could be managed by 'uncommon men' (1978: 326–7). From this was born the need for a form of mass communication enabling elites to communicate with, and manipulate, the masses. From the Jacksonian experiences of managing the birth of liberal democracy emerged those communication skills from which were to grow the hype-generating mass media of today. Pessen argues that the Jacksonian elite had to learn to manage the social powder-keg they had created, i.e. the economic activities of US liberal oligarchs created new cities that drew together a complex mix of people into socially tense environments characterized by rapid social change, disorder and crisis (1978: 55–7). This created a fear of potential revolution among the propertied classes. Their solution was reform and social-management – i.e.

the propertied oligarchs enfranchised their masses; built an education system to inculcate an 'appropriate' value system and work ethic; and developed the earliest mass media ('penny press') to communicate with the masses (1978: 62–3). Liberal democracy was born as a means to prevent revolution through controlled reform. From a Gramscian perspective, the middle class confronted two possible options – maintaining hegemonic control over the masses through violence, or developing methods for communicatively 'steering' the masses. Reformers promoted the latter option – the masses were enfranchised, and the policy elites learned to communicatively 'steer' (rather than shoot) them. Henceforth, an integral part of the liberal democratic system was a mass media facilitating the discursive management of the masses (see chapter 5). This reformist pattern was replicated in Britain as England's propertied oligarchy managed their way out of the social powder-keg created by the industrial revolution. This model was then exported to those places in the British Empire where members of the Anglo oligarchy had settled.

3.3.1 John Stuart Mill

If Locke's seventeenth-century writings captured the spirit of the emergent oligarchs of the early Anglo liberal system, John Stuart Mill's (1986) writings captured the spirit of Anglo middle-class liberal reformers of the nineteenth century. Mill's *On Liberty* deals with these reformers main concerns, i.e. firstly, the liberal oligarchs were caught between two fears – a fear that if the political system was not reformed the masses would seize power through revolution, versus a fear that electoral reform would see middle-class (minority) views swamped by the views of the (non-middle-class) masses (with the danger that this might generate policies unfavourable for wealth and property accumulation or generate leveling-downwards pressures). Mill expressed this fear in the form of a concern about a 'tyranny of the majority' – the fear that minorities would be persecuted within emerging liberal democracy. For Mill, mechanisms were needed to check the potential tyranny of the masses. He concluded that the best mechanism was guaranteed freedom of expression. Fundamental to Mill's liberal vision was the notion that liberal political systems needed to protect diversity of opinion and everyone's right to express their view – this being a mechanism to prevent democratization from producing majoritarian repression. Secondly, there was a concern that democratic representatives might abuse their positions of power. Mill concluded that the best blocking mechanism against a tyranny of politicians was a press free to expose any political abuse, e.g. corruption or the emergence of despotic practices.

For Mill, open communication (facilitated by a free press) was the means to tame some of the potential excesses of mass representative democracy. An (unstated) assumption underpinning Mill's argument is that the educated and propertied middle-class burghers would most likely operate such a press. Mill in fact states that within liberal democracy the 'will of the people' is not necessarily equivalent to the will of the majority. Instead, it meant the will of the most *active part* of the people. In practical terms it meant the will of that part of the active minority who succeeded in getting themselves accepted by the majority. From this emerged the need for a communication vehicle the minority could use to persuade the masses. Not surprisingly, a mass media catering to the newly enfranchised masses followed quickly on the heels of democratic reforms. Importantly, at the very core of liberal reformism lay the principle of an active minority getting themselves accepted by the majority – the idea that the middle classes could continue to dominate the political process (after extending the franchise) because they would be skilled at using the machinery of liberal governance (including the media) to sway and lead the masses. Mill's pro-burgher interests are revealed in the fact that he discussed mechanisms to tame both the tyranny of the masses and the potential tyranny of politicians, but failed to address the mechanisms to check any potential tyranny of capital.

Ultimately, for Mill, the best protection against tyranny was a free press and the vote within a liberal democratic system. This combination, he argued, empowered individual citizens by providing two interlocking mechanisms for ensuring good governance – one ensured that citizens were constantly kept informed about what their political representatives were doing and another allowed for the removal of bad politicians and governments. Mill's writing captured the spirit of nineteenth-century liberalism – encoding a recognition (and concern) that moving from liberal oligarchy to liberal democracy held potential dangers for the reformers. However, Mill was confident that the burghers could successfully reform their (liberal) system such that 'majoritarian tyranny' and 'extremism' were kept in check. Significantly, the emphasis was placed on the media as a mechanism for achieving this. So what is the role of the media within (Mill's) liberal democracy?

3.3.2 The media and liberal democracy

Liberal theorists have been keen to discuss two roles for the media, both based on the utilitarian notion that despotism is not good for the majority of people. Liberals propose that the symbiosis between a free press and liberal democracy keeps despotic government in check (Keane, 1991: 16).

Significantly, the origins of liberalism's call for a free press were associated with the struggle against feudal despotism. Liberal theorists traditionally defined the media as a counterweight to discourse closures associated with feudalism (e.g. the despotic power of monarchs, aristocrats and ecclesiastics).

Further, the media are seen to check power abuses and corruption on the part of politicians and bureaucrats. In this regard the media's role is to ensure the maximal flow of information within society to create an informed citizenry.

On the other hand, liberal theorists have been less keen to openly discuss another role for the media within liberal democracy, namely the role associated with countering a 'tyranny of the majority'. Once universal suffrage was granted, the affluent propertied elite (always a minority) necessarily faced the danger that the enfranchised non-affluent could use democratic majoritarianism to create a mass 'despotism' that would challenge their property rights/affluence. The middle classes have always recognized this danger and, going back to Jacksonian America, have developed communication strategies for dealing with this problem. Hence, it should be no surprise that a mass communication industry of professional image consultants, spin-doctors, pollsters and impression managers grew up to try and steer the masses (see 3.4 on p. 52). In this sense, the popular mass media's role – far from serving to create an informed citizenry – often serves as a vehicle for circulating the hype required to deliver mass publics to mainstream political parties, and thereby stabilize liberal democratic political processes. The result is the emergence of a hype-ocracy.

For the middle class/burghers, there were three issues of concern:

- Monitoring mechanisms were needed to ensure that those staffing the machinery of liberal governance did not transform themselves into self-serving despots;
- Ensuring that remnant (conservative) aristocratic influences were kept in check;
- Taming and controlling the (revolutionary) aspirations of the underclasses.

Managing each of these problems had implications for the liberal media, but the issue of managing the underclasses was especially important if burgher hegemony was to be preserved.

So how did we end up with mass media (geared to hype-circulation) which neatly complement the needs of liberal democracy? The story of Britain's nineteenth-century press is instructive in answering this question. Britain's liberal democracy was born through gradually extending the vote (to males) through the Reform Acts of 1832, 1867 and 1884–5. The press was integrally involved in this reformist process. The first half of the nineteenth century was a period of political turmoil in Britain. Urbanization and industrialization, plus the success of the American and French revolutions, produced restive urban underclasses. William Cobbett's *Political Register* gave voice to this underclass' revolutionary demands for political change. The *Political Register*, consisting only of a political comment written by Cobbett, a radical anarchist, had an enormous impact among the British working class because it was widely read aloud in public houses each week (Williams, 1984: 68–9). Because it sold for a mere 2d. the *Register* achieved record sales figures despite government attempts to repress it. While the *Register* was stirring up the underclasses, the editor of *The Times*, Thomas Barnes, used his newspaper (which serviced the liberal oligarchy) to convince the middle classes that they needed to reform their oligarchy into a liberal democracy to avoid revolution. Conservatives within the liberal oligarchy resisted extending the franchise and opposed journalists like Cobbett (who encouraged revolt) and Barnes (who insisted on publishing stories about mass unrest). In struggling against these conservatives Barnes was not only instrumental in getting the electoral reforms accepted, but also established the principle that a (liberal) press was independent of government and free to publish stories and opinions that governments did not like (Williams, 1984: chapter 6). But it was the enfranchisement of the urban working and lower middle classes that really changed the nature of the newspaper industry.

Reformists within the liberal oligarchy recognized the need to manage this mass of new voters, and turned to education and the media to achieve this. In Britain compulsory elementary education was introduced in 1870 as a vehicle for inducting the masses into habits and predispositions 'appropriate' for industrial society. One effect was to generate mass literacy. This created a market for mass newspapers. The first newspaper geared towards trying to 'tame' the newly enfranchised masses was *The Star* (launched in 1888). This London evening (mass) newspaper was the brainchild of Irish journalist T.P. O'Connor, who persuaded a group of affluent liberals that the way to make liberalism successful was to make democracy attractive (1984: 133). *The Star* ran easy-to-read short stories with jazzy headlines. From this early attempt to appeal to the newly enfranchised masses grew a new genre of hype-oriented mass media – a genre ultimately associated with Joseph Pulitzer (1847–1911) in the USA and Alfred Harmsworth (Lord Northcliffe) in Britain. Northcliffe (1865–1922) invented a new genre of profitable mass journalism when launching the *Daily Mail* in 1896 – a mass circulation newspaper that became financially successful by running easy-to-read hype stories attracting the (newly enfranchised) lower middle classes with enough disposable income to interest advertisers. Northcliffe contemptuously called his new halfpenny newspaper 'a newspaper for office boys written by office boys' (1984: 144). The *Daily Mail* pioneered a new way of reporting politics – focusing on personalities and gossip rather than principles, and on trivia rather than policy issues. Northcliffe drove his staff to seek out news that ordinary people would want to talk about on buses, trains, and in their offices (1984: 144–5). Northcliffe's innovation was a watershed in journalism because it produced two media genres – serious media for Britain's elite and popular media for the masses. The former circulates information and opinion valuable to elites concerned with policy formulation. The latter circulates hype which entertains and 'distracts' the masses and steers them into following those politicians running liberal democracies. This distinction between an elite and popular media continues to this day and has been exported to liberal democracies across the globe.

For the liberal oligarchs, Northcliffe's press was a godsend because he created a genre of hype journalism able to sway the masses through a form of mass suggestion based on repeating slogans until they were naturalized. Complex situations were reduced to short emotive phrases, which were beaten home day after day (1984: 150). Northcliffe derived personal political power from the way his press swayed the masses. Simultaneously, he made his propaganda machine profitable by building huge circulations and selling packaged mass-audiences to advertisers. Part of his success was learning to advertise and sell his own sensationalized product by developing stunts to attract readers, and by applying the media-hype notion that what you say about your product is as important as the product itself (1984: 137). Northcliffe was an innovator, a pioneer of the sensationalist-hyped mass media of today, and thereby a pioneer of the mass media machine required to make liberal democracies function.

This raises the question: are the two roles of the mass media – creating an informed citizenry (Mill's ideal) and circulating hype (the **Northcliffe/ Pulitzer press model**) – incompatible? Purists adhering to the Fourth Estate/ watchdog view of journalism would presumably regard them as incompatible. However, in contemporary liberal democracies the reality is that the media is a mixed system. Some journalists fulfill the watchdog role, and sections of the media circulate information that produces informed citizens. However, it is also true that political spin-doctoring is a growth industry. This presumably means that spin-doctors are deemed worth employing because they are successful at using the mass media to steer public opinion. Essentially, liberal democracy is a multifaceted system, and one part of the system involves hype making, geared towards taming mass publics and managing public opinion for policy elites.

3.4 Managing democracy: taming Western publics

Liberal democracy was born when nineteenth-century liberal oligarchs incrementally reformed political processes without losing control. The twentieth century saw Western elites become masters at managing democracies and taming their publics through developing a culture and spin industry, which includes PR, advertising, public opinion pollsters and image consultants (who construct celebrities for the masses to follow).

Stuart Ewen (1996: 60–5) traces the origins of PR to middle-class fears in early twentieth-century America that Western democracies faced an impending social crisis. Gustav Le Bon's (1922) study of crowd psychology (translated into English in 1896) fed into mounting middle-class panic about looming popular unrest. This panic was driven by Russia's 1917 Revolution, which created the world's first communist state and which was seen to increase the prospect of communist militancy everywhere. Among the Americans influenced by, and responding to, this fear of mass unrest were Walter Lippmann and Ivy Lee, who between them effectively invented the management of public opinion. Lippmann (1985) believed that social engineers and social scientists needed to apply their expertise to help to stabilize liberal democracies. Social scientists like Lippmann (1965), Gabriel Tarde (1969) and Ferdinand Tonnies (1988) concluded that public opinion could be manipulated by communication professionals armed with applied social science methods, and using the mass media as tools for social control. Lippmann argued that professionals could manufacture consent and so help to stabilize liberal democracy. This complemented middle-class desires for social mastery and the notion that 'the crowd' (an assembly of people who threatened to take over the streets) could be transformed by professional communicators into 'a public' (people who were separated from each other, and subject to manipulation via the mass media) (Ewen, 1996: 73). Ivy Lee translated the academic work of Lippmann, Le Bon, Tarde and Tonnies into a set of practical communication tools for manipulating public opinion. Lee (an employee of the Rockefellers) effectively founded public relations (PR) at the turn of the twentieth century (1996: 74–5). After the Russian Revolution of 1917, Lippmann persuaded Woodrow Wilson to deploy Lee's methods for government propaganda purposes. The result was the creation of the Committee on Public Information (CPI) in 1917, under the leadership of George Creel, which produced both foreign and domestic propaganda during the First World War. The CPI's domestic section produced news releases, films, pamphlets, cartoons, newsletters, and mounted exhibitions at state fairs (1996: chapter 6). Ultimately, it was Lee and Creel – both ex-journalists – who invented the basic methods and practices of PR, from which has grown the contemporary industry of communication consultants, spin-doctors and political image makers.

The effect has been a growing twentieth-century **Machiavellian**ization of political communication. So although the Jacksonian system pioneered demagoguery and showmanship to flatter and manage mass electorates, it was the twentieth century that saw the growth of a sophisticated professionalized system of demagoguery – combining the arts of public opinion measurement and spin-doctoring with a mass media machine (especially television) possessing an almost universal reach in Western democracies.

Because there are never enough resources to meet the demands of all citizens, manipulation seems inevitable within liberal democracies. Locke's proposed good liberal governance (geared towards facilitating wealth creation and property accumulation) would necessarily be undermined if mass citizenries could really influence resource-allocation policies. If unmanipulated democracy were implemented, liberal capitalism would experience what Habermas (1976) called steering problems, because the masses would inevitably make resource demands the system could not fulfill. Hence, not surprisingly, those running liberal democracies have found it necessary to try and manage the democratic process by using communication to try and tame their publics (with varying degrees of success). By the end of the twentieth century, Western democracies tended to be characterized by two-party systems representing different *factions* of the political elite. Although the system of political parties institutionalizes differences of opinion within ruling elites and facilitates competition between factions, many contemporary two-party systems now have political parties that have become increasingly indistinguishable. Convergence between the mainstream parties suggests that all political insiders may now be adhering to the same steering needs of 'effective' Lockean (liberal) governance, and both parties may now be deploying the same communication strategies to manipulate public opinion. By the turn of the twenty-first century, this 'sameness' between the players was generating, among Western electorates, a growing **alienation** from the political process (as witnessed in declining voter turnouts). These growing alienation levels serve to debunk any notion that mass publics can be 'routinely' steered/'manipulated' – i.e. not only is the work of 'steering' difficult; it can fail. It is possible that, in order to overcome contemporary alienation, it may be necessary to manage some 'difference' (and 'competition') back into the system, if only at the level of perceptions.

3.5 The media's evolving role in liberal governance

By the beginning of the twenty-first century liberal democracies were highly stable, managed affairs. To ensure that effective Lockean (liberal) governance is not undermined by pressures from below, the management of public opinion through spin-doctoring and impression management has been integrated into the very heart of the political process. The mass media have become fundamental tools of liberal democratic governance. Members of Western political elites now have to be skilled at using this mass media, or at least employ staffers who are media-savvy. In the intense competition for power between *factions* of the political elite, the faction most adept at using the mass media for impression management and the deployment of hype will generally triumph. This is a far cry from the relationship between the media and the political elites during the era of the early liberal oligarchies.

The relationship between liberals and the media has undergone a number of shifts over the past three and a half centuries, i.e.

- Liberalism was born of a struggle by burghers to free themselves from feudal overlordship. During this struggle the early print media were a revolutionary tool in the hands of the burghers. This is why the two dominant forces in Europe at the time – the monarchies and the Catholic Church – invested so much energy into trying to control and censor this early print media;
- Once the burghers established hegemonic control over certain territories, they began using the print media to circulate information/ideas within the oligarchy, e.g. early Parliamentary representatives operated small-circulation propaganda periodicals targeted at their constituencies. During this second phase, the print media became in-house communication vehicles for oligarchy members. There was no hype and no concern for the interests or opinions of the (unenfranchised) masses. During this phase, journalists had to struggle for the right to report Parliament and for freedom of expression rights. During phase two, the emergent liberal media were still a revolutionary force within Western society because liberalism was still struggling for survival against the (stronger) conservative feudal forces of Absolutism; and liberal hegemonies had not, as yet, congealed into conservative establishments;
- During phase three, liberal oligarchies became the established order. Hence, the liberal presses – which were still only concerned with in-house oligarchy matters – became conservative;
- During phase four, liberal oligarchies faced a new threat, namely, potential revolution from the urban underclasses created by nineteenth-century industrialization. Liberal oligarchies responded by reforming themselves into democracies. This necessarily shifted the relationship between liberals and the media. Effectively, the fourth phase saw the development of a two-tier press system – an elite 'quality' press (used by elites) and a mass press, associated with 'popular' and 'tabloid' journalism (McNair, 1999: 54). The latter circulated titillation, sensation and hype geared towards taming the newly enfranchised masses. This two-tiered system has remained in place ever since, being evident in the contemporary **information rich/information poor** dichotomy (see Table 3.2).

- Phase five – during the twentieth century – witnessed the professionalization of the hype machinery (PR, advertising, spin-doctoring and public opinion polling) and a dramatic expansion of the mass media machine (especially radio and television) as a tool for manipulating public opinion. During this phase, Parliaments declined in importance as television studios became more important than Parliaments for staging political performance, and power shifted away from the (open) legislative level to the executive level (behind closed doors).

Table 3.2   *Two-tiered media system*

	Popular media	Quality media
Audience	The masses	Social, political and economic elites
Content	Entertaining stories, sensation, hype and titillation, e.g. tabloid journalism's focus on crime, celebrities and sports competitions	Information required for policy making plus analysis and debate of policy issues

The effect of these shifts has been to alter the nature of journalism and the mass media within the political process. During the liberal oligarchy period, the media were used by decision makers (as an insider mechanism) to circulate information and opinions useful to the decision-making process. Within this system, journalists became part of the policy-formulation process – circulating information of value to policy makers. But, with the arrival of democracy, came the emergence of a different sort of media – a culture industry emerged, geared towards taming and distracting the masses through the circulation of sensation, hype and entertainment. This culture industry is not part of the policy-formulation aspect of governance, but is an integral part of the (external) hype dimension of the political process. Contemporary Western elites now have to invest considerable energy into this hype dimension of politics. Because of the difficulties and complexities of using communication to try and 'steer' the masses (and journalists), a professional spin industry has grown up to help politicians interface with the mass media. Employing professional communicators, expert in the practices of the culture industry, has become vital for Western politicians because this media machine has become the central mechanism through which the active minority (political elites) try to get themselves accepted by the (politically passive) majority. The result has been a media-ization of politics, and a growing symbiotic relationship between journalists and the spin industry. Effectively, a spin industry has become essential for trying to 'steer' the masses, which has become a precondition for making liberal democracy function.

Summary

You should now be familiar with the following key themes and concepts:

feudalism; liberal democracy; liberal oligarchy; Jacksonian democracy; mass liberal democracy; managed democracy; John Locke's notion of good governance; representative government; press freedom; tyranny of the majority; Fourth Estate; franchise reforms; 'steering' the masses; mass media; two-tier media system; hype journalism; Northcliffe's and Pulitzer's 'popular journalism'; public opinion; public relations; and demagoguery.

For further consideration

1 Chapter 3 presented a constructivist reading of liberal democracy. Locate a liberal empiricist reading of liberal democracy and compare the two approaches. Consider what such a comparison reveals about the construction of ideas (whether academic or journalistic);

2 The American Revolution is often portrayed as creating democracy. Yet it created an oligarchy (which was later reformed into a democracy). Who has promoted the 'democratic portrayal' and why?

3 Does liberal democracy help wealth creation? If so, how?

4 Identify those who argue that the massification of democracy was:

(a) a good thing and
(b) a bad thing;

Consider the way each of these two schools justifies its position and compare the logic of each position;

5 It could be argued that the liberal media simply reports the facts and has nothing to do with assisting in wealth creation. What do you think?

6 J.S. Mill saw the media as crucially important for making liberal democracy function. Did he perhaps overstate the capacity of the media/journalists to play the role he assigned to them?

(Continued)

For further consideration　Continued

7　To what extent does the Northcliffe/Pulitzer press model conform to J.S. Mill's notion of an ideal press?

8　Is the notion that public relations emerged from a need to 'tame' the masses overly cynical?

9　Is demagoguery compatible with democracy?

10　Does it matter that the media serving the information poor focuses on 'hype' rather than policy?

4 Political Media Practice: An Outline

Chapter 3 noted how mass media systems emerged to service the needs of mass democratic systems. Chapter 4 examines the role and functioning of the media and media practices within mass democracies. This chapter probes two of this book's key themes, namely the media-ization of politics and the evolution of *journalist–politician relationships* within the liberal democratic system. The self-portrayal journalists have of themselves as 'watchdogs over politicians' is critically examined and discussed in relationship to a number of journalistic genres. The chapter deconstructs journalistic practices, and argues that a *de facto symbiotic relationship* has grown between journalists, politicians and spin-doctors, which has led to a new form of *cynical journalism* (that is proving dysfunctional for liberal democracy). It is argued that the industrialization of journalism has been centrally implicated in the way journalist–politicians relationships have developed. Chapter 4 focuses on the journalistic side of the politician–spin-doctor symbiosis, whereas chapter 7 will look at the same relationship from the spin-doctor's side (chapters 4 and 7 should be read as a couplet). Chapter 4 starts by sketching out journalism's journey from a Fourth Estate into sensationalized watch-dogism, and describes the emergence of (televised) 'entertaining spectacle' journalism. Thereafter, journalistic practices are deconstructed; the institutionalization of politician–media relationships described; and the extent of 'journalistic power' within the political process assessed.

The evolution of liberalism into a democratic form coincided with the emergence of mass media technologies able to simultaneously communicate with millions, even billions of people. These technologies created the possibilities for politicians to communicate with the masses, and hence facilitated the building of mass democracies. Not surprisingly, the symbolic component of mass democratic politics became enmeshed with the mass media. Consequently, mass media journalists became key players in producing and circulating political symbolism. Journalists specializing in politics have, over time, related to the political system in various ways. Each pattern of interaction between journalists and politicians left residues of practices and myths that continue to impact on today's interface. The characteristics of these practices are important because they set the parameters for how politics is presented to the masses. The ethos of the political ideologies, myths and beliefs, and the portrayal of political players is to a great extent governed by the nature of media practices and the media's self-understanding of its relationship to the political process.

Unpacking the media's role in the political process is facilitated by examining four themes – the nature of the relationships (institutionalized and informal) between journalists and politicians; how commercial pressures set parameters for journalists; the practices of political journalists; and journalistic beliefs about their role in the political process. The latter, belief component of liberal journalism, can best be understood by examining the notions of Fourth Estate and watchdog journalism.

4.1 From Fourth Estate to sensationalized watchdogism

Central to the way in which the media/politics relationship has been conceptualized within liberal democracies are the two inter-related notions of the Fourth Estate and watchdog journalism. These lie at the heart of liberal journalism's professional ideology – representing for liberal journalists the core principles defining their 'ideal' relationship to the political machine. This 'ideal' encodes three elements liberal journalists ascribe to themselves. Firstly, the media are deemed to be a separate 'estate' within the political process. This implies that the media should be seen to have the same 'rights' as the other estates – as fully fledged participants in the governance process; in fact, be seen as autonomous players within the political process. Actually, the media are deemed a special sort of participant (with 'additional' rights?) because the model grants to journalists the role of watchdogs over the other political participants. So the media not only has 'autonomy' (setting it apart from the other estates), but also has 'special rights' over and above other players, namely the right to have its autonomy protected; the right to monitor the other players; and the right to 'free speech' (i.e. the right to report on whatever it deems fit). From this

Fourth Estate notion grew the idea liberal journalists should be adversarial (towards politicians) to be effective watchdogs.

The *Fourth Estate/watchdog notion* was originally proposed by *The Times* editor, John Delane. Delane formulated this conceptualization of liberal journalism within the context of mid-nineteenth-century British political turmoil (as urbanization and industrialization transformed the social landscape, producing a restive urban underclass). *The Times* serviced England's liberal oligarchy, which was divided over the issue of reform. This paper, since the editorship of Barnes, had worked to persuade England's propertied classes that reform was better than revolution. Delane advocated reforming the liberal oligarchy into liberal democracy, and insisted on reporting working-class political unrest directed at the oligarchy. This created conflict between his newspaper and conservatives within the oligarchy who did not wish for the press to report on unrest. From this context grew Delane's now famous 1852 editorial:

> The first duty of the press is to obtain the earliest and most cor-rect intelligence of the events of the time and instantly by dis-closing them to make them the common property of the nation. The press lives by disclosures ... bound to tell the truth as we find it without fear of consequences – to lend no convenient shelter to acts of injustice and oppression, but to consign them to the judgment of the world ... the duty of the journalist is the same as that of the historian – to seek out truth, above all things, and to present to his readers not such things as state-craft would wish them to know, but the truth as near as he can attain it. (Delane, in Schultz, 1998: 25)

Schultz (1998: 29) notes, in the years since Delane, that the media have, through successful lobbying and marketing, largely naturalized this Fourth Estate journalistic vision within liberal democracies. Conse-quently, liberal journalists now adhere to the following self-definition of their role:

- To be necessarily critical of politicians (adversarial);
- To champion citizen rights against the abuse of state power;
- To provide a platform for debate.

But what is the relevance of this Fourth Estate/watchdog vision of jour-nalism within contexts, where (contemporary) media industries are governed by commercial pressures driving them to favour entertaining, titillating and sensational content (which is far removed from the Delane information/disclosure model)? Many contemporary journalists working for media favouring spectacle and sensation still believe themselves to be adherents of the watchdog principle. This has produced a journalistic genre hybridizing adversarial watchdogism with reports focusing on politics as competition and conflict, mixed with the titillation of personal indiscretions and evaluations of the 'character' of political players. The outcome is a sensationalized watchdogism appealing to entertainment-seeking mass audiences. However, before examining sensationalized watchdogism, it seems useful to unpack the wider picture of political journalism's practices. This requires examining the full range of relationships that can develop between journalists and politicians. In this regard, Sabato (1991: chapters 2 and 3) identifies five types of US journalism. These are useful, not just for understanding American journalism, but also for understanding, in general, the sorts of relationships that can emerge between journalists and politicians. Modifying Sabato produces a six-genre typology of journalist–politician relationships.

The first type of journalist–politician relationship is (pre-watchdog) *partisan journalism* wherein the media support a particular political party, or ideology. This form of media characterized the early liberal oligarchies of Britain and America when middle-class/burgher journalists actively worked to challenge monarchies. Partisan journalists worked collaboratively with those politicians they supported to help to promote their causes. Two famous journalists who operated small partisan presses promoting early liberalism were John Wilkes in Britain and Benjamin Franklin in the USA. Partisan journalism also characterized South Africa's anti-apartheid alternative press (Tomaselli and Louw, 1991).

Pre-watchdog journalism encodes the practices of journalists who are outside the establishment and who position themselves as 'committed' advocates of changing their political system. They flaunt with pride their partisanship and propagandistic role, and are in no way concerned with monitoring politicians (as watchdogs). However, once journalists become insiders within a liberal political system, their self-definitions necessarily shift as they eschew partisanship. Non-partisan journalists can adopt one of three insider relationships to the liberal political system:

- The *journalist-as-loyal-opposition*, or watchdog. This role can take two forms. Firstly, the provider of 'intelligence' (for policy makers). Secondly, the watchdog adversary;
- The *lapdog*, where journalists cooperate with politicians to make the political system work. It is easy for partisan journalists to slide into becoming lapdog journalists when (successful) revolutionary movements they support become governments;
- Seeking out those aspects of political behavior that provoke emotional responses (e.g. anger, shock or outrage) in audiences because these can be sensationalized and hyped up. This type of journalist–politics relationship is associated with *spectacle journalism* (see 4.2 on p. 66),

geared towards attracting mass audiences, rather than an actual concern with politics-as-policy. This type lends itself to politicians working with (or leaking stories to) journalists, in order to undermine their opponents.

These three broad insider relationships have, over the years, taken on five non-partisan journalistic forms, as discussed below.

The second type of the journalist–politician relationship is *Fourth Estate journalism* as envisaged by Delane. In this model, journalists are insiders within the liberal political process – a part of the policy-formulation process in so far as they service the policy-making elites with information, 'intelligence', opinion and a platform for debate. This journalistic genre eschews sensation and titillation, and can lead to conflict between journalists and politicians because Fourth Estate journalists will publish stories politicians would prefer were repressed. But this genre does not cultivate a necessarily adversarial position. Neither does it deliberately pursue politics-as-competition-and-conflict stories as a means to attract audiences. Within Anglo liberalism, it is a genre associated with 'quality journalism' aimed at elite audiences interested in policy issues (see 2.2.4 on p. 23).

Third, there is *muckraking (or 'yellow') journalism* as developed in the USA by Joseph Pulitzer and Randolph Hearst towards the end of the nineteenth century. This journalistic genre, which is commercially driven, strives to build mass audiences through sensationalism. Spectacular, lurid or titillating stories about the rich and famous (including politicians) attract mass audiences, as do stories of conflict, sex and pain. Journalists justify such stories by deploying the Fourth Estate principle, which gives them the right to publish whatever they want. It is an adversarialism driven not by political commitment or a concern with policy issues, but by a search for sensationalist and personally intrusive stories. Conflict between journalists and politicians occurs when 'yellow' stories impact on political players. In nineteenth-century America this journalistic genre also became associated with corrupt journalistic practices in which politicians paid the media to not publish negative stories. President Theodore Roosevelt branded it 'muckraking' journalism – after a rake designed to collect manure. When US muckraking journalism flourished, Britain's equivalent sensation-seeking commercial media avoided the extremes seen in America, largely because of Lord Northcliffe's influence (see 3.3.2 on p. 49). Northcliffe's presses delivered sensationalism to the masses, but tempered this with a British Empire patriotism. Northcliffe's 'new journalism' assumed its audience was a passive public who wanted less politics, more human interest, sensation and sport (Negrine, 1994: 45–6). This produced a genre of mass-circulation titillation journalism more inclined towards a lapdog relationship with politicians than its American equivalent. As Negrine (1994: 57–8) notes, this journalism was part of the entertainment industry (servicing the masses), not part of the 'political press' (servicing the elites). To some extent muckraker journalism de-politicizes the masses due to its focus on human interest stories, scandals and sexual titillation involving (non-political) entertainment or sports personalities.

A fourth type is *lapdog journalism*, i.e. journalists avoid adversarialism and put aside the watchdog approach. Instead, they collaborate with politicians. This collaboration is not necessarily motivated by political partisanship, but is more often driven by a belief that one's society faces 'challenges' serious enough to make adversarial watchdog journalism unhelpful while trying to solve the problems. Sabato (1991) argues that lapdog journalism characterized the US media from the 1930s to mid-1960s. It began when the media opted to assist Roosevelt to implement his 'New Deal'. The 'New Deal' involved the government adopting **Keynesian** policies and investing in huge public works programs to try and solve the Great Depression's unemployment crisis. Possibly the most serious consequence of America's lapdog period was Senator McCarthy's 1950s' political witch hunt of communists. McCarthy could not have flourished without media acquiescence. Because objective journalism advocated simply reporting the 'facts' – McCarthy's hearings – McCarthyism was able to flourish without any critical scrutiny.

A sub-variety of lapdog journalism is *sunshine journalism* – a Third World genre emerging from the New World Information Order/NWIO (Masmoudi, 1979). During the 1970s and 1980s NWIO theorists argued that the problems facing Third World governments were so serious that journalists needed to avoid 'negative' stories which might destabilize them, and instead actively collaborate with their governments by producing 'development journalism'. Development journalism deliberately focused on positive news, and stories that promoted modernist development. Much development journalism mutated into propaganda, while sunshine journalism allowed corruption and maladministration to flourish. Lapdog/sunshine journalism also characterized the journalism practiced by Afrikaner nationalists (at the apartheid era SABC) and black nationalists (at the post-apartheid SABC) (Louw, 2005). Journalists employed by the Communist Party-run media of the Soviet-bloc and China also practiced a form of lapdog journalism.

Fifth, is a variety of watchdog journalism characterized by *adversarial watchdogism* – i.e. the belief that journalists must be deliberately adversarial towards politicians in order to function as effective watchdogs. Although related to the Fourth Estate approach, adversarial watchdog journalism has less of a policy focus than Delane's model. It focuses more on political personalities, partly because personality and character issues are easier to sell to mass audiences than policy issues. Such watchdogism can generate controversy and conflict without necessarily improving the quality of socio-political debate or policy making.

Sabato (1991) argues that American journalists abandoned lapdog journalism in favour of an adversarial watchdog approach as a result of the Ted Kennedy Chappaquiddick accident and Watergate. The former involved the attempt to cover up a car accident in 1969 in which a female passenger died after Senator Kennedy drove off a bridge at Chappaquiddick. Watergate involved the scandal of Nixon and his White House staffers being caught covering up their attempted 1972 burglary/espionage at the Democratic Party's Watergate HQ. After these incidents, American journalists were no longer prepared to look the other way, and because of Chappaquiddick were especially no longer prepared to ignore the sexual behaviour of politicians, and their alcohol and drug use. After the Watergate scandal and the *Pentagon Papers* (a 1971 book which exposed hidden truths about US policy making during the Vietnam War), an automatic mistrust of politicians became encoded into American political journalism. The resultant adversarial watchdogism affected more than America, e.g. Australian journalistic practices were powerfully influenced by adversarial watchdogism. In fact, Watergate was a myth-making event of global importance – entering journalistic folklore across the entire Anglo world, and transforming the professional ideology of liberal journalists everywhere. The mythology of Watergate plus post-Watergate adversarial watchdogism has, as Sabato (1991: 62) notes, been attracting a particular kind of person into journalism ever since. The results of this sort of recruitment, combined with mounting commercial pressures, have generated a new genre called junkyard journalism.

The sixth type, *junkyard journalism*, marries aspects of muckraking to adversarial watchdogism. Sabato says that this genre of attack journalism, which emerged in the mid-1970s, produced 'political reporting that is often harsh, aggressive, and intrusive, where feeding frenzies flourish, and gossip reaches print. Every aspect of private life potentially becomes fair game for scrutiny as a new, almost "anything goes" philosophy takes hold' (1991: 26).

Junkyard journalism is even less helpful than adversarial watchdogism for promoting the exploration, discussion and debate of policy issues. This form of journalism is especially well suited to the needs of commercial media chasing mass audiences because it is a highly sensationalist genre lending itself to voyeuristic stories about conflict, pain and sex associated with the lurid and titillating events in the lives of the rich and famous. This form of journalism reached new lows during Clinton's presidency. In fact, so routinized was junkyard journalism by the time of the Monica Lewinsky affair, and so 'immunized' had Americans become to junkyard 'revelations', that Clinton's presidency survived the US media's titillating muckraking of Clinton's sexual relationship with Lewinsky.

Junkyard journalism is inherently unconcerned with politics as policy making. Because this journalistic genre is concerned with 'storytelling' rather than Delane's 'information and intelligence' (Nimmo and Combs, 1990: 27) it can become a highly de-politicizing force in society – because it focuses on entertainment and sports celebrities, and (non-political) human interest stories geared towards sensation, titillation, voyeurism and human emotions. The global Anglo media have found Princess Diana and Prince Charles especially valuable in this regard. Even when junk-yard journalists concern themselves with politics, they focus on hyped up politics, celebrity players and sensationalized watchdogism. Junkyard journalism portrays politics as an entertaining spectacle, as a competitive sport, or a backdrop for stories revealing – preferably in ways television can exploit visually – heroic victories, pathos, human foibles, sexuality, aggression, or greed. Ironically, for political elites (concerned with policy making), this is not a bad thing because, although it means they must employ professional communicators to create the hype beloved by junk-yard journalists, it also means that the media distract and entertain the masses, which enables the policy elites to get on with the business of governing while the masses have their attention focused elsewhere.

The late twentieth century saw junkyard journalism diffused within lib-eral democracies across the world. This occurred partly because American journalism (especially the televisual form) was shared globally across the Anglo world, and so came to serve as a (globalized) journalistic model. Further, successful organizations like Rupert Murdoch's News Limited (which produces newspapers, television, cable television, satellite televi-sion, magazines and movies in the USA, UK and Australia) did much to hone and internationalize this genre which is simultaneously highly prof-itable, entertaining for mass publics, and effectively deflects public scrutiny away from the sites and processes of political policy making.

4.2 News as entertaining spectacle

McNair (1999: 67) noted how the arrival of cable and satellite television increased competition in all media sectors. This in turn increased com-mercial pressure on all media workers. Enhanced commercialization of journalism, including political news, has been the result. Even the BBC has been affected by the resultant shift in news values.

Commercial pressure on newsrooms has seen the adoption of a racy style of journalism, well suited to reporting entertaining spectacles. This genre (although not lapdog journalism) comfortably confirms liberal hegemonies. It is news

> crucially lacking in substance, dealing only with the spectacu-lar, epiphenomenal aspects of social and political problems, while avoiding the discussion of solutions. The viewer is

shocked, or entertained, or outraged, but nor necessarily any wiser about the underlying causes of the problem being covered. The entertainment value of events begins to take precedence over their political importance ... In an intensifying commercial environment, therefore, the political process comes to be seen by journalists as the raw material of a commodity – news or current affairs – which must eventually be sold to the maximum number of consumers. Inevitably, those aspects of the process which are the most sellable are those with the most spectacular and dramatic features, and which can be told in those terms. (McNair, 1999: 67–8)

The result is 'news as spectacle' (Fallows, 1997: 52), epitomized by the *60 Minutes* genre of USA and Australian television journalism. This genre turns the anchorman into something of a celebrity, who takes on the persona of an adversarial watchdog 'journalist' who 'protects' ordinary people against the rich and powerful. This is apparently achieved through sensationalized exposures of petty scandals (1997: 57) and adopting hyped-up pseudo-adversarial postures. As Fallows (1997: 58) notes, anchorman-as-stars ask questions from briefing papers and operate more like actors than journalists. These performers lack the background to ask good follow-up questions or recognize when interviewees say something new or surprising. This is greatly advantageous to politicians because it lends itself to manipulation by PRs and spin-doctors.

Because news as spectacle is about entertaining audiences, much 'spectacle' content involves stories about the entertainment industry and celebrities (see chapter 8). The line between news and entertainment, and journalism and anchorman performances, becomes blurred as stories are geared to entertainment, conflict, drama or titillation. It has been suggested by Jon Katz that this has produced a 'new' kind of news discourse which blends Hollywood films, television culture, pop music, pop art, celebrity magazines, tabloid telecasts and home videos (Underwood, 2001: 109). This new news genre is associated with the tendency to 'empty' stories of substantive news content. The OJ Simpson, Rodney King and Monica Lewinsky sagas – which became televisual dramas across the Anglo world – are examples of this 'spectacle' news genre. Such stories can have major political ramifications, despite having little to do with governance, and everything to do with ratings-driven entertainment, e.g. the OJ Simpson trial whipped up racial tensions in the USA because an African-American (OJ Simpson) was on trial for the murder of his white wife. The Rodney King affair whipped up similar racial tensions after video images showed white policemen beating King (an African-American). The Rodney King story was also a first-rate example of how televised stories can be skewed by what is *not* recorded by cameras. And although the Lewinsky saga was little more than a hyped-up story about office sex and indiscretion, it severely destabilized US governance by distracting the Clinton administration from its policy-making functions.

This makes TV celebrity journalists ideal partners for the symbiotic relationship that has grown up between the media and spin-doctors. TV celebrity journalists need dramatic stories as backdrops for their (entertaining) performances, while spin-doctors need vehicles to air their hype and get publicity for their celebrity politicians. The result is a collaboration between TV celebrity journalists and celebrity politicians – they work together, creating shallow entertainment for the masses. This symbiotic relationship benefits the media industry, celebrity journalists (and their backroom research staffers) and celebrity politicians (and their backroom PRs). Effectively, they are all communication professionals, aware they are part of a hype/entertainment industry. Both journalists and spin-doctors know that many of the stories created by PRs are simply 'hype', crafted as entertaining spectacle to service story-hungry media. Journalists, PRs and advertisers call such stories 'puffery' or 'fluff' (Preston, 1994: 26). But because news airtime/space must be filled, many will be broadcast/published. For spin-doctors the advantage of this journalistic genre is its inherent shallowness – well-crafted hype can effectively bury stories that may cause problems for policy makers. The result is 'talk-show democracy' (Blumler and Gurevitch, 2001: 394).

Importantly, this news genre thrives on stage-managed conflict. Media audiences love the drama of competition and conflict, hence the appeal of competitive sports. But real political conflict is both destabilizing and potentially dangerous. Liberal democracies have precisely stabilized themselves by managing much real conflict out of the system – as examined in Marcuse's (1964) discussion of American society.

The Frankfurt School (e.g. Marcuse and Adorno) was concerned that the culture industry's discourse-closing capacity produced one-dimensional societies (Louw, 2001: chapter 1). Adorno and Horkheimer (1979) examined how the culture industry created 'pseudo' choices by presenting similar phenomena (e.g. ten brands of soap powder, or three political parties) as being 'different'. This generated the appearance of alternatives, when no substantive choice was really available. So, instead of facilitating the consideration of (and conflict over) substantive alternatives, the media actually narrowed options – presenting only a limited range of possible issues and opinions. Entertaining spectacle news precisely achieves discourse closure because it facilitates stage-managed conflict. Politics, as reported by this genre, presents a series of hyped-up stage-managed conflicts in which politics is effectively presented as just another (managed) competitive sport.

Sport as entertainment is perfect material for commercial television because of the competition between two teams, players, racehorses and so on. The drama of deciding a winner (who remains unknown until the very end of the competition) creates tension. This is a great audience-puller. Better still, the tension tends to escalate as the game proceeds, so audiences stay glued to their televisions. For the media, sports spectacles have a number of great features – they are cheap to produce (measured against the mass audiences attracted); can be made to fit planned media timetables (i.e. are largely predictable); can be managed and 'scripted' through a collaborative process involving the media and sports managers/PRs. But despite being 'managed', they create an audience experience of (seemingly unmanaged) drama and frenzy. Further, sports competitions generate heroes who can be crafted and packaged into celebrities by publicity managers. These celebrities can be turned into marketable commodities by publicity agents who craft their scripted personas into entertaining spectacles in their own right, providing yet more material to fill the media's insatiable appetite for entertaining news.

Since sports competitions have become so profitable for the commercial media (especially television), it is not surprising that these media have opted to read politics through a competitive sports framework, adopting the news frames of horseracing and (sports) celebrity. Jamieson (1992: 165–7) notes how this news genre, which frames politics into a 'game' or 'war', focuses on strategy. This *strategy schema* leads journalists (and their audiences) to focus on the following questions: which politician is 'winning' and what tactics and strategies are politicians using. It 'encourages voters to ask not who is better able to serve as President but who is going to win' (1992: 167). This turns politicians into performers (akin to sportsmen/women or actors) of carefully designed messages (Watson, 2003: 55). It turns voters into spectators or audiences. For journalists, it reduces politics to a story about just another form of competitive sport. Political reporting is emptied of substantive questions, as journalists focus on 'persons rather than situations' (Cappella and Jamieson, 1997: 84), i.e. journalists concern themselves with the personality traits and motivations of politicians rather than issues of governance. And because the strategic interpretive frame is premised upon the sports model, it encodes the (unjustified) assumption that winning the game is the (only?) motivation driving politicians. From this emerges a cynical view – permeating the strategic schema of journalism – that all politicians are Machiavellians concerned with winning, not governing, and all political actions, no matter how noble, are motivated by strategic intent (1997: 19). This slides easily into the watchdog notion of journalism – providing journalists with a justification for mistrusting politicians; reaffirming their need to adopt adversarial positions towards politicians; and boosting journalists' egos because they see themselves as the defenders of democracy against Machiavellian politicians. This causes some journalists to become patronizing towards their audiences (Jamieson, 1992: 173) because they believe they have special insight into the political process and the motivations of politicians.

The strategy schema for reporting elections generates a string of stories with much in common to competitive sporting series like World Cup Soccer or American Football. Political reporters use the language of competition, strategy and tactics. This is mixed with 'objective reports' about polling results and (stage-managed) events like leadership debates. A symbiotic relationship tends to develop between journalists, pollsters and spin-doctors. Political journalists evaluate political performances much like sports journalists evaluate players in sports matches. In the process they pick winners and losers. This tends to influence audience perceptions, driving up the popularity of politicians rated 'good players' (through a journalist-driven bandwagon effect). The ability to play 'the media-game' is reflected in the polls. Spin-doctors spring into action on the basis of polling results, generating the next wave of strategy and tactics stories, and journalistic evaluations of political performance. The cycle is repeated (see Figure 4.1). This results in sports-like competitions, filled with drama, winners and losers – all mediated by journalists – which generates revenue for the commercial media. It also empowers journalists, turning them into 'experts' on political strategy, and licensing them to evaluate the (media) performance of politicians (which gives journalists the power to boost or undermine political careers). This

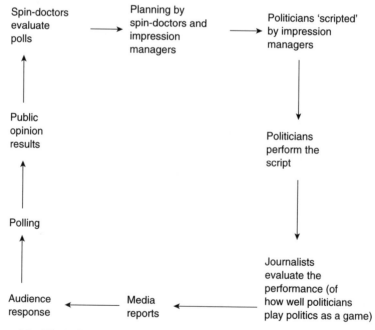

Figure 4.1   *The 'politics-as-strategy' cycle*

produces a watchdogism not based on evaluating policy making or abilities at governance, but based on evaluating personalities, impression-management skills, and politicians' abilities as performers within the media's strategy schema. The advantage of this genre is that it slides easily into a racy, easy-to-understand reporting style that accommodates 'human' stories about endurance, conflict and rivalries, or titillating voyeuristic stories involving human failings, and sexual or financial scandal. Producing such stories does not require high-quality journalists able to engage with the complexities of policy making and governance.

Less complex stories neatly complement the needs of profit-driven media managers because it means that less skilled, and hence cheaper, journalists can be hired. News as entertaining spectacle is profitable because it simultaneously appeals to mass audiences and facilitates the de-skilling and downsizing of newsrooms, because ever-greater volumes of stories simply involve the less complex task of re-processing the hyper-news generated by PRs.

This news genre appeals to the masses precisely because it is entertaining and easy to assimilate. Idealistic intellectuals – with ideological commitments to the notion that democracy should entail active mass publics engaging with politics as policy – will be critical of this shift to infotainment and news as spectacle. But media organizations, seeking profit maximization, necessarily ignore this idealism and cater to the masses' preference for entertainment over in-depth coverage of policy issues. Those staffing the political machine have a vested interest in supporting this commercially driven racier genre of political coverage for two reasons:

Firstly, for politicians, publicity and profile are the fuel for success. The commercialization of political news has dramatically increased the demand for hyped-up stories which politicians are particularly well placed to provide (McNair, 1999: 69). So the new genre has created enhanced opportunities for publicity-minded politicians prepared to script themselves in accordance with the new political news frame. Secondly, for political managers it creates the potential for reducing public scrutiny over policy making. This is achieved by creating a division of labor within the political machine – some specialize in staffing the publicity/spin-doctoring machine which distracts the hype-seeking journalists (and mass public); while others staff the policy-making machinery. Those staffing the publicity machine need to constantly monitor the media as a function of being communication specialists servicing these mass media (see 12.3.6 on p. 264). However, those staffing the policy machinery can largely ignore the mass media (with their shallow hype) and focus instead on the elite media (which provide the information, intelligence, analysis and opinion required for policy work).

For most people in liberal democracies, their awareness of politics is provided by journalists working for the mass media. Hence, understanding the view most people have of politics requires unpacking how journalists construct the mass media's news window.

4.3 Constructing the news window 1: journalistic practices

News is the product of a set of institutionalized work practices. Practices, originally born at Pulitzer- and Northcliffe-owned presses, have become generic across the Anglo world's newspaper, radio and television newsrooms. Journalists are socialized into these practices that are enmeshed with discourses about the 'profession' of journalism (i.e. self-image) and discourses about audience.

Journalists are confronted by huge volumes of information and an enormous array of phenomena that could qualify as news. Creating news involves sorting through these and selecting which will actually be allowed to reach audiences. So news making involves a process of selection, emphasis and de-emphasis. Journalists refer to this process as knowing what is 'newsworthy'. Effectively, journalists are gatekeepers (White, 1950), allowing some information through the gate, but blocking other information. So journalists become agenda setters (Cohen, 1963), setting 'the agenda' or 'parameters' for what is discussed within a society. Noelle-Neumann (1991) has noted how agenda setting can set in motion a 'spiral of silence', i.e. social discourse is progressively closed as people fall silent when their views do not coincide with what the media portray as 'majority opinion'. Hence the 'gatekeeper' or 'agenda setter' role holds great social significance. Gatekeeping has been institutionalized in sites called newsrooms, where the process of selection, emphasis and de-emphasis has been industrialized into a set of systematized routines. Significantly, the very routinization of the process has tended to render it opaque to journalists themselves. Anglo journalists (working within an essentially empiricist worldview), believe news is 'out there', and they simply 'find it' (see chapter 1). They apparently find it because they 'know' what is 'newsworthy'. Constructivists, such as Tuchman (1978), however, argue that journalists 'construct reality' rather than 'find it' (see chapter 1).

News, as Tuchman (1978) says, is a 'window on the world' (see Box 4.1) – journalists, through their work practices, construct a window opening through the wall, hence creating a partial view of the overall panorama – i.e. only one portion of 'reality' is available through the 'window'. The rest, outside the window-frame, is hidden behind the wall.

Box 4.1 Thinking about news as a window

- Consider for a moment the room you are currently in and how the presence or absence of windows changes your relationship to the world around you (e.g. do you know what is behind each of the walls?);
- If the room you are in had no windows and you had never been outside the room imagine how that would change the understanding of the world. In this regard consider Plato's cave (see chapter 1);
- Now mentally place yourself in a windowless room you have never been outside of, and imagine that someone comes and breaks a window through one of the walls. Consider how your understanding of the world would be constructed by the position, size and shape of this window – i.e. how would your understanding of the world be altered by what you *could* see and were still *unable* to see?
- Consider any window in the room you are in. Think of this window as a television screen – if that window were a television screen its position, size and shape would have been created by a camera angle (i.e. what the camera *was* pointed at and what it was *not* pointed at);
- Consider the extent to which moving a camera is equivalent to moving the position of the window;
- In a society which gets most of its news from television, would it be valid to say that switching off the camera (or television) is like blocking up the window?
- Consider how television images seem to be as realistic as looking out of a real window, whereas newspapers do not have this effect;
- Why do television 'windows' create this sense of 'reality'? And is this sense of reality in any way problematic?
- If journalists construct news 'windows', what is the role of spin-doctors?

News is consequently always skewed by the size, shape and position of the window frame. This skewing is not (usually) caused by conscious decision making aimed at deliberately creating partiality. Rather, the window is the outcome of whatever set of practices, work routines and discourses journalists have been trained and socialized into accepting as 'the way things are done'. The partiality of news derives from the news frame built by journalists applying their particular conception of newsworthiness.

Once a journalist has internalized the appropriate vision of 'newsworthiness' (and the work routines accompanying this vision), the model becomes 'naturalized' and 'self-policing'. Thereafter, journalists need not confront the fact they are constructing a partial 'window on the world'. This window is made through a process of selection, emphasis and de-emphasis routinized in the following way.

Firstly, journalists are trained to work according to a set of formulas – they repeatedly look for the same things; routinely ask the same questions. The formulas narrow the options for what can become news by 'guiding' the information-gathering process. There are two key formulas, namely the inverted pyramid and the six-question-formula ('who' does 'what', 'when', 'where', 'why' and 'how'). Journalistic training privileges the writing of 'hard factual news' that the six-question-formula delivers. These six questions are an excellent shorthand method for capturing the essence of 'immediate' events-based stories (e.g. motor accidents or fires). However, the formula becomes a great hindrance when trying to report on complex issues embedded in convoluted contexts (e.g. the reasons for warfare). The formula does not equip journalists to report on complex situations, but does serve to confirm the 'professional discourse' of 'objectivity'. The idea that journalists are 'objective' because only 'the facts' (delivered by answering the six questions) are reported is a powerful self-image and 'value system' central to Anglo journalism. In essence, because hard concrete facts are privileged, stories acquire 'tangibility' and so appear 'factual' rather than 'constructed' – Tuchman calls this 'facticity' (1978: 82). It allows journalists to hide from themselves the 'constructed' and 'partial' nature of their stories. In addition, television journalism has developed a standardized matrix of 'action' images that are sought out and combined with the six-question formula. Effectively television news has developed a visual formula driving journalists to produce news seeking out 'action' and/or the visually spectacular. Television news, because of this visual formula, the six-question-formula and the inverted pyramid formula produces radically simplified news constructs that eschew complexity and ignore nuances.

Journalists also learn to deploy the inverted pyramid formula. This directs journalists to grab audience attention at the start of the story ('the introduction'), and pack the heart of the story into the first few paragraphs. Arguments (building towards a conclusion) are not constructed; rather, journalists put the 'conclusion' at the beginning. This focus on 'the intro' mutated into the television 'sound bite' – television journalists seek out contacts providing 'snappy one-liners'. This makes television news even less able to report on complex situations than newspapers. PRs use their knowledge of journalistic formulas and the demand for 'soundbites' to maximize their chances of placing stories (see 7.4 on p. 163).

A second feature of routinizing journalistic practices is the importance that time plays in imposing certain practices onto journalists. Time necessarily plays a significant role in news selection processes because news making takes place within the parameters of deadlines. News has to be produced regardless of what is actually happening outside the newsroom because newspapers are printed at fixed times and radio and television news bulletins go on air at fixed points in time. Further, Tuchman's 'window' is largely built during office hours. So newsworthiness is enmeshed with journalistic work hours, newsroom time management and meeting production deadlines. There are also some periods (certain days of the week or year) which are traditionally slow news periods. Spin-doctors use their knowledge of such time constraints to maximize their chances of placing news stories.

A third aspect of routinizing journalistic practices is inducting new staffers into newsroom procedures. Each newsroom will have a set of procedures (and related organizational culture). Some of the routinized procedures for collecting, writing and submitting are idiosyncratic in one newsroom, while others will be found across whole media groups. All procedures set parameters on news production, and so socializing journalists into an organization's procedures helps to steer their production into conformity with the genre associated with that organization. Similarly, journalists are socialized into accepting the newsroom bureaucracy, hierarchical pecking orders and the particular style of office politics operative in their newsroom. A relationship will exist between hierarchical chains of command and the operative bureaucratized procedures. It has been suggested that this is a defining characteristic of news production, i.e. news is the ultimate bureaucratized meaning making, because news is simply the outcome of the highly routinized process of collecting and processing information guided by formal rules. Hence news takes on the characteristics of an 'eternal recurrence' (Rock, 1981) – it is meaning that looks repetitive, precisely because it is meaning emergent from a repetitive set of bureaucratized procedures. For spin-doctors this is useful – it means news is highly susceptible to manipulation given the existence of predictable journalistic routines and procedures. Spin-doctors can employ their knowledge of procedures to 'plant' stories at the right time and with the right person so as to maximize the chances of stories being used.

Further, commercial mass media necessarily want to attract the largest possible audience. In practical terms this means that it is unwise to alienate any segment of the potential mass audience. Hence, in commercial newsrooms, journalists are socialized into making 'appropriate' news judgments – people and ideas that may alienate the great mass of people in 'the middle' because they are seen as 'extreme' or 'unconventional' are reported in a particular way in order to avoid offending the intended

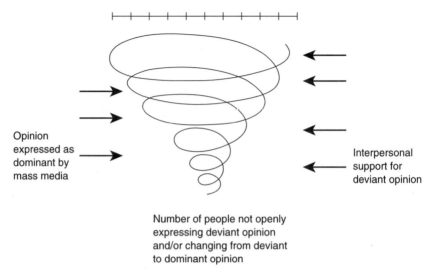

Opinion
expressed as
dominant by
mass media

Interpersonal
support for
deviant opinion

Number of people not openly
expressing deviant opinion
and/or changing from deviant
to dominant opinion

Figure 4.2 *Spiral of silence*
Source: McQuail and Windahl, 1981

audience (McNair, 1999: 77). People and ideas fundamentally threatening to the 'sensible center' are either not reported, or reported with a 'sneer' – so audiences are made aware that these ideas are 'extreme' and 'unacceptable'. This effectively steers the commercial media towards the 'sensible center'. Conflicts and controversies that are reported are of the stage-managed 'hyped' variety, (which conform to Cappella and Jamieson's (1997) strategic view of politics), and reported in ways that help journalists to distance themselves from unacceptable/extreme' positions so audiences do not become annoyed. Ultimately, what is reported are 'unthreatening' (middle ground) controversies and conflicts which do not fundamentally challenge the (safe centrist) conventionalness fostered by the liberal mass media. This 'sensible center' tendency is achieved by socializing journalists to seek out what is believed to be 'popular' with 'the public'. The construct of 'the public' widely deployed by liberal journalists encodes the idea of 'the average'. By seeking out stories that will be 'popular' with this 'public', journalists actually construct that which is popular, and effectively inculcate into their mass audiences an 'average' middle-ground set of perspectives. The effect is to restrict the socio-political debate in society to 'centrist' positions. Entman (1989: 67) notes, the bigger a story grows the more homogeneous does coverage become across the media. Noelle-Neumann (1991) calls this a 'spiral of silence' (see Figure 4.2).

Journalists, operating as a pack, create closure towards 'the center' as they effectively construct 'public opinion' by eliminating views and sources deemed to be out of step with their definition of what the average reader/listener/viewer wants. So journalists produce a sort of mass bandwagoning towards the (bland average) center. In political terms, the commercial mass media have consequently played a significant role in creating two-party systems where differences between the two mass parties become ever more difficult to find. This has steered politicians towards 'staged interviews to fit all situations, sanitized statements to offend nobody [and] bland non-controversial personae' (Nimmo and Combs, 1990: 53). But because this (average) 'public' is an artificial construct, a backlash against 'sensible center politics' emerged in a number of Western liberal democracies at the turn of the century. A manifestation of this alienation is that politicians and journalists are lumped into the same category of 'out of touch' and 'elitist' peddlers of ideas that do not resonate in many sectors of society. Essentially, during the twentieth century, the mass media learned to construct 'popularity' around a 'sensible centrist' position. That which was 'popular' did not grow organically (in a bottom-up way) from the masses, but was manufactured by the culture industry and supplied (top-down) to the masses by the mass media. This has been an important feature of managing liberal democracies.

The result has been political news as predictable as a soap opera or 'ritualized drama' (Nimmo and Combs, 1990: 53) – politics is covered as an emotionally compelling story where political actors swap clichés, all agree with the happy medium of middle-ground politics and (like the commercial media) avoid saying controversial things which might alienate potential mass electorates. Nimmo and Combs (1990: 49) note that coverage of politics by television is even more like a soap opera because television news is constructed as melodrama with an appealing story-line, preferably ending in a tidy resolution. The overall 'sameness' is, however, modified by slight thematic differences between the news frames adopted by different news organizations, e.g. Nimmo and Combs (1990: 38–41) note how American television networks produce slightly different variations on a theme by hanging their political stories on different 'pegs' – 'who are the political managers'; 'who are the victims'; and 'who are the political wizards'. These formulaic frames are useful to spin-doctors because once PRs identify a journalistic frame, they can craft ('spin') stories to fit the simplified story-lines used by a particular organization's journalists. For competent spin-doctors, journalists (and their preferred news frames) should be transparent, and hence easy to exploit. Essentially, political players have learned that to be popular they must play the game of impression management, and craft their image to fit into the comfortable ritualized story-lines the mass media believe to attract audiences. Hence, the mass mediated game of politics becomes *formulaic*, built on the symbiotic need journalists and politicians have for each other. At the heart of this symbiosis is the need journalists have for sources as the basic raw material for producing their stories.

4.4 Constructing the news window 2: choosing sources

A core feature of the professional ideology of liberal journalism is the notion of being objective. **Objectivity** is apparently achieved through quoting sources outside the newsroom (Roshco, 1984: 16–17) because this supposedly ensures that journalists write stories based on external referents, rather than with reference to their own views. From this liberal journalism derives the dichotomy between objective reporting (quoting expert sources) and subjective editorializing (where writers express their own views). Objective journalism also promotes the idea of (ideally) quoting two (countervailing) sources so as to achieve balance, fairness and neutrality. Roshco (1984: 19), however, notes that source-driven journalism merely creates the potential for liberal journalists to disguise (even to themselves) that they have biases because all any journalist needs to do is find sources confirming the views they wish to promote. As Entman says: 'the problem is facts do not speak for themselves' (1989: 31), and so quoting sources does not guarantee objectivity. What it does is create a comfortable, self-affirming myth for liberal journalists. It also creates opportunities for PRs because liberal journalists must find quotable sources – essentially PRs set themselves up as professional sources, available round the clock to provide journalists with quotes on demand. Similarly, it creates a gap for politicians (and their spin-doctors) to develop symbiotic relationships with a media industry hungry for sources. In this regard, Cunningham has noted that the pursuit of 'objectivity' can trip journalists up on the way to 'truth' because objective reporting excuses 'lazy reporting' (2003: 26). The pursuit of 'objectivity' also makes journalists passive recipients of spin-doctored news rather than 'aggressive analyzers and explainers of it' (2003: 26). In effect, 'objective' reporting can become a form of 'stenography' (Miller, 2003: 26) because journalists 'stick to the facts' provided by public officials. Cunningham (2003) suggests that it was the pursuit of objective journalism that prevented the US media from asking critical questions about the Bush administration's spin-doctored reasons for going to war in Iraq.

Sources are people journalists regularly consult when wanting information or 'quotes'. Each newsroom tends to develop a pool of regularly consulted sources. News is effectively made through the symbiotic relationship developed between journalists and this pool of sources – journalists need contacts to provide quotes and information; sources need journalists to develop their 'profile' or to promote a particular idea/product/organization. For many, becoming a regularly consulted source is vital for their career – politicians, for example, need 'profile' and the media are the 'dispensers' of profile, celebrity and fame. So aspirant politicians must develop relationships with journalists, both directly and through the ever-expanding teams of PRs, spin-doctors and media consultants (see chapter 7). Becoming a successful politician means learning to play the media game. If one can become a regular media source one gains 'profile' which is the basis for being electable and re-electable (see chapter 8). The ideal situation is to become a 'media darling' (Stuckey, 2003: 164), i.e. politicians whom journalists adore. Examples of media darlings have been Jimmy Carter, Colin Powell and Nelson Mandela. Spin-doctors all work tirelessly to try and make the politicians they work for a 'darling', but ultimately 'darlings' are 'picked' by journalists rather than 'made' by spin-doctors. Spin-doctors working for media darlings have an 'easy ride' because journalists tend not to ask them difficult questions.

The massive growth of the public relations industry during the twentieth century means that journalists now have an array of professionalized sources to choose from. PRs/spin-doctors are in *competition* with each other – in politics they represent different politicians (who are in competition with each other) and different factions of the ruling elite (that are in competition with each other). This provides good journalists with some opportunity to 'use' PR machines rather than be 'used' by them. However, all too many journalists simply slide into a comfortable symbiotic relationship with the PR industry and use it as a resource to simplify their work (and ease their time-pressures) – i.e. they usually consult the same limited range of people known to deliver the best stories and quotes, namely:

- Professionalized sources (PRs);
- Professional celebrities (in politics, entertainment and sport);
- Predictable events arranged by PRs (press conferences, speeches and hearings);
- Revisiting the same limited number of sites where stories can be routinely found (e.g. the hospital, police, courts and sports beats).

Paletz and Entman (1982: 19) note that chasing the same limited number of story sources produces 'pack journalism' which causes the perceived 'sameness' of so much media content.

The pool of sources used by any newsroom constitutes a very small minority of the overall population. Ultimately, the choice of sources reflects how newsrooms see the community they report on – the choice of contacts being fundamental in defining the shape and position of Tuchman's 'window'. A key mechanism for creating this window is on-the-job socialization of journalists, which involves senior staffers passing on 'appropriate' sources to junior journalists as they are inducted into the newsroom. Learning whom news editors and editors consider to be 'appropriate' sources constitutes an important part of the staff-cloning process in any newsroom – this will be learned by having sources 'passed on' and by encountering disapproval when 'inappropriate' sources are used. Using sources narrows the 'window' in three ways: firstly, there is a tendency to favor quoting the elite, partially because they are already deemed 'important' people, and hence 'newsworthy'. Also as Entman notes, relying on 'legitimate political elites for most information' (1989: 18) is actually the cheapest way to generate news for mass audiences. Further, elite views and information are privileged because already existent social/political/economic elites tend to have the resources to staff publicity machines. The ability to run PR machines has become increasingly important in order to become a 'reliable' source for journalists. Reliability involves always being 'contactable' and delivering 'appropriate' quotes in a timely fashion (i.e. understanding journalistic deadlines and their need for quotes to fit their organization's 'in-house style' and editorial policies).

Secondly, journalists tend to stop calling their sources when the first one tells them what they want to hear. When constructing a story, journalists will work through their contact list, starting with the person deemed the most 'appropriate' source. Consequently, news construction favors (and hence promotes) certain kinds of people – those with the resources to maintain publicity machines, and/or able to deliver 'quotes' and an 'image' concurrent with media requirements. Chapters 6 and 7 will explore whether this has created a new genre of successful politicians – those with the publicity machinery and personal skills required to craft the images appropriate to journalistic news frames.

Thirdly, relying on sources creates a dependence on the likes of government and corporate spokesmen and politicians each of whom have some vested interest in 'censoring' what they say (Paletz and Entman, 1982: 20).

In their attempt to lessen dependence on sources with clear vested interests, journalists have also turned to another kind of source: the ('non-involved') expert-observer or commentator, e.g. academics (in universities, think-tanks and the policy sector). This practice grew to also include other 'non-involved' sources, e.g. pollsters, other journalists; campaign/communication consultants; and retired politicians and officials (Nimmo and Combs, 1990: 171–82). Using these people as sources gives them profile and status, and transforms them into something of a 'priestly caste' of 'experts', 'sages' and 'oracles' (Nimmo and Combs, 1992). Effectively, by selecting them as sources, the media transforms them into *'professional commentators'* or 'pundits'. They are thereby given a platform to influence public opinion. For Nimmo and Combs (1992: chapters 6 and 7) this creates a new kind of mediated politics driven by a 'punditocracy'. The way in which the media now use other journalists as 'expert commentators' is especially revealing of what Nimmo and Combs (1990: 171–3) call journalism's group-mediated fantasy about themselves as objective 'inside-dopesters' working on the citizens' behalf, and as political trendsetters who can (and should) inform the public discourse on politics. This has generated a genre of political journalism (mostly televised, but sometimes on the radio) which brings together political journalists, editors, talk-show hosts and anchors to discuss politics. Through such forums, as well as interviews, journalists effectively promote other journalists into the role of (apparently objective) soothsaying experts. This can transform some journalist soothsayers into celebrity experts and/or sources.

The media (especially television) do not just need any kind of source, they need smooth talkers – people who can think on their feet and produce coherent sentences, even if the content is glib and superficial. Pierre Bourdieu (1998: 29) calls these people 'fast-thinkers who offer cultural "fast food" – predigested and prethought culture'. Bourdieu notes that television rewards those people who can play its language-games:

> The game ... has tacit rules, since television shows, like every social milieu in which discourse circulates, allow certain things to be said and proscribe others. The first, implicit assumption of this language game is rooted in the conception of democratic debates modeled on wrestling. There must be conflicts, with good guys and bad guys ... Yet, at the same time, not all holds are allowed: the blows have to be clothed by the model of formal, intellectual language. Another feature of this space is the complicity between professionals ... The people I call 'fast-thinkers', specialists in throw-away thinking – are known in the industry as 'good guests'. They're the people whom you can always invite because you know they'll be good company and won't create problems. They won't be difficult and they're smooth talkers. There is a whole world of 'good guests' who take to the television format like fish to water. (1998: 35)

PRs/spin-doctors specialize in supplying the media with smooth talkers – people who can perform; and (because they are glib-speakers) can gloss over problem areas and thereby set agendas. In a situation were different *factions* of the political elite are in *competition*, spin-doctors increasingly work to ensure that the politicians they work for say nothing that may offend potential voters. The spin-doctors are, of course, in competition with each other (trying to ensure their employers out-compete the opposition). Ironically, this competition has led to a political system geared towards 'pseudo-competition' – i.e. the scripting of professionalized 'sources' who say as little as possible that may be offensive. PR-ized scripted politics become simultaneously 'bland' and 'hyped' as spin-doctors direct their employers (politicians as performers) to work with journalists at playing the 'sound bite game'. So competition between PRs, between politicians, and between journalists has worked to generate the media-ized 'sources game', which became a mechanism used by skilled spin-doctors to manipulate news agendas.

Ultimately, journalism involves choosing sources, and selectively deploying source-comments to construct stories. Paletz and Entman (1982: 124) note that journalists treat potential sources (interest groups and opinions) in one of three ways: they ignore some, promote others, and turn others into pariahs. These choices necessarily skew news frames because they involve emphasizing some perspectives and de-emphasizing others; treating some favourably, and others unfavourably. This involves attaching 'hooray' words (Hartley, 1982: 21) to sources/opinions rated favourably; and attaching 'boo' words (1982: 21) and journalistic-sneers to interest groups/opinions to be turned into pariahs. The selection, emphasis/de-emphasis process is the outcome of a complex set of human interactions, involving editors encouraging the use of certain sources; (some) journalists struggling to introduce new sources; and a range of professional sources (e.g. PRs and politicians) struggling to promote themselves.

4.5 Constructing the news window 3: newsroom struggles

Each newsroom produces an identifiable news window derived from deploying a particular set of practices, discourses and sources. However, creating news frames is always a complex process because newsrooms are never homogeneous. As Gramsci argued, there will always be struggles taking place over meaning (Louw, 2001: 20–4). Consequently, there will always be individual journalists out of step with their editor's world-views. However, favoured news frames do emerge from the contextually rooted complexity of newsroom relationships, including struggles between competing individuals over power and dominance. But, in general, senior journalists and editors are the most influential in building dominant newsroom discourses, in part, because they control staff recruitment and promotion (Louw, 2001: 156–7). Editors also control newsroom practices which have an enormous impact on the genre of stories produced.

Within Anglo liberal democracies, the mainstream commercial media's preferred news frames generally conform to (and confirm) the dominant discourse(s) of liberal capitalism. In part, this is because newsroom struggles tend to mirror wider hegemonic struggles, and such struggles tend to be resolved in favour of society's hegemonically dominant groups. Within contemporary liberal democracies two discursive frames are dominant within commercial newsrooms: (a) 'conventional spectacle' news; and (b) sensationalized adversarial watchdog news.

Conventional 'spectacle' news is the most widely produced genre. It delivers entertaining and intellectually unchallenging stories, comfortable for both audiences and journalists occupying the 'sensible center' of socio-political opinion. The 'sensible center' actually tends to be skewed slightly left of center because (as research around the Western world reveals) journalists are inclined to this political position (Fallows, 1997: 49). Producing spectacle stories is easy because the PR industry is geared towards producing a constant flow of entertaining information and hyped-up staged spectacles for journalists to report on. Mainstream journalists, operating as 'packs', are generally content to chase PR-created leads for three reasons:

- The PR industry has become highly adept at generating stories appealing to commercial media audiences;
- Ignoring such leads carries the danger (for individual journalists) of missing a good story that one's competitors might run instead;
- It is simply cheaper to use these PR 'gifts'.

Sensationalized adversarial watchdog journalism delivers stories encoding an emotional oppositional dimension portending to have relevance for policy formulation. There are conservative and left-wing versions of this sensational news frame which seek to draw the authorities' attention to the need to act on a particular issue. The conservative variety often takes its cue from issues aired on talkback radio, e.g. the need to exclude illegal immigrants or get tough on crime. Left-wing varieties revolve around issues like environmentalism, or human rights. Emotional oppositional watchdog stories tend to come in waves of 'concern' for a particular issue – e.g. migrants; minorities; genetic engineering; sweatshop labor; protecting forests or whales; or whatever issue is currently in vogue (Tibet; Palestine; Burma; Muslim women; or racism). As with 'spectacle news', these waves of emotional watchdogism are associated with pack journalism. Many adversarial watchdog journalists believe that their stories break the dominant news frame and challenging those in power. In reality, these stories seldom stray far from the sensible center, and actually serve to confirm liberal democracy and liberal watchdog journalism. Stories straying 'too far' are culled by the editing process, while those that are 'oppositional', without being 'revolutionary', can be managed, contained and tamed within the liberal framework of governance – given that such oppositional watchdog stories tend to become just another spectacle for the masses or another hyped-up mass media fad, making, at most, a marginal impact on the world of politics as policy making. For this reason, wise (liberal) newsroom managers tolerate a range of perspectives in their newsrooms, including 'committed' progressive oppositional journalists. Essentially, allowing a measure of discursive struggle within liberal newsrooms should not (if well managed) undermine the dominant news frame; indeed, it can potentially add value to the news-product by delivering stories that can anger, shock or outrage. This can be an audience-puller. In fact, for the commercial media, adversarial watchdog stories can (as a sub-variety of sensationalized, hyped-up spectacle news) be profitable if the controversies are well handled so as to push the right emotional buttons.

But overall, 'conventional spectacle' stories constitute the mainstay of the liberal mass media. So it is this news genre that mainstream politicians must learn to understand if they are to be successful in working with journalists.

4.6 Institutionalizing the media–politician relationship

Some kinds of news lend themselves to be routinized. Parliamentary politics, hospitals, and crime (courts and police) can be organized into beats because journalists know that there will always be a steady stream of stories from some sites and that these sectors produce news in a fairly predictable way, so it is simply a matter of developing procedures for gaining regularized access to those who produce the news within these sites. In the case of political stories newspaper journalists formally institutionalized their access to Parliament during the nineteenth century. The arrival of television modified the original relationship.

The relationship between journalists and politicians within the liberal system has passed through five stages:

- Initially, liberal oligarchs discouraged the reporting of Parliamentary debates;
- A second phase was born in the 1770s when Westminster Parliamentarians grudgingly accepted that they would no longer be able to prevent Parliamentary reporting taking place. However, no formal access or facilities were provided to journalists (Lloyd, 1988: 11);
- Thirdly, access was formalized. The first Parliament to grant formal access to journalists was the American House of Representatives – granted two days after this House was established in 1789 (Emery, 1962: 186). The more secretive American Senate only followed six years later. In 1803 the British did the same when Prime Minister Pitt ordered a bench be set aside for journalists. From 1834 a reporters' gallery was made available in the British Parliament (Lloyd, 1988: 14). As liberal democratic Parliaments were cloned around the British Empire, so too was the gallery-notion exported – the institutionalized reporting of parliamentary debates became a feature of liberal democracies;

- A fourth phase dawned when television cameras became a part of Parliamentary politics, both in the form of cameras inside Parliament recording actual debates, and with the establishment of Parliamentary television studios. These studios altered the nature of the gallery–politician relationship – as politicians came to focus more effort on their television 'sound bite performances' than on their Parliamentary work (Riddell, 1998: 9);
- A fifth phase saw the growth of an industry of communication consultants, spin-doctors and impression-management coaches employed to help politicians to perform better as the political process was increasingly televisualized. This phase first emerged in American politics (Mickelson, 1989: chapter 5); and the USA remains the pacesetter for the evolving triptych relationship between politicians, spin-doctors and journalists (Swanson and Mancini, 1996: chapter 1).

At any rate, journalists have come to be accepted as an integral part of the Anglo-American parliamentary process – with the relationship between politicians and journalists formalized in the institution of the Parliamentary Gallery. This grants the mass media regularized access to politicians, and the formal right to report on debates. In Britain, a unique twist to the politician–media relationship emerged in the nineteenth century – the Lobby – and has remained an important part of the way journalists gather information about British politics ever since. The Lobby's birth was an accident. After a slow news-day, a Westminster reporter was sitting on the lobby stairs one night with no story to file when Prime Minister Gladstone came down the stairs. The next morning's newspaper carried a column beginning 'meeting Mr Gladstone this evening in the Lobby I had a brief but interesting conversation with him'. From this was born the British journalistic tradition of writing political 'think pieces' based upon seemingly exclusive access to insider knowledge of the political process. This insider knowledge was derived from the practice of 'lobbying', or informal loitering – i.e. waiting for Ministers who might pass on political tit-bits. Lobbying was formalized in the 1880s (Lloyd, 1988: 19). Interestingly, Lobbying was not exported to other Anglo parliaments in the way the gallery was. B. Franklin (1994: 16) regards the Westminster Lobby as a good example of the sort of mutual adaptation both politicians and journalists have had to make to accommodate each other over the years. Franklin notes that political news is a mutual construction based on politicians and journalists using each other. He uses the metaphor of journalists and politicians 'sleeping together' – i.e. they keep shifting positions, so no one partner is constantly dominant (Cook, in Franklin, 1994: 16). The Lobby is useful to politicians because it allows them to 'fly kites', 'test the waters', try and set news agendas, and plant story ideas favourable to themselves and their allies (1994: 17).

Significantly, the Lobby provided politicians with a mechanism to develop a 'cosy' symbiotic relationship with journalists. For some journalists a cosy relationship with the powerful can be a great ego booster (Parker, 1990: 4), something skilful politicians can exploit. The Lobby's structuring of this relationship facilitates a regularized informal (off the record) dialogue between politicians and journalists – or what Bernard Ingham (1991: 165) calls 'a bridge' based on mutual respect. This makes it possible to manipulate news frames anonymously through 'background briefings' given by politicians and their PRs. This bridge also provides both journalists and politicians with valuable intelligence. Ingham certainly masterfully used the Lobby to promote Margaret Thatcher (1991: chapters 11, 12 and 13). But the Lobby is not the only mechanism facilitating overly cosy relationships between politicians and journalists. For example, Australia's Parliament has a gallery, but no Lobby. Nonetheless, cosiness emerged between politicians and gallery journalists due to the nature of the design of Canberra's Parliament which generates close proximity between politicians and journalists (see Simons, 1999). This is exacerbated by Canberra being a small claustrophobic city, geographically isolated from mainstream Australia, where politicians and political journalists are thrown together and there is not much to do but talk to each other. The result has been the emergence of a Canberra 'club' with its own (closed-shop) political discourse, strangely disconnected from the rest of the country (Parker, 1990: 176–8). Not surprisingly, given the disconnectedness of this 'club' from the world beyond Canberra, the emergence of Hansonism (a right-wing backlash against mainstream liberal democracy) initially saw Australia's political journalists completely baffled by Hansonism. And falling back upon their usual gallery sources made their reporting worse, which demonstrated that there are times when the journalists–politicians symbiosis can become counter-productive.

Ultimately, for journalists, the political beat requires the development of on-going relationships with politicians and their PR staffers. What makes these relationships work is that both journalists and politicians have a vested interest in sustaining the relationship and in creating, and maintaining, a set of rules and practices facilitating the smooth operation of their interactions. It has been argued that because journalists and politicians have to develop such a close working relationship they eventually come to 'share' each other's culture (Larsson, 2002: 29). Franklin (1994: 19–22) identifies three factors influencing the relationship, which any competent editor would take into account when deploying journalists:

- The more ideological agreement between a journalist and a politician, the more their working relationship can be consensual;
- There exist both newsroom and political hierarchies. 'Matchmaking' to ensure a similar status between the journalist and politician facilitates a better symbiotic relationship;

- If one person in the relationship has more resources the interaction is skewed. So politicians with the resources to establish large PR operations have more capacity to dominate the relationship. Generally, only journalists working for prestigious and affluent newsrooms have any chance of not being overwhelmed by the (ever-expanding) hype-making machinery of well-resourced politicians. At the other extreme, journalists working for suburban knock-and-drops have virtually no chance of being anything else than 'processing clerks' for media releases. Franklin (1994: 33) notes that poorly resourced local media do, indeed, provide political PRs with much scope for influencing public opinion.

The routinization and institutionalization of the journalist–politician nexus is an established practice in liberal democracies. The question is, has this institutionalization, when combined with the growth of the spin-doctor/PR industry, permanently transformed journalists into the symbiotic partners of mainstream politicians?

4.7 Journalists: watchdogs or symbiotic-partners?

Central to liberal journalism's professional ideology is the notion that journalists serve the public by acting as watchdogs. Nimmo and Combs (1990: 226) note that this notion has grown into a package of fantasies political journalists now believe about themselves, i.e.

- A self-image of themselves as tough, rugged individuals fighting for truth and justice;
- The 'inside-dopester fantasy' in terms of which journalists award themselves both special knowledge about the political system and special skills in accessing the 'truth' about what is 'really' going on. This myth justifies journalists interviewing other journalists about politics, thereby turning their colleagues into (apparently) expert pundits;
- Journalists position themselves as 'insiders'. US political journalists, for example, position themselves as part of the Washington power elite – i.e. the 'Inside the Beltway Fantasy' (Nimmo and Combs, 1990: 226). The same phenomenon can be observed in London, Ottawa and Canberra. These fantasies blur into the Fourth Estate self-image – of being part of the political process with the right to intervene to influence decision making and public opinion. These fantasies generate a sense of being an elite group among political journalists. This has the (unintended) effect of encoding into many of their stories an 'air of superiority', and even a professional 'sneer' towards both politicians and their audience.

The above fantasies are ultimately all premised on the belief that journalists know how to pick good sources; are skilled at judging whether sources are 'truthful' or 'untruthful'; and are too smart to be 'taken in' by sources (like politicians, senior civil servants, consultants, spin-doctors and pundits). Some journalists are good enough to do this – i.e. *not* all journalists are routinely taken in, and not all PR/spin-doctoring is successful. However, an enormous percentage of spin-doctoring is successful. The problem is that political sources are inherently going to be manipulative and engage in demagoguery (Entman, 1989: 125) because they have a vested interest in manipulating the media machine, and worse, are precisely employed because they are skilled at 'spinning a line' and 'hoodwinking' journalists. Many journalists are taken in. Others know that their sources are trying to manipulate them, but do not try and discover what they are not being told (Knightley, 2002: 168). Spin-doctors obviously seek out those journalists who are most 'compliant', or approach journalists when they are known to be under pressure. The success of contemporary professional demagoguery is precisely based upon spin-doctors understanding journalists and how they work (many spin-doctors are ex-journalists). (See 7.4 on p. 163.) Understanding the practices, conventions and beliefs of journalists, renders journalistic behaviour highly predictable, which makes it remarkably easy to steer the news-gathering process. It is the practices, conventions, fantasies and egos of journalists that renders them susceptible to being co-opted into a *de facto* symbiotic relationship with those professional political demagogues they rely on as sources. Effectively, journalists, politicians and spin-doctors all operate within a shared culture and shared set of news-making rules – they are effectively partners, unable to function without each other (Negrine, 1994: 16), and locked into a mutual dependency radically diminishing the ability of journalists to function in accordance with Fourth Estate/watchdog principles (Entman, 1989: 29). Journalists may be free from state control, but they are not free of political manipulation; and their own practices both encourage and facilitate such manipulation. As Entman notes, the very nature of the symbiotic partnership leaves politicians no choice but to manipulate journalists:

> Elites who want to succeed politically cannot afford to debate complicated truths in a marketplace of ideas. Nor can officials volunteer information for the public to use in holding them to account, in the naïve faith ordinary people will understand the complexities. If politicians do make the mistake, their competitors ... will almost certainly pounce and seize the advantage. So news organizations wind up depending upon elites whose primary goal when talking to reporters is to manage publicity rather than illuminate truth ... The media system encourages elites to fashion rhetoric and to take actions that accord with journalistic values and limitations rather than with responsive public policy. (1989: 20)

The problem is that journalists rely upon the political sources they are supposed to hold accountable (1989: 73). Politician responses are now usually mediated through a PR machinery. Key political players now have well-funded political PR machines. These machines can heavily shape news agendas simply by how they choose to respond to journalist's questions. This does *not* mean that PRs always succeed in manipulating journalists; does *not* mean that PRs and spin-doctors have 100 percent control of news agendas; and does *not* mean that journalists have no influence over news agendas. Clearly they do. In fact, news is ultimately the outcome of a three-cornered relationship between journalists, spin-doctors and politicians. Circumstances may give one of the players (e.g. journalists) dominance in a particular context. But dominance within the relationship is never fixed. What is fixed is that:

- Politicians need publicity;
- The importance of the media within the political process causes politicians to build PR machines;
- Journalists have no choice but to work with these PR machines;
- The resultant symbiotic relationship means that political news is built upon a mutually reinforcing 'game' (and shared discourse) between journalists and politicians/spin-doctors which Cappella and Jamieson call 'the strategy-conception' of politics:

It is impossible to know which came first – the conflict driven sound bite-oriented discourse of politicians or the conflict-saturated strategy-oriented structure of press coverage. Whatever the answer, each now feeds the other with politicians providing a menu that includes what the press seems most likely to cover and the press arguing that it simply is reporting what is being offered. (1997: 9–10)

This symbiosis is reinforced by the pressures of commercialism which drives journalists to produce 'spectacle' news – a genre requiring celebrities and dramatic or entertaining stories (see 4.2 on p. 76). The result is a collaborative arrangement in which political PRs supply journalists with celebrity politicians and hyped-up news to entertain the masses. As Schultz (1998: 96) notes, although the commercial press once gave journalists independence from governments, commercialism has created new problems, e.g. the pressure placed on journalists to work symbiotically with political PRs. For political journalists, this generates dissonance between the reality of being semi-insiders within a political process driven by political PR hype, and the mythology of themselves as watchdogs and 'truth finders'. In an attempt to resolve this dissonance, some journalists turned to cynical reporting – where journalists work with political PRs, but simultaneously 'expose' the nature of the spin-doctored political 'game' to their audiences. As Cappella and Jamieson (1997) note, this appears to be de-legitimating mainstream liberal politics in Western societies.

4.8 Journalistic 'power'

Journalists potentially have the power to disrupt and undermine the work of spin-doctors by refusing to accept the line they are spinning and by trying to unearth issues the spin-doctors are attempting to bury. Some outstanding journalists do succeed in doing this when their organizations give them the resources to do so through investigative work (although even investigative journalism can be infected by spin-doctoring when it begins with a leak planted by the spin industry). However, the media has increasingly become an industry geared towards profit maximization rather than 'investigation'. This has driven many newsrooms into effectively becoming media release processing centers.

Generally, the power that journalists have to influence the political process comes not from being watchdogs, but from the fact that politicians (and their PRs) need the media (Ingham, 1991: 160). There is a mutual interdependence. Neither side can afford to break the relationship, nor fundamentally alienate the other partner. Franklin (1994: 14–15) notes that the resulting relationship between political PRs and journalists is complex and often tense. It is a relationship in which journalists are never political insiders nor fully in control of the story-telling process (see 4.2 on p. 76). Hence, neither the Fourth Estate nor watchdog concepts accurately describe the real relationship. However, even though journalists are never in control (because they must collaborate in order to retain their sources), neither are they powerless. But their 'power' and status is of a second-hand variety – derivative of their relationship with the real power holders. It is also a 'negative power', because journalists do not have the power to make policy or allocate resources, but they can (in certain circumstances) undermine those with such power. Hence, journalists have (sometimes) the power to frighten politicians and to mobilize 'moral panics' and 'groundswells of hostility' to policies.

It could be argued that communication professionals inside the political machine acquire a variety of power from their direct relationship with policy makers and party functionaries, while those outside the political machine (e.g. journalists) acquire a variety of derivative power because politicians are dependent on them to disseminate the hype. This raises questions about the political consequences of the symbiotic relationships that have apparently developed between politicians, their PRs, journalists and media owners. Representative democracy advocates have some cause for concern given the influence that non-elected communication professionals seem to have accumulated from driving the mass hype machinery.

Essentially, politicians need journalists and PRs to help them to circulate appropriate political myths, stories and visions; build appropriate political-identities; build their own profiles and celebrity status; and sell policies, belief systems and worldviews. With journalists having become the key storytellers in contemporary Western society (Nimmo and Combs, 1990: 14), and with television (the key storytelling mechanism) able to 'cultivate attitudes' (Gerbner et al., 1984), it is not surprising that politicians now systematically seek to develop symbiotic relationships with those driving this (televisualized) storytelling process – working together, politicians, their communication staffers and journalists construct the myths, beliefs and identities holding the political system together (see chapters 5, 8 and 9).

Summary

You should now be familiar with the following key concepts and themes:
fourth estate; partisan press; muckraking journalism; lapdog journalism; adversarial journalism; junkyard journalism; sensational journalism; entertaining 'spectacle' journalism; cynical journalism; industrialized journalism; celebrity journalists; televised storytelling; how Parliamentary reporting has evolved; how news is constructed; how journalists work; the importance of journalistic sources; how news can be staged managed; and how and why a symbiotic relationship has grown up between journalists and politicians.

For further consideration

1   The notion of a Fourth estate can be seen as:

   (a)   A worthy ideal;
   (b)   An existing reality;
   (c)   A myth;
   (d)   An historical model that no longer holds true.

   Consider each of these views.

   (Continued)

For further consideration   Continued

2   Even investigative journalism can begin with a spin-doctored leak. Can you identify examples of this?

3   What is good about spectacle journalism? What is bad about spectacle journalism?

4   The objectivity model of journalism facilitated the McCarthy witch-hunt and made it possible to plant the weapons of mass destruction story in the media before the 2003 Iraq War. How and why?

5   Can spin-doctors use the following to 'spin a line' and/or 'plant' stories:

   (a)   Journalistic cynicism?
   (b)   Watchdog journalism?

6   Do you think a system that allows journalists to become celebrities and pundits is flawed?

7   What is the alternative to seeing politics as a competitive sport?

8   Are spin-doctors and public opinion pollsters damaging for democracy? Or are they part of a process that serves to make democracy function?

9   Do you think it is an inherently bad thing that journalists and politicians need each other?

10   The constructivist school argues that the media makes mass public opinion. The empirical/objectivist school argues that the media reflects existing opinion. What do you think?

PART 2 ● ● ●

Identity, Politics and the Media

Part 2 of this book examines a sub-theme within political communication, namely the role of 'political identity' as a kind of 'conceptual glue' that holds political systems together. Because this glue is *communicatively constructed*, unpacking how identity is actually produced serves to illustrate the central role that communication plays in the political process.

Part 2 focuses on a different set of issues to the ones examined in Parts 1 and 3 of this book. Whereas Parts 1 and 3 both look at the way politics has been *media-ized*, Part 2 focuses on a different sort of communicative dimension to the political process, namely, how political identities (especially national identity) are *communicatively formed* and the role this has played within liberal democracies. Parts 2 and 3 of this book both build on Part 1, but they do so in divergent ways – i.e. Part 2 looks at the importance for political systems of *constructing political identities*, while Part 3 looks at the way *media players* (spin-doctors, journalists and politicians) actually 'sell' ideas, justifications and excuses to mass publics. However, because 'political identity' is so central to the political process, many of the themes discussed in chapters 5 and 6 feed into chapters 8, 9, 10, 11 and 12.

It will be argued that nation states have been highly functional for liberal capitalism, which is why liberal democracy (as discussed in chapter 3) has been so closely associated with nation states and nationalism. In this regard, chapter 5 examines the notion that one of the core tasks of liberal democratic politicians and their communication staffers has been to engage in a form of political communication that serves to generate a sense of national identity. The mass media and journalists have necessarily become complicit in *constructing* such national identities. Chapter 5 will examine how national identities have been communicatively constructed. Chapter 6 will explore the proposal that new media technologies necessarily alter the communicative environment and consequently result in the emergence of new kinds of identities, which will, in turn, alter the political environment.

5 National Identity and Communication

Chapter 5 is concerned with hegemony building within the fulcrum of nation states, and *how ruling groups construct national identities* within such states. The way intellectuals, politicians, journalists and teachers are all implicated in constructing such collective (national) identities, and the myths associated with them, is discussed. Different theories of nationalism and nation identity formations are discussed. It is argued that constructing national identities has been a central feature of the Anglo model of building modern societies, states and economies, and that the mass media has been a crucial dimension of the project of building liberal democratic nation states. Chapter 5 begins by examining the concepts of identity and hegemony then examines the mechanics of national identity construction, and the role played by journalists in this process. The chapter pays particular attention to the emergence and evolution of national identity in Britain and the USA.

Humans live and work in groups. They build collectivities and communities while interacting with one another. People interact for many reasons, e.g. being born into a family or clan; working together to achieve the same end-goal; or worshipping the same god. Collectivities formed in this interactive process become sources of identity – i.e. individuals come to associate themselves with these collectivities and the discourses and practices underpinning these associations. When individuals internalize these discourses and practices they effectively construct an (individual) identity out of their relationship to this (collective) group and its values. An identity is thus a set of meanings emerging from how one constructs one's relationships (associations) with others. **Symbolic interactionists** (e.g. Goffman, 1971) contend our very sense of self is constructed from a communicative sharing process derived from having to operate within such relationships.

Many varieties of associations and collectivities have been built over time, each providing meaning and identity for those associating with it. Because humans are complex beings, an individual may potentially associate with different groups (and hence identities), although usually one group (i.e. relationship) tends to predominate at any one time.

For those born into Western societies during the past two centuries, one particular type of collectivity – nation states – emerged as a powerful agency for structuring relationships between people. Liberal democracy, capitalism, the nation state and national identity evolved in unison as a consequence of the West European burghers outmaneuvering their feudal overlords and establishing their own hegemonic dominance. Central to their liberal-capitalist project was the construction of nation states. From this flowed a plethora of national identities. Some, such as Castells (1997), have suggested that nation states are an anachronism in the contemporary era, and globalization will sweep away nation states and hence national identities. However, predictions of the demise of nation states seem somewhat premature, and derive from a failure to recognize that the emerging Pax Americana (which underpins contemporary globalization) is not being built upon the destruction of nation states. Instead the Pax American a is being forged upon a global networking of nation states, each of which is built upon an Anglo liberal democratic model of governance that the Pax American a seems intent on imposing as a global model of governance. The Anglo-liberal model of nation-state building is alive and well (although the model is opaque to Americans because they conceptualize their governance-and-identity model as a 'pan-human universalism').

5.1 Building political identity

Those seeking to build hegemonic dominance must construct (and hold together) a political community – i.e. build a collective identity. Theorists like Berger and Luckman (1979) argue that identity is an 'individual' rather than 'collective' phenomenon. Certainly individuals construct their own identity, but they do so in interaction with 'others', drawing upon (and helping to construct) identities that are collectively shared, e.g. the sense of belonging to a political community. Constructing communities involves creating a sense of 'groupness' and getting people to identify with this group. This involves constructing a sense of 'self' (individual identity) that draws upon the stories, memories, mythologies and beliefs of the constructed group (collective identity). Politicians and their spin industry necessarily attempt to construct such collective identities (and the accompanying individual identities) by manufacturing stories, memories, myths and beliefs. Building liberal democratic hegemonies has long been associated with creating political communities based on 'national identity' and 'citizens' identifying with these collective identities. Such identities are but one variety of (mass) 'political belonging' emerging from 'drawing the masses together' (as publics). This involves individuals constructing themselves as 'citizens' involved in an 'imagined' relationship with a collectivity/community called a 'nation'. This variety of individual identity ('the citizen') has been a core feature of liberal democratic states where capitalist industrialization flourished (see chapter 3), and so presumably is an 'identity' helpful for facilitating liberal capitalism's political and economic processes. Because, in contemporary Western society, the media (especially television) has become the main storytelling vehicle, journalists have become the key (but not only) players in myth making and identity building.

A core feature of liberal democracies is mass enfranchisement. Mass enfranchisement has produced a two-tiered political process – i.e. political elites participate in politics as policy making, while the masses are involved in politics as hype (see chapter 2, Table 2.1). The latter involves building a (passive) 'public' through the processes of mass communication. The growth of a political hype industry bears testament to the fact mass politics is very much about perceptions and perception management. Ultimately mass politics is about building political collectivities through the sharing of discourses. For this, politicians need the mass media to help them to circulate appropriate political myths, preferably as entertaining stories designed for mass consumption. Effectively, journalists – as part of the hype industry – are implicated in constructing mass identities.

Professional communicators are central to creating the sense of 'belonging' and 'identity' which underpins legitimate hegemonies. Journalists are especially important sources of representations (stories, memories, myths and ideologies) from which mass publics construct their images of the world; their sense of 'available' collectivities and 'identities'; and ultimately the representations from which individuals build their identities. Building hegemonies, and collective and individual identities is part of an intermeshed communicative process. Not surprisingly, those seeking to build hegemonic dominance must engage in perception management which means working with journalists to co-construct representations 'appropriate' to the needs of the hegemony builders.

5.2 Building hegemony

All societies have dominant and dominated groups, and dominant groups necessarily prefer to remain dominant. Becoming hegemonic means becoming the dominant or 'leading' group (or, more likely, alliance of groups) in a society. This entails becoming the 'ruling group' (or elite) whose 'concept of reality' then sets the tone. Hegemonic groups are able to set the over-arching intellectual agenda in society and steer discourses.

According to Gramsci (1971), becoming the ruling group requires performing well in three spheres: firstly, building and maintaining political alliances (i.e. constructing a 'ruling group'); secondly, generating consent ('legitimacy') among the ruled; and thirdly, building coercive capacity (e.g. police, courts, prisons and military forces) to generate 'authority'. The more legitimacy rulers have, the less coercion they need to employ. However, even the most legitimate systems rely on some coercive underpinning – even if it is only the threat that police/legal machines may be used against individuals breaking the law. Each of these three hegemonic functions relies on communication. But the legitimacy/consent sphere is entirely communicative, and is also the sphere most obviously associated with mass media production. Ultimately, becoming dominant requires ruling groups to learn, mobilize and organize three key skills – the arts of coercion; negotiation (to 'politic' alliances); and mass communication (to build mass 'consent'). The latter involves circulating representations which help inculcate identities, beliefs and behaviours confirming the practices and discourses of the ruling group. The art of mass political communication has become increasingly 'institutionalized' (and 'hyped') around a set of complex symbiotic relationships between politicians, spin-doctors and journalists. At the heart of these relationships is the growing 'spin industry' of political communication consultants, PRs and impression managers who effectively 'link' the political machine to the mass media machine.

But becoming hegemonic is not enough. Gramsci (1971) notes that hegemonic groups have to work at staying dominant. In part, this involves:

- Operating discourses that hold the ruling alliance together;
- Maintaining a 'leading position' in society relative to all other groups such that the dominated accept the 'leading' group's dominance;
- Generating consent among the ruled – i.e. ensuring that the discourses, practices and 'authority' ('coercive capacity') of the ruling group are seen as legitimate (and ideally as 'natural') by the ruled.

In liberal democracies, this discursive dimension has been institutionalized in the form of mass education and mass media, staffed by an institutionalized intelligentsia of teachers and journalists. Ruling groups necessarily strive to develop mechanisms for 'steering' the discourses being circulated among the masses by this institutionalized intelligentsia. For hegemonic groups, the more **naturalized** and 'obfuscated' the discourses and practices become, the better, because naturalized hegemonic discourses/practices effectively position people into 'hidden' power relationships. When discourses/practices become 'naturalized' and 'opaque' for teachers and journalists, an especially closed form of discourse is achieved. The discourses/practices embedded in, and 'governing', institutions (as described by Foucault, 1972) produce an especially obfuscated and opaque form of discursive control.

Liberal democratic hegemony building has long been associated with a particular variety of consent, i.e. the construction of a 'mass public' of citizens identifying with a 'nation'. National identity emerged as an especially useful legitimating mechanism for building the modernizing administrative entities (states) which served as fulcra for capitalist industrialization. Such identity provided a sense of 'belonging' and 'meaning' based not upon active citizenship, but upon the creation of (mass-mediated) 'mass publics' – i.e. passive and 'isolated' individuals who 'imagined' themselves to be involved in active relationships with collectivities of fellow-nationals. But as Benedict Anderson (1991: 26) notes, citizens only get to meet a handful of their millions of fellow-citizens. There is certainly no basis for an active relationship with them. Instead, the 'relationship' is 'imaginary' (1991: 6–7). The media are centrally implicated in building these imaginary relationships and passive publics of individuals who effectively only 'interact' with their fellow citizens via media representations.

5.3 Building national identity

Identity can take many forms, and many forms of identity have impacted upon the political process. The form of political identity with an especially long-standing (and core) relationship to Anglo liberal democracy has been national identity. In fact, liberal democracy, the nation state, the mass media, liberal journalism and national identity effectively shared an intermeshed evolution. This evolution came to be termed political 'modernization'. Unraveling 'national identity' offers a way of exploring

- 'Identities' as political phenomena;
- Relationships between political systems, the mass media and legitimacy building;
- The evolution of Anglo liberal political processes.

Greenfeld (1993: 6) argues that the first nation was England. She notes how this was precipitated by the rise of burgher merchants and their destabilization of feudal definitions of political identity (1993: 16). This instability caused a crisis of identity leading to the search for new ways of conceptualizing the self within a political collectivity. This, according to Greenfeld (1993: 14), generated a new identity, called 'national', in England and Holland. From the outset, this identity was strongly associated with print media representations circulating among a literate minority. National identity took strong hold in England, from where it was exported to its colonies (see chapter 3). It thereby came to form the basis of the US polity. Significantly, this identity was the outgrowth of burgher struggles against feudalism and monarchy. Consequently, the idea of 'the nation' fixed sovereignty with 'a people' residing in 'a country' rather than with a small hereditary group who rule over a territory (1993: 32–3). National identity, the nation state, liberal democracy and capitalism all emerged and evolved together because they were all rooted in the same struggle by burghers to seize power from hereditary rulers and reshape the power relations of Europe. Not surprisingly, the concept (central to liberal democracy) of 'enfranchisement' does not literally mean 'getting the vote'; rather it means 'to be made French'. This derives from the fact that England's hereditary rulers were Norman-Frenchmen. Enfranchisement effectively referred to redefining political participation – acceptance into the governing elite was no longer to result from being born into the Norman nobility. Instead, the burghers (i.e. 'ordinary' non-noble English people) now demanded the right to become part of governance by virtue of being born into a 'nation' (the English) who occupied a defined 'national territory' (England). So the assertion of nationality was intertwined with demanding the right to participation in the political process – a right formerly held only by nobles (1993: 44–5). The early print media, circulating these sorts of ideas, were regarded as dangerously revolutionary by Europe's nobility and clergy. This resulted in widespread censorship. This saw Holland (as a toehold of burgher hegemony) become the source of the early liberal revolutionary printed media in a number of the new vernacular languages, including English, French, German and Flemish. Locke's ideas of liberalism, governance and free speech were born out of this context.

The English conceptualization of enfranchisement, discussed above, brought about a new political process based on (a) the right to political participation; (b) the fact that one resided within a defined national territory ('country'); and (c) the shared language and cultural characteristics of the people living in that 'nation'.

Greenfeld notes the role played by burgher literacy; the printing of an English-language Bible; and the Protestant struggle against Catholic nobles, in helping to shape the emergence of this English national consciousness. Initially it was not a 'mass' consciousness, but an identity associated with the literate landed gentry, burghers and bureaucrats. It was these groups who first demanded the right to participate in the political process. During the nineteenth century this consciousness (plus literacy) expanded to become a mass phenomenon.

The English notion of 'national' political participation was exported to the USA ready made. Because Americans did not have to build ('struggle for') this national identity, it simply became a 'given' (1993: 402). Hence transplanted Anglo notions of governance became taken-for-granted 'givens' that were necessarily opaque to Americans. Because they were effectively de-contextualized ideals in the USA, and new migrants were simply assimilated into these given ideals, it became possible to believe that 'national' political participation was a 'universal' (1993: 423). This (Anglo) ideal was systematized into a (teleological) model of political modernization. By the mid-twentieth century this, and the notion of modernizing nation states, had been unproblematically adopted by many members of the Anglo intelligentsia who (as teachers and journalists) popularized this modernist vision as representing 'necessary' progress towards a 'rational' future. The world was to be made 'rational' and 'modern' in accordance with the Anglo model of good national governance. Americans were especially instrumental in transforming this (decontextualized) Anglo model into a 'pan-human universalism' (1993: 446). From the mid-twentieth century, the USA set about imposing this model onto the rest of the world. The same transplantation, decontextualized opaqueness, and universalization of the Anglo model occurred in Australia. In the USA, Australia, Canada and (more recently in) Britain waves of migrants were assimilated into these dominant Anglo discourses/practices, which served to further obfuscate the Anglo-ness of this model. In contexts like the USA and Australia the discourse of multiculturalism has obscured the underlying Anglo-ness of US/Australian 'national identity'. The media in these societies have circulated this multicultural discourse – a discourse highly compatible with the needs of the emergent global networker elite driving the rise of globalized capitalism (Louw, 2001: 60–7).

The early relationship between the growth of national identity and (print) media-ized communication is clear. Two influential theorists of national identity, Ernest Gellner and Benedict Anderson, both formulated (highly compatible) constructivist, language-based theories of national identity. Gellner's argument is a more modernist-constructivism than Anderson's. Gellner argued that nation states were the necessary outgrowth of capitalist industrialization because states are the administrative units within which such economies can be organized most efficiently. Modernizing states effectively organized people into 'large, centrally educated, culturally homogeneous groups' (1983: 35) – groups bound together not by the old feudal-loyalties (of monarchy or religion), but by 'culture' (1983: 36). Significantly, the earliest national cultures were constructed by print media circulating texts not in Latin (the trans-European language of feudal elites), but in local languages spoken by the burghers (e.g. English, Dutch and French). Literacy provided access to these representations (and practices and rituals). Around these grew language-centered 'national' identities. Once burgher hegemony was achieved, literacy was deliberately diffused (through centralized and standardized education systems) so as to systematically incorporate the masses into the 'cultural identity' being constructed within each nation. Mass education simultaneously inculcated practices and values useful for industrialization; and taught literacy (so enabling mass 'access' to the common culture). Literacy also facilitated the emergence of mass newspapers, which disseminated the national cultures being constructed. Anderson (1991: 44) notes how print capitalism effectively 'assembled' vernacular 'national languages' and 'nationally imagined communities' and notes the powerful relationship existing between imagined communities and print languages (1991: 133–4). He discusses, for example, the role newspapers (which served different economic zones) played in building South American nations (1991: 52–3). Anderson (1991: 119–23) also examines how the Dutch East Indies (literacy-focused) education system similarly assembled the Indonesian imagined community.

In the literature on the formation of national identity there is almost universal recognition of the role played by language, literacy and (literate) intellectuals, or what Smith (1998: 194) calls 'vernacular mobilization'. Smith argues that an intelligentsia assembles national identity in one of two ways.

Firstly, an intelligentsia appropriates already existing myths, symbols and traditions of a particular 'core *ethnie*' and rediscovers, reappropriates and reworks their ethno-history and memories into a national formation, e.g. Englishness was constructed out of an Anglo-Saxon core. This highlights the difference between an *ethnie* and a nation. 'A nation' is an identity formed through building a modern state. National identities thus emerge in relationship to organized states; bureaucracies; codified laws/rules and codes; institutionalized education and media systems staffed by a professionalized intelligentsia; and codified languages. This produces an institutionalized, manufactured mass solidarity commonly associated with an organized symbolic exchange that manufactures (passive) public opinion. An *ethnie*, on the other hand, involves identity formation via a group of 'people' (better expressed by the German word *volk*) sharing symbols, experiences and interactions in a non-institutionalized way. An *ethnie* involves sharing discourses, beliefs and practices that are not necessarily formally codified; identifying with an emotionally laden landscape/territory (not state); and sharing a language and 'way of life' which is experienced as an in-group solidarity. This produces a 'popular' active (not 'mass') solidarity born of in-group interactivity rather than bureaucratized, codified or institutionalized relationships. *Ethnies* are associated with grassroots-'popular' myths; nations are associated with constructed 'mass' ideologies (which often parasitize the myths). An *ethnie* is an in-group solidarity associated with a sense of kinship, often based on the 'myth of collective ancestry' (Horowitz, 1985: 52). Van den Berghe (1978: 405) contends that this solidarity is experienced as a form of super-family based on an ethnocentric process of 'kin selection'. Although a nation and an *ethnie* are not reducible to one another, relationships between the two phenomena are common.

Secondly, an intelligentsia can assemble a new *ethnie* from collectivities of people thrown together by circumstance such as migration, e.g. the USA, Australia, Canada, South Africa or Jamaica.

Another route to nation building is bureaucratic incorporation (Smith, 1998: 193). English middle class/burghers successfully constructed an English state, a British state, and eventually an empire precisely because of their early achievements in establishing effective territorially based administrative, legal and taxation systems (Smith, 1991: 59). These territorial bureaucracies deployed local codified print-based vernacular languages (e.g. English) – hence 'bureaucratic incorporation' and 'vernacular mobilization' routes were actually intertwined. Sometimes 'bureaucratic incorporation' involves forcefully widening the core 'national' *ethnie* through territorial expansion, **assimilation** and incorporation, e.g. incorporating the Welsh and Scots into the (Anglofied) UK; Native Americans and African-Americans into the (Anglofied) USA; and Aboriginals into (Anglofied) Australia. However, not all forceful incorporations result in successful assimilation because some groups resist assimilation e.g. the Irish, Québecois and Afrikaners. This was often based upon constructing ('resistance') 'nation' or 'ethnic' identities which essentially replicated the Anglo 'national' model. Not all bureaucratic incorporations have produced successful nation states – e.g. many African states, created from the deconstruction of the British and French empires, failed when the Westernized elites (who inherited these bureaucratic-entities) proved unable to build viable (national) political communities within the inherited boundaries. The reason for the failure of these states is instructive:

- As purely empire-derived administrative-bureaucratic entities, they lacked core *ethnies* from which to construct the representations of a national identity. This may suggest that national identities cannot be invented from scratch;
- These states had only very small middle classes, and so lacked both an intelligentsia (to build a national identity) and economic entrepreneurs;
- They lacked the communication infrastructures required for circulating identity-building representations – i.e. much of the population was both illiterate and not fluent in the 'national language';
- Cultural infrastructures (media and education) were poorly developed. Effectively the Westernized elites were 'isolated from' and unable to communicatively 'reach' their mass populations. These elites were also perceived as (Westernized) 'outsiders'.

Ultimately it was the Anglo-American model of constructing nations, national identity, and liberal democratic states that became something of a prototype around the world. This model has the following features:

- The nation is conceptualized spatially or territorially. It occupies a 'historic' land or 'homeland' which is the repository of historic memories and associations (Smith, 1991: 9). This land becomes the bounded market the middle class/burgher can legitimately use to produce wealth from 'their' national territory. In Australia, this led to the state being officially named the 'Commonwealth of Australia';
- The nation is institutionalized as an administrative and coercive entity, with a bureaucracy, taxation system, and legal and policing framework facilitating territory-wide enforcement of policy decisions (Smith, 1998: 70). Politicians use this state machinery to enforce their will internally and enforce boundary maintenance (or expansion) through warfare (Smith, 1998: 76). The state machinery becomes all-pervasive in modern nation states. Nation states often tie their founding myths to memories of military mobilization (Smith, 1991: 26);
- All members of the national community share a legal equality and reciprocal rights and obligations (1991: 10);
- Members of the nation are deemed to share a set of common understandings, aspirations, sentiments, ideas, symbols, myths, traditions and memories, i.e. a common culture and/or ideology (1991: 11). This common culture/ideology is acquired through 'shared' socialization within a standardized education system. Education serves to maintain standardized national languages, and assimilate migrants into the national language and common understandings. The mass media also plays an important role in developing and circulating sets of common understandings. The print medium (books, newspapers and magazines) played an especially crucial role in the early formation of Anglo national identity, and remains important for the creation of contemporary public opinion and identity. However, when it comes to the formation of contemporary identities, television has become as important as print. In fact, the former is arguably now more important for public opinion formation and for drawing the boundaries around contemporary imagined communities.

5.4 National identity: constructed, imagined, consumed or pre-existing?

National identity has a long association with liberal democracy presumably because this form of imagined community has proven especially valuable for constructing, holding together and 'steering' political communities based on mass publics. Although some argue nations 'exist' in a natural, organic and essentialist way (i.e. national identity is not constructed),

Table 5.1 *Perennial/essentialist vs modernist/constructivist view*

Perennialism	Modernism
The nation as	
Cultural community	Political community
Immemorial	Modern
Rooted	Created
Organic	Mechanical
Seamless	Divided
Quality	Resource
Popular	Elite-constructed
Ancestrally based	Communication-based

modernists propose that nations are communicatively constructed. They place great emphasis on the role played by the media and intelligentsia (such as journalists) in the formation of nations and identity. Smith (1998: 23) provides a useful summary of the differences between the perennial/essentialist versus modernist/constructivist views in Table 5.1.

Smith's dichotomy can be extended such that national identity can be conceptualized as arising in one of five ways:

1   As a primordial *'naturally existent'* entity. Such perennialism would say we identify with nations because they exist, and we are naturally members of them;

2   Modernists argue that nations do not just 'exist'. They are *invented* as modernist projects. These projects construct language-based communities into which people are socialized. Literacy and the print media have been centrally implicated in constructing these national identities. Gellner offers the classic statement of the constructivist argument;

3   Postmodernists see nations as the outcome of a process of *contextually bound* **semiosis**. Nations are linguistic representations, arising as people relate to each other within a matrix of power relations. Hall (1996), for example, argues that our identities mutate as we shift our relational positions, producing a multiplicity of fragmented identities. In essence, we continually construct and reconstruct ourselves as we go along. From Hall's perspective, 'national identity' becomes simply another form of 'temporary attachment' to discursively constructed 'subject-positions'. For postmodernists, the media have become key vehicles for the circulation of the discourses/representations individuals use to invent their identities;

4   There is the *consumption model* of identity which explores how identities are formed as a consequence of media consumption. There are two versions of this model – a modernist and postmodernist version. The seminal modernist version was developed by Frankfurt School members, e.g. Adorno and Horkheimer (1979), who examined the growth of

passive mass publics. The passivity of these publics was attributed to their consumption of commercial mass media products. The Frankfurt School's critique of **'mass culture'** was precisely based upon the perceived passivity of mass media audiences (who simply consumed 'culture' manufactured by an intelligentsia working for the culture industry, rather than organically constructing their own culture). The mass media were seen to circulate representations confirming the needs of mass consumer culture and a mass polity based on passive consumption rather than active engagement; National identity was built upon such a consumed mass media-derived passivity. Lash and Urry (1994) formulated a postmodern version of this consumptionist model around the notion of citizenship being constructed within a fragmented (nichized) consumer culture. For Lash and Urry, mass 'national' identities would be replaced by a multiplicity of niche identities because mass consumer culture was being replaced by niche production, niche marketing and niche media;

5   Benedict Anderson (1991) has developed the notion of *'imagined communities'*. Anderson's understanding of national identity remains grounded in a modernist view that nations are constructed. However, Anderson moves some way towards the postmodernist notion of nations as linguistic representations – i.e. he hybridizes the modernist idea of an elite-constructed, communication-based project of nation building with the postmodernist idea of semiotic 'imaginings'. Hence, national identities are not reducible to modernist constructions. But neither are they simply reducible to subjectivist 'unreality'.

For Anderson, communities can be 'invented' and 'imagined', but that does not mean they are not experienced/perceived as intensely 'real' for those inside them. Anderson's work does not fall into the trap of regarding national identity as simply some form of 'false-consciousness' or 'mystification'. Rather, the 'imagined community' notion makes it possible to regard national communities as valuable entities which can assist their members to interact more effectively with each other and the environment. Anderson's work is also useful for grappling with the role of 'identity' within the political process, and for examining how identity formation and maintenance emerges from the complex interplay between politicians and their hype industry; the media; the intelligentsia (journalists and educationalists); and (mass and niche) publics. Effectively, Anderson recognizes that imagined communities are not simply reducible to manufactured 'external' entities that position and construct citizens, because people can enter into subjective relationships with these communities – i.e. they effectively construct their own 'selves' in relationship to these entities. In this way, Anderson recognizes the dual nature of national identities – i.e. that although identities can be invented and constructed by an intelligentsia/elite, these identities/representations can also become detached from intelligentsia inventions, and develop a self-sustaining popular life of their own.

Ultimately, the various conceptualizations of national identity leave us with the following picture of how this identity is formed.

Firstly, both Gellner and Anderson argue that a modernizing state-building elite constructs national identity. Gellner contends that nations were created by literate elites who constructed the tamed, cultivated 'garden cultures' (which he differentiates from 'wild' undirected cultures). These elites deployed standardized mass education to tame and modernize the masses. Within this model, intellectuals, journalists and teachers generate and circulate the discourses and practices necessary to create 'publics' compatible with the needs of liberal capitalism. There is some overlap between this constructivist view of national identity and Gramsci's notion of hegemony building.

Secondly, elites build cultural infrastructures (media and schools) to disseminate identity-building representations. Anderson argues that national formation was originally associated with the development of a capitalist print medium which circulated nation-building representations. This required constructing three interlocking phenomena: a codified vernacular (to serve as a 'national' print language); mass literacy (to provide audiences for print capitalism and to give the masses access to nation-building representations); and a media industry (books, newspapers and magazines). From this emerges 'a nation' – from the language we are embedded into; the representations taught at school; and media representations. This 'nation' can assume a trans-state (and global) dimension – hence, in the British Empire a 'British nation' was effectively dispersed across the globe. This (Anglo) 'nation' lived in different administrative-bureaucratic entities (e.g. the UK, Australia, Canada, New Zealand, South Africa and India), yet were embedded in the same language, and shared the same 'British' representations. The various administrative-bureaucratic entities were networked into one political entity (the British Empire). At the end of the twentieth century this global Anglo-*ethnie* (but not 'nation') still existed. However, the core generator of this *ethnie*'s representations had shifted from Britain to the USA. The contemporary phenomenon of 'globalization' (underpinned by the Pax Americana) effectively represents this globally dispersed Anglo-*ethnie* re-networking itself (Louw, 2001: chapter 6).

Thirdly, the intelligentsia creates identity in the following ways. They manufacture 'publics' (who share the representations and identities manufactured by the elite). These can be 'mass publics' (discussed by the Frankfurt School) or (networked) 'niche publics' (discussed by Lash and Urry (1994)). The intelligentsia also creates 'in-groups' and 'out-groups'. This involves creating symbolically constructed boundaries separating 'us' from 'them' – i.e. ethnic identification involves symbolically building 'bounded' imagined 'spaces' with 'special' shared 'meanings' for the in-group. Education and media representations are especially important in constructing and circulating emotionally laden landscapes, time-scapes and cultural artifacts as 'memories' which position people inside shared symbolic communities. These include narratives and constructed memories (books, television programs, music, etcetera); symbolic constructions (Big Ben, Statue of Liberty, Sydney Harbour Bridge, Ottawa Parliament House, Voortrekker Monument); symbolic landscapes (Dover Cliffs, Grand Canyon, Uluru/Ayers Rock, Canadian Rockies, or Table Mountain); and symbolic rituals (Britain's 'Proms'; America's 4th July parades, or Australia's Anzac parades). But creating imagined 'spaces' can also occur more mundanely – e.g. the ritualistic watching of television weather bulletins can build a sense of 'national boundedness' (i.e. the 'geographical range' of your in-group). So national identity is not only the result of deliberate nationalistic constructions. It can arise from journalists and teachers 'unconsciously' circulating representations which have become naturalized and taken for granted.

Centrally implicated in constructing national identities is the manufacture and dissemination of stereotypes, especially by the media/culture industry. This is always associated with a positive stereotyping of 'we', which may be (but is not always) associated with defining 'we' as superior to 'them'. Similarly, it is often (but not always) associated with negatively stereotyping 'them'. Further, the 'we' being constructed is necessarily conceptualized as 'unified' – i.e. 'we-ness' involves making that which may divide the group (e.g. class) less important than that which unifies them (e.g. shared language) (see Pickering, 2001: 89–95). Journalists are especially prone to deploying stereotypes because journalistic practices call for shorthand simplifications and sound bites. This is also the reason why journalists are often implicated in creating 'moral panics', folk-devils, pariahs, scapegoats and heroes – all rooted in their tendency to deploy shorthand stereotypes. As both Anderson and Hall note, media representations and stereotypes become the raw material people use to create their sense of 'self' and to construct their 'imaginings' of their relationships to 'others'.

5.5 Journalism and political identity

The intelligentsia are crucial agents in building political identity because they are key players in circulating the meanings from which identities are built.

The human capacity for language, sharing and comprehension involves an ability to make meaning – we are able to absorb perceptions, process them, comprehend them and share them with others. We effectively swim in a sea of meanings. But meanings do not just exist – they are actively made and remade as circumstances change. All humans make meaning and all humans consume meaning. However, meaning-production and circulation is the full-time occupation of some. These professional meaning makers – the intelligentsia – include academics, teachers, journalists, and other communication professionals (e.g. those in the entertainment industry, advertising and public relations). They exercise an influence in society disproportionate to their numbers because they are the primary communicative gatekeepers.

When it comes to politics, journalists have an especially powerful influence because the news media lies at the heart of circulating political meanings. Journalists have therefore played a significant part in constructing national identity reaching back to the earliest days of mass-circulation presses. Unpacking this contribution serves to illustrate the role the intelligentsia play in building political identities such as national identity.

National identity is a form of mass consciousness highly functional for steering democracies. Inculcating mass populations into identifying with national consciousness became possible with the birth of the mass (print) media. Hence, building reading publics was crucial for constructing liberal-capitalist democracies because this created the foundations for the two-tiered political process within which the enfranchised masses posed no danger to ruling elites (see chapter 3). 'Taming' the masses required they be embedded within sets of 'appropriate' representations circulated by the mass media and be inducted into politics as a form of mass entertainment (i.e. second-tier 'politics-as-hype') (see chapter 2). Nowadays the electronic media are the key embedding mechanism, but in the early days of liberal democracy, it was the print media. Journalists were thus, from the outset, implicated in the process of distributing 'appropriate representations' (i.e. those from which national identities could be constructed) and writing the entertaining sensationalist stories from which 'politics-as-hype' is constructed. The masses became publics who, as audiences, were steered by the hype journalists produced. The Hearst and Northcliffe presses epitomized this hyped, entertaining, sensationalized journalistic genre which simultaneously encouraged the growth of both politics as demagoguery and steered publics (see 3.3.2 on p. 49). Northcliffe contemptuously characterized this journalist genre as newspapers 'for office boys, written by office boys' (Williams, 1984: 144). Crucially, this journalistic genre was greatly beneficial for the elites who governed democracies because it simultaneously helped to legitimate the political system; 'pacify' and 'tame' the newly enfranchised masses; and incubate those political identities and 'imagined communities' which generated 'loyalty' towards the states being built.

Essentially, the mass media (originally print, but later also electronic) and journalists played a core role in building liberal democracy because they provided the vehicle(s) for:

- Gathering together mass publics in ways facilitating the hegemonically dominant communicating with the enfranchised masses; but not facilitating members of the public communicating with each other. This made 'publics' manageable in ways 'crowds' were not;
- Creating identities valuable for liberal capitalism. This involves disseminating stories, myths and symbols which the masses can use to build their identities;
- Marking (and maintaining) the boundaries of group identities. Anderson (1991) describes how vernacular language-based 'print communities' became national identities. The contemporary print and electronic media are able to produce many varieties of (bounded) identity, ranging from mass to niche identities. The commercial media specialize in constructing and selling mass and niche audiences to advertisers. Just as the media are valuable to business seeking audiences as consumers, so they are valuable to politicians and their spin-doctors because the media builds and delivers identifiable (bounded) 'mass' and/or 'niche' publics;
- Politicians to communicate with mass electorates so as to promote themselves and their policies;
- Leading 'public opinion' by highlighting some issues and ignoring others (agenda setting); demonizing some individuals, groups and ideas (often associated with building 'folk-devils' and/or 'moral panics') while praising other individuals, groups and ideas. This is often associated with the journalistic deployment of binary oppositions ('hooray' and 'boo' words) and stereotypes;
- Circulating representations legitimating liberal capitalism, the state and its political, legal and bureaucratic frameworks;
- Circulating representations which help promote practices valuable to liberal capitalism;
- Naturalizing those discourses and practices which underpin the smooth functioning of liberal-capitalist states.

Journalists became centrally implicated in circulating the myths, symbols and stories underpinning the building of modern nation states and liberal capitalism. Intellectuals and politicians generally invented these myths, symbols and stories (see 9.2), while journalists (and later on, also spin-doctors) became specialists in packaging and presenting them to mass publics (see 9.3). (See Table 5.2).

The twentieth century saw this creation and packaging process increasingly professionalized within a political myth-making and impression-management system involving an increasingly complex division of labor between politicians as policy makers; politicians as celebrities (facades/faces); spin-doctors/PRs; impression managers/coaches; communication

Table 5.2 *Players and their roles in myth making and circulation*

Intellectuals	Politicians	Spin-doctors	Journalists	Teachers
• Create myths • Systematize myths into ideologies	• Select already-created myths and ideologies and sell them • Package myths • Create myths • Struggle with other politicians over which myths become dominant • Circulate myths	• Help politicians package and sell myths	• Report on politicians circulating myths • Package myths for media audiences • Circulate myths (in society)	• Package dominant myths for pupils • Circulate myths (in schools)

consultants and advertising specialists; journalists as researchers; and journalists as celebrities. Collectively, these people symbiotically construct the patterns of political communication underpinning liberal democracy. In earlier eras, the communicative process may have been less complex, but every era has involved politicians, and journalists interacting to collectively construct the political identities, practices and discourses underwriting the political process.

5.5.1 Liberalism and Anglo identity: the seven phases

Liberal capitalism in the Anglo world has traveled through seven phases to date, each underpinned by a political identity. In each phase journalists have played a central role shaping the political processes and identities of that era.

First came the revolutionary phase when England's burghers (in alliance with the landed gentry) challenged the monarchy and aristocratic privilege. The print media played a crucial role in circulating liberal ideas among the emergent liberal oligarchy, giving rise to a literacy-based revolutionary bourgeois public sphere. This led to the emergence of a new kind of political identity – 'English national identity'. The print media were effectively the fulcrum within which this new identity took shape.

In phase two, England's liberal oligarchy built a pioneering liberal-capitalist state. This involved codifying a 'national' language; building a rational administrative/legal system to serve as the territorial fulcrum for a single market; and building a 'national identity' to underpin the exercise of state and economy building. The print media and journalists played a central role in the process of 'inventing England', and building liberal hegemony over England and its North American colonies. Journalists helped to construct a new identity (associated with liberal capitalism and Englishness) and deconstruct and delegitimize the old feudal identities. ·

Phase three emerged from the American Revolution in England's colonies (1775–81). This revolution, which 'invented' both the USA and liberal democracy, influenced more than the USA – it affected the whole Anglo world. Journalism was centrally implicated in these revolutionary events, and in the subsequent invention of American identity. The consolidation of US liberal democracy and American identity during the nineteenth century was associated with the growth of three inter-related phenomena, namely, a commercial mass media industry; a new journalistic genre; and mass public opinion. All were subsequently exported to the rest of the Anglo world. Journalists circulated meanings helpful for assembling American identity (based on transplanted Anglo notions of identity and governance). American journalists were instrumental in taking these Anglo notions, and turning them into de-contextualized and universalized ideals.

Phase four saw England's liberal oligarchy reform itself into a liberal democracy. This coincided with the invention of 'British national identity'. British identity was globalized when carried by settlers to places like Australia, Canada, New Zealand, South Africa and India. This identity underpinned imperial conquest; a huge global market; an Empire-wide administration system; and the economic integration of the British Empire. Interestingly, 'British identity' involved constructing an 'assembled' identity transcending the idea of a homogeneous nation because it necessarily had to accommodate the assimilation of the Scots and Irish, and the idea of developing loyalty towards a global multi-ethnic trading empire. None the less, within this Empire, Anglo-ethnocentricism was apparent in the shape of a complex ethnic-ranking system which placed Englishmen at the top, followed by other Europeans, then Asians, then black people at the bottom. During this phase, Empire builders replicated liberal democratic practices (tied to 'white-British' identity) in some of Britain's Australasian, Canadian and Southern African colonies. This phase saw the building of mass education systems across the Empire designed to inculcate practices and values useful for the Empire's economic development, and to teach literacy thus enabling 'access' to school text books and newspapers disseminating 'British' and 'Empire' values. Newspaper stories were shared across the Empire (by Reuters), which helped to cement a shared 'British' identity in Britain and among settlers across the Empire. Media such as *Boy's Own* magazine also played an important role in constructing this identity. During the early twentieth century, BBC radio and its Empire clones deepened this shared identity.

During phase four, journalists (and teachers) circulated meanings helpful for assembling the new British identity in the UK and among overseas settlers. Assembling this new identity required deconstructing old identities and especially for *ethnies* to be assimilated (e.g. Scots, Irish, Welsh, Québecois and Afrikaners). It also involved justifying:

- Conquest;
- Destroying some *ethnies* (e.g. Aboriginals, and native Americans);
- Assimilating their remnants;
- The Empire's ethnic ranking system which facilitated using some groups as cheap 'ethnic' labour (e.g. blacks and Indians);
- The repression of those groups resisting the above (e.g. the Irish).

Journalists provided many of the representations justifying/naturalizing the above.

Phase five derived from the USA's post-Civil War nation-building project – constructed upon mass migration from Europe; westward expansion; and the assimilation of non-Anglo migrants. 'American identity' came to transcend the idea of a homogeneous nation because it had to accommodate massive inflows of non-Anglos. By assimilating migrants, the USA grew into the largest society in the Anglo world and this saw the demographic and cultural center of the Anglo world begin its shift across the Atlantic from England to the USA. This shift impacted upon the whole Anglo world – i.e. Anglo-American cultural practices; US-developed modifications to liberal democratic practices and discourses; US-developed innovations to liberal capitalism; US media practices; and US media products (e.g. Hollywood movies; books; music; and eventually television) were dispersed throughout the Anglo world. Ultimately, no one in the Anglo world was untouched by how 'American identity' evolved. This happened because the USA became the Anglo world's demographic and political core, and because the US-media system exported so much to other Anglo countries.

During phase five, journalists (and teachers) circulated meanings helpful to assemble American identity. Journalists helped to systematize transplanted Anglo notions of identity and governance into a teleological and 'universal' model of political modernization – i.e. journalists began popularizing the notion that 'what was good for America was good for the world'. Assembling American identity involved deconstructing the identities of migrants being assimilated into the 'melting pot' of dominant Anglo-American discourses and practices. It also involved justifying:

- Western territorial conquests and American colonization of these;
- The destruction of native Americans;
- Assimilating their remnants;
- The forceful assimilation of Hispanics;
- An ethnic ranking system (paralleling in some ways the British ranking system) which facilitated using some groups as cheap labour (e.g. blacks, Irish, Hispanics).

Journalists provided many of the representations justifying/naturalizing the above.

Phase six was launched by the Atlantic Charter (Anon, 1941), which initiated British (and French) de-colonization and the incorporation of these imperial possessions into a system of US neo-colonialism. This initiated a period of identity reconstruction in the Anglo world. The British had to deal with the trauma of losing their Empire (between 1947 and 1967). This meant simultaneously adjusting to 'becoming European' and to the influx of (dislocated and traumatized) migrants/refugees from the collapsing Empire. These Empire migrants/refugees were diverse – descended of colonial settlers and former slaves and 'natives' who had been assimilated. Many had internalized identities 'more British' than the British. Anglo-derivative settler societies (like Australia and Canada) had to adjust to the end of British hegemony (and the associated collapse of 'Empire identities') and simultaneously cope with integrating migrants/refugees from the collapsing Empire, plus migrants/refugees from post-World War II Europe. All had to cope with the new ascendancy of the USA and American political and cultural values. Inside the USA, identity politics ironically involved constructing an American identity as an anti-colonial/democracy builder while, in reality, the USA began building the neo-colonial Pax Americana from the remnants of the British and French empires. This American self-identity also became enmeshed in the politics of the 1945–89 cold war between liberal capitalism (led by the USA) and communism (led by the Soviet Union).

During phase six, journalists (and teachers) helped to reconstruct identities all over the Anglo world. American journalists helped to transform the decontextualized Anglo model of governance and identity into a 'pan-human universalism', and justified (to Americans) imposing this 'universalized' and '**teleology**-ized' American model/vision of 'modernity' onto the rest of the world. This 'pan-human vision' was adopted by Australian and Canadian journalists and propagated and naturalized in these countries. This vision was also promulgated in Japan and West Germany while they were under US military occupation. Further, during this phase (neo-colonial), Westernized elites promulgated versions of the US nation building and modernization model across the Third World. Because the Anglo-American intelligentsia had naturalized this model into a 'pan-human universalism', its Third World promulgation was widely acclaimed as 'progressive' by US, Canadian and Australian journalists (even when repression was deployed to form and hold these states together, as in the case of Indonesia). The neo-colonial imposition of 'pan-humanism' was a process of 'cultural homogenization' experienced as repression by many around the globe. For Anglo journalists promoting this 'pan-human' vision, the emergence of 'anti-Americanism' (as a response to US neo-colonialism) was jarring, but was 'rationalized away' as a cold war phenomenon. When many Third World modernizing projects mutated into patrimonial cleptocracies or failed states (Hoogvelt, 1997: 175) these same journalists averted their gaze, presumably because reflecting on these events challenged their universalized/teleologized 'pan-human' model (of state and identity building).

Phase seven saw the consolidation of the Pax Americana and America's 'pan-human universalist' model. By the turn of the century UK identity had been substantially 'Americanized'. This was facilitated by three developments:

- The widespread sharing of US television programming/news across the Anglo world diffused and naturalized American social, political and economic discourses and practices;
- The emergence of global network capitalism signaled the effective rise of a global networker elite dominated by Anglos (in North America and the UK), and their OECD allies;
- The Soviet collapse meant the USA became the globally dominant military power.

The seventh phase saw a growing convergence in the practices and values of journalists across the Anglo world. Something of a shared liberal 'cosmopolitanism' emerged from the 'pan-human universalist' vision underpinning US hegemony. The OECD's intelligentsia began circulating representations serving the interests of global network capitalism – i.e. the 'integrative' discourses of 'globalization', 'multiculturalism', 'universal rights' (i.e. American 'pan-humanism') and 'peace keeping'. Ironically, although their value system was effectively Anglo-centric, its Anglo roots were often 'opaque' to many journalists (who preferred to think of themselves as 'cosmopolitan' and/or 'multicultural'). As in phase six, these journalists effectively naturalized Anglo-American modernizing and/or post-modernizing processes into a universal, teleological model. Once these globalizing liberal 'cosmopolitan' values were naturalized as inherently teleological/progressive, many in the Anglo media adopted a 'journalistic sneer' towards individuals and groups not conforming to their worldview. Al-Qaeda's 9/11 bombings represented a radically symbolic refusal of this 'universalized' and 'teleologized' vision. Phase seven has come to be characterized by the emergence of a Pax Americana which underpins globalization. Globalization has seen OECD nation states networked into a shared set of economic and political arrangements. Inside this global network, the discourses of liberal 'cosmopolitanism' are hegemonic. Those outside this network have effectively been placed into one of four categories by the discourses of OECD politicians and journalists:

- States deemed capable of being relatively easily 'developed' into liberal democracies and then admitted into the OECD club (e.g. Rumania);
- States deemed to have long-term potential of being reformed/developed into liberal democracies (e.g. China);
- 'Hostile' states needing to be coerced into becoming liberal democracies (e.g. Iraq, North Korea);
- Failed states which are either 'policing'/peacekeeping problems for the Pax Americana (e.g. Afghanistan) or simply 'irrelevant' for liberal capitalism (e.g. Rwanda).

In each of the above stages, journalists were complicit in manufacturing representations inculcating identities valuable to that phase of liberal capitalism. Journalists, whether aware of it or not, were part of the process of hegemony formation in each phase of building liberal capitalism. They – as professional storytellers – have effectively always naturalized the political and economic practices of each era by circulating the myths, ideologies memories and symbols from which people construct their political identities and justify their political actions. The fact that politicians now employ spin-doctors as their interface with journalists is testament to the importance placed on media-ized storytelling within the process of hegemony building and identity formation.

Summary

You should now be familiar with the following key themes and concepts:
identity construction; hegemony; naturalized discourse; mass publics; modernization; building national identity; nation building; imagined community; pan-human universalism; *ethnie*; language-based theories of national identity; the role of education in constructing national identity; the role of the mass media in constructing national identity; reading publics; how journalists circulate myths, symbols and stories functional for building identity.

For further consideration

1 Why did the nation state emerge as such a useful fulcrum for liberal capitalism?
2 Why has 'the citizen' been so useful for the functioning of liberal capitalism?
3 Has the role of the media in creating 'nations' and 'citizens' been exaggerated by some theorists?
4 What best describes the role of most individuals in society – active citizens or a passive public? Why?
5 Could one build and maintain a national identity without the mass media to share symbols?
6 Some argue that nations simply 'exist'. Others argue that they are 'imagined'. Are these mutually exclusive?
7 Could the growth of a globalized media system herald the 'reintegration' of globally dispersed Anglos (in the UK, USA, Canada, Australia and New Zealand) into a new united Anglo *ethnie*?
8 Does television necessarily create a different identity from newspapers?
9 Are journalists always complicit in manufacturing national identity?
10 Is the building of national identity part of the 'policy dimension' or the 'hype dimension' of the political process?

New Media: New Politics? New Identity?

Chapter 5 examined how national identities were communicatively constructed within mass media fulcra. This raises questions like: does the development of new media forms change the way identities are constructed? And will new media forms bring about the demise of national identity? Chapter 6 examines the proposal that *new media technologies are altering the communicative environment* and the associated argument that altering the communicative environment will generate new kinds of identities and new political forms. This chapter will argue that the actual impacts of new media on politics and identity are likely to be less significant than many have suggested. Chapter 6 will begin by examining the construction of the 'information age' thesis and how 'boosterists' (including the media) promoted this thesis. Responses to this thesis will then be examined. Thereafter, the actual effects of new media on political practices, politicians, spin-doctors and identity formation will be examined.

The last quarter of the twentieth century witnessed the growing popularity of the notion that Western society was experiencing an era-shift as revolutionary as the transformation from the agricultural to the industrial era. This notion was associated with the interchangeable concepts of 'postindustrialism', 'information age' and 'communications age'. At heart, the postindustrial thesis argued that information processing characterized the new era, just as agriculture and industrial production had characterized the previous two eras. The era-shift hypothesis was premised on the view that new communications technologies and new media were radically altering human interactions and socio-economic organization. This led to a view that politics, governance and identities would be altered due to the deployment of new media technologies.

Undoubtedly new media technologies have impacted upon socio-economic processes, and it seems reasonable to argue for a postindustrial/informationized periodization based upon this impact. However, whether the break between industrial and postindustrial society is as profound as some have argued is a moot point (see Cohen and Zysman, 1987). Further, some writings on the information/communications age became boosterist – sliding into promotional salesmanship for rapidly deploying new media technologies on the assumption that this will generate 'progressive' ('post-modern') change associated with, for example, more democracy, new identities and the death of the nation state and national identities. Optimistic boosterism was popularized by writers like Toffler (1990). This chapter will explore whether the proliferation of new media does actually produce new political genres and/or new political identities.

6.1 What is the postindustrial/information age?

Daniel Bell (1973) was first to propose that a postindustrial era had dawned. In its earliest form, the postindustrial thesis confined itself to examining the emergence of a new economic mode of production wherein service-sector and information-processing work expanded disproportionately relative to the industrial and agricultural sectors. This was seen to alter work practices and consumption practices. However, postmodernists colonized and altered the postindustrial thesis. Postmodernists – who wallow in notions of disunity, disorder and incoherence (Featherstone, 1991) – believed postindustrialism heralded the arrival of a new ('improved') era wherein 'modernist' institutions (e.g. the state) and 'modernist' identities (e.g. national identity) would be replaced by **postmodern** practices and discourses. A great complementarity developed between the (highly media-centric) thinking of the postmodernists and the boosterists, both of whom welcomed the dawning of a 'new nirvana' to be born from the new media's undermining of **modern** states, modern politics, modern economics and modern identities. From this would emerge the (postmodern) information age – an era based upon the following developments which place 'information' at the heart of social organization:

- New media technologies alter the flow and increase the volume of social communication by decreasing the cost and distance sensitivity of moving information; increasing the speed and volume of communication; increasing channel diversity and user control over content; increasing system upgradeablity and interconnectivity; and increasing possibilities for two-way communication (Neuman, 1991: 53–71). The exchange of information became potentially instantaneous, globally.

The new media alter the time and space dimensions of communication flows, human interactions and the decision-making processes (Abrahamson et al., 1990: 42–5);

- New media technologies alter the means of economic production. This has been characterized as a shift from fordism to **postfordism** – i.e. towards an informational economy. Computer-integrated manufacture (CIM) means that 'flexible' short production runs are possible – hence, consumers can be offered a choice because communication systems facilitate collecting their demands; channeling these to CIM facilities (for customized production), and delivering products back to the consumers. So communication becomes central to production itself – the system becoming reliant upon telecommunications/computer networks and the conceptual, communication and coordination skills of the people driving the system. As Lash and Urry (1994: 61) argue, the economy becomes 'reflexive' – with reflection, information/symbol processing and cultural capital now crucial to success. The emergence of an informational economy also sees a rapid growth of the service sector, and knowledge and information-processing jobs;

- The shift to postfordism alters power relationships and generates new socio-economic winners and losers, both in individual and geographical terms (see Louw, 2001: chapter 6). For those with access to new media technologies, information becomes hyper-abundant. But this generates new socio-economic cleavages between the information rich and information poor. The information rich (with access to the new technology) can access a wide variety of user-pays information channels, including interactive media and high-quality sources. But the information poor only access low-grade sources, e.g. the tabloid press and free-to-air 'tabloid' television;

- New media technologies change the work practices of professional communicators – e.g. the abundance of easily accessible information on the Internet means that journalists gather ever-larger qualities of information from on-line data sources (Hall, 2001). New technologies such as mini-cams, satellite hook ups, **digitization**, laptop computers (that can be networked into 'newsrooms without walls') plus long-haul jet travel, alter news collection and processing practices. These technologies make it possible to downsize and de-skill newsrooms, by increasing reliance on pooled information fed into the information net by news agencies and PRs. New technologies also alter the nature of PR because the emergence of on-line environments create the need to maintain web-sites and answer e-mails. Overall, on-line journalism greatly increases the possibilities for PRs/spin-doctors to manipulate journalists because of the ease with which information can be trawled off the Internet instead of interfacing firsthand with the world (Fallows, 1997: 148–9);

- New media technologies potentially allow for increased interactivity, with both senders and receivers having greater control over their interface with the communicative process. Boosterists/optimists have used this feature of the new technology to argue that the information age will witness less propagandistic use of the media, and greater individuation of opinion (Neuman, 1991: 104). The Internet and personal computers are seen as especially important examples of such media-ized interactivity facilitating personalized control over communication, self-actualization and intellectual pluralism (1991: 13);
- New technologies create the potential for shifting away from mass media markets towards the growth of economically viable niche media markets. Postmodernists/optimists argue that the resultant proliferation of niche media (serving smaller markets) creates a fulcrum for new niche identities (and pluralism) to grow. This meshes with the view the information age will promote individualism, self-realization and consumerism (Masuda, 1980), and the new media will undermine (modernist) 'mass society'. Neuman, however, has cautioned against assuming that niche identities will result from this 'technological push', because, he argues, the economies of mass marketing and the psychology of mass audiences remain deeply entrenched (1991: 13). In some senses, the emergence of niche media/markets simply reinforces the overall media-ization of Western society in ways complementing rather than challenging the survival of a consumerist 'mass society', surrounded by a plethora of niche identities. Each niche remains connected to, and reinforces the political economy of the core 'mass society'. Further, niche members are just as manipulated/steered (as members of the 'mass') by marketers, advertisers and PRs;
- New media technologies greatly enhance the possibilities for global networking. These have been successfully deployed by global corporations who use new communication technologies to manage their activities across the world from global cities inside the OECD. This has greatly facilitated the 'service-zing' of OECD economies, as industrial production has been progressively relocated outside the OECD (where labour is cheaper). The networking possibilities have also been successfully deployed by the US military to construct a global system of intelligence gathering and global coercion management. The contemporary Pax Americana is substantially constructed upon successfully utilizing all the networking possibilities inherent in the new communications technologies;
- It is argued that the above developments all point to the birth of a new kind of postmodern politics which will see the withering away of state and national identities, coupled with declining possibilities for the mass-propagandistic manipulation of citizens. Proposals for building new sorts of (post-mass) politics are premised upon the view that new

media technologies create possibilities for building active civil society; grassroots plebiscitary democracy; and new forms of resistance-politics (Ganley, 1992). The postmodern politics thesis became especially popular with those sections of the Western intelligentsia ideologically opposed to nation states, nationalism and so on – who found in the notion of an information age a vehicle for (post-Marxist) theorizing about a new utopia.

Although the idea that we have entered a new era has achieved widespread currency, responses to this era-shift have not been uniform. Essentially, three broad responses have been forthcoming – one proposing that major changes are underway, and that these are beneficial/'progressive'. Another set of responses has been more cautious and incredulous about both the depth and the value of the changes: While acknowledging that changes are underway, they have been somewhat skeptical of the utopian interpretations of these changes. A third (Luddite) response has been hostile to the changes.

6.2 Responses to the information age thesis

Of the above three responses, the optimists and boosterists have been the most vocal. Neuman (1991: 164) notes that the most articulate new media champions have been investors and salesmen, who have the most to gain if these media are adopted. Their boosterist visions were strengthened and promoted by postmodernists eager to believe a new utopian age was dawning. The result was the dissemination of optimistic (utopian) visions of the future based upon believing that new information technologies provided a means for undermining all that was bad in the modernist-industrial world. By the start of the twenty-first century such 'transformation thinking' had become very chic among large sections of the OECD's intelligentsia.

At heart, the optimist view is premised upon Daniel Lerner's 1950s notion of development – i.e. media usage is deemed key to transforming society. Lerner (1958) argued that modernization would result from teaching literacy to pre-modern people. This would, he argued, lead to the growth of (print) media, from which would spring political modernization. (Because Lerner operated within the American model of 'pan-human universalism', he regarded US democracy as the teleological end goal of development.) Lerner's media-ized theory of development influenced Gellner (1983) and Anderson (1991). The information age optimists simply modify Lerner's basic model – i.e. if modernization grows out of literacy/print media, postmodernization will grow out of the new media (and learning the new 'electronic-literacies' required to drive new media forms). By extension, if modernization led to mass society, then postmodernization would lead to post-mass society. Or so the theory ran.

6.2.1 Optimistic view of the information age

The optimistic view proposed that the new media would generate six (inter-related) social 'improvements':

1 New media were seen to facilitate two-way communication in contradistinction to mass communication's uni-directionality. The interactivity facilitated would undermine top-down commanderist communication. This would end mass society, because 'massness' resulted from the passivity of traditional mass media audiences;
2 An active participatory democracy and citizen control could be built upon this interactivity because citizens could now be regularly consulted about their views – i.e. instead of being spoken to by the mass media, the new media made it possible for citizens to make their voices heard;
3 New media's interactive nature provided new communicative spaces where people could discover common concerns and discuss possible solutions. It was suggested that this would generate an activated civil society and re-invigorate democracy;
4 The new media were seen to deliver a greater abundance and greater diversity of information than ever before. This, it was argued, would generate a more democratic society because citizens with information would be less open to manipulation;
5 The new media offered the means to break up the mass media market into smaller niche media markets. In this, postmodernists saw the possibility for multiple new niche identities and localisms. This would create the basis for an active civil society built upon pluralist diversity;
6 Because new media facilitated interactive communication on a global basis, it was argued that new niche identities would grow as global phenomena – i.e. like-minded people in each of the 'niches' would find each other via the Internet no matter where they lived in the world. The result would be a globalized pluralist cosmopolitanism, because national identities (and nationalism) would be undermined by proliferating niche identities and localisms (i.e. an active civil society) and by the networking of these localisms/niche identities into a cosmopolitan globalism. Although the early (optimistic) teledemocracy work now seems rather dated – Arterton (1987); Becker (1981, 1993); Hollander (1985); and Pool (1983) – its themes proved remarkably resilient, resurfacing in later works like Abrahamson et al. (1990); Castells (1997); Elgin (1993); Grossman (1995); and Varn (1993).

6.2.2 The skeptical view

But the boosterists failed to persuade everyone. Some remained incredulous, or even pessimistic, about the likely impacts of the new media on society for the sorts of reasons discussed below. Firstly, although new media technologies can facilitate interactive two-way communication, the mass media (using uni-directional communication) show no sign of being displaced. Most people appear to prefer to receive information edited and packaged by others rather than sort through massive amounts of information themselves. Even the Internet increasingly offers packaged information, with sections now adopting mass media formats. Essentially, the idea that citizens will become active communicators because technology allows it seems dubious. Hence, predictions that people would bypass traditional news media (and seek their own information on the Internet) have not come to pass. Instead, mass audiences remain a core feature of contemporary Western society – these audiences still draw most of their information from mass media sources (especially television); this information is still delivered in top-down fashion and is still produced by media professionals. Much of this media content results from deliberate manipulation by social elites and their 'spin industry', and much content is still geared to producing pseudo-realities, infotainment and hype. What is more, professional communication manipulators have turned their attention to new media forms, like the Internet, because skillful communication manipulators can use two-way interactive communication just as effectively as uni-directional communication to steer people. Essentially, mass society, as described by the Frankfurt School, remains alive and well – contemporary mass-citizenries are now reached by traditional mass media as well as new media forms. As Neuman notes, the 'new' audiences (of the new media) remain just as helpless and susceptible to steering as the 'old' audiences (1991: 80–9) and social elites are just as likely to use new media as old media to persuade, propagandize, educate, cajole, manipulate and steer people. Neuman (1991: 158–63), in fact, suggests that market conditions will ensure that the new media never stray that far from the mass media model. We can expect more of the same.

Secondly, boosterist logic predicts greater citizen participation in politics because new media enable people to connect in new ways. Enhanced democracy and pluralism, where a greater range of opinions would be heard was predicted (1991: 40–1). However, as Neuman (1991: 42) notes, just because the new media make such developments possible does not mean that technologies will actually be used in these ways. A study by Hill and Hughes (1998) confirmed that the Internet has simply been used by people to reinforce traditional politics rather than build new forms of participatory politics. Further, Abrahamson et al. (1990: 165–86), Etzioni

(1972) and Malbin (1982) point out that even if new technologies were deployed to build direct democracies, this can generate a number of negative consequences associated with producing 'pseudoparticipation'. Essentially, far from enhancing either pluralist democracy or communitarian democracy (Abrahamson et al., 1990: 18–31), such media-ized politics tend instead to generate electronic plebiscites, where quick polling produces, at most, a partial kind of participation. Instead of real deliberation, debate and engagement with the issue/s, this form of 'democracy' produces something more akin to entertainment and a media-ized spectator sport. It also tends to facilitate a curious mix of crude majoritarianism, elite manipulation (because elites decide on the plebiscite questions), and enhanced factionalism (because niche media facilitate people only exposing themselves to opinions they approve of). Ultimately, boosterist arguments about new media improving political processes seem dubious.

Thirdly, new media generated an explosion in available information and access to a greater diversity of sources (for those with access to the technology). Boosterists argued that citizens would consequently become more informed and aware of a greater diversity of opinions, which would generate higher levels of informed social debate and reduce the possibilities for demagoguery and manipulation of the masses. In reality, new technologies produce a glut of information (of mixed quality), which greatly enhances the difficulties of finding appropriate information and evaluating its quality. Neuman (1991: 94) notes that new media technology and more information do not transform people into more attentive, alert and active information seekers. In fact, information gluts may increase the possibilities for manipulation because audiences are swamped and exhausted by information overload, and many will welcome others making editorial decisions for them, i.e. filtering, interpreting, formatting and packaging information (1991: 163). Neuman suggests that information gluts may increase the demand for packaging because it is easier to have help to navigate huge quantities of information and opinion. Hence the suggestion that new media forms have undercut the old media's gatekeeping role may be exaggerated. Clinton's PR team (who initially focused their energies on the new media) certainly discovered that the old media still mattered – a discovery confirming a 1998 Gallup Poll that showed that most Americans still relied on the old media as their primary source of news (Maltese, 2003: 11).

Fourthly, it has been argued that the new media create fulcra for new niche identities to flourish. Boosterist arguments imply that these new identities will be more organically grassroots in nature and less prone to manipulation than were the identities associated with mass media/society. This is based on a romantic notion that new media facilitate some sort of 'return' to a communal nirvana, where small communities of people interact with each other (in a sort of electronic village). In reality, the trend towards people living in large mass cities grows unabated and *de facto* mass urbanization continues to provide the contextual framework for most OECD living. There appears to be no return to communal village nirvanas (if these ever existed). Further, niche media are just as prone to manipulative interventions by marketers, advertisers and PRs – and many new niche identities are simply fads produced by marketing interventions aimed at generating 'lifestyle' consumption. Essentially, what has happened is that the mass audience (served by a mass media) has been fragmented into a series of smaller niche audiences (served by niche media) due to communication professionals becoming more sophisticated in understanding how to reach audiences more effectively. Politically, niche media facilitate the targeting and mobilization of single-issue groups, and/or to allow spin-doctors to reach more narrowly defined audiences with tailor-made messages. Far from heralding a new genre of politics, this has simply served to reinforce the American model of pluralist democracy. Overall, the old mass market/mass identity/mass media survives, but is now surrounded by an ever-shifting mélange of niche markets/identities.

The view that new identities would emerge was accompanied by three predictions:

- That web-based niche communities would overtake more traditional communities. This has not come to pass. At most, web 'communities' have simply intersected with, and complemented, older community forms;
- That localism (balkanization) would blossom because, it was assumed, niche and interactive media would facilitate grassroots communication and a re-discovery of local issues and loyalties. Some went as far as to predict that 'local politics' would replace 'national politics';
- That the global Internet would generate a new form of global cosmopolitanism in which individuals would discover like-minded persons globally. This would lead to new 'electronic communities' stretching across the globe. This notion was premised upon the American 'pan-human universalism' model – it implicitly assumed that US pluralistic democracy and urban cosmopolitanism (associated with cities like New York, Los Angeles and London) are destined to become globally hegemonic. At most, such globalized electronic communities have grown up among the globally dispersed Anglo intelligentsia. To date, predictions of localism and globalism replacing nationalism have not come to pass.

In broad terms, Gellner and Anderson's theories of development/social organization have much to recommend them – i.e. industrialization led to particular organizational, political and communicative forms which, in turn, generated identities complementing these organizational formations. It is easy to see how the postindustrialization thesis could generate the view that we are about to experience dramatic organizational, political and identity shifts. What is less clear is whether the shift from industrial to postindustrial is as far-reaching as some propose. Are we witnessing a radical break, or a mutation of industrial capitalism? If it is only a mutation, we can presumably expect only a series of mutations in political organization and identity formation, rather than the massive shifts predicted by boosterists and optimists.

6.3 New media and political and identity changes

The argument that deploying new media technologies will create a 'better' (postmodern) world is the outcome of the promotional hype of boosterist salesmanship. Neuman (1991: 14) argued that introducing new media technologies would not necessarily change either the mass psychology or the commercial logic underpinning US communications. To date he has been proven correct – new media have not resurrected the communication, values and lifestyle of small town and rural society (1991: 9); not given birth to a new participative democracy nor produced new actively engaged citizenries; not ended spin-doctoring and steering of mass audiences; nor produced better journalism. As Neuman said: 'although new media make possible new forms of political and cultural communication, in the main they are not likely to be used that way' (1991: 42). Instead, power elites will deploy new media in ways simply reinforcing their old behaviors and many people will continue to be susceptible to mass media influence of the sort seen in Orson Welles' 1938 'War of the Worlds' radio broadcast which generated mass hysteria because audiences believed an alien invasion from Mars was underway. So although new media make it possible for people to connect to each other in new ways, the reality is that the mass media remain firmly in place and continue to effectively 'disconnect' people from each other.

However, new media have impacted upon aspects of socio-economic organization as well as some of the practices of OECD political players. The extent to which this has influenced governance and identity is open to interpretation. When considering the impact of new media on political processes and identity, it is important to avoid media determinism – i.e. new technologies do not determine change; at most they create new possibilities. The extent to which these possibilities are taken up, how they are deployed, and the impact they have in various sectors is related to a myriad of human decisions and how these decisions interact with other variables. Perhaps the most important variable is the distribution of social power. The extent to which new technologies are deployed, and how they are deployed, is strongly influenced by decisions made by existing power elites. But new technologies also alter power relationships, because once adopted, they necessarily alter power distributions by producing new economic winners and losers. The adoption of new information technologies has already seen the emergence of new winners ('global networkers') positioned at the heart of a new form of capitalism – global network capitalism (Louw, 2001: 60–3). As the new (postfordist) winners insinuate themselves into power elites, decision making will tend to become more favourably disposed to the further deployment of new technologies.

Boosterist predictions of greater democracy and radically altered political identities may not have come to pass. But this poses the question: what changes have been wrought? Have political practices been altered? And have political identities been altered?

6.3.1 New media influences on political practices

Because new media technologies provided OECD political players with new tools, some of their practices have been modified. This has generated some impact on political conduct. But the changes wrought in no way conform to boosterist predictions. So what have been the changes to date? Significantly, most of the 'changes' in political practice since the 1980s simply involved a deepening of changes already evident in the 1960s–70s. This lends credence to the idea that postindustrialism may not be as profound as an era-shift. Instead, we may be witnessing a mutation within capitalism (towards global network capitalism) that involves mutating some practices (towards postfordism). Nonetheless, the arrival of new information technologies has been accompanied by some noteworthy mutations to the practices of political players.

The new OECD political game has seen a deepening of televisualized politics (with the USA leading the way). This has generated three key effects: changing political leadership styles; a growing 'spin industry' of political communication professionals; and a growing need for money to pay for television airtime and professional communicators.

6.3.1.1 Politicians as televised personalities Abrahamson et al. (1990: 68–91) describe the mutating style of US political leadership as the shift from statesmen to politicians to personalities. A shift to personality-based politics has been associated with the televisionizing of politics. Abrahamson et al. ascribe this to two causes: firstly, one cannot televise an entire political party. One can only televise an individual (1990: 17). Secondly, television has an intrinsic 'personalizing' nature. It enters into people's private homes and establishes a 'seeming intimacy' between viewers and communicators. It also inherently focuses viewer attention onto the personal qualities of politicians (1990: 83).

The result has been a 'personalization' of politics in which leaders are now chosen for their televisual skills – the ability to look good on television; speak in sound bites; convincingly match body language to sound bites; and resonate with TV audiences by televisually projecting appropriate personalities/masks. This has seen politicians-as-actors assume the characteristics of celebrities – the line between politicians, pop stars, movie stars, supermodels and sports stars has blurred as politicians have taken on the guise of popular culture celebrities (Street, 2001: 276). And because politicians have become celebrities, there has been a growing need to script their televisual performances and professionally construct their (televisual) faces. Hence, the growing need for backroom professionals specializing in electronic communication, i.e. minders/handlers, spin-doctors and a support staff of speechwriters, make-up artists and visual designers who are all experts in the arts of communicating with mass audiences through mobilizing flattery and demagoguery (Abrahamson et al., 1990: 13).

The shift to personality-based politics also modified political parties. Old-style party organizations comprising politically committed citizens were eroded. In their place came specialists (communication professionals, consultants and so on) employed to get celebrity candidates elected (1990: 87–9) so back-room policy staffers can get their hands on the machinery of power.

6.3.1.2 The 'nationalization' of politics
Significantly, the televisualizing of the political process has deepened the 'nationalization' of politics. This occurred because technology facilitated transmission images nationally and in real time, making it possible to build national political spheres within which leaders as celebrities, and their messages, could be simultaneously shared by all citizens, no matter how big the country. National TV news is a powerful vehicle for a ritualized and virtualized 'coming together' and 'sharing' in which 'nations' can imagine themselves as 'existent' in the Benedict Anderson sense. The way 9/11 Twin Towers imagery bonded Americans together is a case in point. Abrahamson et al. (1990: 11) draw attention to the way US televisualized governance has been centralized and nationalized as television networks concentrated their operations in New York and Washington. Similarly, the 'spin industry' has been located in these core media centers. The same pattern is true in other countries, e.g. London, Sydney/Canberra, Toronto/Ottawa, Tokyo and Paris. This contradicts predictions that the information age would cause the demise of national politics.

6.3.1.3 The growth of a spin-machine

It was further predicted that the information age would activate citizenries and civil society. Instead, we witness an ever-expanding 'spin industry' underpinning politicians as actors. This machinery scripts the performances of televisualized politics. In addition, it works with all the other new media technologies, including computers, the Internet and niche media outlets. This machinery underpinning celebrity politicians has made increasing use of computer databases as intelligence and marketing tools. Politics has become 'informationized' – information is gathered and stored in computer databases about voters, potential financial contributors and opposition candidates (Abrahamson et al., 1990: 91–3). It is used for a variety of purposes – e.g. discrediting opposition candidates; targeting specific potential voters or financial contributors; and telemarketing. Computers make it possible to define a specific niche group as a target audience; compose a message geared to that niche; and design publicity material or even direct-mail letters with the appearance of being personally directed and even personally signed (whereas, in fact, they are mass produced). Videos are also used as a form of 'direct mail'. In addition, communication professionals have become adept at using cable-TV, local radio, local presses, the Internet, e-mail and even mini-cable systems on private property for '**narrowcasting**' their messages to niche groups (1990: 6). Some of these narrowcasting strategies are specifically geared at bypassing journalists so as to enable politicians to talk directly with their constituency, and it has been suggested that new media technologies have helped to undercut the gatekeeping roles of traditional 'old media' journalism (Caprini and Williams, 2001: 174). Ultimately, the information age has proved to be an era of enhanced PR manipulation, with professional political communicators learning to deploy the full spectrum of media technologies to manipulate, flatter and cajole people.

This informationization and media-ization of politics has made politics a very expensive business because it involves employing high-cost experts to script and produce quality televisual images; public opinion research; computer databases; and marketing and advertising. Consequently, politicians must now have access to large amounts of money to pay for these experts. Even incumbents have experienced difficulties raising the huge sums required. In the USA this led to the phenomenon of Political Action Committees (PACs), specializing in raising money from individual donors, corporations, business associations and labor unions (Abrahamson et al., 1990: 16). Those making contributions expect 'access' to (and 'favors' from) elected politicians. This confers on those with enough wealth to make such contributions (the power elite) undue influence over future policy making.

6.3.1.4 The new media and revolutionary groups The practices of some revolutionary groups have also been altered by new media. Ganley (1992) provides examples of revolutionary groups learning to deploy new technologies – e.g. the Ayatollah Khomeini's successful use of tapes in his 1970s Islamic fundamentalist struggle against the Shah of Iran. Essentially, revolutionary groups have learned to use an array of new media such as personal computers; laser printing and desktop publishing; Web Pages; e-mail; audio and videocassettes. Some revolutionary and oppositional groups also learned the arts of televisualized and informationized PR as vehicles for stirring emotions, creating favourable publicity and creating celebrity 'struggle leaders' e.g. Tibet's Dalai Lama, Burma's Aung San Suu Kyi, South Africa's Nelson Mandela and Palestine's Yasser Arafat. By 'personalizing' their struggles, in ways resonating with Western audiences, some revolutionary groups became highly adept at stirring Western publics into demanding that Western governments act against foreign governments. Mobilizing foreign opinion constitutes the 'external maneuvers' of revolutionary groups. ('internal maneuvers' are activities on home territory.) Among the most successful external maneuvers ever conducted were the ANC's 1980s 'Free Mandela' and anti-apartheid campaigns, which turned Mandela into a global celebrity and mobilized high levels of Western pressure (including sanctions) against South Africa's government. An external maneuver involves three activities:

- Activating foreign opinion through PR activities generating media coverage favourable to the revolutionary group, while demonizing the government being opposed;
- Lobbying foreign legislators/governments and transnational organizations (e.g. the UN);
- Mobilizing single-issue collective action groups to support their cause, e.g. 'Free Tibet' groups. These groups are immensely valuable for generating publicity, and for 'pressurizing' foreign legislators.

6.3.1.5 New media and 'grassroots lobbying' Single-issue collective action groups in the OECD – e.g. 'right-to-life' organizations and conservation and Green groups – have also learned to use new media technologies to arouse public opinion. New media provides an array of vehicles for PR. In the USA this spawned the growth of a new industry of 'grassroots lobbyists' (Abrahamson et al., 1990: 129) – i.e. firms hired by interest groups, foreign governments and revolutionary groups to publicize public opinion on an issue. This puts indirect pressure on US legislators and/or the White House. These grassroots lobby firms use the same new media and PR techniques as establishment politicians – e.g. computer-aided targeting of audiences; phone banks; and direct mail (using letters and videos).

In fact, direct mail is becoming the ultimate niche-media political tool because it lends itself to delivering highly partisan messages to target audiences, pre-selected for their likely support. This generates an interesting form of political behavior identified by Theodore Lowi: a highly fluid and agitated politics can be mobilized, sometimes leading to collective action not based on the recognition of mutual interest (Abrahamson et al., 1990: 160). Essentially, OECD populations increasingly live 'isolated' lives, with media (e.g. television and the Internet) providing the social 'connectivity' between isolated individuals. Abrahamson et al. (1990: 160) note that this means that OECD citizens receive ever-less political information in face-to-face human contact situations. Instead, information is received while isolated and out of social context. This means that communication professionals, skilled at manipulating media images/messages, can exploit **anomie** to politically mobilize coalitions of individuals who never actually interact with each other. Television and the Internet are especially well suited to manipulating blocks of voters into 'collective action' on the basis of single issues given an emotional charge. Such mobilization lends itself to both 'national' issues (e.g. health care systems) and to trans-OECD issues (e.g. save the whales). And because new media networks are globalized, it is possible to run trans-OECD PR campaigns. However, even when this happens, the collective action is still steered towards pressurizing national governments. Politicians find it difficult to ignore such single-issue collective action, hence, they often find themselves having to respond (in knee jerk fashion) to single-issue emotionally charged PR campaigns run by pressure groups and/or grassroots lobbyists. Often their responses are equally PR-ized and media-ized rather than substantive (e.g. condemning Israel).

Overall, it is possible to identify some changes to OECD political practices wrought by the deployment of new media technologies. However, these new practices have at most generated evolutionary mutations to existing OECD political processes, rather than caused revolutionary ruptures to Western liberal democratic political systems. When it comes to political identities, a similar pattern is found – i.e. new media technologies have impacted upon some communicative interactions, and these changed interactive conditions have facilitated some new patterns of political identity formation. However, these new patterns have not constituted epoch-like ruptures to political identity formation. In fact, post-cold war balance of power shifts are a more likely source of recent identity changes than new media technologies.

6.3.2 New media and identity shifts

Those suggesting that identity shifts would be associated with the information age have made five key proposals.

Firstly, because new media encourage interactivity and facilitate niched narrowcasting, the era of top-down mass communication was over. Further, the demise of the mass media would end mass society and 'mass identity'. In its place would emerge an active civil society built upon a proliferation of (niche) collective action groups, each using its own (niche) media to promote its issues.

Secondly, proliferating collective action groups would produce an explosion of niche identities, often grounded in local issues – i.e. new (niche) media would lead to a blossoming of new niche identities and the proliferation of 'identity politics'. From this would emerge a revived pluralist democracy based upon an activated civil society of many niche groups. Local (niched) identities would become more important than national identities and the era of national mass publics would end. With this would come a 'new politics' associated with groups mobilizing around single issues (e.g. halting the building of a nuclear power plant), or groups grounded in identity politics (e.g. ethnic minorities, gay lifestyles and so on).

Thirdly, nation states would be eclipsed by a combination of 'local (niche) politics', and transnational and global politics (e.g. EU, UN, WTO, World Court and so on). The argument was that information age economies no longer needed nation states as organizing fulcra. The new organizing fulcrum was global governance. Nation states would therefore wither, and so would national identities (fostered by national mass media systems). National identities would also wither because the new media facilitated and encouraged niche (local) communication and global communication. Hence the prediction that these new (niche and global) identities would grow at the expense of national identity as new media forms and political contexts proliferated.

Fourthly, new forms of global identity would emerge as like-minded people (e.g. those opposed to whale hunting) 'found each other' via the Internet no matter where they lived in the world. The result would be globalized identity/ies based upon a pluralist cosmopolitanism. National identities (and nationalism) would be undermined by the proliferation of niche identities networking themselves globally. This prediction amounted to the 'American dream' writ large – effectively US 'pan-human universalism' was (unconsciously) adopted as the teleological goal of a twenty-first-century globalization project.

But to what extent are the above four identity shifts occurring?

To date, the demise of mass society has not taken place. If anything, mass-appeal content has expanded in the media. The 'spectacle' genre of political news, geared to mass-audience entertainment and titillation is widespread. Neuman's (1991: 158–9) prediction that the mass genre of news would survive (and even grow) because of commercial pressures within capitalist news organizations has proved to be more accurate than boosterist/ postmodern predictions of the demise of mass audience/mass society. Mass communication remains a feature of contemporary OECD political processes, with spin-doctors and celebrity politicians still using the mass media to cajole, influence and 'steer' public opinion and mass audiences.

The prediction that niche identities would proliferate, and local concerns, single-issue politics and identity politics arise, has proved to be valid. Undoubtedly, new media technologies facilitated this by making smaller niche media economically viable; making it easier to start and operate small media; and encouraging interactivity. However, it would be overly media centric to see these new identities as solely derivative of the new technologies. Rather, it is necessary to recognize contextual reasons for the emergence of some of these niche identities, e.g. OECD de-industrialization caused a demographic decline in working-class populations. This impacted negatively on political parties traditionally relying upon working-class voters (e.g. British Labour Party, Australian Labour Party and US Democratic Party). During the last quarter of the twentieth century these parties responded by seeking out new (non-working class) support bases, and built 'rainbow coalitions' from the alliances they forged with gays, lesbians, ethnic minorities, feminists and indigenous groups. In the process, these parties encouraged and (when in power) even funded the growth of this new 'identity politics', and so were as instrumental in promoting these niched 'identities' as were new media technologies.

The prediction that nation states and national identities would wither, and be replaced by supra-national (global) identity/ies, proved to be greatly exaggerated. The 'end-of-nations' prediction appears to have four sources.

Firstly, the globalization of capitalism (facilitated by global media technologies) required a free flow of capital and goods so industrial plants could be moved where labor was cheapest. Consequently, nation states' power to impose capital/currency/labor/trade barriers was diminished. This led some to hypothesize that nation states were no longer needed as organizing fulcra for capital accumulation and so they would wither. But this hypothesis failed to recognize the other equally crucial state functions, e.g. law and order; security; and the maintaince of collective infrastructures required for the reproduction of labor, capital and cultural capital (which could not be effectively carried out by supra-national bodies).

Secondly, the creation of the EU plus the widespread collapse of many African states, in the latter part of the twentieth century, appeared to confirm the 'end-of-nation-states' hypothesis. But neither had much to do with the globalization of capital, or the globalization of new information technologies. Instead, both were tied to contextually specific issues – the EU was born of a concern to 'contain' Germany with a network of EU infrastructures, while the African phenomenon derived from the weaknesses and failures of the ruling elites who had inherited post-colonial Africa. Outside of Africa and the EU, nation states showed no signs of withering away. In fact, post-9/11, nation states (including those inside the EU) appear to have acquired renewed vigor.

Thirdly, it was assumed that because the globalization of capitalism seemed to require global regulation/organization (e.g. WTO, IMF, World Court, World Bank, UN peacekeeping and so on), a new form of 'global identity' would grow up associated with this new global governance (just as 'national identity' had grown up in association with national governance). But this assumption ignored the connectivity between globalization and the rise of the Pax Americana. The Pax Americana roots lay in the Atlantic Charter signed by the USA and UK in 1941. This Charter secured US assistance for the UK during World War II, in return for which post-war decolonization was agreed to. The Charter effectively killed Europe's empires; transferred global hegemony to the USA; and proposed a new world order based on ending mercantilism. However, the US's global hegemony, envisaged by the Atlantic Charter, could not be fully realized until Soviet power unraveled in the 1980s. Significantly, the Pax Americana was never envisaged as a form of global governance. Rather, in terms of the post-World War II treaties (e.g. 1944 Bretton Woods and 1947 GATT agreements on economic matters, and 1944 Dumbarton Oaks agreement on the UN), the Pax Americana was premised upon independent nation states whose ruling elites would operate as compradors within a US-led economic and political hegemony. A key feature of the Pax Americana's original (1940s) conceptualization involved building national states (and national identities) (see chapter 5) replicating the US governance model. This remains a central feature of the operationalization of the Pax Americana occurring since the collapse of the Soviet Union. This model has informed globalization. Those boosterists and postmoderns who proposed the formation of new 'information age identities' have generally ignored the impact of these underpinning contextual power relationship and ignored the way the new information technologies simply facilitate the implementation of the Pax Americana model originally drawn up in the 1940s.

Fourthly, the prediction that supra-national (global) identity/ies would emerge was premised upon an assumption that new media technologies facilitated instantaneous global communication and global networking. It was assumed that like-minded people would find each other on the Internet and from this would grow a global civil society. This global identity-formation hypothesis was boosted by the fact that OECD intellectuals, especially those in the global Anglo diaspora, (who produced these theories) used the Internet in this way. These intellectuals effectively universalized their own preferred practices and discourses (i.e. cosmopolitan 'pan-human universalism'); and promoted ('boosted') the new information technologies as the means to achieve their 'idealized' world of cosmopolitan globalism. The bulk of the human race do not interact in this informationized/mediated way. Hence the envisaged 'global identities' remain, at best, the preserve of the world's informationized networking elite.

6.4 Beyond boosterism

Undoubtedly, new information technologies have impacted upon economic and political practices in the OECD. But boosterist arguments that the information age is somehow radically different, and a new utopian age, seems exaggerated. If anything, there are many continuities with the past, and core features of the modernist project seem to have been declared dead rather prematurely.

Modernity has been about Western industrial civilization imposing itself upon, and colonizing, huge swathes of the globe. New information technologies are simply facilitating a new phase of this phenomenon – as industrial plants are relocated to wherever productive labor is cheapest. This has seen the emergence of a sophisticated information-based global management system operated out of the OECD heartlands. This system uses new information technologies to coordinate the new globally integrated economy and network globally dispersed players into global network capitalism. New information technologies did facilitate the development of postfordist production practices, and the globalization of production, marketing and distribution. But global network capitalism was not caused by this new technology. Rather, new technologies made it feasible to speed up the implementation of globalizing capitalism, and make the system of globally integrated production more efficient. This produced a new international division of labour as OECD economies (where the coordinating functions were located) were de-industrialized, 'service-ized' and informationized. Global network capitalism was also made possible by the collapse of the Soviet Union, which left the way open for the USA to finally implement its plans for spreading American models of modernity and governance to the rest of the world as originally envisaged by the Atlantic Charter, Bretton Woods, GATT and Dumbarton Oaks agreements.

In looking for breaks with the past, the boosterists and postmodern theorists ignored the continuities between global network capitalism and its forerunners. The Pax Americana appears to remain grounded in the notion of building modern states (which replicate US models of governance) across the globe. The 'regime change' wars in Afghanistan (2001) and Iraq (2003) were premised upon exporting the US governance model to these states. If this model of governance could be replicated across the globe, the resultant states would provide the fulcra within which global network capitalism can continue to grow, by facilitating the process of expanding and diversifying a globalized international division of labour. This means that the work done by Anderson (1991), Gellner (1983) and Smith (1991, 1998) retains explanatory value for understanding identity formation under the Pax Americana.

Ultimately, deploying the new information technologies has, at most, hyped up modernity and made it more feasible to make the system global. Suggestions that we have entered an information age, associated with a radical (postmodern) shift in political processes and identities, seem overdrawn. Instead, the political process and identities associated with liberal democracy and capitalism remain strongly in evidence in contemporary OECD countries. Overall, what seems to characterize the start of the twenty-first century is a global system premised upon universalizing the core principles of Anglo liberal democracy (see chapter 3). This entails the following:

- Globalized information networks constitute the communicative matrix of global network capitalism and the global military infrastructure underpinning the Pax Americana. This communicative matrix lies at the heart of contemporary US power. The global information network also ('virtually') 'brings together' Anglos who have been globally dispersed by the British and US empires over the past four centuries;
- Identities associated with Anglo culture (see chapter 5) are dominant within the Pax Americana and global network capitalism, and other identities have to effectively 'negotiate' a space for themselves in relation to this core;
- Anglo culture is assimilationist (see 5.5.1 on p. 111). The existence of niche media, niche identities, multiculturalism and so on, in no way undercuts the overall trajectory of Anglo's incorporation of 'others'. The process of 'incorporation' (which involves some cultural hybridization) takes place on terms set by the (powerful) Anglo core. Incorporation/ hybridization simultaneously encourages the idea of a 'universalist' culture and obscures the maintenance of an essentially Anglo cultural formation;
- The media are widely perceived as a part of the political process (see chapter 4), tasked with the function of watchdogs over the executive and legislators;
- The mass media remain a powerful part of the cultural machinery of global network capitalism – this media industry is an important

homogenizing cultural machine (see chapters 5, 8 and 9). Politicians and their spin-doctors are greatly concerned with influencing the content of this mass media because of its enormous influence within the political process;

- The proliferation of niche media sources is seen to increase opportunities for the development of heterogeneity and pluralism. Politicians and their spin-doctors have turned their attention to also influencing the content of this niche media (see 7.3.4 on p. 156);

- Lockean principles – which encode seventeenth-century Anglo burgher values (see 3.2.1 on p. 42) – continue to underpin the political processes of 'liberal democracy' that the Pax Americana is attempting to universalize;

- The core function of Anglo liberal democracy is to secure the conditions necessary for capital accumulation (see chapter 3);

- It is a social order underpinned by the following core organizing values (with their roots in the Enlightenment): individualism, materialism, secularism, rationalism and empiricism (and cosmopolitanism among the urban elite) (see chapter 3).

Because the above principles have assumed the status of a 'pan-human universalism' within the Anglo-American lexicon, the Pax Americana is not seen to be imposing 'Anglo culture' onto the world. Hence, many Anglo-Americans appear to find it difficult to understand how some people feel their identities are threatened by the Pax Americana, and why some therefore engage in acts of resistance (such as al-Qaeda's 9/11 bombings) (see chapter 11). In some ways both boosterists and postmoderns contributed to making Anglo-American culture opaque to itself because they helped to popularize the notion that 'rooted' cultures and identities had somehow been 'transcended' by the 'progressive nature' of the information age, and that cultures and identities within information age networks were somehow 'universal' in their 'rootlessness'. This discourse was widely popularized within the new media networks, and by many journalists – and served to suggest that Anglo-American culture (and its associated identities) was universal, and represented some kind of pinnacle of evolutionary development.

Ultimately, new media technologies have simply reinforced tendencies already inherent in Western culture, rather than precipitated a radical break. The modern became hyper-modern; capitalist accumulation became truly global; and the USA acquired the power to impose its preferred political and economic order globally. The 1940s' dreams of globalizing capitalism and modern American governance began to be realized in the 1980s–90s as Soviet power waned and information technologies provided the coordinating matrix to make the dream realizable. It could be argued that the information age is simply the American dream writ large.

Summary

You should now be familiar with the following key themes and concepts:
information age; postindustrialism; modernist; postmodernist; modernization; postmodernization; postfordism; mass society; mass identity; niche identities; teledemocracy; participatory democracy; 'informationization' of politics; 'nationalization' of politics; grassroots lobbying; Lerner's theory of political modernization; and how PRs/spin-doctors have learned to use new media to enhance their impacts.

For further consideration

1 To what extent is it valid to regard much writing about the information age as a form of salesmanship geared to promoting the adopting of new media technologies?

2 Is it a form of media determinism to argue that the new media will produce new identities?

3 The new media offer a host of new opportunities for spin-doctors. Do these necessarily undermine democracy? Or can they assist democracy?

4 Does new media technology necessarily undermine states? Or does it strengthen states? Or can it do both?

5 Why have new media technologies not displaced mass media forms as some theorists had predicted?

6 Does the new media allow for the construction of new varieties of political performers?

7 Does the proliferation of niche media serve to enhance democracy or not?

8 Some have argued that globalization is a radical break with the past. Is it?

9 Does the existence of new media promote the spread of spectacle journalism, or not? Why?

10 Has the emergence of globalization altered journalism in any way?

PART 3 ● ● ●

The Media-ization of Politics

Part 3 of this book is geared to illustrating how different parts of the political process have been substantively media-ized. Six themes will be discussed to demonstrate how deeply the media now impacts on the political process, and the extent to which some dimensions of politics are now substantively conducted in, and through, the media. Part 3 will begin with an examination of how political spin-doctoring works (in chapter 7). Thereafter five dimensions of the political process will be looked at in terms of how much they have been media-ized, namely: (1) how politicians are scripted and celebrity-ized in order to sell them to voters; (2) how political belief systems and policies are sold to voters; (3) how war is sold to voters; (4) how terrorists use the media; and (5) how the media impacts on foreign policy.

7 Spin-doctoring: The Art of Political Public Relations

Chapter 7 examines how Western politics has been PR-ized. It is argued that as politics became a televised activity (first in the USA, and then spreading to the rest of the Western world), politicians were increasingly transformed into *television performers*. This gave rise to a new industry of communication professionals – called spin-doctors – who *stage-manage* televisual performances and events in order to 'steer' public opinion. Chapter 7 begins by describing the rise of the profession of spin-doctoring. The chapter examines a number of particularly innovative moments within the growth of PR-ized politics, namely, the presidencies of Kennedy, Nixon, Reagan and Clinton, as well as the prime ministerships of Thatcher and Blair. Thereafter the way spin-doctoring has actually changed the political process is examined. The chapter also describes how spin-doctors do their job and the tools they use. Chapters 7 and 4 should be read as a couplet because they examine the two sides of the journalist–spin-doctor symbiotic relationship.

One of the dimensions of mass democratic politics is hype making. Just as magicians use smoke and mirrors to distract their audiences and conjure up illusions, so too does the political machine and its media staffers. In today's Western democracies, television is the primary (but not exclusive) vehicle for this smoke-and-mirrors show. This show involves four sets of players:

- Politicians as performers;
- The spin industry;
- Media workers (journalists, presenters/hosts and researchers);
- Media audiences.

A fifth set of players are:

- Policy makers. But these policy makers remain deliberately back stage, shielded from as much scrutiny as possible by the smoke-and-mirrors show.

Demagoguery is not a new phenomenon, but televisualized politics generated many new demagogic arts for steering mass publics and building 'popularity'. Entman (1989: 128) blames the media and journalists for encouraging and feeding this spiral into demagoguery. In reality, all four sets of players are equally 'guilty'. Further, given the impossibility of substantive mass participation in policy making, it is difficult to see another way of dealing with mass democracy's demands, except to 'steer', and 'tame' the masses by whatever means are available. Television is today's available mechanism, so not surprisingly it is used by the hype machine to 'deflect' and 'entertain' the masses. Consequently, politics (or at least one dimension of it) becomes stage managed for (largely) tele*visual* audiences – scripted by spin-doctors and handlers; performed by politicians as performers; and reported by journalists who, sometimes, play the role of stage hands, and sometimes the role of celebrities in their own right.

Spin-doctors as demagogues are unpopular with journalists and voters because no-one likes to believe they can be manipulated. Hence, political performance scriptwriters are criticized for being practitioners of deceit and manipulation, and for undermining democracy. In reality, journalists and voters are equally complicit in the smoke-and-mirrors game, and the spin industry simply services the needs of the mass democratic machine. It is also worth noting that political deceit has a long history – as far back as 1625, the classic Western legal text by Hugo de Grotius (1922) said that planned and deliberate lying and secrecy were legitimate vehicles for achieving political ends. The twentieth century has simply seen the 'arts of deceit' become more sophisticated and institutionalized, as America's PR industry grew to meet the US power elites' needs to try and control and steer their enfranchised masses (Ewen, 1996). The resultant PR-ization of politics subsequently spread from the USA to other Western liberal democracies.

7.1 The rise of PR professionals as political players

Although now a global phenomenon, political PR's roots are American. In the 1920s, Walter Lippmann described the emergence of a new professional class of 'publicists' and 'press agents' standing between US politicians and the media (McNair, 1999: xi). Sabato (1981: 11) traces the first consultants engaging in today's genre of political PR back to 1930s' Californian politics. However, the PR-ization of politics really took off in 1950s' USA (1981: 12). Jamieson (1984: 59) agrees: the Democrat Adlai Stevenson's defeat at the hands of Eisenhower/Nixon in 1952 and 1956 occurred because Stevenson, as the last of the old pre-television politicians, could not adjust to the requirements of televisualized politics. Eisenhower, on the other hand, was 'made over' by his media consultants, who televisualized his style (1984: 60). His media consultants had a candidate who understood the importance of PR – during World War II General Eisenhower had learned to use propaganda as an adjunct to warfare and had been very successful in mobilizing PR to promote himself as a war hero (see 10.1.4 on p. 216). The Stevenson/Eisenhower campaigns were the turning point. After the 1950s, PRs, specializing in scripting televisual performances, became an ever-expanding feature of US politics – proliferating numerically; honing new tools; and becoming ever more influential. This phenomenon subsequently spread beyond the USA.

The resultant 'PR-ization of politics' has brought the demagoguery underpinning the political process into the open. This occurred partly because political consultants emerged as public actors in their own right, rather than merely behind-the-scenes advisors. It is now clear that a spin industry (spin-doctors, minders, plus specialists in crafting visual-media appearances and advertising) undergirds the political processes of mass democracies. In fact, to be taken seriously, politicians must now possess communication campaign machines – i.e. consultants have become status symbols (and media stars), performing alongside politicians-as-performers and alongside celebrity journalists (see Sabato, 1981: 19–20). As Boorstin says: 'most true celebrities have press agents. And these press agents sometimes themselves become celebrities. The hat, the rabbit, and the magician are all equally news' (1971: 75).

But why did this class of communication professionals arise? Firstly, liberal democracy is grounded upon the notion of legitimate governance. And legitimacy requires the consent of the governed. But as McNair says: 'consent can be manufactured' (1999: 26). Ultimately, policy makers within liberal democracies have two (contradictory?) needs:

- To try and prevent the masses from disrupting and convoluting the policy process by keeping them at arms length from the actual decision-making process;
- To try and make the masses believe they are actually participating in governance as a way of building consent.

Part of the solution for generating consent, while simultaneously keeping the masses disengaged from the real process of governance, is to pursue 'calculated strategies of distraction' (Jamieson, 1992: 205). And this is where the spin industry comes in.

Another reason for the rise of political consultants was the arrival of television. The pioneer political consultants (in 1950s' America) were technical advisors about television (Jamieson, 1984: 35). From these (not verypowerful) technical advisory positions evolved media advisors, and the (highly influential) US campaign strategists of today (1984: 36). Television has made the difficult process of 'mobilizing' and 'steering' citizenries much easier, because it delivers low-involvement viewers to political players who understand how to use its manipulative powers (see Jamieson, 1992: 52–3). Effectively, television can splice together, speedily and seamlessly, images and ideas that are in reality unrelated. And it creates such linkages in ways defying scrutiny and logic. These can have enormous political impacts because of the emotions generated by **montage** (1992: 54–6). So, not surprising, televisualized politics first emerged in the USA which has a very visual culture (see Adatto, 1993: chapter 1). Ewen (1996) devotes his entire chapter 10 to the examination of the filmic optical illusions PRs use to arouse, assemble and magnify viewer emotions. This 'optic-power' has become a central tool for steering public opinion. And as televisualized politics spread from the USA to other liberal democracies, so spin industry techniques followed.

A further impetus for the rise of US political consultants was the capacity of the 'eastern establishment media' to influence political agendas (Maltese, 1994: 42). If these journalists disliked a particular politician they could negatively impact upon his/her political career through their agenda-setting role. Journalists do not have 'power', but in certain locations (i.e. key media) they have 'influence' derivative of being authorative – i.e. as authors they can authorize certain versions of 'reality'. This gives journalists opportunities to:

- Disrupt the agendas policy makers wish to pursue by raising issues that undermine policy planning;
- Intimidate policy makers;
- Trivialize some issues and hype up/exaggerate others (i.e. direct attention one way or another).

Obviously, politicians wish to retain as much control over policy agendas as possible. This requires reducing journalists' capacities to do the above. From this emerged their impetus to employ communication professionals who deploy their knowledge of media practices to side-step the establishment media and facilitate un-mediated communication voters.

Certainly Richard Nixon regarded 'eastern establishment' journalists as hostile. Not surprisingly, President Nixon was a central facilitator of the revolution that saw campaign strategists emerge as powerful players within US politics. He stood for President three times – losing to Kennedy in 1960, but beating Humphrey in 1968 and McGovern in 1972. His loss in 1960 because of a poor television profile taught Nixon to take the media seriously. Consequently Nixon's Republican administration sought ways to use PR, tame the media, and develop mechanisms to communicate directly with voters over the heads of 'hostile' journalists (especially the elite Washington and New York presses). Nixon's presidency (1968–74) was important for the evolution of spin-doctors, who ultimately became political players in their own right due to their demagogic skills of deploying media (especially visual media) to build consent and steer public opinion. By the 1990s there was a large US spin industry, skilled in using the media as partners; or side-stepping 'hostile' journalists and communicating directly with voters (when necessary). Serious political players needed media-teams (see Figure 7.1). Bill Clinton's Democrat media-team adopted and masterfully deployed this knowledge to use a range of media and popular cultural forms to success-fully reach 'ordinary people' (Newman, 1994: 5–7). These US techniques migrated across the Atlantic and were 'Britishized' by Tony Blair's Labour media-team. Australia's adoption of these techniques has been fed by influ-ences from both the US and the Blair versions.

Effectively, Nixon's belief that the media were hostile led to a range of media management and 'spinning' techniques that eventually became commonplace political practice in many Anglo countries (although the USA remains the pace-setter for developing new techniques). What has emerged is a political process investing considerable energy into produc-ing stage-managed and largely (but not exclusively) televisualized 'faces' (see chapter 8). These stage-managed faces are ultimately the outcome of a (often symbiotic) relationship between two sets of communication professionals – those working for the media (e.g. journalists) and those working for the political machines (e.g. spin-doctors). Politicians are the third party to the 'face-manufacturing' process. There is a constant strug-gle for dominance within this relationship (between journalists, poli-ticians and spin-doctors). Depending on the contextual conditions, spin-doctors sometimes have the upper hand. On other occasions journalists are dominant, while at other times, politicians assume control.

Sometimes power is shared. Who dominates at any moment depends upon the following variables:

- The resources available to the players. Generally, the player with the most resources has an advantage over the others;
- How skilled the spin-doctors are at dealing with the media. The more skilled, the more they are able to dominate relationships;
- The level of political agitation among the mass public. An agitated and unhappy public generates challenges for politicians and spin machines which often increases the bargaining position of journalists;

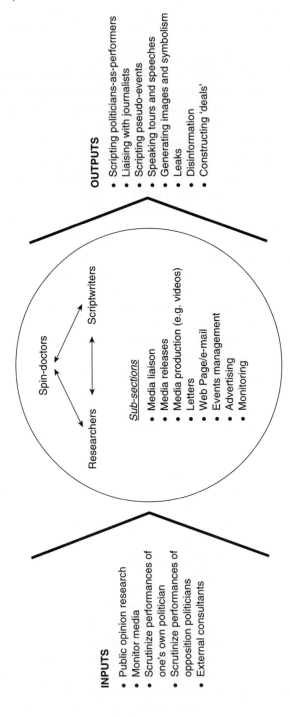

INPUTS

- Public opinion research
- Monitor media
- Scrutinize performances of one's own politician
- Scrutinize performances of opposition politicians
- External consultants

Spin-doctors

Researchers ⟷ Scriptwriters

Sub-sections

- Media liaison
- Media releases
- Media production (e.g. videos)
- Letters
- Web Page/e-mail
- Events management
- Advertising
- Monitoring

OUTPUTS

- Scripting politicians-as-performers
- Liaising with journalists
- Scripting pseudo-events
- Speaking tours and speeches
- Generating images and symbolism
- Leaks
- Disinformation
- Constructing 'deals'

Figure 7.1 *Political spin-teams*

- How skilled spin-doctors are at steering mass public opinion. The more successful they are, the more power they accumulate;
- The nature and intensity of the struggles between politicians. The more intense the struggle, the more politicians need their spin-doctors and journalists. This diminishes the bargaining position of politicians.

However, in general terms (although journalists have not been rendered completely powerless), the capacity of journalists to frame and interpret the news has been declining (Graber, 2001: 440) because:

- New media forms have provided alternative sources of information;
- The PR/spin industry has been growing at the expense of journalists (as news production is increasingly outsourced);
- Spin-doctors have grown increasingly skilled at using both old and new media forms to bypass 'problem' journalists.

7.1.1 Journalist–PR tensions

The PR/spin industry is geared to planting stories in the media by using journalists to disseminate stories serving the spin-doctors' agenda (i.e. agenda setting). Good journalists resist being used, and do their best to turn the tables on spin-doctors by using PR machines as resources that can serve their own agendas. For example, journalists can use the fact that all serious politicians now have PR machines that are in competition with each other. Good journalists can potentially use this competition to play the various PR machineries off against each other in their search for stories. This is one reason why the PR/spin industry is not always successful. The PR/spin industry has a particular problem when ruling elites are deeply divided over policy options. Not surprisingly, during periods when elite consensus breaks down, journalists are more likely to unearth 'damaging stories' (e.g. the USA's torturing of Iraqi prisoners) than during periods of policy consensus (e.g. 2001 Afghan War). On issues where there is broad consensus among the policy elites, journalists are unlikely to find exploitable cracks in the spin machine because the line being spun will be uniform and the consensus difficult to crack. Perhaps more troubling is the fact that are many issues where policy elites and journalists share a joint consensus – in these instances the symbiotic relationship between journalists and PRs will generate a total closure of discourse.

In general, Margaret Thatcher's Chief Press Secretary, Bernard Ingham, described the relationship between PRs and journalists as one of symbiotic tension: 'the relationship is essentially cannibalistic. They feed off each other but no one knows who is next on the menu' (Ingham, in B. Franklin, 1994: 14). However, on balance, the spin industry probably has the edge over journalists because spin-doctors are well paid and so their industry attracts very talented people who know exactly how to steer journalists (given many are ex-journalists lured by higher salaries). Ultimately, whoever dominates the journalist–PR relationship, one thing is clear: spin-doctors are now integrally part of the political processes of Anglo liberal democracies.

7.2 Changes to the political process

So what changes has PR-ization wrought to the political processes of liberal democracies? To some extent, each country has been impacted differently because of the different political cultures in each, and because PR-ization was launched at different dates in each country. The country that has moved farthest down the PR-ization route is the USA. Because the US has been (and remains) the trendsetter in developing spin techniques, it will be focused upon when examining the changes wrought by PR-ization – on the assumption other liberal democracies will probably eventually follow the US lead.

Firstly, PR-ization has changed political parties, as power shifted away from party bosses and hacks towards consultants and spin-doctors (Newman, 1994: 15). Party machines once fulfilled the role of delivering voters – i.e. party bosses cajoling the grassroots party faithful to work so as to ensure voters turned up on election day. Party bosses acquired power by being able to deliver and organize functioning election machines. PR-ization professionalized the whole process, reducing the importance of party hacks. The new power brokers are no longer faithful party members. Rather, brokers now need to possess media and research skills in order to analyze and steer public opinion. People with these skills expect to be paid as professionals. These professionals are also increasingly involved in selecting political leaders, based not on party faithfulness, but upon how well they can perform televisually. The changes wrought on political parties have progressed farthest in the USA. Changes to parties within the Westminster system, like the UK (Blumler et al., 1996: 58), have (to date) been less pronounced.

Secondly, political leaders now require different attributes to be selected as candidates – they need to be credible (convincing) television performers, be visually appealing to voters, and be able to speak in soundbites. They must also be able to follow scripts designed by spin-doctors. Leaders possessing these skills can (with the help of spin-doctors) jump over the heads of party hierarchies to appeal directly to voters. Hence, aspirant leaders with televisual charisma, backed by good spin-doctors, can force the hand of party nominating processes. This has also altered party power relationships in favour of those who best understand the mechanics of the PR-ization and televisualization.

Thirdly, PR-ization has made politics a very expensive business because of the cost of the spin industry and opinion pollsters, plus media production costs (e.g. direct mail, TV spots, Web Pages, video media releases and so on). This has placed an enormous burden on political parties to raise money. The result, in the USA, was a professionalized fund-raising industry of Political Action Committees (PACs) (see Sabato, 1989: 145–51). The cost of running this PAC industry is also high. There has been considerable concern in the USA that the resultant drive for funds has distorted the political process by forcing politicians to 'sell themselves' to large campaign donors. Attempts to regulate PACs have not altered these underlying financial pressures – pressures evident in all liberal democracies that have gone down the PR-ization path.

Fourthly, PRs learned to systematically mobilize popular culture to reach voters (see Street, 1997). This generated a new genre of scripted politics, requiring politicians to step outside the 'normal' genre of political performance and adopt a new range of (popular and populist) faces, e.g. Bill Clinton playing saxophone on *The Arsenio Hall Show* (Newman, 1994: 135). Among those displaying a real flair for this televisualized populism are President Clinton, Prime Minister Blair and Queensland's Premier Peter Beattie.

Fifthly, since television can reach mass publics and stir emotions (by presenting audiences with simplified and idealized presentations), it is well suited to deflecting voter attention away from policy problems by:

- Mobilizing support for a person or position;
- Demonizing people;
- Creating pariah groups;
- Building selective outrage, indignation and hostility.

Essentially, television provides the perfect vehicle for politics as hype. Hence, it has become a valued spin industry tool. This has driven political spinning into an ever more visual art – (tele-)visual performances have become the preferred tool for reaching and steering voters. Those unable or unwilling to play the game of (tele-)visual smoke and mirrors will find it difficult to achieve political success in today's democracies.

Sixthly, the combination of PR-ization and televisualized politics undermined local political meetings where voters were addressed face to face. The arts of oratory, making policy speeches, and question-and-answer formats of discussion and debate, do not mesh easily with the techniques of spinning sound bites and slick images (designed for passive mass audiences). So politicians skilled in 'working a meeting' are no longer required, and have been replaced by politicians skilled in 'working' mass television audiences. Television has pushed politicians away from engaging in debate, discussion and selling policies, towards simply reciting/performing lines scripted by others (Selnow, 1994: 142).

Seventhly, the press' power within the political process has declined. As Selnow notes, PR-ized politics now reaches voters either via television or by deploying marketing techniques using individualized media like direct mail. The latter is becoming especially important and, as Selnow (1994: 147) notes, falls beneath journalists' radar screen. Consequently, print journalists (who used to be so influential within the political process) are increasingly bypassed. Essentially, the press can no longer monitor the multitude of political messages generated, because of the complexity of the spin industry's communication activities.

Lastly, PR-ization produces a 'politics of avoidance' (1994: 178) because the new process is governed by on-going opinion polls. PR-ized politics involves running a permanent campaign (1994: 177). Building legitimacy requires not just manufacturing consent, but maintaining it. This translates into trying to avoid any issue that might destabilize 'consent'. The spin industry not only constantly tests and monitors public opinion shifts, but also runs focus groups to test the 'acceptability' of issues before publicly flighting them. Issues that look too contentious, or which focus groups reveal may 'cause problems' with important sections of the electorate, are avoided. The result has been the 'bland-ization of politics' – i.e. politics driven towards the comfortable (non-controversial) center of the spectrum, while real debate is stymied in favour of smoke and mirrors and distraction. This produces political machines effectively geared towards avoiding the emergence of real controversy. Pseudo-controversy (manufactured by sensationalized-PR or hyped-up pseudo-adversarial journalism) is acceptable. The result is politics as a (poll-driven) smoke-and-mirrors show, geared towards permanently entertaining and distracting the masses within a 24-hour, multi-channel television environment.

7.3 The innovators of PR-ized politics

Although PR-ized politics was born in the USA, it is no longer an exclusively US phenomenon, because the 'Americanization' of politics has become a global export, influencing both other Anglo democracies, and a wide range of other societies (see Swanson and Mancini, 1996). For Swanson and Mancini this 'Americanization' represents political 'modernization'. Their case studies demonstrate how different countries selectively absorbed and integrated American influences in unique ways, and how some even created their own local innovations.

7.3.1 The pioneers of televisualized politics

Jamieson (1984) argues that it was the arrival of televised US presidential campaigning that set the stage for transforming the political process. The pioneers in exploiting television's possibilities were those in Eisenhower/Nixon's 1952 and 1956 campaigns. Significantly, they turned to America's top advertising agencies in New York's Madison Avenue. The new political style they developed involved shifting away from making speeches about issues, towards the deployment of sound bites, visual grabs and slogans. This occurred because the essence of television rhetoric involves avoiding complex argumentation and static images (e.g. 'talking heads') in favour of verbally simple messages mixed with exciting (moving) imagery. Eisenhower's campaigns successfully used television spots to drive home the message of Eisenhower as a World War II hero. Simplistic slogans such as 'I like Ike' were deployed to great effect. Equally, Eisenhower's team learned that using television required adjusting to the demands of this medium – e.g. learning to use the teleprompter to deliver scripted rhetoric convincingly. Eisenhower's team also adjusted to the needs of TV schedules and to the practices of television journalists – e.g. Nixon flew from Portland to Los Angeles simply to appear on networked television. Nixon was, in fact, a pioneer in understanding television's value – his 1952 Checkers speech representing an early masterful deployment of television as a smoke-and-mirrors tool. This television performance made Nixon appear humble, as he seemed to engage in self-disclosure while actually revealing nothing. Perhaps not surprisingly, Nixon was to play a key role in promoting the further evolution of spin-doctoring 20 years later when he became President.

7.3.2 Kennedy's PR

The 1960 Presidential election, won by John Kennedy, was another crucial moment in the development of PR-ized and televisualized politics. The Kennedy team's PR problem was his Catholicism. Television was used to transform this negative into a positive by spinning religion into an issue of tolerance – i.e. not voting for Kennedy was made equivalent to being intolerant. This was achieved through a series of short television adverts deploying question-and-answer formats to address the religious issue. Kennedy's team also scripted a 30-minute television exchange between him and Franklin Roosevelt Jr. on Catholicism. This was followed by a masterful performance in Houston where Kennedy attended a gathering of Protestant ministers and answered their questions. Jamieson quotes

Halbersam as saying that this represented the new art of televisualized spin at its best: 'deliberately allowing someone else to rig something against you that is, in fact, rigged for you.... The Houston audience was, much to its own surprise, a prop audience' (1984: 130). Kennedy's team recorded the Houston session and screened it in 39 US states. In crucial cities it was aired twice. Further, Kennedy's team mounted a PR campaign around his World War II naval experiences on PT109, a high-speed attack vessel used in the Pacific. Kennedy was cast as a war hero through the production of a documentary, television and print adverts and brochures. Thousands of copies of a *Reader's Digest* PT109 article were reproduced and distributed by his team. Kennedy's media-team performed brilliantly. However, as Jamieson (1984: 162–5) notes, although this team pioneered many televisualized spin techniques, it was far from some of today's well-oiled political PR machines.

One especially significant moment in the 1960 election was the first Kennedy–Nixon television debate. Although Nixon had been a 1950s' pioneer in using television, he ironically lost this crucial debate because he failed to pay attention to his TV appearance – he would not wear make up; his shirt was too large; his suit the wrong color; and he slouched. Kennedy's appearance, on the other hand, was masterfully executed: 'the image millions saw was that of a nervous, haggard, sweating Nixon versus a relaxed, robust, confident Kennedy. What the two candidates said no longer mattered' (Maltese, 1994: 16). Kennedy won the election, and Nixon learned a lesson for the future. So too have all other politicians – the Kennedy–Nixon debate became a PR benchmark in what to do, and not to do, in television appearances.

7.3.3 Nixon's PR

Richard Nixon and his media-team were perhaps the most significant innovators with regard to PR-izing politics – it was Nixon, after all, who created the White House Office of Communications in 1969. The reason he formally incorporated spin-doctoring into US executive governance is not hard to find – American politicians were confronting an alarming breakdown in the legitimacy and 'consent' required for liberal governance to function. In 1968 Martin Luther King Jr. and Robert Kennedy were assassinated. There were race riots, student demonstrations and mass protests over Vietnam. Opposition to the War even spread to middle America after the Vietcong's 1968 Tet Offensive. Ewen (1996) contends that PR was originally developed to manage the US crises of the turn of the twentieth century: 1968 was another such crisis period and Nixon responded by institutionalizing spin-doctoring at the heart of US governance. In the process, Nixon's media machine developed a range of successful PR techniques (Maltese, 1994: 15–74) including:

- Sophisticated advertising;
- Direct mail;
- Carefully orchestrated use of the media including lobbying columnists and editorial writers; developing ties with small local publications and broadcasters; and stimulating letters-to-the-editor;
- Using network television plus local media to communicate with the American masses over the heads of media deemed 'hostile' – i.e. 'problem' journalists were frozen out;
- All television appearances were carefully scripted and orchestrated. A Television Office was created. Nixon had a full-time television producer on hand to advise him on staging his television performances;
- Staged television events using scripted question-and-answer methods where Nixon answered questions from 'ordinary people' (what he called the 'man in the arena' concept). The media were excluded from asking questions;
- Press conferences were avoided (in favour of scripted television appearances);
- News flow was coordinated from all departments and Cabinet Ministers;
- Speaking tours were run across the country, speakers were carefully chosen and dispatched such that local media would pick up stories. These were carefully scripted performances with detailed briefing notes and prepared questions and answers;
- Members of Congress and Senators were supplied with briefing material and speeches, and with 'attack material' produced by researching opposition weaknesses;
- Nixon, his Cabinet and White House team were coached in televisual performance;
- Television news was monitored on an on-going basis and 'reactions' (negative and positive) lodged with TV stations and networks;
- The 'silent majority' (who supported Nixon) were engineered into existence by orchestrating letters to the editor, phone-in callers and supportive telegrams to the President;
- Hollywood stars were used to endorse Nixon;
- Nixon's media-team learned to script the Republican Convention for television leaving nothing to chance.

After Nixon, White House politics would never be the same again. The sophistication of his media machine was demonstrated by its institutionalized division of labor – the Press Office worked with the media; the

Office of Public Liaison worked with special interest groups; while (the heart of the operation) the Office of Communications engaged in analysis, long-term planning, and the development of a media strategy. Ironically, Nixon's career was ultimately terminated by print journalism; his PR machine proving unable to save him. However, his legacy to Washington was a pool of spin-doctoring talent and practices that others – such as Reagan, Clinton and Bush – have been only too happy to deploy.

7.3.4 Reagan's PR

Ronald Reagan was one of the great beneficiaries of Nixon's revolution – with Reagan's team adopting Nixon's spin techniques to great effect. Although Reagan's team were not great innovators, they did refine spin-doctoring tactics, and deployed these with great success. Such was their success that the term 'spin-doctor' was, in fact, first used with reference to Reagan's media-team in a 1984 *New York Times* editorial (Patterson, 1997). As with Nixon, Reagan's team put television first, but they also put energy into building relationships with local media and grassroots organizations. They were so successful with the latter that they mobilized a 'Coalition for a New Beginning' which was used to spread the word about Reagan's economic program using direct mail and speaking tours (Maltese, 1994: 194). At the heart of this media-team's strategy was maintaining Reagan's profile on television. An oft-heard anecdote serves to illustrate this strategy. CBS's Lesley Stahl ran a story critical of Reagan. When she received a phone call from the White House she expected to be chewed out. Instead she was praised. On enquiring 'why?' the White House official replied: 'you television people still don't get it. No one heard what you said. Don't you people realize the picture is all that counts. A powerful picture drowns out the words' (Fallows, 1997: 62).

So Reagan's spin-machine developed techniques for ensuring that journalists kept feeding the public powerful pictures. One of the most successful devices for achieving this was the 'Rose Garden Strategy' – Reagan would fly to the White House's rose garden by helicopter (looking commanding, but friendly). He would shout out a few scripted sound bites to waiting journalists, but would be unable to field questions because he was rushing to do something important. And for PR's, the great beauty of Reagan, was that (as a former actor) he knew how to look presidential and follow a script (Maltese, 1994: 179). His PR team worked hard developing good sound bites. These were tested on focus groups before being flighted (1994: 213). The Rose Garden Strategy summed up the Reagan team's approach – 'control the agenda, control access, control the sound bites, and control the visual image' (1994: 214).

Besides the Rose Garden Strategy, Reagan's team also made other adaptations to the Nixon revolution. These included (1994: 200–3):

- Using the Internet;
- Using satellites for 'live' television feeds of presidential statements;
- Using niche-ized marketing techniques to target the proliferating niche media sector, e.g. cable television and ethnic media;
- Creating Republican Television Network – which provided free good quality images of the Republican Convention. Cameras were positioned in the best spots to provide continuous image feeds – these naturally showcased the Convention in a way complementary to the PRs' agendas. They also allowed television stations to send their anchors along and provided them with a camera (rent free) and good locations in the hall to conduct interviews. Thousands of television stations broadcast the results of this PR exercise. Many others have subsequently picked up this sort of strategy for spinning favourable televisual images, including players outside America (see Louw and Chitty, 2000).

Overall, excellent PR characterized Reagan's term – Nixon's spin revolution had come of age. Not surprisingly, Reagan's PR success catalyzed the further diffusion of PR-ized politics and political marketing – not just to other sectors of America's system of governance, but also to other countries – including the UK and Australia.

7.3.5 Thatcher's PR

Margaret Thatcher pioneered the introduction of American spin and political marketing into Britain. Thatcher's ideological closeness to Reagan, and her admiration for his PR success, led her to import elements of his PR-ized style beginning with her appointment of Saatchi and Saatchi in 1978. However, as Scammell (1995: 271) notes, although Thatcher opened the door to US-style political marketing, she never adopted the US system holus bolus; never replicated all aspects of Reagan's PR-machine in Britain; nor allowed her PR-machinery to exercise as much influence over her as Reagan's exercised over him. In particular, Thatcher did not have a PR expert sit in on her policy meetings in the way Reagan did and did not copy the US Political Agenda Control System – a computerized system for tracking public opinion responses to Presidential actions (Scammell, 1995: 271–2). Essentially, 'in British parties … communication specialists did not simply slide smoothly into positions of publicity command' (Blumler et al., 1996: 65). For Thatcher, PR/marketing was her tool, not her master

(Scammell, 1995: 286). However, during Thatcher's era the following elements of spin-doctoring and political marketing were introduced into the UK system:

- Public opinion polling and market research, especially the use of focus groups and other qualitative methods. However, Thatcher never allowed market research to dictate policy; only to suggest the tone and tenor of her policies (1995: 272). Blumler et al. (1996: 64) agree pollsters have less power within UK politics than in the USA;
- Political advertising dramatically increased under Thatcher (1996: 50);
- Political marketing techniques geared towards targeting populations/niches (1996: 52), e.g. using niche media and direct mail;
- Deploying PR techniques targeted at journalists with a view to spin-doctoring media content (1996: 51, 56). Thatcher's Press Secretary said he tried to manage the news (Ingham, 1991: 187);
- Image consultants specializing in making-over politicians and adjusting their images to make them more marketable – so objective reality was overridden by perceived image (Blumler et al., 1996: 52);
- Image consultants specializing in organizing Party conventions and Rallies. The Conservative Party employed Harvey Thomas (who previously worked for evangelist Billy Graham) to hype up their rallies and conferences with slogans, lighting, video screens, colourful backdrops, flags, music and warm-up acts (Scammell, 1995: 275);
- Gordon Reece coached Thatcher and her Ministers about television appearances, and introduced them to the television autoprompt – which Reece's team called the 'sincerity machine' (B. Franklin, 1994: 148). Thatcher's image was rescripted after polling revealed her voice was too shrill and upper class, her style too hectoring, and her appearance too school marmish. So she was transformed into an 'ordinary housewife' by rescripting her speeches; employing a voice tutor; changing her dress, jewellery and make-up style; and having her hair tinted and teeth capped (1994: 149–50);
- Staged photo opportunities designed by Reece (Scammell, 1995: 281–2);
- The growth of populist politics which has seen politicians appear on human-interest television programs, e.g. *The Jimmy Young Show* (1995: 275);
- The careful scripting of sound bite-driven speeches and restricting opportunities for politicians to speak in an unscripted way (1995: 276);
- A news management system was developed to coordinate all government media releases, advertising and the liaison between the Cabinet and the journalists' lobby. This system of news management was initiated (at Thatcher's behest) by Angus Maude; but perfected by Thatcher's Press Secretary, Bernard Ingham (1991).

The introduction of PR-ized politics into the UK certainly transformed British politics. However, Thatcher's revolution did not represent the complete Americanization of British politics. Rather, it represented a mutation of the British system because:

- Core elements of the British process remained unaltered – e.g. the civil service remained 'un-media-ized' compared to the US system;
- British political parties remained more hierarchical than US parties with British party leaderships able to exercise greater control over their party machines (Blumler et al., 1996: 58, 63);
- British politicians have been far less inclined than their US counterparts to simply acquiesce to the notion that public opinion experts know more about their constituencies' feelings than they do (1996: 65).

But even if Thatcher's revolution did not represent the full Americanization of British politics, it represented a substantial PR-ization of the process. One significance of this was that Thatcher's style became a conduit for transferring many political marketing techniques into the rest of the EU and to countries like Australia – e.g. Thatcher's PR style strongly influenced Australia's 1996 election campaign which John Howard's Liberal Party won (see Williams, 1997).

7.3.6 Blair's PR

The Labour Party under Tony Blair subsequently took this PR-ization of British politics further. Three spin-doctors – Peter Mandelson, Alastair Campbell and Charlie Whelan – played a key role in this PR-ization process. Because of their success these three became very influential within the Labour Party. Labour's media-team, headed by Mandelson, set about transforming the Labour Party – away from its working-class cloth cap image (which was alienating, and even threatening to the non-working class), and towards a center–left social democrat image more inclusive of other classes (B. Franklin, 1994: 132). Mandelson's team transformed not just the Labour Party, but British politics by introducing 'political marketing' and 'professionalized' communication into the heart of the party machine (Bartle and Griffiths, 2001).

Mandelson reconstructed the Labour Party's new profile around the symbol of a red rose. To achieve this metamorphosis, he first had to overcome the unease felt towards 'marketing' by many Labour Party members. Mandelson, a former television producer, built a volunteer organization – the Shadow Communications Agency (SCA) – out of Labour's sympathizers within the advertising, PR and media industries. SCA worked closely with Blair on a day-to-day basis to script his smoke-and-mirrors show. Under Mandelson, image became everything – as he rescripted the Labour Party's message and moved the Party towards the bland center of the political spectrum. Opinion polling and marketing considerations took precedence over political principle. Under Mandelson, SCA successfully coached and televisualized the performances of Labour politicians pushing telegenic performers like Blair to the forefront (B. Franklin, 1994: 133). The result was that Blair became Prime Minister, thus confirming the fact that British politics has become a televisualized, PR-ized affair. Significantly, the scripted performances of Blair, Clinton and Bush, reveal a growing trend towards trans-Atlantic borrowings – as innovative spin-doctoring techniques travel in both directions. This trend was greatly enhanced by the joint Bush–Blair scripting of the reasons for invading Iraq in 2003 (see 10.4.1 on p. 227).

But Blair's PR machine came under great stress as a result of the Iraq War, with his spin-doctor, Alastair Campbell, even being forced to resign in 2003. Campbell was part of the Mandelson revolution, being Blair's personal spin-doctor from 1994 to 2001, after which he was promoted to Labour Party Communications Director. Campbell's resignation revealed much about how British politics had been PR-ized. His resignation followed a BBC journalist's report that a Defence Ministry weapons expert had claimed an intelligence dossier on Iraqi 'weapons of mass destruction' had been 'sexed up' as part of a PR drive to justify the 2003 Iraq War. This precipitated a chain of events that turned spin-doctoring into an issue within British politics, and led to the 2004 Hutton Commission of Inquiry into the suicide of the weapons expert (after Blair's government leaked his name to the media). The Hutton Report (www.the-huttoninquiry.org.uk) exonerated Blair and attacked the BBC for poor journalistic practices. However, although the BBC was forced to apologize to Blair's government for its handling of the matter – sparking considerable debate among journalists (see *British Journalism Review*, 14 (3) 2003) – Blair's political credibility was damaged by the story of the 'sexed up' intelligence documents. Campbell's resignation – to try and take the pressure off Blair – revealed much about spin-doctoring, i.e. that

- PR must be opaque in order to work. PRs must not get caught actually practicing demagoguery/spin. Once caught, PRs cease to be functional;
- Spin-doctors are disliked by journalists, and so if 'caught in the act' the media will relentlessly pursue them;
- Spin-doctoring is focused on building and maintaining a 'positive profile' for the politicians who employ the spin-doctor. Campbell's actions revealed that when a politician's profile is in danger, the PR will be scapegoated to try and save the 'face' that has been constructed;
- The media's response to the 'sexed up' dossier and the Hutton inquiry revealed the extent to which some journalists have difficulty accepting their own complicity in the symbiotic relationship between the media and

spin doctors. Before the Iraq War US, British and Australian government spin-doctors successfully used the media to convince their populations that the Iraqi weapons of mass destruction (WMD) posed a real threat to world peace. The media's attack on Campbell, Blair or Hutton constituted a form of spin – i.e. an exercise that focused blame on spin-doctors and politicians, which then conveniently deflected ('spinned') attention away from the media's own complicity in making the WMD lie possible.

Campbell's resignation did not end the PR-ization of British politics. He was simply replaced by a new Labour Party spin-doctor who then faced the challenge of trying to reconstruct Blair's damaged 'face', or at least trying to save the Labour Party's credibility for the next election. On the other hand, PRs working for Britain's Conservative Party naturally worked equally hard trying to 'spin a line' that undermined the Labour Party by keeping the pejorative 'spin tag' attached to Blair and his team.

7.3.7 Clinton's PR

Bill Clinton, like Reagan, inherited the legacy of Nixon's PR revolution. Clinton has been one of the great beneficiaries of the way politics has been transformed, because his style and persona mesh so well with the televised spin revolution. Clinton was a model telegenic celebrity politician because of his gift for television performance and ability to follow spin-doctored scripts in crisis situations. Essentially, he could play television audiences such that the members of mass audiences felt a (pseudo) 'personal' rapport with him – i.e. Clinton was like 'the old-style politician who is the student of human nature and focuses on the voter in front of him. The premium is on the personal encounter. But, unlike the old-style pol, Clinton can perform this seduction in front of cameras' (Blumenthal, quoted in Maltese, 1994: 225). Clinton's success derived from the fact he was both telegenic and a wizard (television) performer. However, this should not detract from the impressive PR machinery that James Carville built to support Clinton. This PR machine replicated many of the features of Reagan's machine, which only serves to illustrate how 'naturalized' PR spinning has become within the US political process (1994: 225–7):

- When Clinton first ran for President, his image was made over by his media-team when polling revealed he had an image problem. Focus groups found that even hostile voters could be converted by telling them about his alcoholic stepfather; small town upbringing; childhood poverty; how he worked his way through college; and about his wife and daughter. The result was a campaign ('the Manhattan Project') to promote this image (Bennett, 1995: 108);

- Clinton's media-team conducted 'War Room' meetings twice daily. These analyzed media coverage; discussed how to script Clinton's responses; and engaged in strategic planning;
- A core feature of Clinton's media machine (both during election campaigning and as President) was the 'rapid response strategy'. This involved running an 'opposition research' unit and 'special events' (dirty tricks) unit. Opposition research constantly monitored opposition politicians (including background research, plus on-going monitoring of off-air satellite feeds and on-air performances). This research enabled Clinton's team to anticipate opposition moves and so have communication strategies in place before events broke. Clinton's team worked to anticipate 'bad news', so when 'problem' stories broke an immediate positive spin could be disseminated;
- Clinton's Communications Director held at least two meetings a week with public information officers throughout the executive branch of government, to try and project a coordinated public profile;
- Clinton would not appear on television until his team had negotiated with producers concerning which topics could be discussed and which were disallowed;
- Clinton's team did background research for the media as a strategy to try and set agendas and manage content;
- Clinton's team placed great emphasis on local media outlets and 'narrowcasting' as part of their effort to send targeted messages to specific niche audiences. In addition to using locally targeted media releases, his team organized surrogate speakers to take Clinton's message directly into local communities. Nixon's strategy of jumping over the heads of the Washington/New York press was used. Ultimately, both Clinton and Nixon's PR-teams under-estimated the importance of working with mass media journalists;
- Video news releases were produced in the White House's TV studio. These were distributed by satellite feeds;
- Use was made of the Internet, enabling people to communicate directly with the White House by e-mail;
- Every Presidential policy initiative was treated as requiring a communication campaign. Clinton's team operated on a 'permanent campaign' footing.

During Clinton's term, PR-ized politics came of age, with both the Democrats and the Republicans playing the same game:

- Trying to put a positive spin on their own activities and a negative spin on the opposition;
- Trying to undermine the opposition with 'dirty tricks';
- Deploying spin techniques to undo the damage wrought by dirty tricks directed at them.

Further, Mark Gearan's appointment to head Clinton's White House communications operation served to reveal how far US political PR had been professionalized – because Gearan had previously served the Republican Party's Nixon, Ford and Reagan. His appointment to Clinton's Democrat Party staff demonstrated how far politics had moved away from being controlled by political parties governed by 'principle'. What counted in the new political process was being a professional communicator, not being a 'believer' or a party hack.

In general, Clinton's team were not great PR innovators. However, they demonstrated how PR techniques developed by Nixon and Reagan could be used to script a political celebrity based upon 'populism'. Clinton's PR team learned to mobilize his saxophone playing, youthful rebellion and even sexual indiscretions, to make him both 'hip' and a 'nice guy'. They masterfully deployed PR techniques and populism to manage public opinion.

7.4 What is political PR?

Political PR involves a multi-prong set of strategies and tactics geared towards putting a positive spin on the politician one works for and a negative spin on the opposition. Different factions of the political elite are in competition with each other, and spin-doctors work for all the competing politicians and factions. As political PR has become professionalized, spin-doctors increasingly change teams, working for whoever pays the most – after all it makes no difference which political faction they work for, given they are not employed on the basis of party loyalty/commitment but for their professional communication skills.

Spin lies at the heart of PR-ized politics. The ability to spin a story means:

[The ability] to manipulate not only what administration officials are saying but also what the media are saying about them. Spinning a story involves twisting it to one's advantage, using surrogates, press releases, radio actualities, and other friendly sources to deliver the line from an angle that puts the story in the best possible light. Successful spin often involves getting the media to 'play along', by convincing them – through briefings, backgrounders, or other methods of persuasion – that a particular spin to the story is the correct one. Sometimes the spinner can accomplish the same result not by persuading reporters but simply by making life easy for them: that is ... [by doing the] reporters' work for them. Press releases, radio actualities, satellite feeds, fact sheets, and the like provide a torrent of easy news for the media to relay to their audience.

> Briefing and press conferences serve as a watering hole for packs of journalists in search of news. Well-choreographed photo opportunities provide striking visual images that reinforce the messages White House officials want to convey, but they give the producers of television news ready-made opportunities to get exactly what they need most: good pictures. (Maltese, 1994: 215–16)

PR not only suits politicians, but also suits contemporary media organizations faced by pressures to be economically viable. Contemporary media economics has produced a tendency towards downsizing and de-skilling newsrooms – i.e. pressures to employ fewer and cheaper staffers. Consequently, editors and producers have to produce news with ever-higher proportions of people not experienced to produce quality news and images. However, these staffers are able to process media releases which become a cheap way of producing 'news'. In a sense, growing pressures to use PR material is simply a form of journalistic outsourcing, which makes good economic sense for media corporations. Spin-doctors take advantage of this – i.e. the more media corporations downsize and outsource, the more spin-doctors are able to place their stories. Not surprisingly, this outsourcing phenomenon has seen the number of journalists fall relative to PRs/spin-doctors – e.g. in the USA there were estimated to be 130,000 journalists and 150,000 PRs (Bennett and Manheim, 2001: 284).

So a core feature of spinning is understanding how the media works and exploiting one's knowledge of journalistic practices and discourses to provide newsrooms with what they need. A good PR knows how to place stories by making it as easy as possible for journalists to do their job, i.e. by:

- Supplying journalists with the sorts of stories and images they need to please their bosses;
- Doing background research for time-pressed journalists to supply the information needed to produce stories. This allows journalists to believe they have control and ownership over their stories;
- Leaking stories to journalists who are not experienced enough to know they are being 'used';
- Leaking stories to experienced journalists with whom one needs to develop/maintain a symbiotic relationship – i.e. providing them with an exclusive story. This can create a 'debt' PRs can use to negotiate future 'favors'. Developing such relationships requires great care and tact (and mutual trust) so that journalists do not get the impression they are being 'used' or 'spun a line' (i.e. journalists must be handled in a way which allows them to maintain their 'professional ideology');

- Scripting speeches to provide sound bites and leads making the journalistic task easier;
- Arranging photo opportunities guaranteeing good, cost-effective images. This often involves arranging staged pseudo-events geared to the needs of time-pressed newsrooms. Pseudo-events are often used as 'bait' to catch journalists – i.e. designed to attract media attention. Once attracted, other information can be supplied;
- Arranging news conferences to make the collection of 'quotes' as easy as possible. Well-arranged news conferences supply good sound bites, good visuals and a good information package (i.e. background research) – making it as easy as possible for journalists to construct the news with what is supplied. In some instances, news conferences become pseudo-events. News conferences can also be constructed so as to make it difficult for journalists to ask questions.

Of course, PRs/spin doctors are not always successful in placing their stories, setting agendas and steering journalists. But the more profit-driven news organizations reduce spending on experienced investigative journalists in favor of spectacle journalism or newsrooms employing less experienced (cheaper) journalists, the greater become the opportunities for the PR-ization of news and agenda setting.

Because journalists do not like to believe they are being, or can be, manipulated a crucial element of spin-doctoring is hiding one's own spin. Equally important is the need not to be caught unprepared. This requires the early identification and analysis of potential communication problems. Once future potential problems are known, spin-doctors prepare contingency plans (strategies and tactics) to deal with them should they ever become known to journalists (often because opposition 'dirty tricks' teams leak them to the media). This allows for a rapid response to crises – i.e. journalists are spun a new line to minimize damage, create 'plausible deniability', or (if possible) to deflect attention elsewhere. As soon as the Iraq War began going badly for the Western coalition, American, British and Australian spin-doctors began trying to deflect attention elsewhere and concocting 'plausible deniability'.

Sometimes the best strategy is 'jumping over' the heads of journalists deemed 'problematic'. Both Nixon's and Clinton's teams used this approach to communicate with the public via local and niche media, cable TV, direct mail and advertisements, as a substitute for dealing with 'negative' White House media corps. PRs call this 'going public', 'disintermediation' or 'end-running' journalists (Maltese, 1994: 216). This tactic must be used with great care to avoid overly alienating the elite media. Nixon's demise demonstrated the danger of using 'end-runs' to excess.

But there are other ways spin-doctors use the media, namely:

- Organizing teams to write letters to the press. Even if not published, the impression can be created within newsrooms of a groundswell of public opinion (what Nixon called 'the silent majority');
- Organizing teams who monitor and phone radio talk back programs;
- Lobbying key people – e.g. columnist and editorial writers;
- Providing journalists with 'off-the-record' backgrounders. This can involve politicians (rather than their staffers) having personal meetings with 'negative' journalists to try and charm them, and/or give them off-the-record information;
- Journalists' career paths can be influenced by providing stories to those deemed 'friendly'; while 'squeezing out' the 'hostile'. This works when journalists have to cover certain stories (e.g. the media cannot ignore Presidents or prime ministers). In such instances, if journalists assigned to cover these beats are 'frozen out', they face career problems;
- Running smear campaigns against opponents. This involves running an effective research department to gather information about the opposition. This information is leaked to journalists to undermine opponents. The Republicans used information about Clinton's sexual exploits in this way. Although smear campaigns are more commonly deployed against those in opposition political parties, they are also used inside political parties (e.g. during struggles to select candidates);
- Staged ('planted') questions when politicians 'meet the public' in shopping malls or during question-time in televised Parliamentary sessions.

But political PRs do more than engage with journalists. They are also in the business of creating celebrities (see chapter 8). This involves being able to spot and recruit latent talent – i.e. those who are telegenic; can speak in sound bites; sound sincere; and have the discipline and theatrical abilities to follow a script. It also involves training politicians to be televisual performers, to use autoprompts, and to only give 'appropriate' answers to journalists. PRs also teach them to dress appropriately and possibly improve their appearance through dentistry, contact lenses, hair implants, diet changes and so on. Further, some politicians need to be accompanied by handlers and minders to help them 'manage' their micro-relationships with the media.

Contemporary political PRs are also involved in marketing and advertising because politicians have become products to be 'sold' to audiences (see Newman, 1994). This involves scripting celebrity performances to 'position' the politician as a 'brand' matching a particular voter profile. 'Candidate positioning' often involves mobilizing the icons and symbols of popular culture and linking politicians to these, so as to make them more appealing. PRs obviously prefer to gain free access to (mass or niche) audiences by getting journalists to use media releases, cover their pseudo-events and pick up their scripted sound bites. But PRs cannot afford to rely exclusively upon free media coverage – sometimes they must pay to ensure access is gained to the audiences they want to reach. Hence, political PRs also engage in the business of paid marketing and advertising, and this involves them in audience and public opinion research. This dimension of selling politicians has seen the growth of a political PR industry that is increasingly expensive to run.

Finally, political PRs are also involved in internal communication – i.e. communication within political parties. Such internal communication can take many forms, including internal lobbying, rumours, direct mail or scripting party congresses. Further, stories placed in the media (e.g. leaks) are sometimes actually designed to influence people inside one's own political party, e.g. manipulating party members when candidates are being selected.

Overall, political PRs deploy their communicative expertise to try and achieve the following effects:

- Try and shift audience (journalists and/or public) perspectives about a chosen topic to move it as close to one's own perspective as possible. This often involves 'recasting' stories by putting one's own 'spin' on the topic. Spin-doctors are often engaged in trying to get journalists to look at damaging stories from a different angle;
- Distracting the masses as much as possible so they do not create 'steering problems' for policy makers by demanding 'real' participation in the policy process. Distraction is also deployed to try and focus voter attention away from issues politicians would prefer them not to think about. This agenda-setting role is a fundamental part of PR – i.e. the objective is not to tell people what to think, but to try and influence what they think about (Cohen, 1963: 13);
- Try and steer voters to vote 'appropriately'. This is often associated with inventing celebrity leaders or heroes, but can also be associated with undermining opposition candidates (e.g. smear campaigns);
- Using stories to put 'pressure' on policy opponents – e.g. PRs work to whip journalists into a frenzy over issues that, if reported, will undermine their opponent's position. In such instances, journalists are effectively used to mobilize public opinion. Although not part of insider policy making, the masses can (if hyped up) be used to impact on policy making in an indirect way – e.g. over the years spin-doctors have successfully 'encouraged' Western journalists to 'mobilize' public support for Palestine; Tibet; anti-apartheid, anti-whale hunting; banning the sale of ivory; anti-Nike sweat-shops and so on;
- Try and get voters to support (or at least not oppose) Government policies;

- Try and win the support of interest groups, and/or reduce the support interest groups give to one's opponents;
- Maximizing the support one's employer has within his/her own political party (and/or undermining the position of detractors within the party) – i.e. political PR is partially involved in internal communication and relationship building.

Although political PRs may not be successful 100 percent of the time, they have obviously been deemed successful enough to have given rise to a huge spin industry – i.e. serious politicians now spend huge amounts of money to employ spin-doctors. Presumably they must believe they are getting value for money.

7.5 The tools of political PR

A key PR tool is knowledge of journalistic practices because much PR is about two-step communication – getting journalists to run one's story (with as few changes as possible). When PRs are successful at this they help to set the agenda for what people talk about. Agenda setting via the media involves knowing what journalists regard as newsworthy, and understanding the institutional and time constraints faced by journalists. Effectively, spin-doctors have to be able to:

- Write press releases meeting the needs of different news organizations. Good PRs know the different newsroom styles;
- Produce good quality photographs and/or video releases meeting the media's image requirements;
- Provide good photo opportunities;
- Stage pseudo-events or 'gimmicks' (see Scalmer, 2002) to provide events attractive to the media;
- Organize, manage and script events (e.g. political party conventions) in order to maximize the control one has over images and stories flowing out of these events;
- Provide a good and reliable background research service for journalists, so that one becomes a dependable source of (free) information;
- Be reliable contacts for journalists so as to make their job as easy as possible – i.e. be available 24 hours a day to deliver good sound-bite 'quotes'. This involves developing a symbiotic relationship with journalists;
- Plant leaks (see Negrine, 1996: 29–30). 'Leaking' can actually become institutionalized, as is the case with the British Lobby system (Cockerell et al., 1984).

Secondly, political PRs should be media experts – i.e. know which media attract which audiences. This increasingly requires a working knowledge of 'narrowcasting' – i.e. using niche media to reach target audiences (e.g. cable-TV and media serving local areas, interest groups, ethnic groups, lifestyle groups and so on).

Thirdly, political PRs must be able to conduct research (or manage research teams). Qualitative and quantitative public opinion research, and the use of computerized databases, have become a central feature of PR-ized politics (see Sabato, 1981; Selnow, 1994: chapter 2). Effectively, political PRs must match politicians to those constituencies most appropriate for them. This involves demographic profiling and voter segmentation research; researching what messages work best with different voter profiles; and researching what messages trigger unintended or negative responses. Research has consequently become an on-going dimension of the scripting and re-scripting process from which emerge stage-managed celebrity politicians.

Fourthly, researching the opposition is an important dimension of politics. At its most sophisticated this involves gathering as much information on the opposition as possible, plus constructing computerized opposition databases. This enables spin-doctors to speedily undermine the opposition by, for example, referring to a speech made five years earlier that contradicts a recent speech. Opposition research involves trying to develop a complete database on everything someone has ever said or done. This often becomes the basis for 'smears'. 'Opposition' research can also be geared towards detractors within one's own political party.

Fifthly, PR-ized politics is increasingly developing into a branch of marketing (see Maarek, 1995; Newman, 1994). Politicians are increasingly sold like 'branded' products – their profiles based upon candidate positioning and public opinion research. This has seen political PRs jump over the heads of journalists by deploying other means to reach audiences – e.g. direct mail, telemarketing, the Internet and advertising. Targeted television advertising has, in particular, grown into a specialized form of political rhetoric – with the USA leading the way in designing negative spot adverts, based upon the findings of market research (see Diamond and Bates, 1992; Newman, 1994: chapter 1). In many ways, these political spots represent the most sophisticated form of political communication (see Nelson and Boynton, 1997): mobilizing an emotional mix of visual stimuli, sounds and – what Jamieson (1992: 137–41) describes as – 'adbites'. Political PRs, in fact, script 'adbites' as part of their overall strategy of feeding journalists with catchy sound bites.

Sixthly, spin-doctors anticipate that things go wrong, e.g. political performances sometime fail; zealous journalists dig up negative stories; or opposition spin-doctors plant stories that inflict damage. Spin-doctors necessarily spend much of their time dealing with communication crises – i.e. breaking stories that inflict damage on their employer. When a 'negative story' emerges, PRs necessarily try and 'bury it' as quickly as possible.

This generally involves trying to deflect attention elsewhere, and/or inventing some sort of 'plausible deniability'. Good spin-doctors try and build 'plausible deniability' into all of their Machiavellian work. And all spin-doctors develop a repertoire of techniques to try and refocus television cameras on new (distracting) issues far removed from any issue they are trying to 'bury'.

Lastly, political PRs engage in the business of impression management – managing the way their politicians are perceived. This is achieved by carefully scripting their performances (especially television performances). An important dimension to this is speech writing – with each speech tailored to appeal to the particular audience it is geared to reach and constructed around one or two carefully crafted sound bites. Some politicians are masterful at following such scripts. For those who are not, handlers and minders are provided to try and keep them on-script, and/or intervene when they threaten the integrity of intended performances. In part, spin-doctors are counselors – they must win the trust of politicians and then advise them about the media. Spin-doctors are employed to be the experts in journalistic behaviour – their job is, in part, to explain to politicians what will, and will not work with journalists. In the process, they modify the behavior of politicians in order to try and achieve the most positive media coverage possible (by playing to a journalistic audience). In this respect, journalists partially set the parameters of the political game by compelling politicians and their minders to behave in certain ways. The outcome is that PRs become expert demagogues – scripting politicians as televisual performers – and so helping create the celebrity politicians who entertain and distract the masses (see chapter 8).

Summary

You should now be familiar with the following key concepts and themes:

spin industry; politician as performer; televisualized politics; stage-managed politics; creating political 'faces'; Political Action Committees; bland-ization of politics; pseudo-controversies; pseudo-events and PR gimmicks; 'planting' and 'leaking' stories; Americanization of politics; Nixon–Kennedy debate; Nixon's key role in PR-izing politics; how television pictures drown out words; the relationship between spin-doctors and public opinion pollsters; news management; PR techniques when working with journalists; PR techniques to bypass journalists; the tension between journalists and spin-doctors.

For further consideration

1 A symbiotic relationship has grown up between journalists, politicians and spin-doctors. Is this a 'necessary' function of mass televisualized democracies?

2 Journalists blame spin-doctors for corrupting the political process. Is this a reasonable portrayal of the situation?

3 Are the notions of 'manufacturing consent' and 'distracting the masses' inherently conspiratorial? If so, identify the conspirators.

4 Constructivists would argue there is no conspiracy. To what do they attribute the emergence of 'consent'?

5 Habermas argues that mass democracies 'steer' the masses to facilitate smooth policy making. If such 'steering' did not take place what might happen?

6 Britain's Hutton Inquiry (in 2003) emerged from the failure of spin-doctoring. Blair survived the resultant crisis; his spin-doctor did not survive. What does this reveal about how spin-doctoring works?

7 The professionalization of a spin industry has altered the organization and funding of political machines. Was this inevitable? Could the political machine be organized in any other way?

8 Some argue that politicians are performers acting out a script. Others see this as an exaggerated portrayal. Consider the two positions by considering the political process in your own area.

9 Who is responsible for sound bite politics – spin-doctors or the media?

10 Pseudo-controversy can be used to cover up a multitude of problems including spin-doctoring gone wrong. See if you can identify instances of pseudo-controversy.

8 Selling Politicians and Creating Celebrity

Chapter 8 examines how, in the age of television, *impression management* has become important for politicians. The chapter will argue that spin-doctors have *celebrity-ized politicians* in order to *sell* them to voters. This means that politicians have had to become experts in creating 'faces' (or 'masks') by *performing* scripts written by spin-doctors for television audiences. Chapter 8 examines what a celebrity is, and how celebrities are constructed. The chapter describes a number of different types of political celebrity. Chapter 8 is an examination of one of the key 'products' of successful political PR; consequently, this chapter is an extension of a number of themes developed in Chapter 7.

Celebrities are famous because they are media personalities – their fame derives from having their image constantly in the public domain. Celebrities appear important because the media make them important. They are in the media because the public is interested in them; but the public is interested because the media generate that interest. During the twentieth century, celebrity-ness became a consciously organized and manufactured phenomenon associated with the industrialization of culture. Boorstin (1971: 47) notes that the manufacturing process can synthetically fabricate 'well knownness', making someone a household name overnight. Significantly, fame no longer necessarily requires doing anything 'great', it simply requires gaining widespread media exposure. Gaining such exposure increasingly results from an industry of 'fame-game' specialists, e.g. publicity agents, image specialists and minders, producers and spin-doctors. Boorstin suggests that success is increasingly a function of impression management geared towards crafting a working mask:

The hero was distinguished by his achievement; the celebrity by his image or trademark. The hero created himself, the celebrity is created by the media. The hero was a big man; the celebrity is a big name. Formerly, a public man needed a *private* secretary for a barrier between himself and the public. Nowadays he has a *press* secretary, to keep him properly in the public eye…. In the democracy of pseudo-events, anyone can become a celebrity, if only he can get into the news and stay there. (1971: 60–1)

Consequently, we have filled our world with 'artificial fame' (1971: 47). Our media world is now peopled with celebrities, famous simply for being famous. Because becoming a celebrity requires on-going media exposure, it is not surprising that celebrities emerge from occupations where exposure occurs – e.g. movie/television actors, sportsmen/women (preferably televised sports), supermodels, musicians and television hosts. However, as Alberoni notes, celebrities emerging from film, television and sports, have traditionally constituted a 'powerless' elite (Turner et al., 2000: 9). This powerlessness set them apart from politicians. However, it is a moot point whether this 'power' distinction remains, because the end of the twentieth century saw a new phenomenon emerge – a growing convergence between politicians and other forms of celebrity: 'Film stars like Arnold Schwarzenegger share the stage with politicians like George Bush; Gorbechev appears in a film by Wenders; Michael Jackson hangs out on the White House lawn with Ronald Reagan; Nelson Mandela fills an entire issue of Vogue' (Marshall, 1997: 19).

This convergence assumed three forms – politicians and other types of celebrity increasingly hang out together (often because spin-doctors believe that politicians could benefit from this); actors and musicians cash in on well knownness to move into politics; and politicians increasingly become scripted performers. The latter means that the line between a politician as actor and other types of celebrity blurs. The celebrity best illustrating this blurring is Ronald Reagan who built his political career on being a scripted performer (Cannon, 1991: 53–4). It is a moot point whether, under these circumstances, power resides with on-stage performer-politicians (the scripted 'face'); with those scripting the 'face' (back-stage spinners); or with faceless policy makers inhabiting the off-stage machinery. But as politicians as celebrities increasingly become specialists in performing for the masses, they have ever less time to play policy-making and power games. Consequently, convergence between politicians and other forms of celebrity may well be more than appearance – it may represent a real decline in the actual power possessed by celebrity politicians. Conceivably celebrity politicians are becoming more like other celebrities – i.e. perhaps those allowing themselves to become 'hyped' and 'puffed' celebrity performers thereby lose power to off-stage and back-stage political players? One example would be South African President Mandela, who in performing the celebrity role of 'Madiba' abrogated power and responsibility to party machinery run by Thabo Mbeki (Jacobs and Calland, 2002: 13). This served to make Mandela a better celebrity performer because he thereby stepped outside the constraints imposed by day-to-day power politics.

So why did the twentieth century give birth to celebrity-ness? At the risk of oversimplification, two explanations suggest themselves: firstly, celebrity-ness is a phenomenon tied to the rise of visual mass media (pho-tojournalism, film, television and videos). These visual media have become ubiquitous in Western (and many non-Western) societies. So inte-gral to our lives have mass media become, that images of celebrities are now omnipresent features of our daily existence. Celebrity faces are liter-ally mass-produced, and because of close-up photography, are often larger than life. The phenomenon was invented by Hollywood's studio system and involved constructing photojournalism images to promote movie actors. During World War II, this produced pin-up girls, of whom Betty Grable – a completely constructed chimera – was the most famous. The 1950s continued this intermeshing of photojournalism, magazine exposure and movie appearances to construct celebrity-ness with sexiness at its heart – e.g. Marilyn Monroe and James Dean. Because these con-structed faces filled our (mass media-ted) world and even entered our homes (via television), they became 'familiar' – we believe we 'know' these people even though we do not.

Secondly, in the hands of spin-doctors, manufacturing 'familiarity' becomes a powerful tool for steering mass publics – hence, political oper-ators moved into celebrity construction. This is the second reason for the rise of celebrity-ness – public opinion management originally arose in response to middle-class American fears that Western democracies faced a crisis (Ewen, 1996: 60–5) (see 3.4 on p. 52). Drawing upon Le Bon, Walter Lippmann and his followers developed the notion that 'the crowd' is open to suggestion and influence (Marshall, 1997: 32). From this grew a culture industry geared towards influencing and managing the masses – and the manufacture of celebrity has featured strongly in the repertoire of tools used to grab and hold mass attention. Constructing a celebrity system became a means for controlling the crowd/mass/popular will (1997: 204). This phenomenon was born in the USA but subsequently spread globally. The diffusion of television dramatically enhanced this celebrity pheno-menon; in fact, today's celebrities are increasingly creatures of television – e.g. Kylie Minogue, Oprah Winfrey, Madonna, Cher and Michael Jackson. However, the continuing importance of photojournalism and maga-zine exposure within the process of creating celebrity-ness must not be underestimated. The 1970s' Farrah Fawcett-Majors phenomenon serves to illustrate this – Farrah's fame derived not merely from her televisual appearance on *Charlie's Angels*, but from pin-up posters. Significantly, Fawcett-Majors became the first pin up to become rich from posters, because unlike previous pin ups, she retained control of her image of which she sold millions of copies.

8.1 Constructing celebrity

Marshall (1997) argues that the culture industry learned to package aspects of personality into celebrity form. These packages are scripted to have maximal audience appeal, which makes them bankable commodities within the culture industry. Manufacturing successful celebrities is a profitable industry. For power brokers, constructing a successful celebrity politician is just as bankable.

For spin-doctors, manufacturing a popular celebrity politician represents the ultimate success. This involves constructing a distinctively *branded celebrity* who appeals to the target constituency, and constructing a personality the media keeps giving 'profile' to. Ironically, all those involved in manufacturing celebrity politicians have a vested interest denying celebrity-ness is an organized construction – journalists deny complicity because that would be an admission that spin-doctors can manipulate them (Turner et al., 2000: 38–9); PRs deny complicity because of negativity towards their 'dark arts' (2000: 30–1); and politicians deny they are 'constructed' because that would undermine their 'leadership' image (2000: 39–40).

So how does one make a celebrity? Constructing celebrity means constructing (scripting, staging and acting) 'appearances'. It involves:

- Communication professionals deciding what face will attract/appeal to the desired audience (i.e. branding);
- Scripting the face to be projected;
- Staging that face;
- Working to get that face maximal televisual and magazine cover exposure.

So building celebrity-ness is about systematically staging a series of *visual* exposures to mass publics. The aim is to plant a particular 'look' in the public's mind. In this regard, Althusser's (1971: 162–3) notion of 'interpellation' is helpful for understanding celebrity construction. Interpellation means 'hailing' (or 'calling') – an analogy being the way we always respond when our names are called out. Althusser argues that each of us 'knows' who we 'are' *within relationships* because each of us is 'interpellated' as we speak;

and other people around us are similarly 'interpellated' as we speak to each other. Effectively, our identity (who we think we are) and our status are embedded within representational systems – i.e. we are positioned within a system of language. When we respond to someone 'hailing' us, we (unconsciously) accept our social position, and the position of the person calling us. The point is, these positions are socially constructed – they are 'meanings' made in, and through, the language we share.

Celebrities are similarly constructed – through the 'language' (signs and codes) of visual media (especially television). Celebrities effectively **interpellate** us – they 'hail' us, and so 'position' both us, and themselves, within a relationship. Celebrity-ness is the construction of a particular kind of status – celebrities are famous within sign systems designed to appeal to mass publics. Celebrity-ness is an interpellation based upon an *'ideology of egalitarianism'*. Essentially, we all implicitly know celebrities are famous only because they have been 'recognized' (and promoted) by the media, not because they have necessarily done anything 'great'. Denton notes that when one examines successful television performers one is struck by the fact they are 'really smaller than life ... [they are] soothing, attractive, and everyday' (1988: 72). Celebrities are precisely 'ordinary' people (the more ordinary the better) who have been elevated to 'fame'. Encoded in celebrity-ness therefore is the implicit notion that life is like lotto – it is based on luck. The way fashion models get 'discovered' illustrates this. Simply being selected to be cover girl of the swimsuit edition of the USA's *Sports Illustrated* magazine exposes one to millions, and hence instant visual fame. This has launched many careers.

As politics was televisualized, spin-doctors recognized the importance of constructing celebrity politicians with the sorts of 'ordinary' features voters could identify with – this was a feature of the scripting of US Presidents Jimmy Carter, Ronald Reagan, Bill Clinton, George Bush Jr., British Prime Ministers Margaret Thatcher, John Major and (Australia's Prime Minister) John Howard. Their aura derives from a curious mix of 'specialness' and 'ordinariness' (Marshall, 1997: 226), plus familiarity mixed with hierarchical distance (1997: 227). If well scripted and performed, mass publics 'attach' themselves to celebrities because they identify with the script being acted out. For today's celebrity politicians, the recipe for success is to use television appearances to project an aura of being 'in command', but simultaneously 'in touch with ordinary folk' (i.e. never haughty or 'superior'). Clinton and George Bush Jr. were masters at performing this role.

Constructing celebrity-ness is about creating (and popularizing) a 'face' and personality the masses can identify with in two senses: firstly, celebrities are admired because of their elite status – i.e. fame and success. Secondly, celebrities interpellate ('hail') 'ordinary' people into a fantasy world – holding out the promise anyone can become famous. They are precisely admired for being *ordinary* people who have managed to achieve what everyone would like – a better status based upon success and fame. This fantasy makes the real world more bearable – i.e. celebrities interpellate the masses into fantasy relationships by providing personified 'illusions' to make up for the deficiencies of real life (Boorstin, 1971: 9). They become a 'celebration' of individual success and 'individuality' in an increasingly 'massified' world, where people live anonymous lives in mega-cities. Celebrities stand out of the crowd (see Marshall, 1997: 43, 57). And because the celebrity system allows some individuals to 'stand out', it becomes possible to 'hope' for fame – a fantasy which helps to legitimate liberal capitalism. Ultimately, scriptwriters simply tap into deep-seated needs people have when constructing these pseudo-personalities to draw mass audiences into 'imaginary relationships' with celebrity personas.

The way soap opera characters appeal to mass audiences is instructive for understanding how celebrity functions. Audiences come to identify with soap opera characters in multiple ways – identifying with one character (effectively 'becoming' that character); hating another, liking another and so on. Effectively, audiences are interpellated into various 'relationships' with fictional television characters. Celebrities are scripted into existence in the same way – brought into being to provide a media 'personality' to whom audiences can relate. Much has to do with 'appearance' – celebrities need to 'look the part'. Significantly, when actors are auditioned for film, television or advertising roles they are selected because their appearance triggers certain responses – i.e. audiences respond to (are 'interpellated' by) stereotypes based upon how they 'look'. Celebrities must have the 'right' appearance – they are chosen because they are deemed able to trigger appropriate responses in target audience/s. Generally, those chosen for television performance tend to be attractive (or at least not unattractive), partly because sexuality is an element within constructing celebrity-ness. Constructing celebrity-ness tied to beauty, glamour or ruggedness offers scriptwriters various interpellation possibilities associated with getting audiences to project their aspirations, fantasies or dreams onto the screen personalities – i.e. celebrities are constructed in ways enabling them to host audience desires (Turner et al., 2000: 11). Not surprisingly, the televisualization of politics generated a shift towards selecting on-screen politicians who are *televisually attractive*.

But attractiveness is not enough for celebrity politicians. They must also be good *televisual performers*. Their performances ultimately give structure to the political environment and frame the political culture. Effectively, celebrities (including celebrity politicians) help the masses make sense of the world. Interpellating the masses into relationships with celebrities builds social cohesion by ideologically positioning people. Celebrities are in the business of *myth making* and *fantasy*. From a Lippmann/Le Bon perspective, celebrities are a highly functional and cost-effective form of 'crowd-control'.

Celebrities 'hail' audiences into imaginary relationships – people identify with these constructed personalities. Significantly, a well-constructed celebrity is precisely not a fully rounded character – the ideal celebrity's constructed 'personality' has minimal substantive content. Ideally celebrity personality should be **polysemic** (open to as many interpretations as possible), to facilitate multiple kinds of people identifying with the celebrity. Constructing a well-rounded character makes the celebrity 'too easy' to understand. This removes the 'mystery' and closes off interpellation possibilities (i.e. narrows the appeal of the personality). Constructing celebrity-ness (see Table 8.1) is an art form that, when successfully executed, serves as a 'crowd'-manipulation device in the following ways:

- Celebrities are mysterious. On the one hand they seem familiar, yet audiences are constantly aware they do not 'know' the 'whole' person. In fact, a key component of the mystique is intuitively knowing that celebrities are 'constructed' chimeras. Hence audiences are constantly trying to 'get behind' the mask to discover the 'real person' (Turner et al., 2000: 12). This is partly driven by a desire to work out 'the secret' of their success to try and emulate it. The drive to find out more about the 'real life' of celebrities underpins an industry of junkyard titillation journalism. Audiences invest much time into 'following the lives' of their favorite celebrities, which supports a publicity and magazine industry. In its extreme form this behavior becomes 'fan clubs' and can even lead to celebrities being enshrined in highly profitable 'museums' (e.g. Elvis Presley's Graceland). Much media content is geared towards circulating celebrity-based 'hype' and 'puffery' of the sort that entertains and distracts the masses;
- Celebrity-ness is fame grafted onto ordinary people – celebrities are 'nothing but ourselves seen in a magnifying glass' (Boorstin, 1971: 61). Hence, celebrities provide the masses with the (false) hope they too might one day become famous (and hence rich);
- Celebrities can become (pseudo-) 'heroes' for their followers – role models the masses turn to for solutions to life's problems (Turner et al., 2000: 164). This can be used as a device for steering public opinion – e.g. Elvis Presley was used to legitimate military conscription;
- Celebrities help to reduce information overload by acting as a kind of prism through which social complexity is reduced to simple moral codes attached to easily understood 'humanized' messages (2000: 166). Celebrity-ness conforms to the mass media's preference for visualized simplicity, binary oppositions and titillation, and hence contributes to the production of social 'one dimensionality' (Marcuse, 1964). Celebrities

Table 8.1 *Crafting political celebrity*

Role of spin-team	Role of politician
Research target audiences to find what sort of personality is appealing	Analyze target constituency and work with spin-doctors to understand this target group
Script a personality that appeals to target audience/s	Help to construct the script
	Understand and internalize the script
Find and/or create a 'face' that appeals to target audience/s	Work at building and maintaining an appropriate 'face' and 'persona' – i.e. build 'profile' (that is 'recognized' and 'known')
Develop gimmicks and pseudo-events that attract audience attention	Develop a 'fantasy' relationship with audiences – i.e. gather audiences and turn them into 'followers'
Transform 'issues' into 'personalities'	Help followers to 'make sense' of the world by simplifying complex issues into slogans and symbols – i.e. provide a 'leader'
Concretize myths into an identifiable 'leader'	Perform a personality/'face' that embodies myths
Work back stage to build celebrity	Perform 'the script' front stage to build celebrity

help the masses 'make sense' of a rapidly changing world through the melodrama of popular journalism (Turner et al., 2000: 15);

- Celebrities provide the masses with an endless supply of material for gossip (2000: 14). Stories churned out about celebrities by their publicity agents and media give people something to talk about. Given the bland and sterile routines of suburban life, gossiping about celebrities becomes one of the few sources from which people can construct conversations. So discussing celebrities and scandals has effectively become the basis for 'social bonding' – a form of social cohesion and 'community' building based upon pseudo-personalities and pseudo-events;
- Constructed celebrity-ness constitutes a form of mass distraction by focusing people's attention on hype and puffery;
- Well-constructed celebrities attract audiences. This funds the culture industry. Liberal capitalism has not only developed machinery for building legitimacy and consent, it has made this machinery both entertaining and profitable.

8.2 The game: playing to a televisual audience

Television transformed politics, partly because of the demagogic possibilities it offered for building mass popularity and consent. Further, the growth of the television industry generated an insatiable appetite for a certain genre of material – visually stimulating images; attractive people; and entertaining and titillating stories, especially stories that can be 'personalized'. Packaged celebrities filled television's need for visual titillation and 'human interest' stories. From this grew a symbiotic relationship between spectacle journalism and publicity agents crafting the 'personalities' and 'looks' required to fill the airwaves.

Political machinery staffers noted the fascination that journalists, and their mass publics, had for celebrities – so why not manufacture some political celebrities for them? From this emerged politicians as television actors cum celebrities. Politicians were increasingly scripted into the role of popular culture celebrities (Street, 2001: 276) as the spin industry crafted their appearances. Spin-doctored politicians grew from the recognition that television offered an array of new communicative possibilities – televised spectacle journalism provided a potential vehicle for manipulating millions.

Significantly, television emerged into a post World War II world wherein a particular ideology was being popularized – 'belief in the power of the common people to govern themselves, which has brought with it a passion for human equality...[and] a distrust, or at least a suspicion on individual heroic greatness' (Boorstin, 1971: 49). Television played an interesting dual role with regard to this new ideology – it:

- Helped to popularize the 'ideology of commonness' and celebration of 'averageness'; yet
- Became a tool to both steer mass public opinion and tame the dangers of mass democracy. Television effectively helped to 'tame' the ideology of commonness, and so ensured that egalitarianism never became a real threat to capital accumulation or the existence of a de facto power elite.

Television actually helped to build mass consent for liberal capitalism by deploying the 'ideology of commonness' and celebrating 'averageness' within a new genre of televisualized politics – a genre that saw television celebrities crafted as tools to entertain, titillate, distract and steer the masses.

A significant part of televisualized politics was geared towards finding and training people into the role of politician celebrities – those able to perform in front of television cameras to project the curious image of being simultaneously 'ordinary' and a 'leader' – of being 'special', but not too special. As with other celebrities, celebrity politicians are special for being famous, not for being superior. The role requires someone with an attractive personality (i.e. someone who can get on with 'ordinary folks') and is also (tele-)visually appealing. Politicians now attempt to portray themselves as 'Mr. Everyman' or 'Ms. Everywoman'. If the role is played well, celebrity politicians confirm that the democratic myth any citizen can become the leader – i.e. citizens must be able to fantasize themselves into that role if they wish.

For politicians, the new game involves playing to television audiences. To become politically successful requires developing 'profile' – finding a way to get onto television and staying there (Boorstin, 1971: 60–1). Such constant exposure requires recruiting politician-performers able to deal with the stress of continually maintaining a mask and performing in a never-ending smoke-and-mirrors show. Those not able to cope with being constantly in the limelight, or those uncomfortable with smoke and mirrors, become political liabilities. An example was the poor media image (in the West) of South Africa's President Mbeki because he refused to play the sort of media game played by his predecessor, Mandela. Mbeki failed to play the game of Western PR-ized politics – refusing to simplify issues like South Africa's Aids crisis and the Zimbabwean crisis into the sort of sound bite solutions preferred by liberal journalists. In this respect, Mbeki has emulated South Africa's apartheid rulers who also refused to play the Western 'media game'. Both Mbeki and the apartheid politicians paid a heavy price for refusing to play the sound bite game. Negrine (1994: 10) goes as far as suggesting that, in the West, political credibility has become simply a function of how politicians present themselves in the media. He notes how, due to good media performances, Sadat and Gorbachev achieved high credibility in the West while being unpopular at home (Negrine, 1994: 11).

So how is a successful celebrity politician constructed? Denton (1988: 55) suggests that it involves:

- Developing name recognition;
- Studying the art of self-promotion geared towards turning oneself into a televised fantasy figure the masses can identify with;
- Projecting an aura of warmth and sincerity;
- Learning to substitute 'personality' for 'issues' because 'personalities ... are more salient and easier to understand than issues' (1988: 55);
- Learning to appeal to mass television audiences by staging performances that 'reduce complexity';
- Crafting appearances open to multiple different audience interpretations/ identifications (1988: 47).

Television is the ideal medium for this, because it allows audiences to 'fill in' character details. So crafting less clearly delineated and vacuous personalities is preferable to crafting strongly defined characters. Strong characters become targets for those who do not like that personality 'type'. Hence, the shift towards celebrity politicians complements the shift towards bland-centrist politics – it is the politics of vacuousness born from trying to simultaneously make oneself a 'small target' and popular with as many people as possible.

Celebrity politicians must be good actors because, as Postman (1985) says, politics has become show business. Politicians are in the business of crafting and performing televisualized personalities. In this respect, Boorstin makes the useful distinction between character and personality. He notes that constructing celebrity involves manufacturing *personality*. This is why entertainers and actors make good celebrities – because 'they are skilled in the marginal differentiation of their personalities' (1971: 65). With the growth of televisualized politics and celebrity politicians, politicians have cuddled up to entertainment celebrities (Street, 1997: 46) and copied their practices. Street describes this political genre as 'a matter of "performance" – it is about giving life and relevance to ideas, about evoking trust and claiming representativeness. This creates obvious affinities with popular culture' (1997: 51). Playing to television audiences is an art form. As Street says:

> Some politicians 'work' their audiences better, have a more effective rapport with the 'folks' … Politics, like popular culture, is about creating an 'audience', a 'people' who will laugh at their jokes, understand their fears and share their hopes. Both the popular media and politicians are engaged in creating works of popular fiction which portray credible worlds that resonate with popular experiences. (1997: 60)

Politicians who do this well, interpellate audiences into *fantasy relationships* within which audiences believe they 'know' these constructed personas. The resultant artificial familiarity can be used to turn audiences into followers. Celebrity politicians who can play (and attract) audiences are – like entertainment celebrities – valuable commodities because they effectively 'collect', organize and steer the masses. They function not unlike the Pied Piper of Hamelin.

Politicians in democracies have always been actors – always had to play the crowd. But contemporary politicians play the crowd in new ways – through television. Political success nowadays means understanding and exploiting the possibilities that television offers to project one's profile and reach and manipulate mass publics. This constitutes a particular genre of performance (see Hawes, 1991).

8.3 Genres of political celebrity

The twentieth century gave birth to a new type of politician – those who learned to exploit the mass media's potential, especially the visual media of photojournalism, film and television. From this emerged celebrity politicians.

Celebrity politicians are culture industry products – they are manufactured. Some achieve media-prominence thanks to skilled scriptwriters (and the spin industry supporting them); some achieve media-prominence because opposition scriptwriters tried to undermine them; others achieve prominence because they stumbled onto a profile or gimmick appealing to journalist gatekeepers. During the twentieth century a whole array of celebrity politicians emerged. Categorizing these into five genres helps us to understand how political celebrity works.

8.3.1 The media managers

At the heart of political celebrity lies the need to exploit the interpellation potential that the mass media offers. This requires developing strategies to manipulate and manage the media. From this grew the PR industry.

Successful politicians have always exploited the communications technology of their era. The earliest form of mass medium to impact upon political practice was the press. The press' capacity to sway the masses was demonstrated by how Hearst's 'yellow press' provoked the 1898 Spanish-American war during which Spain was driven out of the last remnants of its empire – Cuba, Puerto Rico and the Philippines. This war transformed the USA into a great power by establishing US hegemony over Latin America (and the Philippines). Significantly, Hearst used artists to sensationalize and hype up Spanish 'atrocities' in Cuba – producing an early form of visualized mass propaganda to justify the USA attacking Spain. This war was also used by Theodore 'Teddy' Roosevelt to promote his political career – making him an early pioneer in the art of mass media impression management. Roosevelt skillfully used the press to promote himself as both a war hero (during the war against Spanish Cuba) and compassionate. Roosevelt's compassionate persona was masterfully symbolized by the 'teddy bear', which was named after him as a result of a story about him refusing to shoot a bear cub on a hunting trip. The media skills honed by Roosevelt during the Spanish-American war eventually won him the US Presidency in 1904.

The next medium technology politicians needed to master was radio. Among those pioneering the use of radio were Franklin Roosevelt, Eva

Peron and Adolf Hitler. As US President, Franklin Roosevelt (1933–45) masterfully used radio. His radio 'fireside chats' were a brilliant use of this medium to sell his New Deal Keynesian program and to calm Americans during the 1930s' Great Depression unemployment crisis. The Argentinean politician Eva Peron (previously a radio soap actor) demonstrated how radio could be used not to calm the masses, but rather to stir up emotions. After she married the leader of Argentina's Peronistas movement, Eva deployed her radio acting skills to rally workers into this fascist movement and simultaneously transform herself into an early version of a celebrity politician. Eva's radio skills were instrumental in helping her husband Juan Peron to become Argentina's President in 1946. In Germany, Hitler was equally masterful in deploying radio to mobilize mass support during the 1920s–30s.

Hitler's rise to power as German Chancellor in 1933 marks him out as an early innovator of mass mobilization using impression management and the media to sway mass public opinion. Hitler's chief propagandist, Joseph Goebbels, was a pioneer in building political PR machines (see 10.1.3 on p. 214). Goebbels' Ministry for People's Enlightenment and Propaganda became specialists in using the press, film, radio and mass rallies to agitate and steer the masses. These media were often used in unison, e.g. the mass rallies were broadcast and filmed – the filmed documentary versions becoming important tools for mobilizing those not attending rallies. Goebbels and Hitler clearly understood the power of visually stimulating images and visual gimmicks (e.g. the swastika and military parades). Nazi rallies were choreographed down to the smallest detail, and heroic Aryan symbolism crafted and deployed to maximal effect. Significantly, Hitler was scripted in accordance with the methodology of celebrity-ness. His appeal to the masses precisely lay in being a curious mix of greatness and ordinary-ness – i.e. he was scripted to be a 'man of the people', yet simultaneously a 'great leader' (Bramstead, 1965: 206–16, 197).

But ultimately, Americans have been the real masters in scripting celebrity performances; developing PR media-management techniques; and successfully deploying the media to steer the masses. US Presidents and their staffers have led the way in pioneering political PR and spin-doctoring in the televisual era. But the arts of political PR were not only developed by those 'inside' US government or involved in elections – American leaders 'outside' mainstream politics, such as Martin Luther King Jr., were equally instrumental in honing and deploying the arts of political PR. King and his team developed various strategies during the 1950s–60s' civil rights struggle (to end US racial segregation) that masterfully captured media attention through 'passive resistance', 'mass action', 'sit-ins', picketing and the 'weapon of love'. Reverend King was skillfully projected as a decent God-fearing man standing up against unjust laws. He was brilliantly scripted to appeal to white northern liberals – King's performance interpellated liberals (including liberal journalists) into a relationship with a decent moderate black man heroically standing up against Southern racist rednecks, and someone offering an alternative to Malcolm X (whose 'black power' radicalism frightened US liberals). By deliberately courting arrest, King projected this persona nationally via the media. He got into the news and he stayed there. Importantly, King's team carefully crafted performances to provoke Southern political-legal police systems into acting in ways that cast themselves into the roles of heavy-handed villains. As King noted, his movement consequently learned to mobilize 'righteous indignation' (Garrow, 1986: 265). Key players in King's team, Andrew Young and Wyatt Walker, both commented on how they worked to manage the media in their campaigns: 'In essence,' Andrew Young commented, 'we were using the mass media to try and get across to the nation what our message was,' that southern segregation was far more vicious than most white Americans had ever realized. 'The movement was really about getting publicity for injustice'... As Walker later boasted, 'there never was any more skillful manipulation of the news media than there was in Birmingham' (Garrow, 1986: 264).

These media-management strategies were copied and successfully deployed by the United Democratic Front (UDF) during South Africa's 1980s' anti-apartheid struggle. The UDF created a very successful media profile through creating celebrity spokespersons like Reverend Allan Boesak and Archbishop Desmond Tutu. By investing considerable resources into PR (Van Kessel, 2000: 56), the UDF developed a highly 'symbolic' struggle which played a huge role in undermining the apartheid state and its reform-agenda (Seekings, 2000).

The rewards of successfully crafting a political persona that works and managing the media into constantly giving this persona exposure are great – one can become a political celebrity, or even a political icon.

8.3.2 The sympathy managers

Newsroom practices inherently simplify the world (Louw, 2001: chapter 7). Journalists seek out the dramatic and sensational – pressures to produce stories appealing to mass audiences mean that journalists are trained to generate news which necessarily compresses, simplifies, and eschews complexity and ambiguity. Journalists prefer news that:

- Can be presented as easy-to-understand linear narratives;
- Includes binary oppositions ('good guys'/'bad guys');
- Is 'concrete';
- Can preferably be 'personalized';
- Has interesting or unusual dimensions which can be used as a 'hook' or 'angle' to attract audience attention.

The political spin industry can use these journalistic preferences to construct scenarios and 'hooks' for journalists. A 'recipe' for scripting political profiles likely to capture journalist's attention would include:

- Transforming 'issues' into 'personalities';
- Giving these personalities identifiable 'hooks' or 'gimmicks';
- Catering to the fact that journalists generally hold political views to the left of the social norm (Henningham, 1988: 106–7).

So a good strategy for grabbing the attention of Western journalists is to script a political persona combining: an identifiable visual gimmick; someone who engenders sympathy (preferably for being a 'victim'); someone who struggles against villains.

The pioneer of scripting a political persona which evoked sympathy was Mohandas 'Mahatma' Gandhi (1869–1948) who mobilized 'passive resistance' against the British Empire (firstly in South Africa and then in India). In the 1920s–30s the Indian National Congress used Gandhi to generate mass support and publicity for their campaign to end British rule of India. Gandhi's performances were magnificent – scripted around a brilliant visual gimmick of a half-naked little man in a white shawl, holding a bamboo stave who looked like a victim rather than a skilled political operator. Gandhi was a photojournalist's delight – and images of him were splashed across the pages of the world's press. Gandhi was a 'televisual performer' before television existed. His carefully crafted image evoked sympathy in its target audience – i.e. liberal journalists and the Western liberal intelligentsia. Gandhi and the Congress Party understood that the real decisions about British India were made in London. It was UK decision makers who needed to be persuaded that the liabilities of Empire outweighed the benefits. And so Gandhi invented symbols (e.g. the spinning wheel) and staged performances to embarrass India's British rulers, and provoke them into arresting him, thus making themselves look like heavy-handed villains. (Martin Luther King copied Gandhi's strategy.) Gandhi's non-cooperation campaigns, geared towards generating 'moral' pressure, successfully created the binary opposition of poor non-aggressive Indians victimized by an unjust, aggressive and bullying imperial machinery – his performances served to simultaneously highlight the coercion underpinning British rule; disguise how the Congress Party served India's Westernized middle classes; and disguise his own position as a Westernized lawyer who had accumulated considerable wealth in South Africa. Ultimately, Western journalists fixated so much on Gandhi's performance that they paid insufficient attention to the real power brokers, organizers and opinion leaders of India's independence struggle (e.g. Jawaharlal Nehru, Vallabhbhai Patel, and Mohammed Jinnah). In 1947, when Britain withdrew from India, Nehru became India's first Prime Minister and Jinnah became Pakistan's first Governor-General.

Gandhi was a brilliant sympathy manager. His performances during the 1930s' Salt Marches; visit to the British Viceroy's New Delhi house (from which emerged the Gandhi–Irwin Pact); and visit to London were skillfully executed media events. His presence during these media events personified (and simplified) the struggle for journalists – providing the movement with a celebrity face for photojournalists to use; a carefully crafted face that was a public relations disaster for British imperialism. Gandhi's performances made him not only a hero-victim and celebrity politician, but an icon of anti-colonialism. Gandhi's use of the media helped to make colonialism unfashionable, especially in the USA. This made it difficult for Europeans to resist the USA's post-World War II drive for global hegemony built upon a US model of economic hegemony that required ending European Imperialism (in order to make way for US hegemony).

Gandhi's success as a sympathy manager led to others copying him in their struggles, e.g. the Dalai Lama's struggle against Chinese rule of Tibet; South Africa's Archbishop Desmond Tutu's struggle against apartheid; Aung San Suu Kyi's struggle against Burma's military government; and Martin Luther King's struggle against US racial segregation. Sympathy managers often make use of religious symbolism and scripts encoding non-violent resistance deployed against opponents who are provoked into being heavy handed. Those scoring these performances attempt, as much as possible, to deploy the binary oppositions of good vs bad; victim vs villain; peaceful vs aggressive; and justice vs injustice. These performances are often geared towards mobilizing foreign pressure against one's opponents – and because of US global power, this means influencing American public opinion. For this reason, sympathy managers often gear their performances to appeal to American liberal values, or to appeal to specific caucuses within the US Congress – e.g. anti-apartheid activists targeted African-Americans (Louw, 2004: 134, 146), while the Free Tibet movement crafted the Dalai Lama's performance to appeal to the human rights lobby (Goldstein, 1999: 76).

The anti-apartheid movement skillfully mobilized Nelson Mandela to evoke sympathy. But unlike other sympathy performers who achieved celebrity status, Mandela did not perform the role himself. Instead, during the 1980s, he was cast into the role of an absentee performer; his role scripted and played out by anti-apartheid activists. The 1988 Free Mandela concert demonstrated the power of global television to popularize a celebrity who was not even present. That Mandela was in jail turned him into an extraordinarily powerful 'celebrity' because his own character and performance abilities did not get in the way – Mandela could be scripted as the ultimate polysemic persona: his image became available to be read in multiple ways by different constituencies making up the global anti-apartheid movement. He became 'pure imagery' – a mass media image constructed from photographs taken prior to imprisonment, onto which was grafted an heroic mystique and the notion of a hero-victim fighting tyrannical villains. This portrayal neatly complemented the media's emotional construction of South Africa's 1980s' anti-apartheid struggle as a 'morality play' (Hawkins, 2002: 225). That the media allowed the anti-apartheid movement to construct Mandela as a 'virtual' performance, unsullied by real politics, helped strengthen the 'morality play' scenario being portrayed. The crafting of the absent Mandela into a global celebrity serves to demonstrate how 'artificial' the whole process of scripting a celebrity is. So successfully was the absent Mandela constructed as a celebrity, that both his release from prison (in 1990) and his inauguration as South African President (in 1994) became globalized spectacle television events. Foreign journalists, in particular, became so infatuated with the Mandela construct that it distracted them from the real political game being played in South Africa.

Even in the print and newsreel era, Gandhi had demonstrated what a powerful public relations tool sympathy performances can be. Television enormously enhances the capacity of skilled spin-doctors to evoke such sympathy because, as Sadkovich notes:

> Television seems able to portray only a limited range of emotions because it lacks linear development and nuance. It homogenizes and reduces complex situations, events and emotions to simple standard items that are almost mythic ... Television precludes careful exegesis in favor of simple explanations of group conflict and reality in general. It invokes and evokes, it does not inform or explain. If Television is a dream, it also decides what is real ... As the tube creates and idealizes some groups and ideas by focusing on them, it makes other disappear by ignoring them. (1998: 60)

Skilled spin-doctors are able to deploy these characteristics of television to generate enormous levels of sympathy for politicians portrayed as victims. If well performed, the resultant celebrity can take on the aura of a secularized saint, and so becomes exempt from the scrutiny other politicians can expect. For their opponents this becomes a public relations nightmare.

8.3.3 The demonized

Celebrities are well known because they are media personalities. It is common to think of celebrities as persons of (manufactured) repute – i.e. those scripted to be appealing to mass audiences. But people can also become well-known media entities because someone has successfully demonized them. Demonizing enemies has been a long-standing feature of political communication, but in the televisual age it has generated a new kind of celebrity – the well-known demon. They are not 'well known' at all, but like other celebrities their image is well known. And grafted onto this image is the scripted persona of the villain-demon. The last few decades have seen the creation of an array of such villains in the West – e.g. Iraq's Saddam Hussein, Iran's Ayotollah Khomeini, Libya's Muammar Gaddafi, Palestine's Yasser Arafat, Cuba's Fidel Castro, Yugoslavia's Slobodan Milosevic, and Osama bin Laden. The demonized celebrity serves the purpose of making 'the enemy' tangible (a 'face'), and providing a convenient fulcrum into which 'boo' words can be poured – as opposed to the 'hooray' words attached to heroes and victims (see Hartley, 1982: 21).

Normally celebrity demons are unambiguous villains. However, there are instances where the demonization process can become contested – e.g. Yasser Arafat and Fidel Castro. Both Arafat and Castro became heroes in the Third World and symbols of anti-colonialism. And because colonialism had been made unfashionable among the Western intelligentsia, it became possible to destabilize the anti-Castro and anti-Arafat portrayals in liberal newsrooms. The struggle that emerged over Arafat is instructive – Israel and the US Jewish lobby worked to demonize Arafat, while the PLO and US Arab lobby worked to rescript him as hero-victim. The Arafat portrayal was made more complex by the fact that, at one stage, Arafat was rehabilitated by the Western media (and even by the Israelis) as a useful moderate who could be used as an ally against Muslim radicals. This involved recasting earlier villain portrayals. Subsequent attempts to return Arafat to the unambiguous villain category proved to be hard work.

Creating celebrity demons can be dangerous because celebrities (even villainous ones) become well-known icons. The danger is that one can inadvertently create media-rallying points for one's opponents. Arafat is a case in point – i.e. the more Israel attacked him, the easier it became to cast him as a victim-hero among Palestinians. South Africa's apartheid government similarly generated support for Mandela by trying to demonize him. And current Western demonization of Osama bin Laden ironically turns him into a hero across large swathes of the Third World. The point is that well knowness (celebrity-ness) is a valuable currency for politicians, and there are instances where even demon celebrity-ness becomes valuable in the hands of good re-scripting agents.

8.3.4 The inexplicables

An 'inexplicable' is someone not conforming to Western media stereotypes. Journalistic practice encourages the deployment of simplistic role labels. Shorthand labeling becomes a way for journalists to render complex situations understandable for mass audiences. Role labels attached to celebrities help not only to render complexity easier for mass audiences to understand, but also to render the story more 'human' and hence more interesting. Over time, these simplistic labels (and stereotypes) grow into 'truths' for both mass audiences and journalists.

But because role labels and stereotypes fail to deal with complexity, situations arise where something happens that does not conform to 'the script' the media use to describe that situation. These aberrations become problems for the media because they challenge the narrative the media has popularized. In such instances the media has two options:

- Recast the narrative, explaining the complexity leading to this 'aberration'. However, because mass audiences generally find complexity challenging, such an approach would likely alienate audiences (which could reduce audience size). For this reason, the media are more likely to opt for option two;
- Stick with the original narrative and basket of stereotypes, but confer upon this political actor a new role label: an inexplicable. This 'explains away' the aberration in terms of the behavior of one individual; hence, the original media narrative retains its integrity.

Among those who became inexplicables when they behaved 'out of character' (i.e. violated 'the face' conferred upon them by the media) were Russia's Mikhail Gorbachev and South Africa's F.W. de Klerk. Both became celebrities cast into the role of having single-handedly changed history. This meant that the media could create easy-to-understand journalistic explanations (which ignored other role players and issues). They created enigma celebrities, whom media audiences wanted to know more about (so creating more demand for media products). Both Gorbachev and de Klerk discovered that such celebrity status was a bankable commodity – becoming part of the US lecture circuit to explain their 'inexplicable' actions.

8.3.5 The fame-game endorsers

Marshall (1997: x) notes that celebrity status confers upon the person a 'discursive power' within society. When celebrities talk, others listen. So celebrity-ness is a bankable commodity – celebrities can be marketed in their own right, or used to market other commodities (Turner et al., 2000: 12). They can also be used to sell ideas. Celebrity endorsement can be a powerful tool for persuading mass publics to buy commodities or ideas. This has produced a new kind of mass politics where (non-political) celebrities endorse political agendas, becoming tools in the hands of spin-doctors. Effectively, spin-doctors have moved beyond merely generating pseudo-events. They now generate *pseudo-politics* – rendering the boundary between politics and entertainment even more blurred. Pseudo-politics involves building hype upon hype – i.e. already constructed celebrities are scripted into performances designed to popularize political messages. Spin-doctors re-package already existent celebrities, hopeful that the political messages attached to them will grow in stature because of endorsement, plus be absorbed by mass audiences in an uncritical way. This has created fame-game endorsers – where non-political celebrities are used to promote/endorse political agendas.

This new genre of politics emerged in July 1988 with the Free Mandela concert which drew together entertainment celebrities like Whitney Houston, Stevie Wonder, Harry Belafonte, and Roberta Flack to perform before a global television audience. The Mandela concert, attended by 70,000 people at Wembley Stadium, was broadcast by the BBC to a global TV audience of 200 million. This global television event turned Mandela into a global celebrity, even among publics not normally interested in politics. The concert popularized the 'Release Mandela' campaigns and created enormous sympathy for him (as a hero-victim construct); generated invaluable endorsement for the ANC; and further demonized apartheid. The event served to demonstrate the emotional power global television possessed, and the value of entertainment celebrity political endorsement. From this grew a new genre of spin-doctored political hype in which already existent celebrities are enlisted to promote political agendas – e.g. Princess Diana (anti-landmines); Bono (Third World debt relief); Bruce Springsteen (human rights); Bob Geldof (starvation); and Sting (Amazon forest destruction). The result has been the PR-ization of political issues in which entertainment celebrities are now enlisted to whip up mass public opinion. The United Nations also discovered the value of fame-game endorsements – mobilizing non-political celebrities as UN Special Ambassadors. A sub-feature of celebrity endorsement has been Tony Blair's hosting of pop stars at 10 Downing Street and Hollywood celebrities being hosted at the White House.

Fame-game endorsements constitute the ultimate PR-ization of politics based upon pure puffery and hype. The media's preference for glib soundbites, good visuals, and attractive famous faces is exploited to the full to celebrity-ize and emotionalize issues as a tool to steer mass public opinion. This political genre confirms the American penchant for visual glitz, beautiful successful people and happy endings (even if they are staged).

The politics of fame-game endorsement is the clearest form of the politics of illusion and smoke and mirrors. But ultimately, all varieties of political celebrity share a common rootedness in a form of politics driven by visual illusions and packaged, scripted personalities. As Boorstin notes: it is a variety of politics where *image gets mistaken for reality*. In this regard Boorstin says of Americans: 'we risk being the first people in history to have been able to make their illusions so vivid, so persuasive, so "realistic" that they can live in them. We are the most illusioned people on earth' (1971: 240).

As US global dominance has grown, so the phenomenon of televisualized illusion has been exported. It is no longer an American-only phenomenon.

Celebrity politicians are but one manifestation of this world of media-made illusion – where branded and scripted personalities are now performed for mass television audiences, and the gap between entertainers and politicians narrows. The film and television industry uses producers and directors to audition, script and direct celebrity performers. Politics has spin-doctors to achieve the same effect. Both are in the business of crafting performances to sell branded celebrities to mass audiences. But the political machine sells more than celebrities – it also crafts ideas and beliefs and sells these to mass audiences (see chapter 9).

Summary

You should now be familiar with the following key concepts and themes:

manufacturing 'well knownness' and 'recognition'; fame; 'artificial' fame; the relationship between 'ordinariness' and 'celebrity'; how celebrities 'interpellate' audiences; the importance of 'branding' and 'appearance' in constructing political celebrities; the role of images (photographs, film and television) in constructing celebrities.

For further consideration

1 Could spin-doctors create celebrities as effectively if television did not exist?
2 Consider the role that film and visual images played in the creation of the 'cult of personality' in communist countries (e.g. Stalin and Mao). How is this similar, or different, to Western celebrity politicians?
3 How is celebrity-ness used to sell 'ideas'? Find examples from the political process in your area;

(Continued)

For further consideration   Continued

4   It has been suggested that spin-doctors create superficial 'faces' and craft 'personality' (rather than 'characters'). Why would crafting 'characters' not suit their need to manufacture 'leaders' for the masses to follow? Examine the political process in your area for 'personalities' and 'characters';

5   The 'look' required to be a successful politician varies according to context (time and place). See if you can identify such differences, and explain any differences found;

6   Is it an exaggeration to say all politicians are merely scripted performers?

7   Compare the media styles of South African Presidents Mandela and Mbeki, and consider the price Mbeki has paid for not emulating Mandela's style;

8   Why did the following politicians become successful celebrities – Gandhi, Martin Luther King, Mandela, Gorbachev and Clinton?

9   Identify examples of pseudo-politics and pseudo-events and examine how these have been used to manufacture political celebrities;

10 It has been suggested that celebrity-ness is associated with highly visual cultures (e.g. USA). Can you identify any non-visual cultures where celebrity politicians have existed?

9 Selling Political Policies and Beliefs

Chapter 9 examines how governments build consent for their policies and political systems. The chapter focuses on the role of worldviews and ideology in *building legitimacy*, and examines how politicians justify their actions by adopting and mobilizing the worldviews invented by others. It is argued that political elites need to invest considerable energy into managing worldviews as a means to steer mass publics. The worldviews they manage are produced and disseminated within a two-tier intelligentsia system – i.e. intellectuals construct worldviews and the media disseminate the ideas that become dominant in a particular context. Chapter 9 discusses the concept of worldviews; how worldviews are constructed and popularized; and the function of worldviews within political systems. Chapter 9 extends a number of themes developed in chapters 4 and 5.

Governments steer societies in certain directions through regulating how resources flow through society and/or are produced and distributed. Political processes generate policy about resource distribution (i.e. devising and umpiring 'the rules of the game'). These distribution rules produce winners and losers in all societies, including liberal democracies. But liberal democracies are premised upon gaining mass consent both for these policies, and for the ideological frameworks within which policies are embedded. How is such consent garnered? How are resource allocations/distributions, beliefs and policies sold to the masses?

All societies have dominant and dominated groups, and dominant groups necessarily prefer to remain dominant because this gives them the upper hand in deciding the rules of the game. Dominant groups have two mechanisms for creating and retaining dominance:

- Using violence; or
- Creating legitimacy.

Generally, the more legitimacy dominant groups have, the less violence (or threat of violence) they need employ. In situations of serious de-legitimation, ruling groups generally use overt military violence against those not abiding by their rules. In 'normal' situations, ruling groups need not deploy much (overt) violence, because they successfully 'criminalize' those not 'playing by the rules'. This requires getting most people to agree that the laws are 'just', so when the police-courts-prison system is used against 'criminals', this 'violence' is seen as 'legitimate'. Ruling groups employ a mix of violence and legitimacy to maintain their dominance, with legitimacy deemed preferable to violence. Gramsci used the term hegemony to describe how ruling groups build dominance. This involves three tasks:

- Using force or the threat of force through the police (internally) or military forces (externally);
- Organizing alliances and compromises – as institutionalized in parliaments or (international) multi-lateral organizations, where bargains are struck between different interests; deals are done and compromises identified;
- Building consent and legitimacy among the masses. This involves getting as many of 'the dominated' as possible to accept as 'natural' the 'leadership' and 'worldviews' of the dominant group/s, and to accept as legitimate the rules of the game which benefit those ruling groups. Legitimacy-making work is at its most obvious in the media, education and cultural systems.

9.1 Worldviews

Individuals are 'made social' (socialized) by having linguistically constructed 'pictures' put into their heads. Wilhelm Dilthey's notion of a 'world-view' (*Weltanschauung*) encapsulates how people come to 'see' the world through acquiring knowledge, beliefs and language. A *Weltanschauung* provides an individual with a fulcrum around which to construct a 'map' for guiding his/her life. A worldview mixes 'belief' (rational and emotional) and 'lived experience' (action-in-the-world) – a mix of discourse and practice. Over the years many concepts have been developed to describe the phenomenon of how people 'see' the world' and 'act ' in accordance with these visions. Hall (1977: 330) used the term 'maps of meaning'; Rokeach (1960: 18–19) referred to 'belief systems'; George (1969) called them 'operational codes'; and Boulding (1956) said people develop 'an image' of the world. Dilthey's '*Weltanschauung*' or worldview encapsulates all of these.

So where do worldviews come from? What is the mechanism by which political socialization takes place? Effectively, humans become embedded within sets of discourses and practices. Each individual is born into a context where pre-existing meanings and practices exist – these are internalized as individuals imbibe and internalize the signs, codes and practices of their social environment. Although there will be some who are not successfully socialized into the dominant meanings, the majority usually are. Hence, the discourses and practices of liberal democracy are now mostly taken for granted in places like the USA and Australia. At heart, *socialization* is the acquisition of *language* as mediated by the family, media and schooling. Socialization processes position individuals into sets of social *relationships*, some of which are political. So the acquisition of political worldviews is related to the process of interpellation (Althusser, 1971: 162–3). Humans are embedded into, and embed themselves into, belief systems as they interact with their linguistic environment. We come to 'know' who we 'are' because our identities (who we think we are) and status are embedded within representational systems – we are *positioned* within a system of language. Hence, any group seeking to rule, must pay attention to the 'language' used in society – ruling groups will try to ensure that the media and schools make available 'appropriate' representational systems from which citizens construct their identities – e.g. one would not expect to find the mass promulgation of communist or nazi discourses in US or Australian schooling and media systems where liberal democracy is hegemonic. Conversely, liberal discourse would not be found in Iran's, Libya's or North Korea's schooling and media systems.

9.1.1 Ideology

Effectively, acquiring worldviews is the acquisition of ideology. By internalizing representations around us (especially in the media and school), we embed ourselves into those 'pictures of the world' made available to us. Hence, ideology is not imposed upon us – we actively participate in interpellating ourselves, through engaging with our cultural environment. For Althusserians, ideology is a system of *coding* reality – it emerges from a system of **signification** (signs and codes) (see Heck, 1980). This Althusserian conceptualization of ideology emphasizes the 'subjective' dimension of socialization – i.e. the language (signs and codes) we internalize provides us with the material from which to construct our 'visions' of the world, and of our relationship to this world. This constitutes the mechanism for positioning citizens into sets of 'imaginary lived relations'

(Hall, 1977: 329). But ideology is not merely 'subjective'. It also has an 'objective' dimension – i.e. we also learn to interact with a material world by learning practices, e.g. the 'appropriate' use of cultural objects (furniture, work-place tools, roads, 'private property' and so on). Volosinov (1973) pointed to ideology's dual subjective–objective dimension. Deploying Volosinov offers a semiotic approach to ideological analysis (see Louw and Tomaselli, 1991) that corrects the Althusserians overly subjectivist view. The point is that our environments may be 'subjective', but they also have 'objective' dimensions, culturally imposed by coding systems operative in that environment – e.g. gender-based toilets and clothing; codes of behaviour and clothing in work environments; or recreational environments; plus geographically sanctioned behavior – i.e. 'places' set aside to get drunk (pubs and bars); get stoned (heroin shooting galleries); buy sex (red light districts); for removing problem people (prisons, mental asylums, execution chambers) and so on. Places and things have appropriate behaviors attached by ideological coding systems (which derive from political policy making). We are interpellated into these 'appropriate behaviors'. The codings become opaque as they become naturalized – they end up guiding people's behaviors unconsciously because they become embedded into a person's worldview through the processes of socialization and language acquisition. The media and schools play a crucial role in these processes of embedding, naturalization and normalization. What is 'normal' in contemporary liberal democracies is not normal in Muslim society (e.g. pubs, gay bars, and revealing clothing for women). Similarly, segregation based on gender (in Iran), caste (in India), or race (in pre-1960s southern USA or apartheid South Africa) would be deemed abnormal in contemporary liberal societies. Yet liberal capitalism regards a de facto system of class segregation based on housing affordability not only acceptable, but normal. Some liberal societies have de facto religion-based segregation, e.g. Northern Ireland and Israel.

9.1.2 Determination or 'guidance'

Worldviews are a curious phenomenon – on the one hand, each individual actively constructs his/her own worldview through a process of engaging with and drawing upon linguistic material in their environment. Individuals actively construct their own worldviews using pre-existing discourses and practices as 'representational resources'. So worldviews are not predetermined or static. Humans are not encoded automatons, trapped inside a 'prison house of language', because they are capable of struggling over the encoding possibilities of meaning. But worldviews are significantly 'guided' by existing 'pools of meaning' and existing encoding rules. In all societies, it is possible to identify a pool of meaning that has become hegemonically dominant at any point in time – e.g. liberal secularism is dominant in contemporary US, British and Australian society. Huntington (1997) contends that there are nine main 'pools of meaning' in the contemporary world – the West, Orthodox (Russia), Islam, Sinic (China), Japan, Hindu, Buddhist, Latin American, and African. He contends that cleavages between eight of these civilizations are likely sources of future conflict. (The African pool may mature into a ninth.) These 'pools of meaning' (and 'sub pools' within them) are the raw material ('signification systems') from which individuals construct their identities, everyday practices, and understandings of the world. These signification systems also set the parameters for policy makers. Because existing signification systems are the raw material from which individuals construct worldviews, the scope to influence people is great – i.e. most people can be steered by manipulating the available encoding possibilities. Effectively, those staffing key meaning-making sites (like media and schools) are worldview 'agenda setters', because they influence the pool of signs and codes from which the next wave of worldviews will be constructed. Not surprisingly, ruling elites pay considerable attention to this agenda setting function.

So understanding how worldviews come into being requires examining the role played by those who professionally craft and circulate significations – namely, the intelligentsia (academics, researchers, teachers, journalists and cultural producers).

9.2 Making worldviews

Political machines do not make new ideas, but are instrumental in deciding which worldviews (packages of discourses and practices) become hegemonic because political players promote some ideas and undermine others.

Some worldviews become hegemonic. Others struggle at the margins. Others are obliterated. How does this happen? Ultimately, elevating any worldview into a hegemonically dominant position is the outcome of a symbiotic relationship between the following people:

- Intellectuals produce ideas – codifying and packaging signification systems. Inventing new 'packages' and revising/recoding existing packages is carried out by academics, researchers, writers, policy designers, judges, and movie and television producers. This production is often associated with the notion of authorship, although this can be a problem because the process of creating and generating new meanings is often a team activity, especially within contemporary culture industries, research centers, or policy-making machines. Pinpointing an individual author is often difficult. Further, because intellectuals interpellate themselves into signification systems (worldviews) manufactured by earlier generations of intellectuals, authorship is often simply a process of reworking and recycling existing signs and codes;

- Political players 'adopt' worldviews – i.e. politicians interpellate themselves into signification systems (worldviews) manufactured by intellectuals. Political parties/politicians then battle for supremacy. This involves struggling over which worldview will achieve dominance because successful politicians/political parties become governments, who then promote the successful worldview. Worldviews are 'concretized' when codified into government policy. Policies (and the worldviews within which they are grounded) are then disseminated and naturalized within media and education systems;
- Making and circulating worldviews involves a *two-tiered intelligentsia system*. One branch – intellectuals – manufactures worldviews (see 9.2 on p. 198). The second branch – teachers and journalists – circulate and naturalize worldviews (see 9.3 on p. 202). The circulation and massification process is carried out by teachers, who simplify and repackage ideas as part of socializing the young. Journalists simplify and popularize ideas for wider mass publics. Both branches of the circulation intelligentsia specialize in making ideas accessible to mass audiences. Hence they are important within the political process, being crucial players for legitimating (or de-legitimating) beliefs, and generating consent for (or opposition to) policies.

Worldviews become hegemonic when underpinned by political machines. This explains why some are successful, while others are obliterated. The success of a worldview is generally related to it being adopted by a group which successfully achieves power. Such success can be the result of:

- Access to more resources than one's political opponents;
- Skillful leadership and impression management – i.e. attracting supporters;
- Skillful political management – political teams able to build successful alliances;
- Military victories.

Success does not necessarily have anything to do with a worldview being 'inherently' superior to its competitors. But once a group achieves success, it will work to promote and naturalize its preferred worldview. This will often be accompanied by claims that the victorious worldview is superior and/or more (teleological) advanced than other worldviews. Western elites use educators and the media to promote such ideas.

So there is a correlation between worldviews becoming successful (hegemonic) and their relationship to ruling elites – i.e. creating successful worldviews has much to do with building symbiotic relationships between intellectuals and political machines. In this regard, Peter Berger's Pyramids of Sacrifice notion is instructive. Berger (1977) uses the analogy of Aztec temples to explore how ruling groups sacrifice people to their dreams. Aztec priests (who formed a local intelligentsia and served the local ruling elite) would kill ordinary people on top of their temples in sacrificial rites. Because the priests had successfully convinced people that these religious sacrifices brought good fortune upon society, people did not resist family members being sacrificed. Berger notes that intellectuals serve ruling elites by developing the worldviews that guide elite actions. He makes the important observation that it is ordinary people who are usually sacrificed to these plans and discourses, and that intellectuals are usually in a good position to ensure they avoid being made the victims of the sacrificial processes they help initiate with their knowledge building.

Intellectuals need resources to craft their significations – someone must pay for the time and facilities intellectuals need to conduct research, and craft new ideas and cultural products. Ruling elites need packages of significations helpful for governance. The basis for a relationship between intellectuals and political machines is obvious. It is a relationship often built upon a form of (sometimes disguised) **patronage**. Ultimately, all societies develop funding regimes which 'guide' intellectuals towards producing 'appropriate' significations helpful for building consent for the policies and belief systems of ruling elites – i.e. funding is an important mechanism for *intellectual agenda setting*. Funding arrangements vary:

- Funding relationships can be explicit – e.g. politicians or governments directly employ intellectuals as advisors and consultants; or governments pay for propaganda films;
- Government subsidies – e.g. subsidizing universities, research, filmmakers, writers, etc. Such subsidy arrangements involve a relationship between intellectuals and political machines that is less explicit than direct employment. Although subsidy systems grant a degree of 'intellectual autonomy', subsidy arrangements still serve to 'guide' intellectuals away from 'inappropriate' areas. Subsidies often implicitly encourage 'administrative research' (i.e. 'instrumental' research that is politically and economically 'functional'). Governments will also sometimes subsidize foreign intellectuals in an effort to undermine the foreign governments they oppose – e.g. the campaign to overthrow Afghanistan's pro-Soviet government included funding Islamic medrassas (schools) in refugee camps. This anti-communist intellectual engagement facilitated the growth of Islamic fundamentalism and al-Qaeda;

- Non-government subsidies (e.g. foundations established by business corporations, or religious organizations) can 'guide' intellectual activity through forms of patronage;
- The market mechanism is a powerful force for channeling intellectuals towards the production of signification servicing the needs of liberal capitalism – e.g. the film and publishing industries. Effectively, the culture industry promotes certain genres of intellectual endeavor and not others.

Worldviews do not get to be successful by chance. Successful worldviews are those that have been promoted by powerful interests – because their creation, reproduction and dissemination have been funded and institutionalized. Generally, it is not easy to 'see' the worldview into which one is interpellated – because one's own belief systems are usually 'taken for granted' and opaque. So for liberals it is easy to 'see' intellectuals collaborating with communist or nazi systems to produce ideology, but less easy to recognize the same collaborative and ideological processes operative in their own political systems. The reality is, throughout liberal capitalism's evolution, intellectuals have collaborated to produce worldviews serving ruling elite needs, for example:

- During the construction of Europe's empires, intellectuals justified this phenomenon and helped to build appropriate technologies and administrative systems;
- When slavery was required for capital accumulation in Europe's American possessions, intellectuals justified this and helped to build appropriate technologies and administrative systems;
- Intellectuals helped to conceptualize and drive the processes of industrialization and capital accumulation built upon the social dislocation of rural dispossession and urbanization;
- Intellectuals conceptualized and constructed Keynesian state interventionism and the 'consent-making' culture industry in response to the Russian Revolution and Great Depression;
- Intellectuals constructed the discourses of anti-colonialism and developmentalism to facilitate the post-World War II transfer of global power from European empires to a US 'trading hegemony' (in accordance with the Atlantic Charter);
- When labor shortages became problematic, discourses were developed and popularized to widen the labor pool by incorporating women (feminism) and migrants (multiculturalism). When capitalism required new investment opportunities, intellectuals helped to generate new conceptual opportunities, e.g. globalization/IT-boosterism and Green/environmental economics.

Broadly, any era will be characterized by a set of dominant (mainstream) intellectual concerns – research and publishing agendas become skewed so as to conform to answering fashionable research questions. Intellectuals remaining outside these fashionable pursuits face marginalization and difficulties accessing resources, which can translate into career suicide. Not surprisingly most intellectuals opt to join the intellectual industry producing knowledge 'appropriate' to their ruling hegemonies' requirements. This is often not a conscious decision to serve the ruling hegemony. Rather, it is driven by career opportunities which effectively serve to interpellate most intellectuals into mainstream pursuits. However, ruling hegemonies generally tolerate a wider diversity of worldviews among intellectuals than among the masses. Hence, 'spaces' set aside for the production of new ideas – universities and research institutes – are usually more tolerant of oppositional and dissident discourses than the rest of society.

Over time worldviews have emerged, become dominant, and been overtaken by others. In every era, ruling elites and intellectuals develop mutually beneficial symbiotic relationships. In some tribes, shamans provide the intellectual underpinnings of political legitimacy. In other contexts the intellectuals serving ruling elites have been Christian clergy or Islamic Mullahs. With the creation of Western secular states, a new kind of signification system, serviced by a new kind of intellectual emerged, namely, worldviews promoting materialist secularism and rule-governed human interaction based upon written coding systems. Intellectuals have created, interpreted and 'policed' these coding systems or '-isms', e.g. liberalism, conservatism, socialism, communism, fascism, nationalism, imperialism, anti-imperialism, environmentalism, conservationism, feminism, cosmopolitanism, multiculturalism, etc. These '-isms' have become the core worldviews available to contemporary Westerners – the pre-packaged coding systems people can interpellate themselves into, in order to try and make sense of themselves and their positions in society (see chapter 5). Although compatibilities exist between some of these packages, interpellation into one generally means automatically disavowing the others. Neo-liberalism is the signification system currently hegemonic in the West.

9.3 Popularizing worldviews

Producing 'appropriate' knowledge is not enough. Ruling hegemonies require appropriate ideas, discourses and practices be widely *disseminated* – i.e. they need to be popularized and naturalized among the masses. This is the job of the 'second-tier' *circulation intelligentsia*, especially journalists and teachers. It is also the work of information-processing professions

such as those in PR, advertising and cultural production (theaters, entertainment theme parks, video/computer games industry, museums and
so on). The circulation intelligentsia simultaneously makes worldviews
accessible to mass audiences and *naturalizes* them (making them 'taken for
granted' and 'commonsensical'). The circulation intelligentsia is in the
business of interpellating the masses into hegemonically appropriate discourses and practices. Ironically, many are not aware that this is what they
are doing because they themselves have been interpellated into coding
systems (worldviews) that they 'take for granted'. This is one of the key
features of the circulation intelligentsia – they are professional communicators, not 'ideas people'. Hence, unlike intellectuals, they do not focus
attention on where meaning comes from. This is why the circulation intelligentsia can fail to be consciously aware of their role in building hegemonically dominant worldviews.

Journalists and teachers are especially central to building liberal democratic hegemony because the media and schools are key gatekeepers and
agenda setters – selecting some ideas (while ignoring others), and promoting the selected ideas to mass audiences. Journalists and teachers are
effectively in the business of simplifying ideas produced by intellectuals,
and translating these into a form the masses will understand and find
entertaining. This is something university- and research-based intellectuals have traditionally been inept at, although television has produced a
new kind of communication-savvy intellectual – the pundit (see Nimmo
and Combs, 1992). Pundits are intellectuals who have 'popularized' themselves and learned to make their own ideas accessible to mass audiences.
But, in general, intellectuals do not communicate directly with mass
publics – leaving this up to the circulation intelligentsia.

Journalists and teachers are the communication specialists, tasked with
removing complexity, and making messages easily comprehensible and
(preferably) enjoyable – given that well-crafted communication ensures the
media attracts audiences, and pupils pay attention. To be effective they
should be good storytellers. One technique deployed to make communication more accessible and enjoyable is the invention of 'great people' and
'celebrities' because this serves to concretize and simplify ideas down to
'tangible' individuals (see chapter 8). Another involves scripting gripping
journalistic narratives by deploying emotive language and role labels –
e.g. 'well respected', 'justice', 'democratically elected', 'the people', 'heroic',
'victims', 'brutal', 'regime', 'extreme', 'fanatic', 'racist', 'cruel', 'repression'
and so on (see chapter 4). Effectively, sensationalist language – which often
encodes binary oppositions and selective self-righteous indignation –
reduces the amount of energy audiences must invest to interpret stories.
This increases mass audience appeal. In the process, the circulation intelligentsia often inadvertently add additional layers of connotative meaning
to the worldviews being presented to their audiences. This process of

two-step communication can ironically serve to make belief systems more intensely 'felt' by mass adherents than by the people who originally invented the beliefs. These feelings appear to be greatly enhanced when emotive language is combined with powerful images (e.g. television).

Despite sometimes adding connotations, journalists and teachers are not involved in creating *new* ideas. Rather, they are engaged in *two-step communication* – popularizing, naturalizing and circulating other people's ideas. Because they are not 'ideas people', they necessarily acquire the worldviews they promote from elsewhere – i.e. they interpellate themselves into signification systems (worldviews) intellectuals have already manufactured. The three most common sources of such worldviews are: attending university courses; on-the-job socialization; and consuming other media. Journalists are renowned copycats – they constantly develop storylines by watching what other journalists produce. Hence much of what the second-tier intelligentsia produces encodes intertextual readings – ideas borrowed (often unconsciously) from other texts/sources. Effectively, journalists and teachers interpellate themselves into already existent worldviews. Commonly, the circulation intelligentsia are socialized into accepting whatever discourses and practices (i.e. '-isms') are dominant and/or fashionable at the time of their university education. Once socialized, they become (often unconscious) missionaries for whatever worldview they have been interpellated into – e.g. journalists produce media content through a process of selection and emphasis based upon their existing beliefs (i.e. the coding system they have been interpellated into). This is where PRs/spin-doctors enter the picture – it is their job to understand these coding systems, and to try and use them to steer journalists (see 7.4 and 7.5 on p. 163 and p. 168). For example, military PRs have found it useful to 'piggy-back' upon discourses already possessing widespread currency among journalists – e.g. the pool of idealistic discourses born of the 'conscience mobilization' campaigns of 'social justice' NGOs like Amnesty International or Oxfam (see 10.3 on p. 221). Military PRs have found these 'idealisms' to be a great resource when mobilizing OECD populations for war and demonizing enemies. Essentially, mobilizing 'victimhood' discourses already fashionable in journalistic circles means that stories, promoted by military PRs, tend to receive little critical scrutiny from journalists. Stories are more easily 'placed' in the media if they confirm the worldviews that journalists have already internalized (Louw, 2001: 174).

Given the importance of the media and schools within hegemony building, it should come as no surprise that more direct controls are placed upon the circulation intelligentsia than is the case with university and research intellectuals. Editors exercise considerable control over media content, and teachers have no control over the curricula they teach. This is not to say that the circulation intelligentsia simply uncritically reproduce the dominant worldviews in their environments. Aberrant decoding and encoding are always possible – in fact, newsroom struggles against editorial control are common (see 4.5 on p. 82). However, editors have the final say. Also, editors will generally avoid hiring journalists with views radically outside the parameters acceptable within their organization. Another way of policing the discourses circulating in a society is to get the circulation intelligentsia to police themselves. This is partly a function of interpellating the circulation intelligentsia into 'appropriate' worldviews – i.e. exposing aspirant journalists and teachers to 'appropriate' discourses and practices during their training. Political power brokers can attempt (sometimes successfully) to incorporate into such training rules of 'discursive closure' – i.e. the next generation of circulation intelligentsia can be taught not to use certain terminology (e.g. 'political correctness'/PC). If the next generation of journalists and teachers can be taught to police themselves, a very effective form of discursive closure is achieved.

The circulation intelligentsia are central to turning worldviews into a mass phenomenon, and/or making worldviews hegemonically dominant in **mass societies**. Journalism's capacity to achieve this is not derived from the media's power to 'control' or 'manipulate' audience views in a simple stimulus–response way. Much research suggests that the media have no such 'directive' powers (Severin and Tankard, 1988: 323–4). Rather, their capacity to make worldviews hegemonic derives from what George Gerbner calls the *'cultivation' effect* (Gerbner et al., 1984) – influence comes from *repeated, long-term exposure to media storytelling* because embedded in these stories are worldviews. Viewers become gradually interpellated into these worldviews by a slow process of (drip-drip) absorbsion (Reep and Dambrot, 1989: 556). Gerbner's thesis suggests that over time the dominant worldview represented on mainstream television becomes hegemonic because of this cultivation effect. Clearly, political players cannot ignore this phenomenon – they necessarily must either find ways to develop symbiotic relationships with the media, or find other ways to influence or control media workers. The same is true of teachers because the same long-term cultivation effect can be observed in the education sector.

9.4 The functions of worldviews

Societies are huge agglomerations of human beings, held together by linguistic coding systems – effectively individuals within these agglomerations share the same 'pictures' in their heads; 'pictures' internalized as individuals are socialized into, and interpellate themselves into, the coding framework characterizing that social environment. Sometimes these agglomerations are consciously identifiable. Anderson (1991) called these 'imagined communities' – i.e. the members are consciously aware of the existence of their coding system as a community (e.g. a 'nation'). But sometimes, the signification system is not consciously recognized as a bounded 'community' because the codings become a taken-for-granted 'invisible community', – e.g. under the Pax Americana, neo-liberal values are being 'universalized' within the OECD through the rubrics of 'globalization', 'human rights' and so on.

Human agglomerations need some sort of 'glue' to hold them together. Coercion is one such 'glue' – used when aggregates of people are brought and held together against their wishes (e.g. conquest). More commonly, the 'glue' used is linguistic. Ruling groups build and entrench their control by deploying worldviews. If ruling groups can get the masses to interpellate themselves into these worldviews ('signification systems') then their rule and policies can become acceptable to the governed. Although such interpellation is never automatic, much can be done by ruling groups to routinize it as much as possible. The core function of any worldview is providing a fulcrum for constructing social rules, around which society can be organized. So building successful worldviews lies at the heart of any successful political process. Worldviews service political systems by:

- Creating the basis for legitimate governance – i.e. governance based upon consent. Interpellating the masses into 'signification systems' is the basis of organizing consent;
- Making possible the emergence of leadership. Leaders are effectively those able to construct 'visions' of the future, present and past (i.e. 'signification systems') which persuade the masses to follow them. Leaders provide 'conceptual maps' to 'orientate' the masses;
- Providing 'explanations' of the world and 'guides for action'. Worldviews help people to orientate themselves – by providing sets of pre-coded values that reduce the complexity of the world, and so reduce the number of decisions and choices individuals need to make. Many people find that immersing themselves into pre-coded explanations (worldviews) provides comfort, security and reassurance. Political systems constructing such 'comfort zones' for their masses can stabilize themselves for considerable periods of time;
- Providing fulcra into which citizens can be 'incorporated' (Hall, 1977: 331). Worldviews make it possible to conceptualize oneself, others and the relationship between oneself and others. This facilitates imagining 'group coherence' (1977: 340) and 'belongingness', which is the basis of all political entities. One example is the circulation of stories ('history') creating us–them dichotomies. Citizens are often interpellated into (conceptual) relationships with 'others' where others are deemed threatening.

Whether these threats are real or imagined, 'otherness' remains a useful 'bonding mechanism' around which to construct political communities. In this regard, Edelman (1964: 16–18) sees rituals and myths as mechanisms of incorporation. Edelman suggests that rituals, as 'motor activities that involve participants in a common symbolic enterprise' (e.g. ceremonies, voting, and routinized watching of television news), are powerful vehicles for ('concretely') embedding citizens into group identities and mythologies. Humans appear to derive considerable emotional satisfaction from belonging to groups. Political players work to incorporate people into groups they construct, rather than have them incorporated into opposition groups;

- Making it possible for social agglomerations to reproduce themselves (Hall, 1977: 335) by incorporating new generations into existing signification systems, or by reinventing signification systems in response to contextual changes;
- Serving to stabilize human agglomerations through proving chains of linguistic continuity into which successive generations are interpellated. Both these chains of signification, and the processes of being socialized into these chains, function within a process of double naturalization – they naturalize existing social relationships and naturalize the processes of interpellation/socialization itself;
- Masking and displacing social, economic or political domination (1977: 337). Worldviews 'explain' (and 'justify') wealth and power differentials, hence facilitating the continued governance by ruling elites;
- Providing a mechanism for steering mass behavior by arousing, placating or reassuring them, or by suggesting they are threatened (Edelman, 1964: 12–13).

The management of worldviews is an important activity for political elites. Those most successful at managing social discourses and practices tend to become hegemonically dominant. This involves political players learning to manage their relationships with intellectuals and the circulation intelligentsia. Ultimately, all political players attempt to portray their own belief systems and policies as inherently superior, and their worldviews as more just and civilized than their opponents. Generally, political policies are open to some measure of debate and review, but belief systems are less subject to scrutiny – i.e. beliefs tend to exist as 'givens' into which people are interpellated. In fact, ideologies function most effectively when they are precisely opaque and operate unconsciously – i.e. for those 'inside' a worldview, their belief system is taken for granted. Naturally, the most comfortable situation for a political player is when their belief system has become mainstream (dominant and naturalized). Thereafter, their task simply becomes one of enmeshing their proposed policies with such naturalized belief systems, since this reduces the scrutiny such policies will receive. The contemporary tendency in the Anglo world towards two-party systems, where little difference exists between the two parties, is the outgrowth of one worldview becoming so dominant that no political player wants to be seen as straying too far from the mainstream.

Ultimately, the fate of any signification system will be strongly connected to its relationship to the governing elite in that context. The emergence and growth of any belief system is a function of encoding possibilities – i.e. the availability of 'intellectual spaces' and funding. Governing elites are thus heavily implicated in facilitating the growth of new beliefs, knowledge and practices; strangling others; marginalizing some; and allowing others to flourish. Signification systems become successful when they are underpinned by power. Ruling elites may not determine what intellectuals produce but they set the parameters 'guiding' intellectual pursuits. As significantly, governing elites set the parameters of education policies that are instrumental in deciding which belief systems become the mainstream coding systems into which the next generation of schoolchildren are interpellated.

So worldviews become hegemonic thanks to symbiotic relationships between ruling elites, intellectuals and the circulation intelligentsia. For many embedded in this relationship, it is invisible; and dominant worldviews are simply taken for granted. But whether invisible or not, the impact of politics on the beliefs circulating (and not circulating) in any context are profound. Governing elites are in constant interaction with signification systems – they feed off those which they find useful; and encourage the birth, growth, marginalization and/or death of others. Radical belief system shifts are rare, but they help to illustrate the connectivity between political power and hegemonically dominant signification systems. Post-World War II Germany and Japan provide excellent cases – in both, former belief systems were consciously obliterated by occupation forces. In Japan and West Germany, liberal capitalism was imposed, while in East Germany communism was imposed. At such moments of radical change, worldviews are rendered visible, as are the processes by which politicians, intellectuals, journalists, teachers and other cultural workers legitimate some ideas; de-legitimate others; and build hegemonic dominance. A new belief system (and the ruling elite it serves) can be deemed secure when such 'visibility' ends and the 'new' worldview is rendered opaque to the majority of the mass public and as many of the circulation intelligentsia as possible. At that point, the hegemonic elite requires less coercion to remain dominant, and can rely primarily on teachers and journalists to naturalize its position.

Summary

You should now be familiar with the following key concepts and themes:

mass consent; ideology; hegemony; worldview; political socialization; 'pools of meaning'; intelligentsia; intellectuals; circulation intelligentsia; signification; intellectual agenda setting; coding systems as '-isms'; cultivation effect; dominant worldview; naturalized worldview; rendering worldviews opaque.

For further consideration

1 Can you unpack the elements of the 'pool of meaning' into which you were socialized?

2 Map out the roles the media, schooling and university have played in inducting you into the worldview you currently hold;

3 If journalists and teachers are part of the circulation intelligentsia, what are spin-doctors?

4 Identify the key features of the following worldviews: Western neo-liberalism and Islamic fundamentalism;

5 Compare the intellectuals and the circulation intelligentsia of: (a) Western neo-liberalism and (b) Islamic fundamentalism. What are the similarities and differences?

6 What is the role of a worldview in building hegemony?

7 Spin-doctors can use the worldviews already held by journalists to manipulate these journalists. Can you find examples?

8 What is the relationship between worldviews and celebrity politicians?

9 We are socialized into worldviews through storytelling. Find examples of journalism as storytelling which build or confirm a worldview;

10 If the Western coalition is to successfully 'stabilize' Iraq they will need the collaboration of local intellectuals, journalists and teachers. See how much information you can find on what the Western coalition is doing in this regard.

Selling War/Selling Peace

Chapter 10 examines how the media became increasingly implicated in fighting wars during the twentieth century. It is argued that warfare passed through three phases during the twentieth century, namely, (1) wars involving industrialized mass killing which necessitated the development of propaganda machines to legitimate such warfare; (2) the de-legitimation of warfare by the Vietnam War; (3) the re-legitimation of war by the PR-ization of warfare. Chapter 10 begins by examining the three phases of warfare. Special attention is paid to the techniques of propaganda developed during World Wars I and II. Thereafter attention is turned to the impact of television on warfare and the techniques of PR-izing televised warfare. Attention is also paid to how the selling of peace is an adjunct to the selling of warfare. Chapter 10 extends a number of themes developed in Chapter 7.

Wars are nothing new; neither is the need to justify using violence; persuading people to fight in wars; and legitimating the outcomes of victories (i.e. peace). However, three developments did change warfare and the conduct of persuasion and propaganda:

- Industrialization;
- The emergence of mass media;
- The emergence of mass democracies.

Although these phenomena emerged during the nineteenth century, it was during the twentieth century that they produced new genres of warfare and propaganda, first seen in World War I. During the twentieth century, the relationship between warfare; media portrayals of wars; and attempts to build mass consent for political violence have passed through three phases:

- The emergence of mass killing machines requiring mass consent and cannon fodder;
- Vietnam makes warfare unpopular;
- Re-legitimizing war through PR-ization.

10.1 The era of mass consent for mass killing

Industrialization changed warfare because it produced highly effective killing technologies. Killing could be mass produced. The earliest effects of this – i.e. high casualties – were seen in the American Civil War. However, World War I was the first fully industrialized war. Kill rates were extraordinarily high, generating the need for an on-going resupply of soldiers. This required propaganda machines to build patriotism, maintain morale, and keep up the flow of volunteers:

> To enable the war to go on, the [British] people had to be steeled for further sacrifices, and this could not be done if the full story of what was happening on the Western Front was known. And so began a great conspiracy. More deliberate lies were told than in any other period of history, and the whole apparatus of the state went into action to suppress the truth … The willingness of the newspaper proprietors to accept this control and their co-operation in disseminating propaganda brought them rewards of social rank and political power. (Knightley, 1982: 64)

The USA ran a similarly successful propaganda operation.

Knightly notes that propaganda is as old as *The Art of War*, a classic book on strategy written by the Chinese General Sun-Tzu 2400 years ago. But World War I saw the first *systematically* organized mass-propaganda machines. The British led the way. So why did the early twentieth century see the first systematic mass propaganda? The answer lies in the emergence of liberal democracy. Once mass populations were enfranchised, waging war required popular consent. Building World War I propaganda machines was part of the wider growth of early twentieth-century PR as a mechanism to manage and steer the enfranchised masses (Ewen 1996: 60–5). Essentially, in mass democracies, conducting warfare requires whipping up mass public support for war, so citizens will sacrifice their lives and pay taxes to fund wars. This is what underpinned government-directed mass-propaganda techniques, using the mass media to mobilize the masses during World War I. This said, World War I was not the first time mass media were used to whip up popular support for war, because the US press was used to generate mass war hysteria during the 1898 Spanish-American War; and the first fake propaganda newsreel dated back to the 1899–1902 Boer War (Young and Jesser, 1997: 28). William Randolph Hearst's 1898 'private' use of his newspapers to whip up popular support for war with Spain demonstrated the mass media's warmongering potential within mass democracies. Hearst's model for promoting war among mass publics was institutionalized with Government propaganda machines during World War I.

World War I's propaganda machines were concerned with agenda setting – the information made available to the masses was carefully managed and 'appropriate' discourses circulated. The masses were interpellated into worldviews making them prepared to sacrifice their lives. This information management consisted of three parts: eliminating negative news; hyping up positive news; and providing the masses with both heroes and narratives which built us–them binary oppositions and aroused patriotism. The mechanisms developed controlled information flows and censored material deemed unhelpful to the war effort. Simultaneously, positive information was deliberately manufactured. Although this included outright lies, much of this information simply consisted of emphasizing positive issues (i.e. ensuring that 'good news' was widely publicized) or putting a positive spin onto stories. Effectively, journalists were fed 'a line'. This was an early form of PR, in which the mass (print) media became complicit in circulating stories the military wanted the mass to receive. The propaganda machines also produced pro-war newsreels; provided heroes (a form of celebrity) and role models with whom the masses could identify; and circulated stories demonizing the enemy – 'proving' they were a threat and evil.

10.1.1 Britain's World War I propaganda

Many patterns set during World War I have simply been replicated in subsequent wars. The most effective World War I propaganda machine was Britain's. Britain's machine was subsequently copied by the USA's Committee on Public Information (CPI); and by the Germans in World War II (Knightley, 1982: 66). A key problem confronting Britain's World War I propagandists was switching British allegiances from Germany to France. A long-standing history of British–French conflict existed; whereas British–German sentimental ties were strong. This had to be turned on its head in 1914 – former friends had to be demonized and former enemies rehabilitated.

To achieve this, the propagandists systematically propagated the idea of German war guilt – successfully convincing Britons that Germany started the war (Bramsted, 1965: xx). The ability to create and sustain such a myth so impressed Goebbels that he made a special study of Britain's World War I propaganda, and ultimately used Britain's approach to construct the Nazi Ministry of Propaganda. But Britain's propagandists went beyond the guilt-myth. They set about systematically propagating atrocity stories to demonize Germans (Knightley, 1982: 67). In consequence, the war was made to seem both just and essential – propaganda convinced the British and Empire masses Germany was a menacing aggressor, to be defeated at any cost. The war was transformed, in the public mind, into a 'crusade for civilization' (Haste, 1995: 106).

Significantly, Britain's World War I propaganda machine deployed some of the country's most talented writers and communicators, e.g. H.G. Wells, John Buchanan, Rudyard Kipling, Hugh Walpole and Lord Northcliffe (1995: 109). The idea of conscripting such people has subsequently been copied by others. Britain operated both a censorship system and a propaganda delivery system targeted at both Britain and the Empire. Journalist access to the front-lines was controlled, and their stories censored (Knightley, 1982: 80–1). Propaganda was disseminated throughout the Empire under the aegis of the Newspaper Proprietors' Association and Reuters. This was geared towards making the war seem heroic and glorious in order to sustain the flow of volunteers. The British also ran propaganda operations directed at the USA (because of significant pro-German sentiment in the USA) and at the enemy. Ultimately, Britain's propaganda machinery was stunningly successful. Grant (1994: 11–12) suggests it was so successful that this machine was responsible for the way the term 'propaganda' changed its meaning. Before World War I, 'propaganda' (born of the Catholic Church's 'Congregation of the Propaganda' missionary activities) did not have an especially pejorative connotation. However, during the 1920s the publication of memoirs and exposés made Britons aware they had been duped and manipulated. This produced a great unease with propaganda – and the negative connotation was born. Not surprisingly, Anglo democracies no longer officially run propaganda operations – they have been re-badged as **psy-ops** (psychological operations) (see Taylor, 1997: 150). Psy-ops were given a major boost by the cold war, with the establishment of the Psychological Warfare Center at Fort Bragg in 1952 (1997: 165). Fort Bragg remains a key center of US psy-ops expertise.

10.1.2 USA's World War I propaganda

When, in 1917, America created its World War I propaganda machine – the CPI – many features of Britain's machine were copied. The CPI drew together, under one organizational roof, the country's leading journalists, muckrakers, publicists, advertising professionals, novelists and academics (Jackall and Hirota, 1995: 137). This ensured the production of quality propaganda. Goebbels copied this model – building his World War II propaganda machine by drafting Germany's journalists, advertising professionals, filmmakers and so on into his Propaganda Ministry. South Africa's military's propaganda unit did the same thing during the 1980s' anti-apartheid struggle. CPI novelists and short-story writers produced a steady stream of pro-war features and articles for the US press, and CPI journalists wrote an endless supply of press releases. The CPI:

- Produced and distributed cartoons to deliver messages (Jackall and Hirota, 1995: 141);
- Learned to mould public opinion by creating 'front organizations' – e.g. the League of Oppressed Nations (1995: 155–8);
- Produced emotive photographic images, shown at exhibitions around the USA (1995: 141);
- Built an army of 75,000 people to deliver orchestrated speeches in movie houses (1995: 140);
- Produced a flood of emotive pro-war films (1995: 143–4). Used the seductive Christy Girls to suggest men prove their manhood by joining the military (1995: 141);
- Greatly accelerated 'placing news' in post-war America according to Jackall and Hirota (1995: 149);
- Generally sped up the development of PR techniques for steering mass public opinion.

The CPI successfully delivered to Americans a similar message to the one Britons were receiving: the war was necessary because it was a moral struggle against a cruel tyranny, barbarity and German imperialist expansion (1995: 149).

10.1.3 Goebbels

Britons and Americans may have developed impressive (and successful) propaganda machines during World War I, but Goebbels' Nazi propaganda machine was to outshine these. Goebbels initially copied the British and Americans, but ultimately took their techniques to new heights – delivering, in the process, millions of German supporters to the Nazi Party in the 1930s–40s. He was a true pioneer of deploying the latest communication technologies for mobilizing mass publics and became a master of mass politics and moulding public opinion through the mass media. Bramsted argues that Alfred Harmsworth (Lord Northcliffe) and Goebbels were the leading developers of twentieth-century mass propaganda. He notes that both these men shared a number of characteristics – both earned their spurs in mass popular journalism, not highbrow journalism; neither emerged from the old ruling class or bureaucracy. Both were self-made men who intuitively understood the 'masses' produced by industrialization. Both thought in terms of collectives, not individuals. Both intuitively understood how to tame and steer mass publics (1965: xiii).

Goebbels built his propaganda machine on the premise that the masses were manipulable because they were passive and mentally lazy, and so would allow themselves to be manipulated and led. He (successfully) used the principle of repeating simple ideas over and over again until they became taken-for-granted 'truths' (1965: 26–7). Goebbels' persuasive techniques also included a sophisticated understanding of what would nowadays be called 'niche target markets' (1965: 28), and the use of what would now be called public opinion research geared towards understanding different publics, and the best way to communicate with them (1965: 53–4). Goebbels also pioneered other techniques that subsequently became commonplace. He

- Organized election air-trips to enable Hitler to speak in four cities on one day (1965: 23);
- Built a pool of (trained) speakers who could be dispatched to any area where publicity was needed (1965: 73);
- Recognized the value of film, radio and newspapers to reach the masses;
- Made extensive use of newsreels to mould public opinion through deploying emotive imagery (1965: 67);
- Made cheap wireless sets available, and popularized their purchase, so radio could become a nation-building tool (1965: 74–5).

Goebbels mixed Le Bon's ideas on mass psychology with Machiavelli's tactics (1965: 43) – the masses were aroused through showmanship and spectacular smoke-and-mirrors performances. As Bramsted (1965: 22) suggests, Goebbels deployed the showmanship of America's Barnum circus. This was especially apparent in the mass rallies organized to promote Hitler's Fuhrer cult. These were gigantic carefully choreographed events, brilliantly staged managed to allow hundreds of thousands of participants to subsume themselves into semi-religious pageants (1965: 214–15). Goebbels used print media – posters and postcards – to advertise these rallies and draw the crowds (1965: 25). He was a master at using mixed media – deploying the entire spectrum of communication forms available in his day.

Goebbels was also impressed by how the British had controlled and censored the press to mould public opinion during World War I. Hence, he worked to get the German press under control. But not through direct censorship. Rather, intimidation and the use of regularized press conferences (1965: 89) were deployed. A Foreign Press Department – run by Professor Karl Bonner – existed within the Propaganda Ministry (Knightley, 1982: 204). This was a PR department, tasked with making the job of neutral journalists as easy as possible – including arranging their travel to war fronts. This Foreign Press Department made much of Germany's policy of no censorship – *freie berichterstattung* or freedom of reporting (1982: 204). Instead, journalists were controlled through being helpful (PR) or through subtle intimidation. Goebbels also conscripted journalists and photographers into the army's propaganda division, creating the *Propaganda Kompanien* or PKs (1982: 205). These PKs were dispatched to the front lines to report the war – they rode in tanks, flew in bombers, jumped with parachute troops and marched with the infantry (1982: 212). Because PKs were professional journalists and photographers they produced excellent quality news reports and war images as press releases. These were widely used by both German and foreign media outlets. While Germany was winning the war (accurate) PK news stories served to inspire Germans and promote Germany to outsiders as invincible. Once Germany began losing the war, the PK's were pressured to doctor their stories.

But the Germans were not the only ones to run propaganda operations during World War II – Britain and the USA did too.

10.1.4 Britain and the USA's
World War II propaganda

The British Ministry of Information faced an uphill battle during World War II precisely because British propaganda had been so effective during World War I, but then exposed during the 1920s. The US media, for example, would simply not believe any British information during the early years of World War II (Knightley, 1982: 212). Goebbels used this mistrust of British sources – even when Germany began losing the war, he persuaded Germans to dismiss negative reports as just British propaganda of the World War I variety. However, within Britain and the Empire, British propagandists successfully conveyed to their masses an 'appropriate' view of the war. Once again censorship was (successfully) deployed, as was manipulation of journalists. Significantly, during World War II, the British deployed a new method for handling journalists – the pool system (1982: 203). British journalists were selected by a ballot system to go to the front lines, where they were escorted by 'conducting officers' attached to military intelligence. Their stories were then pooled for use by all media.

This method for supervising journalists during warfare has become popular with contemporary liberal democracies.

During World War II the USA built a censorship machine and propaganda machinery which mobilized the USA's public relations expertise. Significantly, during World War II, news rather than views was censored – allowing media debate and criticism fostered the illusion that there was no censorship (Taylor, 1997: 107). Effectively, the USA integrated the manipulation of mass public opinion through propaganda and censorship into the very heart of conducting World War II. As General Eisenhower said in 1944: 'public opinion wins wars ... [and so] I have always considered as quasi-staff officers, correspondents accredited to my headquarters' (in Knightley, 1982: 299). The size of the US military's PR machine gives some indication of how seriously the US regarded the manipulation of public opinion: 'by late 1944 Allied PR headquarters in Paris had a staff and facilities to deal each week with 3 million words from nearly 1000 correspondents, plus 35000 photographers and 100,000 feet of newsreel film' (1982: 299). And that was simply the West European military sector – i.e. the main US military PR machine still operated from Washington where military communiqués were mass produced. The US built a competent propaganda machine, which media-savvy US generals used to promote not only the war, but also themselves. Generals Bradley and Patton turned themselves into celebrities by playing unashamedly to the media. They even deployed the media in their personal struggles (e.g. the Bradley–Monty struggle) (1982: 307–8). General MacArthur was especially adept at playing the media. Defeated in the Philippines, MacArthur fled to Australia where he was appointed UN South Pacific Commander. Having virtually no army, MacArthur turned to PR instead – setting up a PR team under his personal direction at his Brisbane headquarters. This PR team set about (successfully) promoting the idea of a great general at the helm of a great army, and popularizing his 'I shall return' (to the Philippines) hype (1982: 264). MacArthur also ran a tight censorship regime – all stories had to be cleared by censors, and any soldier under his command interviewed by a journalist was to be court-martialled. This censorship regime was to hide McArthur's inability to defend Australia, and his fall-back plans if attacked. And when MacArthur was involved in action, he made sure the media was there to see *him*. He became a celebrity because he controlled the image projected – at a Milne Bay (New Guinea) operation, which MacArthur used to promote himself, 'one Australian officer said he had not known there were so many photographers in the world' (1982: 265). As Knightley (1982: 266) points out, MacArthur's 'Hollywood-style publicity' proved very effective.

By World War II, the Americans had honed the techniques of censorship and PR in order to manipulate mass public opinion. They used this machinery to create the impression of a just and perfect America, led by geniuses who won the war without a single mistake being made (1982: 260–1). The media went along with this, convinced it was in the national interest (1982: 261). Ultimately, the media in Britain, the Empire and USA during World War II simply fell into line with the propagandists – they became willing accomplices in the game of manipulating the masses in order to make mass industrialized warfare possible:

> Thirty years later, Charles Lynch … accredited to the British Army for Reuters, grasped the nettle. 'It's humiliating to look back at what we wrote during the war. It was crap … We were a propaganda arm of our governments. At the start the censors enforced that, but by the end we were our own censors. We were cheerleaders. (1982: 317)

Significantly, one war correspondent has argued that censorship was the reason the military and media built up such a close relationship. Drew Middleton wrote: 'as long as all copy was submitted to censors before transmission, people in the field, from generals down, felt free to discuss top secret material with reporters … the military came to consider correspondents as part of the forces, and it is equally clear many correspondents felt the same way' (in Knightley, 1982: 299–300). This was one of the core differences during the Vietnam War – the removal of censorship meant that generals and everyone else became very wary about talking to journalists (1982: 300).

10.2 Vietnam: a televised non-censored war

The twentieth century produced killing machines with an insatiable appetite for cannon fodder. During both World Wars, and the Korean War, the US military communicatively managed their masses through (successful) 'communication operations' (i.e. propaganda/censorship). But during the Vietnam War things went wrong – America's propaganda machine failed to control the way the war was reported, and many Americans turned against the war. Vietnam showed Lippmann to be correct – failure to communicatively manage the masses in liberal democracies can generate serious hegemonic disruption.

So what made the Vietnam War different? Most significantly, the absence of military censorship. This meant that the military were wary of journalists. This translated into journalists knowing less about what was going on than had been the case in earlier wars, when officers took journalists into their confidence. To make matters worse, Vietnam began as a small exercise on the margins of America's world. Consequently, young journalists were dispatched to cover this war (1982: 348). So, one had in Vietnam young inexperienced idealists, recently trained in the professional ideology of 'watchdog journalism, and working for commercial media seeking sensational news'. John Mecklin, *Time*'s bureau chief in San Francisco, summed up the result – the journalists were inexperienced and unsophisticated, and their reporting was 'irresponsible' and 'sensationalized' (in Knightley, 1982: 346). Because many people in Vietnam were unhappy with the war, journalists could always find sources of information – they had no need to consult with a wide spectrum of sources and/or with official sources. So one had young inexperienced journalists, parachuted into a situation they did not understand, motivated by 'watchdogism', and intensely keen to use this war to boost their careers – not a recipe for good reporting. They also practiced pack-journalism – sitting around in bars together (1982: 391) and consulting the same sources. They did what journalists often do when confronted by complex foreign places – they herded together into expatriate communities of Westerners and invented 'closed-shop' interpretations (see Louw, 2001: 194). As Louw (2001: chapter 9) suggests, the reporting of foreign contexts is often flawed. Vietnam was a case in point – as illustrated by the fact that the US hid the Cambodian War from journalists for over a year. Interestingly, in the early stages of the war, US editors, aware of their own journalists' limitations, preferred to believe official versions offered by Pentagon PRs, not their own staffers' stories (Knightley, 1982: 344). This PR version was propaganda, and so was as distorted as the sensationalist stories filed from Saigon. Ultimately, this illustrates the problem with reporting warfare and political violence – because there are two sides who feel strongly enough to kill each other, everybody will also be involved in disseminating misinformation and propaganda, and engaged in trying to manipulate journalists. At least some of the time, someone will be successful. Hence, just because Pentagon propagandists failed to control the Vietnam news agenda, does not mean that 'the truth' was reported.

But that still does not explain why the media's coverage of Vietnam had such an impact on the US masses. In part, this occurred because Vietnam was the first televised war. Every evening emotive images of dead and bloodied soldiers were beamed into American homes. Vietnam became a communications disaster for the US military. Because they failed to manage the news agenda, a large proportion of America's masses turned against the war. Significantly, the US policy elite were not united about fighting this war. Growing mass discontent, fueled by negative televisual images, served to exacerbate the struggles between the policy makers, and bolstered the position of 'dove' policy makers wanting to end the war. The military establishment discovered that negative television images made it harder for them to manage Washington's policy-making machinery – and in the end 'dove' policy makers triumphed over the 'hawks'. This policy defeat generated a shift in military thinking about the conduct of warfare in the televisual age (Young and Jesser, 1997: 275).

The US military believed it learned two lessons from the Vietnam War. Firstly, if anti-war consciousness develops among one's own civilians, the war will be lost because political pressure grows to end the war (the so called Vietnam syndrome). Secondly, television images can promote anti-war consciousness, and/or can disrupt the legitimacy of using coercion. Further, if war is not carefully PR-ized, television images of the war have the capacity to destabilize the legitimacy of hegemonic orders. The military went as far as blaming television for losing the Vietnam War because television was unable to deal with the complexity of warfare. Instead, the immediacy of television left viewers with negative 'impressions' and 'emotions' (MacArthur, 1992: 82). Hallin (1986: 213) suggests that blaming television for losing the war is simplistic, because television coverage was only one element in the process leading to the collapse of America's 'will to fight'. Hallin's (1986) examination of media content also demonstrated that US media coverage of the Vietnam War was far from uniformly negative. Nonetheless, negative television coverage did impact on Washington's policy-making process by strengthening the hand of the anti-war policy makers (see chapter 12). The outcome was the growth of a new PR-ized genre of warfare developed by the military as a strategic response to the perception of General Westmoreland (1980: 555), US commander in Vietnam, that television coverage of the war produced an inherently distorted perspective.

The US military's belief that television caused their defeat is an exaggeration. However, undoubtedly television is a problem for those employed by ruling hegemonies to deploy coercion (i.e. the military and police). A key problem is that the immediacy of television images makes such images appear unmanipulated. Television viewers get the impression that they are actually privy to what is going on – i.e. TV images seem real. But television images are manufactured. Viewers only get to see what the camera was pointed at, not what was behind the cameraman or what happened when the camera was turned off. They do not see what was edited out, or the countless other gatekeeping decisions. As Knightley (1982: 381–3) notes: television images of warfare (or other news for that matter) do not portray 'reality' (or a 'fair' unbiased perspective on the war); they just seem to convey such a 'reality'. And when conflict and violence is involved, television is almost guaranteed to skew the portrayal of such news. So although television may not have been to blame for America losing the Vietnam War, it contributed to the doves winning the policy debate. Media coverage of the Tet Offensive was a PR disaster for the US military. Tet undermined support for the war and undercut the credibility of military briefings because 1967 US military briefings said the US had almost won the war. Then in 1968 the Vietcong launched massive attacks, including in Saigon (where US television journalists were on hand to record the resultant street-fighting). Tet was a PR disaster because:

- It generated television images of US military brutality;
- In these television images the Vietcong looked far from beaten (although ironically they were militarily in a very weakened state);
- It led to discussion of Vietnamese civilian support for the Vietcong – i.e. the notion that the US was protecting Vietnamese civilians from communists was undermined;
- Tet was a case of bad timing – it occurring when the US ruling elite was internally divided. It may not have had the same negative impact earlier.

The US military took the lessons of Tet to heart and set about ensuring such a PR disaster would not happen again – i.e. they learned to public relations-ize warfare, and to pay serious attention to curtailing negative television images from reaching the public. The Pentagon decided that if they could not institute a system of censorship, then they would need to become hyper-effective PR practitioners instead.

10.3 The PR-ization of warfare

After Vietnam, the US military (and Nato) were concerned with the media's impact on waging war. This resulted in warfare being media-ized and PR-ized. Each war involving Anglo-Americans since Vietnam – the Falklands (1982), Grenada (1983), Panama (1989), the Persian Gulf (1990), Somalia (1992–3), Bosnia (1992–5), Haiti (1994), Kosovo (1999), Timor (1999), Afghanistan (2001) and Iraq (2003) – has seen the military become increasingly sophisticated hegemonic agents, skilled at both killing people and using the media (especially television) as powerful tools of warfare.

The first step in learning to PR-ize warfare happened by accident in 1982. Britain's campaign to recapture the Falklands from Argentina involved dispatching a task force to a remote and isolated location. To cover this war, the British media sailed with the expeditionary force. They effectively became part of Britain's military's PR machine because they were within a 'closed' deployment, 'trapped' on naval ships and dependent upon the military for getting information, for dispatching their stories and indeed for their survival. The military saw how the media could be corralled and hence controlled.

The Falklands became a testing ground for media control (Young and Jesser, 1997: 277). Hence when the USA invaded Grenada to overthrow its government in 1983, the military applied a media-management policy derived from the Falklands lesson – they simply excluded the media from the island effectively creating a news blackout. When four Western journalists reached the island they were arrested and removed (1997: 129). US military PRs released televisual images of the Grenada war which, in absence of other material, were used. For the US military Grenada was a PR-coup, demonstrating they could block negative television images. But Grenada was a small insignificant island easily sealed off from the world. The question was: could this strategy (for depriving the media of 'negative' images) be successfully applied to larger and less isolated theaters of war? The 1989 campaign to change Panama's government demonstrated that the US military could manage the media in non-island contexts. During this war 'news was not actively censored, but passively censored by ensuring lack of access and delay' (1997: 148). Towards the end of the conflict, this media management unraveled because Noriega was not captured as quickly as planned. However, an important feature of the Panamanian campaign was the successfully demonization of Noriega (a difficult task given that Noriega was previously a US ally). This moved the PR-izing of war another step forward.

By 1990 the US military had developed a new model of media-ized warfare in which PR and psy-ops were central features of the planning and execution of the war. As Engelhardt says of the 1990 Gulf War: it was 'the war to reestablish war' (1994: 92). War was once more going to be made to 'appear' acceptable, even in highly media-ized societies. Essentially, all the lessons learned since Vietnam were brought to bear on the Gulf War – war was organized differently to both exclude negative television images, and legitimate one's own coercive actions. As Young and Jesser (1997: 280) say, the Gulf War was constructed in accordance with the 'primacy of politics' – i.e. alliance and legitimacy considerations were as important as military issues.

So the Gulf War was meticulously planned and organized as a media (and psy-ops) operation. Young and Jesser (1997: 292–4) describe these new media-ized wars as involving the following. Long-term forward planning now includes significant media and political/hegemonic strategizing. Warfare planning builds media concerns into its core. Opposition leaderships are demonized in preparation for the war. In fact demonization is usually a good indication that war is coming. And given the strong 'individualist strand' in Anglo thinking, such demonization tends to involve creating identifiable villains, e.g. Saddam Hussein and Slobodan Milosevic. This villainization process often involves associating the person with Hitler as folk-devil – a trend initiated in Noriega's removal from power. Demonization is often accompanied by identifying refugees and exile groups and promoting them as future alternative governments. Demonization also involves the selective portrayal of history, especially where intervention is made on one side of a civil conflict (e.g. Kosovo). The target regime will be destabilized, embarrassed and made to look unreasonable and irrational through political, economic and diplomatic maneuvers.

In addition to vilifying the enemy, binary opposition logic necessitates creating 'victims' to be saved from the villain. Finding 'victims' to 'save' has become an important device for justifying using violence against foreigners. Military PRs have found it useful to 'piggy back' upon NGO 'victimhood' and 'humanitarian' discourses that already have widespread currency with Western journalists – propaganda is more easily 'placed' in the media if it confirms existing journalistic bias and/or fits their news 'frame'. Further, much energy is expended to create public approval and declarations of support for action against the target – e.g. 'flag nation' allies are enlisted, and legitimacy sought from the UN and regional political groupings. (These are achieved through diplomatic lobbying and economic inducements.) The media is targeted with a view to creating public approval for action. The deployment of troops involves building up overwhelming superiority in numbers and firepower to ensure quick victory. This deployment will include media exclusion from the deployment zone. The media will be corralled and managed throughout the actual war. Media manipulation and deception will be practiced, with military PRs providing good televisual images. As soon as possible after the war, the military withdraws and hands over to the UN, a regional grouping or a new government created from former opposition groups, exiles and so on.

The 1990 Gulf War set the pattern for this new PR-ized genre of warfare. To begin with, Saddam Hussein (a former US ally) was demonized – the media being co-opted into this demonizing process. 'Flag nation' allies were brought on board to legitimate US deployment – Arab allies were especially desirable, and induced to join the alliance through having their debts written off. Once military deployment began, the media were corralled and managed. Journalists were formed into 'pools' far removed from the battlefront, where military PRs fed them information. Pool journalists were only granted access to strictly controlled events. Censorship was achieved through denial of access to military engagement, and news blackouts at the start of the war. All interviews had to be conducted in the presence of military escorts, and all copy and images cleared by the military before transmission. Military PRs ensured that a 'flow of favorable military sourced information to fill the vacuum created by media restrictions. Material ranged from information provided at carefully controlled briefings which bypassed journalists on the spot, all the way to carefully sanitized television coverage of high technology weaponry in action' (Young and Jesser, 1997: 280). Military spokesmen were auditioned and selected for their 'media presence'. The media was stage-managed, manipulated and lied to, and they believed the lies (Taylor, 1992: 220–1). The media became a vehicle through which 'the government and the military made direct approaches to the public through the immediacy of television' (Young and Jesser, 1997: 191) – television became a tool for legitimating violence. For the US military, the Gulf War was a tremendous success – they asserted US hegemony over the Gulf region; developed new networked ('coalition') command systems; and not only turned the media into propaganda tools (through deploying PR/psy-ops), but seemingly got journalists to enjoy being co-opted by the military (MacArthur, 1992: 227–9).

A crucial dimension to the military's perception of waging media-ized warfare is the creation of media events that appear as bloodless as possible, so war can be made 'acceptable'. This is based upon a belief that televised images of blood (during the Vietnam War) caused American public opinion to swing against warfare.

Consequently, military PRs aim to sanitize war, 'portraying it as a low risk Nintendo game ... Military-PRs also reflects the American penchant for the upbeat, the happy endings, with a minimum of groans, blood, and deaths' (Pinsdorf, 1994: 49). At heart, creating Nintendo warfare means working to exclude images of dead bodies, blood and brutality. This type of warfare has also seen the development of a new militaristic language aiming to mystify and obscure as much as possible. Taylor calls this the creation of a 'terminological fog' (1992: 45), such as using 'collateral damage' for civilian deaths; and 'sorties' for bombing. Words like 'dead', 'enemy' and 'war' are avoided. Brivio notes how a technical military language is deployed which 'uses acronyms and euphemisms to sterilize the horrors of war' (1999: 516). On the other hand, reports will be circulated of how the (now demonized) opposition uses brutality against their 'victims' (who are to be saved through the intervention).

But PR-izing warfare goes beyond military PR units. Outside PR consultants are also hired by belligerents. In fact, the most spectacular PR success of the Gulf War was the work of a PR firm, CFK/H&K hired by the Kuwaiti Government. This firm arranged for a 15-year-old Kuwaiti girl to lie to a US Congressional Committee that she had witnessed Iraqi troops throw babies out of incubators (MacArthur, 1992: 58–9). The story was calculated to promote the 'Saddam as Hitler' notion, plus feed the need for 'victims' to rescue. This incubator story had an enormous impact on Anglo public opinion. And once planted, spread throughout the global media network. This served to legitimate aggression against Iraq. As importantly, the incubator story (as well as the 'oil-covered sea birds' story, whose plight was untruthfully blamed on Saddam's 'ecological terrorism'), had the effect of co-opting mainstream Anglo journalists into the anti-Iraq camp (since both stories were designed to generate outrage by violating those discourses with widespread currency among journalists). Once co-opted, journalists could be relied on to play the part as functionaries of the PR-ized war effort.

The PR-ized genre of warfare, perfected by the USA in the 1990 Gulf War, has been deployed in all subsequent Anglo wars – i.e. Somalia, Haiti, Bosnia, Kosovo, East Timor, Afghanistan and Iraq.

10.4 Nintendo warfare

The new genre of warfare has got much to do with technological developments. New media technologies not only changed socio-economic dispensations, but also impacted on how wars can be fought. During the 1980s the USA led the world in deploying networked computers as coercive tools. The US also led the way in developing 'smart' killing machines – enormous firepower can now be delivered to any part of the globe thus radically reducing the need for US ground combat. From World War II onwards the US has perfected the art of bombing – aerial technologies (bombers and missiles) are used to pulverize enemy forces and socio-economic (and moral) infrastructure from a safe distance before ground troops are actually committed. Adding digital communication technology to weaponry was a natural extension of this US style of warfare. This digitization of warfare played a role in the Soviet Union's collapse because it is an enormously expensive form of warfare. Partly as a response to trying to keep up with US military spending, the Soviets spent themselves into bankruptcy. By the mid-1980s, Gorbachev recognized that the Soviets were economically unable to sustain this form of warfare, and so effectively called an end to the cold war. From this was born the **New World Order** (NWO), founded upon a (highly digitized) US military machine (Louw, 2001: chapters 6 and 8).

The beauty of this digitized 'smart weapons' warfare is that it can make wars look clean if PRs mobilize it correctly. During the Vietnam War, high altitude aerial bombing lost its 'cleanness' when it became visually enmeshed with images of bloody ground combat. So although US aircrews were portrayed as skilled professionals, with no vindictiveness towards those they bombed (Hallin, 1986: 137), the overall impression of the war was of a bloody, dirty and messy affair. During the Gulf War this was not allowed to happen. Instead, military PRs used the Gulf's aerial warfare to 'create the impression of a "clean" techno-war, almost devoid of human suffering and death, conducted with surgical precision by wondrous mechanisms' (H.B. Franklin, 1994: 42). In place of blood and dead bodies were 'weapons counts' and the blowing up of 'inanimate things' like buildings and bridges (Engelhardt, 1994: 88).

In this media-ized 'hyperwar' what got lost were the physical effects of modern weapons on human beings (Taylor, 1992: 29). For those at the receiving end of bombing the effects are brutal; but when PRs do their job well, these new digitized techno-wars can be made to look like video-games. The very immediateness of media-ized wars is a powerful weapon for military PRs – because when viewers appear to have instantaneous access to real-time images, they seem more real and unmanipulated. The Gulf War, for example, generated the illusion that satellite-age television gave audiences real-time direct access to the action of wars. Because CNN covered the bombing of Baghdad 'the illusion was created that war was being fought out in full view of a global audience' (1992: 278), but this merely served to disguise the processes of selection, omission and propaganda actually taking place as well as disguise the fact that no real information was being provided by the spectacular 'lights show'. It also hid the fact that the real action on the Iraqi front and in Kuwait was not being shown. The Gulf War showed that television, when used well, can be a military PR's dream medium.

As societies informationalized and digitized, so OECD military strategists adjusted and PR-ized their thinking. Military PR and psy-ops machines became a growth industry. The PR machines created for events like the Gulf War are impressive. As Engelhardt (1994: 85) notes, these machines have to be able to organize around-the-clock, on-location support ('minders'/'handlers') for journalists allowed into the area of operations; manage thousands of journalists (allowed into the 'pools' and briefings); coordinate messages released at different sites around the world; schedule information releases to suit the routinized schedules of newsrooms (in many time zones); and provide high-quality images to feed television's need for on-going action. Military PRs have become highly skilled users of all the possibilities opened up by the latest media technologies. During the Gulf War, the military created a global PR machinery of scriptwriters, make-up artists, graphic designers and film editors to back up the performances of their generals-as-actors (Engelhardt, 1994: 86). The Pentagon was at the heart of orchestrating the script for the Nintendo war; the co-ordination and instantaneous sharing of the script and images was made possible by the global communication Net. During the Kosovo War a similar globally networked PR machine was developed, operating out of three centers – Washington, London and Brussels. This machinery developed spokesmen who could be credible digital performers – i.e. who could project the right televisual image, speak in appropriate sound-bites, and look the part of professional digital warfare warriors. In this regard, Generals Schwarzkopf and Powell certainly performed as skilled actors during the Gulf War. But nine years later during the Kosovo War, NATO opted instead for a 'civilian' spokesman, Jamie Shea. Shea was a skilled television performer (with a PhD in World War I propaganda).

During the 2001 Afghan War the Pentagon succeeded in maintaining the integrity of the PR-ized model of warfare, although the model had to be slightly rescripted. Following al-Qaeda's 9/11 terrorist attacks (see chapter 11), the Bush administration created a global 24-hour communications operation called the Coalition Information Center (CIC) with the brief to build public support for the war on terrorism. An interesting feature of the CIC's work was the use made of speeches by the US President's and British Prime Minister's wives, Laura Bush and Cherie Blair to build public support. The CIC ran offices around the world (including London, Islamabad and Kabul) and focused much attention on trying to get Muslims to support the war on terror (Maltese, 2003: 4). During the Afghan War, the USA produced and disseminated high-quality PR images of aircraft carriers, clean-cut young American aircrews and smart 'clean' weapons. Television images of high altitude bombers and *the distant* billowing of smoke and dust caused by huge explosions became the staple fare of the Afghan War. No civilian bodies, no blood, no images of the devastation caused by the cluster or daisy-cutter bombs, and no unhappy civilians *inside* Afghanistan. Journalists were almost completely denied access to US troops in the field (Hickey, 2002). However, an interesting new component to the CIC script was 'low tech' (humanized) images of Afghan Northern Alliance tanks, soldiers and cavalry against the backdrop of exotic-looking mountains and deserts. These (Islamic) Northern Alliance personnel were often shown in prayer. But still no images of blood – no hand-to-hand fighting, tank battles or images of Northern Alliance atrocities. Instead of bloody fighting, the West saw images of tanks driving around – which almost made war look like fun. And carefully crafted images of Northern Alliance ground forces had the added bonus of disguising the failure to enlist Muslim 'flag nation' allies. It also helped to create the image of the Northern Alliance as professional soldiers rather than as warlord militias. Ultimately, the televisual images deployed were examples of well-scripted PR, which the Western media accepted uncritically.

10.4.1 Selling the Iraq War

The USA planned the 2003 Iraq War in accordance with the PR-ized model of warfare, i.e.:

- Saddam Hussein was demonized. He was reported to be a threat to world peace because he possessed weapons of mass destruction (WMD) (itself a highly emotive spin-doctored term). A spurious rhetorical link was also made between Hussein and al-Qaeda. Through innuendo Hussein was 'linked' to the 'war on terror'. Although al-Qaeda/ bin Laden were intensely hostile to Hussein's secular regime, the spin-doctors successfully persuaded a majority of Americans that Hussein was implicated in the 9/11 terror attacks. They also got Americans to believe that Hussein had massive stockpiles of WMD;

- Attempts were made to mobilize refugees/exiles as an alternative government;
- War was justified by creating victims (Iraqi citizens) to be rescued from a villain (Saddam's tyrannical regime). The gassing of Kurds story was endlessly recycled (in decontextualized format) to hammer home this point;
- Overwhelming military superiority ensured US victory and massive US air-power was deployed to obliterate Iraqi forces, thereby minimizing US casualties;
- A clean high-tech 'Nintendo war' was scripted and presented to US/British/Australian publics by deploying sanitized language and minimizing images of death;
- Psy-ops techniques were extensively deployed.

In one respect only was the original PR-ized warfare model substantially modified in 2003, namely, 600 journalists were 'embedded' within US forces during the invasion of Iraq. These 'embeds' lived, worked and traveled with operational units. This essentially revived General Eisenhower's World War II media liaison strategy (Knightley, 1982: 299). Embedded journalists rely on soldiers for their security, and by experiencing the intense comradeship of warfare, come to identify with these troops. This turned World War II journalists into cheerleaders. The same thing happened in Iraq in 2003. Initially, the 2003 'embed' strategy was premised on a belief that US/UK troops would be welcomed as 'liberators' – the 'embeds' would facilitate images of surrendering Iraqi troops and happy Iraqi civilians. When this did not happen the Pentagon simply fell back upon PR media-management strategies. Firstly, the 'embeds' were relied upon to become so psychologically embedded with the troops that they would adopt and disseminate US/UK military's perspectives. The embeds did deliver a stream of sanitized and heroic images, tied to 'enthusiastic' voice-overs, often referring to US/UK forces as 'we'. The embed-management strategy was a great PR success story. Secondly, mainstream US/UK/Australian media were called upon to practice self-censorship, to avoid 'assisting' Iraq, and avoid demoralizing images, or blood and death imagery. The mainstream media complied. Mainstream US television went even further, and became 'patriotic'. Thirdly, military PRs produced a stream of high-quality material (including 'patriotic' imagery and 'backgrounders' stressing clean warfare/ precision weaponry) for the mass media. The mainstream US media uncritically accepted the spin-doctored line (see MacArthur, 2003; Mooney, 2004).

But the original PR-ized model did unravel in some respects, i.e.:

- The villain–victim model came under strain when the Iraqis failed to welcome 'US liberation'. However, once Iraqi law and order collapsed and Baghdad's underclass took advantage to loot and attack the old social hierarchy/order, the spin-doctors quickly resuscitated the villain–victim model;
- The US failed to build a successful flag nation coalition, partly because it failed to project a consistent justification for war. The first justification was Iraq's alleged involvement in global terrorism. This shifted to needing to destroy weapons of mass destruction; then shifted to calling for regime change (i.e. 'rescuing' Iraqis from Saddam); then shifted back to weapons of mass destruction when this was found to be resonating particularly well with US audiences and was deemed at least plausible in Europe;
- The original briefings system at Doha was unsuccessful when General Tommy Franks proved to be a poor media performer. Consequently, briefings switched to Washington (performed by Donald Rumsfeld), while General Vincent Brooks performed scaled-back Doha briefings.

The Pentagon also encountered a significant PR problem in the form of al-Jazeera satellite television (an Arabic-language service modeled on CNN). When other television networks withdrew from Baghdad (leaving remote control cameras on rooftops), al-Jazeera and the BBC remained. Al-Jazeera did not comply with Pentagon self-censorship requirements and broadcast imagery of dead, wounded and angry civilians, plus dead and captured US troops. Al-Jazeera's coverage in Arabic helped to fuel anti-American sentiments in the Arab world. Worse for the Pentagon, al-Jazeera signed up millions of new EU subscribers during Iraq 2003. However, despite PR problems outside the US/UK/Australian coalition, within the coalition countries, the spin-doctors successfully steered mass public opinion because US/British/Australian mass media audiences received a PR-managed, spin-doctored, sanitized and 'patriotic' version of the Iraq War. Consequently, as the war proceeded, support for it grew steadily in the coalition homelands. By the time Saddam's statue was toppled (as a well-executed PR event) and President Bush (prematurely) declared the war over (in another well-executed PR event), the coalition spin-doctors had every reason to feel pleased with how well they had steered their populations (and their mass media).

However, within months of the conventional war ending, the coalition spin-doctors began facing real PR challenges. Four issues, in particular, emerged as PR problems:

1   First, the failure to find any weapons of mass destruction (WMD) undermined the PR justification for launching the war. This became an especially serious problem for Tony Blair (see 7.3.6 on p. 159), but even Bush's administration experienced growing criticism from sections of the US Congress, Senate and media;

Bush-administration spin doctors responded in a number of creative ways:

(a)   Lowering the burden of proof as to what constituted a WMD-find, e.g. finding one truck equipped for chemical warfare research was described as proof of an Iraqi WMD program. Opinion polls revealed that Bush actually persuaded one-third of Americans that WMD had been found; while two-thirds (incorrectly) believed that the Iraqis used chemical/biological weapons during the war;

(b)   Creating plausible deniability by suggesting that Iraq destroyed WMD during or before the war; or smuggled WMD out of the country (to Syria);

(c)   Shifting the focus to the brutality of how Hussein's regime tortured its political opponents. Consequently, it was argued that even without WMD, Hussein was a tyrannical dictator, and replacing this tyranny with democracy was justification enough for war.

2   Second, an insurgency war broke out which undermined the original spin-doctored story that the US would be welcomed by the Iraqis as liberators. The spin-doctors responded in two ways:

(a)   Suggesting that the insurgents were a small minority of extremists and/or a few remnant Hussein-loyalists who were opposed to 'democracy';

(b)   Suggesting that the insurgency/terrorism 'proved' the Iraq war was part of the wider 'war on terrorism' – i.e. rhetorically linking Iraq to 9/11, which served to make the war more palatable to Americans.

3   PR-ized wars need to be short. With the emergence of an ever-worsening Iraqi insurgency war, the coalition was confronted with the prospect of a long war. As a result:

(a)   The Bush administration's PR machine lost the ability to control the images coming out of Iraq (unlike Afghanistan which was still well controlled). This forced the PR machine to constantly deal with negative images/stories that needed crisis spin-doctoring interventions;

(b) Coalition casualties mounted (as the insurgency claimed more lives than the original PR-ized war). This provided anti-war policy makers and journalists with material to exacerbate tensions within the Bush and Blair administrations;

(c) Opposition (among both US and British policy makers, the families of US servicemen, and civilians) began to emerge in the coalition homelands as the insurgency war intensified; casualties mounted; Iraqi (and Arab) opposition to the US occupation grew more vocal; and the refugees/exiles who had been touted as an alternative government looked ever less credible. This produced a host of possible anti-war sources interested in providing journalists with 'leaks', 'leads' and 'plants' (see 12.3.8 on p. 266). The longer the war went on the more the chances increased that a really damaging 'leak' would occur. It came in the form of images of brutal interrogations of Iraqis by US and British troops. The images planted with the British press proved to be forgeries, but the US images were not.

4   Images of US troops torturing Iraqis at Abu Ghraib Prison in 2004 undermined the villain–victim binary opposition that US spin-doctors had previously constructed, precipitating an enormous PR crisis for the Bush administration and its coalition allies. Abu Ghraib not only increased Iraqi (and wider Muslim) hostility to the USA's occupation of Iraq, but also bolstered anti-war factions within the coalition countries themselves, thereby increasing the likelihood of future negative 'leaks', 'leads' and 'plants'.

Abu Ghraib triggered a major Bush administration spin-doctoring exercise consisting of three interconnected elements:

- Unable to deny brutal interrogations had taken place, the spin machine engaged in blame-shifting – the abuse was blamed on a few 'rotten apples' who were scapegoated. The spin machine tried to create 'plausible deniability' – i.e. military command structures, and key decision makers in the Bush administration and occupation government in Iraq claimed they were not responsible for these interrogation methods;
- Publicity on those to be scapegoated painted a picture of people from poor socio-economic backgrounds who, as dysfunctional individuals, became monsters at Abu Ghraib. The scapegoats were effectively demonized, with the spin industry and mainstream media constructing them as 'scum' and 'un-American' – i.e. not representative of ordinary decent Americans who were struggling to bring democracy to Iraq;
- An attempt was made to salvage the shattered binary opposition between democracy (USA) and tyranny (Saddam's Iraq). President

Bush himself delivered the spin-doctor's script when saying there was a big difference between the horrors inflicted by Saddam Hussein and the actions of the US jailers because, although in a democracy not everything is perfect and mistakes are made, in a democracy mistakes are investigated and people are brought to justice.

The problem for the spin-doctors was that the USA has a highly visualized culture, and the Abu Ghraib images not only were extremely graphic and easy to remember, but undercut almost every aspect of earlier spin-doctored explanations for why the US had invaded Iraq. Hence Abu Ghraib precipitated an enormous PR crisis for the US military – a crisis as significant as that posed by the 1968 Tet Offensive television images. Abu Ghraib dramatically reduced support for the Iraq War among coalition populations, but it remains to be seen whether Abu Ghraib ultimately serves to undermine faith in PR-ized warfare in general, or merely results in military PRs learning valuable lessons which results in their spin-doctoring becoming even more sophisticated.

10.5 Selling peace

Peace is the absence of war/conflict. Peace is 'established' by a functioning hegemony – one not seriously challenged by anyone (internally or externally). Power grants one the ability to have one's interests prevail over others, and the ability to prevent oppositional agendas from even being raised. Ultimately, wars are fought over who will be hegemonically dominant, who will have the power to impose peace terms and prevent opposition terms from even being raised. Wars end when hegemony is established, and all parties to the conflict accept who will henceforth be dominant.

Wars have to be sold to mass publics. So too does 'peace' – i.e. the victors must establish, secure and stabilize their peace by:

- Legitimating their rule, leadership and worldviews;
- Negotiating deals and partnerships (i.e. building hegemonic alliances);
- Normalizing and legitimating the coercive (policing) machineries required to stabilize their governance.

Victors write both the peace terms and the history – producing explanations about why they won, and why their hegemony is necessarily better than their opponent's would have been. Binary oppositions and mythologies codified by propagandists during war are naturalized and popularized by victors after the war, through the mass media, popular cultural forms and schooling. Immediately after wars, 'peace' must usually be coercively imposed on the vanquished (e.g. post-1945 occupations of Germany and Japan). But over time, coercive levels can be reduced, as the new hegemonic order sells itself – i.e. legitimates and naturalizes its victory, discourses, practices and worldviews. In the absence of clear victors/vanquished, 'peace' requires negotiating/building joint coercive mechanisms with sufficient legitimation in both camps to end the conflict (e.g. South Africa's post-apartheid Government of National Unity). But building successful long-term hegemony requires stabilizing new post-war discourses and practices, and/or interpellating citizens into new worldviews (see chapter 9), new identities (see chapter 5) and new hegemonic arrangements. The masses must be convinced that post-war distributions of power, wealth and status (i.e. new winners and losers) are legitimate. If such legitimacy is not achieved, on-going violence will be needed to create 'peace'. 'Peace' is created by:

- Making post-war hegemonies legitimate in order to reduce the coercion required. This may necessitate actively de-legitimating earlier hegemonic arrangements, worldviews and leaderships. It always necessitates selling new hegemonic arrangements, leaderships and accompanying worldviews;
- Coercively imposing hegemonic order on the vanquished;
- Convincing groups unhappy with the new hegemonic order they have little option but to accept the existing 'peace'. The third option involves persuasion underpinned by coercion.

A new kind of 'peace' emerged after the cold war – when one state (the USA) became globally dominant because it faced no serious contenders. This produced the Pax Americana. Because US power has been so overwhelming since 1989, Anglo-American political discourses and practices came to predominate within the New World Order (NWO) – i.e. America's model of governance and Anglo-American values were effectively naturalized into a **'pan-human universalism'** (Greenfeld, 1993: 446). From US global hegemonic dominance is coalescing a Pax Americana. In those parts of the globe where the Pax Americana lacks legitimacy, US military power is substituted. Significantly, the USA has preferred not to project such power alone; opting to deploy 'coalitions' built around a US node (because such coalitions are easier to legitimate within the PR-ized warfare model).

A new model of war and peace emerged under the NWO. Previously, 'peace' terms were worked out after the war. Now they are worked out before the war begins, because US power is so overwhelming that it can decide (almost unilaterally) the desired outcomes and impose them.

Effectively, the Pax Americana (as a 'pan-human universalized' worldview) has become a pre-encoded, taken-for-granted outcome of NWO wars. Hence, the difference between the military (as external enforcers) and police (as internal enforcers) begins to blur; as does the boundary between US internal sovereignty and US capacity to project its hegemonic order externally. This blurring is most clearly seen in the evolution of 'peacekeeping'.

Since World War II, 'peacekeeping' has passed through five phases:

1   *Phase one* involved the USA successfully getting the UN to intervene in Korea (thanks to a Soviet diplomatic blunder) after forces from the northern Soviet communist zone invaded the southern US zone. During the Korean War (1950–3), a UN coalition force, under US leadership intervened to maintain a cold war 'peace'/division of Korea;

2   *Phase two* (1954–78) saw the UN deploy peacekeeping forces to stabilize situations born of US–Soviet cold war conflicts. Phase two 'peace operations' were characterized by 'consent building, impartiality, and minimum use of force, and were deployed as interdisposition forces between previously warring parties' (Fiedler, 2000: 18);

3   *Phase three* (1978–88) represented a transition period when (as Soviet power declined) the UN no longer had to mount new peacekeeping operations;

4   *Phase four* (1989–2002) was a period of UN intrusiveness – the UN no longer interdisposed itself between warring parties to 'keep the peace'. Instead, the UN acted to change political landscapes in accordance with its *Agenda for Peace*. This *Agenda* authorized UN violence in the form of armed coalitions led by the major powers, as long as the UN Security Council authorized these (Fiedler, 2000: 14). Effectively, when the USA secured Security Council agreement, it could (by invoking Chapter 8 of the UN Charter), use the UN to militarily 'secure' an area and impose NWO political agendas (Kuhne, 2001: 378–9). The consent of actors in targeted states was no longer required. The absence of such consent means peacekeepers have three options (Fiedler, 2000: 68) – to:

(a)   Allow (or assist) one side to defeat the other;
(b)   Maintain the status quo;
(c)   Intervene to overpower both sides, and impose a settlement.

Phase four saw each of these used to further NWO agendas. Essentially, phase four saw UN ('flag nation') coalitions (under US leadership) impose 'NWO peace'. During this phase, the sovereignty of states could be trumped by the UN's 'human rights' agenda (Fiedler,

2000: 23–4) which was effectively derived from Anglo-American values. During phase four, these values were naturalized into a 'pan-human universalism' within NWO's multilateral-system of global governance (resting upon a mutating mix of US military alliances, the WTO, World Bank, UN and World Court);

5   A new mechanism for imposing 'NWO peace' emerged in 2003 – a shift away from 'UN peacekeeping coalitions' to unilateral US interventionism. When the UN Security Council failed to endorse US plans for enforced Iraqi 'regime change' the USA bypassed the UN and assembled a 'coalition of the willing' to launch a war on Iraq in 2003 to unilaterally impose the Pax Americana. This signaled a shift away from the multilateral system of global governance constructed by the USA after World War II. However, this proved to be a temporary shift because, when the USA ran into difficulties in Iraq, the multilateral peacekeeping approach was restored.

The Iraq War did much to render the relationship between the NWO and US global hegemony (Pax Americana) transparent. During phase four, 'UN peacekeeping' meant the imposition of NWO 'peace'/governance onto communities out of step with the dominant NWO worldview (e.g. Bosnia, Kosovo/Yugoslavia and Afghanistan). The Iraq War did the same. Phase four 'peacekeeping' and Iraqi 'regime change' were thus one and the same thing – both were closer to policing than to conventional warfare; because both involve incorporating 'problem areas' back into the NWO mainstream and imposing NWO law and order/'peace' upon 'problem' populations. Both sought to implant a USA governance model; install government personnel 'acceptable' to Washington; and remove from power former leaders (often criminalizing them). These actions were legitimized and sold to US and allied mass publics through the mechanisms of PR-ized warfare. Hence, these PR machines promoted not only armed action, but also a set of (globalized) political discourses associated with the NWO. NWO wars were sold to US and allied populations as 'missionary' exercises in removing 'dangerous tyrants' and replacing them with 'democracy' and 'justice'. Not surprisingly, military PRs tried to sell this latest generation of NWO wars, 'peacekeeping operations', 'regime change' and 'peace settlements' to the masses using the same old binary oppositions that have long characterized wartime propaganda – and from the Gulf War in 1990 until the toppling of Saddam Hussein's statue in 2003 they had every reason to be pleased with their successes in steering the masses and the mainstream media.

Summary

You should now be familiar with the following key concepts and themes:
propaganda; Goebbels' propaganda techniques; censorship; US generals as media celebrities; Vietnam War reporting; PR-ized warfare; PR techniques used during the 1990s Gulf War; Nintendo warfare; psychological operations; 'embedding' journalists; demonization; villain–victim model; legitimating peace settlements; legitimating peacekeeping; why television inherently skews the reporting of wars and conflicts; and how television can be used by military PRs.

For further consideration

1 Examine how PR and spin-doctoring grew out of the propaganda model;
2 The pioneers of using the mass media to generate war hysteria were: (a) William Randolph Hearst's USA press in 1898 and (b) the British press during the Boer War (1899–1902). Examine this pioneering propaganda and trace out its impact on twentieth-century military propaganda and spin-doctoring;
3 Identify the way the following US generals have used PR to promote their careers – Dwight Eisenhower, Douglas MacArthur and Colin Powell;
4 Some argue that the media were responsible for the USA's defeat in Vietnam. Others argue this is an exaggeration. Identify all the arguments offered by both sides and evaluate their validity;
5 Is television capable of accurately and fairly portraying war and conflict?
6 Map out how the Western media systematically demonized Saddam Hussein and Slobodan Milosevic;
7 Examine the way the Western media have portrayed Pakistan's Pervaz Musharraf since 9/11. Evaluate this portrayal in the light of the situation on the ground in Pakistan;
8 Examine the US media's portrayal of US casualties, plus American reactions to the deaths of US soldiers in (a) the Vietnam War and (b) the war in Iraq in 2004. Explain any differences found;

(Continued)

For further consideration   Continued

9   Consider the view that multilateral peacekeeping is a spin-doctored legitimation device by examining the following: Gulf War (1990), Kosovo (1999), Timor (1999), Afghanistan (2001) and Iraq (2003);

10 Examine how 'peace' was imposed in the following countries after World War II: West Germany, East Germany and Japan. Examine how the media and education were used to plant new worldviews and political systems into these countries. Identify any parallels with contemporary Afghanistan and Iraq.

The Media and Terrorism

Chapter 10 discussed how the media has become increasingly implicated in fighting wars. Chapter 11 will take this theme further, and examine a specialist form of warfare, namely terrorism. The chapter will look at how terrorism is a form of political violence deployed by politically weak groups to draw attention to their cause. It is argued that terrorism is essentially a communicative act that shares much in common with spin-doctoring and political PR (as discussed in chapter 7) – i.e. terrorists are essentially using a form of 'political theater' to sell their messages. Chapter 11 examines the following: the history of terrorism/guerilla warfare; the importance of 'symbolic deeds' in terrorism; how terrorists use spectacular acts of violence to spread their messages to different audiences; how counter-terrorist operations also seek to use the media; and three ways in which journalists can relate to terrorism. Chapter 11 extends a number of themes developed in chapters 7 and 10.

All societies have dominant and dominated groups. Sometimes, dominated groups become so alienated and frustrated they rebel, and opt to deploy political violence against their rulers. Various explanations have been proposed for this behavior (Nieburg, 1969). Essentially, terrorism – one form of political violence – is the weapon of the weak. In situations where dominated groups face overwhelming hegemonic power, they may conclude that there is no other way to get their voices heard in the political process. Terrorism becomes a kind of 'struggle over meaning' (Louw, 2001: chapter 1), with violence used to 'grab attention' and build counter-hegemony (i.e. recruit supporters). Just as PRs and spin-doctors create pseudo-events to grab media attention (see chapter 7), so terrorists use violence to grab media attention and thereby overcome their 'invisibility' (which is a political weakness in any struggle over meaning) – i.e. terrorism is a way of putting (forcing) counter-hegemonic meanings onto the political agenda.

Both hegemonic and counter-hegemonic players use a mix of violence, persuasion and bargaining. Both try and use the media to promote their worldviews, legitimate their use of violence and de-legitimate their opposition's use of violence. But in struggles where ruling hegemonies have overwhelming power, they also have the power to 'define' their opponents – in these situations hegemonic violence becomes taken for granted and normalized ('legitimate policing'); while counter-hegemonic violence is branded non-legitimate ('terrorism'). Hence, to be branded a 'terrorist' precisely implies political weakness. Terrorists achieving power confer legitimacy upon themselves, and eulogize themselves as 'freedom fighters'. Those on the way to success often succeed in having the intermediary term – 'guerilla' – used. So terrorists, guerillas and freedom fighters are the same thing – namely groups of politically motivated people, deeply alienated from the political system, who opt to deploy political violence and 'terror' to try and overturn what they perceive to be political repression.

Deploying 'terror' as a political strategy has passed through four phases:

- Russian and French anarchists developed the idea of deploying 'terror' during the nineteenth century – Paul Brousse and Peter Kropotkin used the term 'propaganda of the deed' in 1877 to refer to the politically weak, finding themselves confronting an overwhelmingly powerful foe, needing to carry out a spectacularly courageous act to draw attention to their cause (Laqueur, 1977: 49). Anarchists and socialists deployed terror in Czarist Russia;
- During World War II partisan guerilla forces carried out acts of sabotage and terrorism against the Nazis in France, Yugoslavia, Poland, Greece; and against the Japanese in China, Malaysia, Vietnam and the Philippines. These partisans (who were often communists) received assistance from the USA or Britain, so becoming surrogate forces. After the war, the Allies lost control of many of these surrogate partisans – e.g. Mao's Red Army captured China and the Viet Minh defeated the French in Vietnam (which precipitated America's Vietnam War). Further, after World War II, the Greek partisans, Malayan Communist Party and Filipino HUKs opted not to end their struggles. The British and Americans pioneered many counter-insurgency strategies through defeating these groups;
- The cold war saw the proliferation of revolutionary guerilla warfare – a form of surrogate warfare, liberally deploying terrorism. This phenomenon was born of opportunism – rebellious groups learned to use the cold war by asking the USSR, PRC or USA to assist them with weapons and training. The cold war produced a burst of guerilla activity around the globe because dissidents could more easily find arms (although

providing arms and training seldom translated into full Soviet, Chinese or US control of these guerilla groups). The Soviets, in particular, assisted many groups – e.g. FLN (Algeria), Viet Minh and Viet Cong (Vietnam), Pathet Lao (Laos), FRELIMO (Mozambique), MPLA (Angola), PAIGC (Guinea-Bissau), ZAPU (Zimbabwe), PLO (Israel), ANC (South Africa), SWAPO (Namibia), and FRETELIN (East Timor). Many of these ran successful guerilla wars and eventually became the governments of their countries. This enabled them to train and assist other guerilla groups. The PRC assisted guerilla groups like ZANU-PF (Zimbabwe), UNITA (Angola), and Khmer Rouge (Cambodia). UNITA later became a South African/US surrogate force. The USA assisted guerilla groups in Angola, Tibet, Nicaragua, Iraq, Cambodia, Ethiopia and Afghanistan. The largest US surrogate guerilla operations were the Contras in Nicaragua and the mujahedin in Afghanistan. The Afghan operation helped to spawn Muslim fundamentalism, which, in turn, precipitated the contemporary Western 'war against terrorism'. The PLO, IRA and FARC were able to continue their struggles into the post-cold war period because of funding sources reaching beyond the superpowers. The cold war phase generated much guerilla warfare theorizing – e.g. China's Mao Tse-Tung, Vietnam's Nguyen Giap, Latin America's Che Guevara and Mozambique's Eduardo Mondlane (see Fairbairn, 1974; Sarkesian, 1975).

- The Pax Americana generated a new wave of terrorism driven by the Muslim fundamentalist network al-Qaeda, which carried out the 9/11 terror attacks on the USA in 2001. Al-Qaeda's worldview is a hybridization of two (overlapping) components – one is hostility to US global hegemony (which they share with many Third World political movements); the other is a uniquely Muslim fundamentalist opposition to Western cultural hegemony. Ali Shari'ati (1980) discusses opposition to Western (both Marxist and liberal) **secularism**, materialism and 'ungodliness'. Al-Qaeda shares with many non-Westerners a sense of victimhood. Western hegemony is opposed because Western political forms, ideologies and (since de-colonization) '**comprador**' ruling elites are seen as foreign impositions. The West is deemed responsible for local minorities of Westernized people becoming 'comprador' ruling elites in many Third World countries. These elites are deemed to be in power (despite often being corrupt, incompetent and brutal) because the West keeps them in power, because they serve the economic interests of the West, and because having become Westernized, they are culturally proximate to those in power in the Western heartland. The West is consequently blamed for the poor quality of Third World governance because of a 'partnership' between Third World elites and their 'partners' in the USA/Europe. The resultant sense of political and economic victimhood is also tied to concern about Western '**cultural imperialism**'. For al-Qaeda, this is enmeshed with a concern that Muslim godliness and morality is being undermined by Western secularism (ungodliness and immorality) and materialism (born of Western-style economic development). Further, in many Third World societies, political and economic instability, crime and warlordism have become rampant. (The contexts giving birth to al-Qaeda, namely Afghanistan and Pakistan, epitomize such unstable areas.) These phenomena are blamed on: US political interference in local issues they do not comprehend; incompetence and corruption of local 'comprador' governments allied to the West; and the negative effects of Western cultural imperialism. Economic and social instability, crime and warlordism, and (in some regions) population explosions have produced waves of Third World migrants and refugees (many of whom now reside in the West), who often carry with them resentments about instability in their former homelands (often deemed to be the outcome of US foreign policy). This chapter focuses on NWO terror because of its topicality.

11.1 Terrorism as communication

Theories about terrorism abound. A common theme in many theories is that communication and symbolism are key features of the terrorist act (Bassiouni, 1979; Schmid and de Graaf, 1982; Thornton, 1964). As Thornton notes: 'the terrorist act is intended and perceived as a symbol ... If the terrorist comprehends he is seeking a demonstration effect, he will attack targets with a maximum symbolic value' (1964: 73–4). The 9/11 targets signaled to al-Qaeda's constituency that it was possible to hit back at those inflicting 'economic' and 'cultural' pain on the Muslim world – i.e. Wall Street (as symbolic heart of global capitalism), and the Pentagon (as symbolic heart of the US military machine). The 9/11 attacks were classic examples of 'propaganda of the deed'. With the arrival of television, 'propaganda of the deed' opportunities are dramatically enhanced.

The 9/11 attacks were textbook acts of symbolic terror. It was predictable that crashing an airplane into a New York skyscraper would attract television cameras, so positioning them for the crash of a second airliner – hence guaranteeing a mass audience of North Americans to simultaneously 'terrorize' and provoke into anger. These terror attacks were executed for maximal symbolic effect. It was violence choreographed with an American audience in mind – not as theater, but as a televisual spectacular for a population that relies on television for its 'understanding' of the world. The attacks simultaneously achieved a number of ends. They:

- Created fear across the USA because the psychological impact of destroying two skyscrapers at the US economy's heart was profound. It was psychological warfare (Kelly and Mitchell, 1981: 282) – the psychological damage wrought going far beyond the actual physical damage inflicted on the USA. As Bassiouni (1979: 752) notes, such violence is specifically designed to 'inspire terror' not as a by-product, but as the central outcome of the terror act;

- Provoked anger and a desire for revenge. Because terrorism is the weapon of the weak, a key objective is to provoke the stronger party into lashing out at the terrorists' perceived support base (Jenkins, 1978: 5). Such acts of reprisal, repression and counter-terrorism often turn the stronger party into a 'recruiting agent' for the terrorist cause (Bassiouni, 1979: 757; Thornton, 1964: 86). Al-Qaeda's objective would have been to provoke US retaliation so that the USA was seen as 'brutally repressive' (Kelly and Mitchell, 1981: 283);
- Served as a global advertising vehicle (Bassiouni, 1979: 757; Thornton, 1964: 82) to propagandize al-Qaeda's cause and grievances. As Crenshaw notes: 'the most basic reason for terrorism is to gain recognition or attention' (1981: 386);
- Demonstrated the USA's vulnerability. For the politically weak, shattering an opponent's image of strength and invincibility is important (Bassiouni, 1979: 757) as a device to give 'hope' to one's supporters, and to mobilize support for one's cause (Thornton, 1964: 73–4);
- Served as a recruiting agent (Crenshaw Hutchinson, 1978: 76) for al-Qaeda and for Muslim fundamentalist movements generally;
- Caused political polarization (Bassiouni, 1979: 757) in both the Muslim and non-Muslim worlds;
- Boosted 'morale' (Thornton, 1964: 82) within Muslim fundamentalist groups (and other anti-American movements) and/or served to release tension and frustration within groups (such as al-Qaeda) feeling helpless in the face of the Pax Americana's overwhelming global hegemony.

11.2 Terrorist audiences

Because symbolism is a key feature of terrorism, successful terrorists must be skilled political communicators. Just as those engaged in PR, advertising, propaganda and psy-ops must understand their target audiences, so too must terrorists. Terrorism, like all other forms of political communication, involves developing message/s 'saleable' to a particular social sector (or mix of sectors). This involves understanding the different social sectors and what messages will trigger what results.

Because political violence is a communicative tool for triggering responses, anyone deploying terrorism needs to consider (and try and 'orchestrate') its likely impact on six audiences.

1 All terrorists try to mobilize a constituency. This may be a tiny constituency – e.g. Carlos Marighela's small 'foco' communist cadre of

Latin American urban terrorists who deliberately isolated themselves to avoid detection. It may be a mass constituency of peasants – e.g. Mao's Red Army in China; Giap's Viet Minh/Viet Cong in Vietnam; Mondlane's FRELIMO in Mozambique; and Mugabe's ZANU in Zimbabwe. Or it may be a small revolutionary cadre trying to use terrorism to 'detonate' mass insurrection – e.g. Guevara's *Fidelistas* in Cuba or Mandela's *Umkonto we Sizwe* in South Africa. Because terrorists are alienated from ruling hegemonies, they will necessarily aim to mobilize other alienated people. Most commonly, they will attempt to communicate the idea that the ruling hegemony is not all-powerful, and can be successfully challenged. Terror is used to advertise the possibility of opposition and begin the process of undercutting hegemonic worldviews and disseminating counter-hegemonic worldviews. Terrorists select targets that grab the attention of their potential constituents, yet avoid injuring these constituents. Ultimately terrorists aim to interpellate their constituents into a narrative that says: 'the existing hegemony does not serve my interests; using violence against this hegemony is legitimate and the terrorist/guerilla organization stands a reasonable chance of victory. If this hegemony is defeated I will derive benefit; therefore I should support the anti-hegemonic struggle';

2 Terrorists also communicate with their own governments when deploying violence. Violence can be geared towards 'encouraging' ruling hegemonies to open negotiations with terror groups. In that case, targets are selected to make governments 'pay attention', but which do not overly antagonize government decision makers. Alternatively, terror can be geared towards deliberately provoking governments into over-reactions (e.g. heavy-handed government actions against those people the terrorists believe they may be able to win over as sympathizers if state actions are sufficiently alienating). In that case, targets are selected to outrage and antagonize government decision makers, in order to get them to lash out in anger;

3 Terrorists also send messages to government supporters, saying: 'you may not know we exist, but we do exist. We're unhappy; your government is responsible for our unhappiness; and unless your government makes changes we are going to inflict pain upon you'. Such a communicative strategy is geared towards getting government supporters to induce changes in government policy. In such instances, the targets selected should cause 'concern' but not overly antagonize government supporters so as to make them too hardline. On other occasions, the aim is to frighten government supporters by making them believe they are personally potential targets;

4 Terrorists must also consider 'neutrals'. Selecting targets impacting on this sector risks driving them into the arms of the ruling hegemony;

5 Terrorist actions can also be designed to send messages to foreign governments and citizens, including the allies and enemies of the target government. Targets may be selected as a 'warning' not to give too much support to a target country; or selected to secure funds and weapons from governments opposed to the target;

6 Terrorists also consider other actors when selecting targets – e.g. tourists, investors, human rights lobbyists and multilateral organizations (like the UN). The aim of this might be to frighten tourists or foreign investors away from a country, to induce economic decline and unemployment and so generate more alienation and opposition to the target government.

Al-Qaeda simultaneously communicated with three different audiences through the 9/11 attacks.

Firstly, a core audience was Americans. The US political system is significantly media-ized. Television, in particular, substantively influences how Americans perceive their world. Al-Qaeda's Twin Towers attack systematically exploited this. The attack was designed to provoke extreme anger such that Americans demanded immediate revenge. This drove US politicians to hit back. This helped to polarize public opinion in the Muslim and Western worlds. For al-Qaeda, reprisals anywhere in the Muslim world would be deemed beneficial because they could be portrayed as another example of US 'bullying', 'aggression' and 'imperialism'. Further, provoking attacks on al-Qaeda bases in the Muslim world, effectively compelled US comprador allies (e.g. Pakistan, Saudi Arabia and Jordan) to reveal their allegiance to Washington against the wishes of large numbers of their own citizens (so further weakening their position). So although the USA's military success in the 2001 Afghan War greatly strengthened US global hegemony, this success ironically served al-Qaeda's political purpose of increasing opposition to the Pax Americana among those perceiving themselves as (economically or culturally) 'marginalized' or 'victimized' within this US global hegemony.

A second audience was al-Qaeda's own constituency. For this group, the 9/11 attacks served as a great morale booster by demonstrating how US power could be successfully challenged. In fact, America's hegemonic machinery was revealed to be vulnerable at its very heart. For al-Qaeda's supporters, destroying the Twin Towers would have been a cathartic experience of the sort discussed by Frantz Fanon (a leader in the 1960s' Algerian FLN struggle against France) – i.e. a catharsis generating a restoration of self-respect as the outcome of successfully hitting back at those perceived as one's tormentors (1965: 74).

A third audience was Muslims generally. For al-Qaeda, the 9/11 attacks were a vehicle to place its ideology and grievances on the agenda of Muslims globally. And if the USA and its allies could be provoked into retaliation (including harassing Muslims in Western countries) al-Qaeda would have hoped such actions would 'radicalize' many Muslims, hence functioning as a 'recruiting mechanism' for Muslim fundamentalism. Significantly, al-Qaeda's potential constituency is globally dispersed. Al-Qaeda demonstrated how – because of globalized television – well-selected terror targets can now serve as propaganda of the deed exercises for such globally dispersed constituencies.

The 9/11 attacks were geared towards radicalizing sections of Muslim and Western public opinion, to create polarization, thus generating the potential for future Muslim fundamentalist struggle against Western hegemony (and secularism). So, for al-Qaeda, even if the USA success-fully hit back and devastated its organization, this might not be perceived as a 'defeat', as long as polarization and radicalization had been generated – i.e. the seeds sown for an on-going struggle against the Pax Americana. Hence, al-Qaeda would not necessarily regard the 2001 Afghan War as a defeat, because this war transformed the Pax Americana into a hegemonic order more *visibly* militaristic and more *visibly* reliant upon using coercion to underpin the processes of globalization. (In fact, the 'war against ter-rorism' may possibly become as transformative of US global hegemony as Robert Clive's 1750s' battles at Arcot and Plassey were for the Pax Britannica. These battles created Britain's Indian empire, and precipitated a shift from an imperial hegemony grounded in trade, to an imperial hegemony grounded in military power.) This effectively serves al-Qaeda's polarization objective.

The 9/11 attacks were successful 'propaganda of the deed' exercises – generating the sort of radicalization, polarization and conflict sought by al-Qaeda. Previous al-Qaeda attacks against US targets (for example, those in Nairobi and Aden) were precisely unsuccessful because they failed to cross the necessary media threshold required to provoke wide-spread American anger. The 9/11 attacks set a new benchmark for how terrorists can use the media.

11.3 Fighting terrorism

Terrorists/guerillas use violence to communicate political messages. Governments fighting terrorists do the same thing. Despite contextual dif-ferences, there is a remarkable uniformity in the messages that have been promoted over time. The message terrorists generally try and promote is that they are fighting for 'liberation/freedom' against a tyranny. Governments have usually responded with a message saying that because terrorists are a radical minority using evil methods, fighting against them is a crusade for civilization. Both sides will find examples of evil perpetrated by their opponents, and use these to interpellate their porters into passionately held us–them binary oppositions. The media often deeply implicated in this struggle over perceptions – with both sides engaged in spinning stories geared to persuading journalists of the rectitude of 'their side'. So just as conventional warfare involves both military and PR battles, so too do terror wars.

The burst of guerilla/terrorist activity during the cold war produced a proliferation of counter-insurgency, anti-terror forces. States which built significant counter-insurgency forces from the 1950s to the 1980s were France, the USA, UK, Israel, South Africa, Rhodesia, Turkey and the USSR. Some societies engaging in these terror struggles slid into civil wars (where both sides used terror to 'communicate' with their opponents) and became societies deeply transformed and militarized by the experience – e.g. Israel (since the 1970s) and South Africa (in the 1980s). Four main approaches to dealing with terrorists/guerillas were developed during the cold war phase. (These approaches still inform the actions of contemporary anti-terror forces.)

One approach argues that terror wars are competitions of 'will', and battles for 'popularity'. French general André Beaufre (1965) developed this approach out of his experiences fighting the Viet Minh in Vietnam and FLN in Algeria. Beaufre argued that guerilla wars involved both direct battlefield engagement and indirect engagement. The latter included diplomatic, media and psychological conflict, and for Beaufre, the indirect conflict (or 'exterior maneuver') was the most crucial dimension of guerilla warfare – i.e. these wars were not won or lost on the battlefield, but were won or lost in perceptual battles (in diplomatic forums, the media, etc). Beaufre's approach developed into a counter-insurgency strategy called WHAM (Win Hearts and Minds); a conceptualization placing great emphasis on psy-ops and media concerns (e.g. PR, spin-doctoring and censorship). Communication operations were deployed to weaken enemy resolve; try and win mass support; and bolster the resolve of one's own forces and supporters. Both sides tried to get their opponents to 'surrender psychologically'. Beaufre argued that no clear lines separated civilians from combatants in guerilla warfare, and fighting terrorists necessitated deploying both civilian and military resources within a unified planned response. Deploying this conceptualization militarized society, e.g. South Africa (see Frankel, 1984). Beaufre's model influenced Clutterbuck's (1981) view that the media should not be allowed to assist terrorists.

A second approach was Coin-ops (Counter Insurgency Operations), which argued that winning such wars required 'authority' rather than 'popularity'. An important Coin-ops theorist was McCuen (1966), whose theory grew out of his experiences in the US Army's war against Viet Cong insurgents in Vietnam. McCuen effectively inverted the revolutionary guerilla strategy developed by Mao Tse-Tung in China. McCuen argued that Mao's revolutionary model involved four phases:

1   A political phase when political agitators were deployed to build local support. The resultant 'political wing' of cadres would support and hide the 'military wing' of terrorists in phase two. Phase one was clandestine because the ruling hegemony's power was overwhelming;

2   A terror (or propaganda of the deed) phase designed to provoke the government into lashing out in the hope this would alienate the local population and so generate populations willing to listen to the revolutionary messages of the political cadres; demonstrate the vulnerability of the ruling hegemony and 'advertise' a (counter-hegemonic) alternative; demoralize government supporters; and intimidate neutrals into withholding assistance from the government and its supporters. During phase two, both the military and political wings remained clandestine, emerging only briefly to conduct terror acts. At the start of phase two, counter-hegemonic power was very limited; but by the end, counter-hegemonic authority had grown to the point where it could challenge the government's hegemony;

3   A guerilla phase evolved from a successful terror phase. Once the 'political wing' had interpellated a majority of the population into a counter-hegemonic worldview, and the 'military wing' was sufficiently numerous and skilled, the clandestine phase could be ended. Hence during phase three, the military wing emerged to fight in uniform and the political wing operated openly and set up legal and welfare infrastructures. During phase three, the state's police and legal infrastructures experienced difficulties operating, because they no longer exercised authority and/or served a functioning hegemony in guerilla-controlled areas;

4   Conventional warfare occurred when the guerillas were strong enough to transform themselves into a regular army and engage in conventional battles with government forces. By phase four, the former government had lost virtually all authority.

McCuen's model involved counter-insurgency forces working out which phase the revolutionary terrorists/guerillas had reached. If the revolutionaries had reached phase four, then the counter-insurgents had to deploy Mao's phase one ('political') strategies. If the revolutionaries had reached phase three, then the counter-insurgents would use Mao's phase two strategies. If the revolutionaries had reached phase two, the counter-insurgents would use Mao's phase three strategies. If the revolutionaries were in phase one, the state could (and according to McCuen, should) fully exercise its military might to crush the insurgents. The aim at each phase was for the counter-insurgents to exercise as much territorial authority as they could muster to wind back whatever hegemonic influence the insurgents possessed.

The Coin-ops approach has less impact on the media than WHAM, because while WHAM strategists are concerned with influencing mass public opinion and the content of the mass media, Coin-ops strategists are focused on deploying coercion to gain authority over territory. This authority is used to eliminate insurgents and their supporters. The USA has deployed this Coin-ops approach in Afghanistan since 2001 and Iraq since 2003.

A third approach mixes the above – i.e. both coercion (Coin-ops) and a struggle over legitimacy (WHAM) are deployed.

A fourth approach involved destabilizing states supplying guerillas/terrorists with training bases, logistical support and so on. The objective is to disrupt guerilla supply lines and training bases. This approach was used by Israel against Lebanon in the 1980s (Laffin, 1985); Rhodesia against Mozambique in the 1970s (Flower, 1987); and South Africa against Angola in the 1980s (Bridgland, 1990). And deployed by the USA against Afghanistan after 9/11. Because such destabilization requires attacking foreign territories, the chances of generating hostile public opinion (both foreign and domestic) is high. Consequently, PR is deployed to justify such actions and/or try and cover up any excesses occurring during such operations.

11.4 Terrorism and the media

Terrorist acts are always symbolic – intended to communicate political messages. The media, as conduits for symbolism, are used by terrorists to communicate with mass audiences in the same way the media are used by more conventional political actors. But not all acts of terrorism are geared to the media, because some terror acts are best carried out at the micro level, and spreading the message to wider audiences serves no purpose, or is even counter-productive – e.g. during the 1980s, black South Africans working for the apartheid state were 'necklaced' (burned alive) on street corners so their painful deaths could be witnessed by their communities. These symbolic acts helped to render black townships 'ungovernable'. Winnie Mandela recognized the effectiveness of 'necklacing' when she said of this non-mediaized, low-tech political theatre: 'we will liberate this country with our boxes of matches'. Widespread media coverage of these acts in the USA or Europe would have been counter-productive for the ANC. However, there will be occasions when mass audiences are highly desirable. On such occasions terror acts will be specifically designed to attract mass media coverage, e.g. the 9/11 attacks.

In societies where the mass media are significantly integrated into the political process, both terrorists and those fighting terrorists necessarily pay serious attention to the media, and how the media can be used to promote 'their side' of the struggle. So the media become enmeshed in terror/guerilla wars whether they want to or not. Schlesinger et al. (1983) describe three schools of thought concerning the relationship between the media and terrorists, i.e. terrorists:

- Successfully use the media to further their ends;
- Are not usually successful in duping journalists, and consequently the media do not generally assist terrorists;
- Seek to use the media. The media sometimes assist terrorists to propagate their symbolism, and sometimes do not.

The media, as gatekeepers and agenda setters, determine the sort of coverage terrorists will receive. But the media are not homogeneous; there are struggles over meaning (Louw, 2001: 20–4); and different views about terrorism (within the community and media sector). The portrayals terrorists receive are at least partially the outcome of meaning struggles, and the media coverage that terror groups receive will be influenced by whatever perspective is currently hegemonic within a media organization. One such perspective has been called 'the official line' (Schlesinger et al., 1983: 12–13). The official line criminalizes terrorists and regards journalists who cover terrorist events sympathetically as the 'dupes' of terrorist criminals. Governments try and get as many journalists as possible to agree with this position. Journalists interpellated into the mainstream hegemonic position will demonize terror groups; draw attention to their atrocities; and support the use of military and police violence against them. Following 9/11, such an anti-terrorist position became dominant within the mainstream Western media. A second perspective, agrees with 'the official line' that terrorist violence is illegitimate, but argues that terrorism is caused by social ills which need to be rectified (1983: 16–17). Journalists agreeing with this position are potentially useful for terror/guerilla organizations especially when such organizations wish to communicate with 'middle-ground' people – i.e. those unlikely to actively support terror/guerilla groups, but who will advocate negotiations between the warring parties. Both terror/guerilla groups and counter-insurgency forces will engage in PR work with opinion leaders (e.g. journalists) in this second category. Third, is an 'oppositional perspective' – those seeing terrorist violence as justified (1983: 27–8). Journalists in this category portray terrorists/guerillas as heroes (freedom fighters) engaged in a legitimate struggle against tyranny. Terror/guerilla groups will try and identify such journalists and assist them wherever they can. Governments, on the other hand, will try and put obstacles in the way of such journalists. In its most extreme form this becomes formalized censorship.

Ultimately terrorists – like all politicians – are in the communication business. And, like other political players, terrorists face an increasingly media-ized political process. So it should come as little surprise that twenty-first century terrorists/guerillas pay attention to the media as a site of struggle. This is not to say that terror wars are reducible to media affairs. In fact, terror wars involve real battles, often out of sight of the media. However, as with other politicians, terrorists have messages to sell – and success or failure depends on the terror organization's perception-management skills, and skill at symbol and belief propagation. As with other political players, terrorists will try and use the media to their own advantage; and as with other politicians, they will sometimes be successful, and sometimes fail. The 9/11 attacks simultaneously elevated the benchmark for terrorists selling themselves through the media, and opened a new terror phase. It will be interesting to see how many of the old terror/guerilla methodologies get incorporated into today's emergent genre of political violence; and how many new methodologies terrorists invent through engaging with the increasingly media-ized contemporary political processes.

Summary

You should now be familiar with the following key concepts and themes:
   propaganda of the deed; terrorist/guerilla/freedom fighter; surrogate guerilla warfare; victimhood; alienation and terror; how terrorists use television; provoking anger and retaliation; generating political polarization; Win Hearts and Minds; counter-insurgency operations; and the three ways journalists have responded to terrorists.

For further consideration

1   In politics 'profile' is everything. Examine how weak political groups have used terror to reverse their political fortunes;
2   Consider the communicative similarities and differences between two forms of political violence: (a) terrorism and (b) conventional warfare;

(Continued)

For further consideration Continued

3 Some would argue terrorism is pure symbolism (propaganda of the deed). Is this simply a media determinist perspective?

4 The cold war produced a form of terrorism associated with insurgencies (e.g. FLN, Viet Cong, and ZANU-PF). What are the similarities and differences between this insurgency terror and al-Qaeda's terror?

5 Can a liberal media avoid being 'used' by terrorists to disseminate their messages?

6 Explore the following notion: television can be both a friend and a foe of terrorism;

7 Those fighting terrorists generally want to prevent the media from carrying messages that 'assist' terrorists. Hence they seek to either apply censorship or get the media to apply self-censorship. Is this strategy helpful or self-defeating?

8 Is the censorship of the media in a terror war ever justified?

9 Put yourself into al-Qaeda's position, and make two lists: (a) what aspects of the Twin Towers attack were successful? (b) What aspects were failures (or had negative consequences)?

10 Terrorist groups who become successful and become governments often mythologize their terrorist pasts (into liberation struggles). And once they are governments they, in turn, regard terrorism used against them as illegitimate. (Examples are: Israeli Irgun regard PLO as illegitimate; Angola's MPLA regard UNITA as illegitimate; Algeria's FLN regard GIA as illegitimate; and South Africa's ANC regard PAGAD and Boeremag as illegitimate). What does this tell us about the role of 'legitimate' violence and 'illegitimate' violence in the political process?

The Media and Foreign Relations

Chapter 12 explores the validity of the argument that globalized television networks (like CNN) impact on the formulation of foreign policy. The origins of this 'CNN effect' thesis are discussed. Thereafter, chapter 12 looks at the debate the CNN effect thesis gave rise to. It is argued that the actual relationship between media reporting and policy making is a complex one – i.e. the evidence suggests that those who argue that the media have massive influence over policy formulation have exaggerated their case. At the same time, it would be incorrect to argue that the media have no influence. Instead, it will be argued they can exercise some influence, but only when the right conditions apply. Chapter 12 extends a number of themes developed in chapters 4, 7 and 10.

Some have argued that the arrival of global television altered the nature of foreign relations because the conduct of foreign policy decision making was media-ized. This is referred to as the **'CNN effect'**. But is this argument valid? Establishing the validity, or otherwise, of the CNN effect involves unpacking the relationship/s between the media, politicians, spin-doctors, consultants/advisors, policy makers and civil servants. Unpacking this will help us to understand what media-ization is, and what it is not. The chapter focuses on US foreign relations given contemporary US dominance.

12.1 The CNN effect

The 1990 Gulf War produced the view that foreign relations were being transformed by the global mass media. During this war, CNN provided all players with round-the-clock information. This appeared to provide:

- A potential source of real-time visual intelligence for both sides;
- A vehicle for the delivery of mis-information (i.e. counter-intelligence deception exercises);
- A 'back-channel' negotiations vehicle via 24-hour television – i.e. during interviews, either side could slip in 'threats', 'warnings', or 'offers' for ending the conflict. This suggested a potential short-circuiting of the role for professional diplomats;
- A means for delivering PR/psy-ops messages directly to the other side's population – i.e. a direct delivery vehicle for potentially turning 'enemy' public opinion against the war, and hence putting 'pressure' on the policy makers to end the war.

Journalists proposed the idea that CNN – the first global television channel – had introduced a new dimension into the conduct of foreign relations (Volkmer, 1999: 153–5). As one CNN employee said:

> I know we have been used by governments in the past to get their point of view across because, my God, we are watched everywhere. We are watched in Cuba, we are watched in Moscow, we are watched in Libya. When Muammar Gaddafi wants to get his point of view across, he picks up the phone and he calls CNN and says, 'Hey, I have got an interview. Would you like to interview me? I have got something I want to tell you. I have a peace plan.' Yasser Arafat does the same type of thing. It was done with Saddam Hussein during the war. (Volkmer, 1999: 153)

Originally 'the CNN effect' only referred to the impact that CNN itself supposedly exercised on foreign relations because all sides used the same information source (Robinson, 2002: 2). Subsequently the notion widened beyond CNN, to mean the impact that all globalized media (print and television) had on public opinion (2002: 2). This view was especially progressed by Freedman's (2000) and Wheeler's (2000) discussions of the CNN effect; and Hoge's (1994) concern that the CNN effect 'pressured' politicians to make poor policy decisions. As the CNN effect thesis entrenched itself, it became commonplace to suggest that US/UN interventions in northern Iraq and Somalia had been driven by emotive media coverage of suffering people and US disengagement from Somalia occurred because of media images of a US soldier being dragged through Mogadishu's streets. The CNN effect thesis was enhanced by the (misplaced) belief that television images of starving Ethiopians were responsible for generating food aid which ended the famine. The media's power to influence foreign audiences, and by extension foreign policy, became taken for granted. But as Robinson (2002: 12) notes, this CNN effect thesis was asserted, not demonstrated. When Robinson examined the Somali and Iraq cases, he found the thesis exaggerated.

Robinson's examination of the Somalia intervention revealed a complex picture. Robinson (2002) demonstrates that media coverage did not directly cause the intervention – in fact, significant US media coverage of Somalia only occurred after it was announced that US troops would be deployed. At most it can be said that aid workers, some middle-ranking officials and Congress members used televisual images when lobbying senior policy makers, but no strong link can be found between these images and policies adopted. Similarly, Robinson debunks Shaw's (1996) thesis that media coverage caused US intervention to establish northern Iraqi Kurdish safe havens. Instead, Robinson (2002: 69–71) discovered that this intervention was driven by the US–Turkish alliance, and Turkey's concern about how Kurdish refugees might impact on its own 'Kurdish problem'. Robinson (2002: 8–9) contends that Western interventions are driven by power politics, not by humanitarian concerns as proposed by the CNN effect thesis. Humanitarian rhetoric is deployed by PRs to justify such interventions (see 10.3 on p. 221) – and the media conveniently disseminates this 'justification hype' to global mass publics.

12.2 Foreign policy making: the players

The CNN effect thesis is premised upon two assumptions:

- The media have influence and power within policy-making processes;
- Mass public opinion (mediated by the media) influences policy formulation.

Both assumptions are empowering for journalists. So it should come as no surprise that journalists promote both assumptions. But how valid are they?

Unraveling the real role of media within policy making requires identifying the locus of decision making – who sets agendas; who decides; and what factors impact on decisions. Overall, the foreign policy-making process involves five sets of players: civil servants/policy officials; politicians; 'unorganized' public (public opinion); 'organized' public (interest groups and their lobbyists); and the media. When considering the role of these players in foreign policy formulation, the following four scenarios suggest themselves.

12.2.1 Elite decision making

Foreign policy decisions are *made exclusively by a tight-knit elite team* of senior cabinet members (e.g. presidents, prime ministers, and cabinet members representing foreign affairs, the military and intelligence agencies) plus senior foreign affairs and security staffers. Outside consultants are sometimes approached before decisions are made. Politicians also increasingly consult with communication professionals before making decisions – i.e. PRs and spin-doctors can also impact on policy making (see 2.4 on p. 26). Within these teams, politicians often lean heavily on their senior civil servants. In fact, it may argued that civil servants set policy agendas by exercising control over what information reaches the table for discussion – i.e. just as the media act as agenda setters for mass publics, so senior civil servants are agenda setters for cabinets, presidents and prime ministers.

The question is, how much are tight-knit elite groups of policy makers influenced by the public or the media? One scenario suggests that foreign policy is made largely independently of both mass public opinion and media reports designed for mass publics – because foreign policy makers have information sources far richer than those available to either journalists or mass publics. Governments maintain foreign affairs bureaucracies; post diplomats abroad; engage in on-going talks with foreign political players; employ analysts and regional specialists; and build intelligence-gathering infrastructures to ensure they have rich information. Hence, no self-respecting government needs to rely on mass media information. Similarly, because governments have multiple information sources, policy makers are presumably not influenced by sensational mass media images to the same extent that (less-informed) mass publics are. Mass publics are more susceptible to sensational journalism, hyperbole, psy-ops and misinformation campaigns (from all sides) than policy makers simply because policy makers are insiders with access to both high-grade officially collected information and (generally low-grade) popular media stories. Further, policy makers presumably have limited time available to consume the sensationalized products of popular journalism (although their spin industry monitors this media for them).

12.2.2 Journalistic influence

A second scenario sees *journalists as possessing influence* over foreign policy formulation. Journalistic influence derives from the following:

- Journalists can undermine the agenda-setting capacity of senior civil servants by publishing stories bureaucrats and/or intelligence agencies would rather were not brought to the attention of politicians;
- Politicians need to keep their constituents on-side. This can be achieved by PR, spin-doctoring and impression-management techniques – i.e. publicizing those policies constituents will find acceptable while minimizing the publicizing of policies likely to displease constituents. Journalists can expose policies (and their consequences) politicians would rather have buried;

- When policy makers are divided over what course of action to adopt, journalists can shift the debate by providing one side with the evidence it needs to out-argue its opponents; and/or shift the debate by mobilizing pressure groups, or pushing public opinion in one direction.

Before journalists can have this sort of influence, they need sources of information. In general, stories challenging the mainstream policy-elite position come to light as the result of divisions within the elite – i.e. those losing policy debates will leak stories to journalists to try and give themselves negotiating leverage, and/or undermine their policy opponents. So journalistic influence is generally 'derivative'.

12.2.3 Public opinion influence

A third scenario *grants the masses influence* over foreign policy formulation. Risse-Kappen (1994: 239) notes that scholars are divided into two camps: those believing that mass public opinion has a measurable and distinct 'bottom-up' effect on foreign policy, and those believing public opinion merely follows the 'top-down' lead of elites who use the media to influence them. Risse-Kappen (1994: 239) makes the interesting distinction between 'attentive publics' (with more than an average interest in politics), 'issue publics' (who can be mobilized on specific problems) and the undifferentiated 'mass public'. Risse-Kappen suggests that talking about an undifferentiated mass public is unhelpful when considering bottom-up influence on policy because it is 'attentive' and 'issue' publics who are active and impact on policy makers.

One way of conceptualizing attentive/issue publics is to think of them as organized interest groups who initiate bottom-up influence on policy makers within a pluralist democracy. Interest groups can try and influence policy making in a number of ways, e.g.:

- Employing lobbyists who specialize in directly interfacing with the policy-making elite;
- Making financial contributions to politicians' election campaigns and PACs to 'buy influence' and 'access';
- Employing PRs and spin-doctors to try and ensure their perspective/s gain media attention, or the attention of selected niche audiences;
- Organizing demonstrations and, in extreme cases, acts of political violence.

But some assume that the broad masses can influence policy making without being attached to organized interest groups – e.g. Bennett (1994) notes that mass publics exercise a 'negative' power over policy, in the sense that policy elites are deemed 'responsive' to public concerns because they anticipate what will be unpopular with their constituents. In democracies, policy elites are deemed to avoid making unpopular decisions.

Whatever the extent of such bottom-up impact, such influence is presumably always circumscribed by other factors – i.e. 'public opinion' and 'public moods' (both domestic and overseas) are but one of many inputs that policy makers have to consider. Ultimately, bottom-up pressures presumably only work if policy elites are receptive, and/or if these pressures do not fundamentally cut across preferred policy opinions already held by policy elites.

12.2.4 A complex mix

A fourth scenario suggests a *complex interaction between policy-making elites and the media*. Within this scenario, the masses are seen as followers – i.e. the elite (or sections of the elite) mobilize the masses (or sections of the masses) by using the media. For example, Graham (1994) argues that American public opinion has a bottom-up influence on US foreign policy, within a complex mix of bottom-up and top-down influences – e.g. US Presidents engineer top-down influence by 'going public' on an issue. This can generate bottom-up public opinion pressure, thus giving the President negotiating leverage over other members of the policy elite. Graham refers to research (ironically) suggesting that 'attentive' and 'issue' publics are more easily swayed by such top-down interventions than 'passive' mass publics – precisely because they are paying attention. As Graham (1994: 194) notes, this means that attentive publics do not necessarily provide the sort of 'democratic check on government policy' suggested by Lippmann – i.e. bottom-up pressure is simply derivative of top-down intervention by one or other section of a (divided) policy elite.

Bennett (1994: 168–9) argues that a core feature of contemporary policy making is the policy elite's (PR) management of the media, geared towards keeping the masses on side. He refers to the way the Pentagon kept the US public on side during the 1990 Gulf War as an example of successful foreign policy news management. News management is a complex business. It involves those pushing a particular foreign policy agenda getting the media to promote their position. If the entire foreign policy elite are unified, this task is made easier. If divided, the dominant faction driving policy faces the problem that disgruntled faction/s may try to undermine them by leaking 'problematic' stories to the media. These stories can be geared towards:

- Disrupting the dominant group – i.e. increasing the energy required to pursue the preferred policy in the hope that if their policy becomes too 'costly' they might back down;
- Stirring some legislators to oppose executive policy makers; and/or
- Mobilizing public opposition to policies.

Hence, a key task in foreign policy formulation is building and maintaining unity within the policy-making team. This involves lobbying and negotiating. If policy elites can achieve unity, their prospects for driving their policies to a successful conclusion are greatly increased. If they become divided – as happened in the USA during the Vietnam War – it is likely that their divisions will eventually cascade into the public domain, setting off a feeding frenzy among opposition legislators and journalists. Once this happens, the task of impression management becomes difficult.

Ultimately, everyone involved in foreign policy making will, to some extent, engage in media management, whether it is the dominant group 'promoting' their policy, or the opposition group/s 'disrupting' its implementation. Media management involves trying to get the media to promote your position and/or trying to ensure that stories are viewed from your perspective/angle. In the foreign policy field this is achieved in three ways:

1   Censorship. Although unpopular in liberal democracies, some censorship is 'accepted' during wartime;
2   PR/spin/psy-ops. There now exists a spin industry working for politicians, government departments, interest groups and so on. These people specialize in news management, impression management, and selling politicians and their policies. Within the foreign policy sector, different (competing) policy factions might each employ their own PRs/ spin-doctors. Each will be trying to manage information flows; engaged in agenda setting; and spinning the story to try and get journalists to view it from their perspective/angle;
3   Negotiating a favorable relationship with media proprietors. All politicians strive to build and maintain good relations with media proprietors who have the power to deny them favorable publicity. On some occasions, proprietors will have the upper hand in the relationship; on other occasions, politicians will gain the advantage. The preferred position of foreign policy elites is when media proprietors are on side (e.g. Lord Northcliffe during the World War I).

Formulating foreign policy is a complex process involving multiple players. The CNN effect thesis suggests that one of these players – the media – plays a leading role in contemporary policy formulation. In reality, the media seem to be but one player among many.

12.3 The media and foreign relations

For most Westerners, politics has become a secondhand reality – encountered in a mediated form (via the media) by passive mass audiences, rather than encountered directly (firsthand) through active participation. Those formulating and implementing foreign policies can generally assume that their mass citizenries will be almost completely reliant on the media for information about the successes, failures and effects of their policies in far away places. So, what is the role of the media in formulating and implementing foreign policy? Eight possible roles suggest themselves.

12.3.1 Media as 'consent manufacturers'

The media simply *promote government foreign policy*. Robinson (2002: 31) suggests that the extent to which the media have any impact upon policy formulation depends upon three variables, namely how united the governing elite are; the extent of controversies within the policy elite; and the extent to which the executive has a firm policy. According to Robinson:

- If elites are united, the media tend to simply help them to 'manufacture consent' for their foreign policies. The media will have no influence on policy formulation;
- If there are controversies within the elite, the media will reflect these. But, if policy makers and the executive can still formulate a policy, the media have no influence on policy formulation. See Hallin (1986) and Bennett (1990).

When these above two conditions apply, the media tend, on balance, to simply affirm government foreign policy directions, largely because there exists a policy direction which the government promotes through its publicity machineries.

This view sees the media as simply helping ruling elites to 'manufacture consent'. Robinson (2002: 12) notes: 'whilst totalizing arguments about manufacturing consent (e.g. Herman and Chomsky, 1988) are controversial, the thesis that news media coverage of "foreign" affairs is "indexed" (Bennett, 1990) to frames of reference of foreign policy-elites receives substantial empirical support'.

There are two explanations for why the media help governing elites. Some see the media as part of the same 'interest block' in society, i.e. media staffers ultimately share the same values as governing elites – they literally 'see' the world through similar eyes. A second explanation is that governing elites invest considerable energy managing the media through PR, spin-doctoring and propaganda. This PR-machinery has become a huge industry in the West, engaged in impression management, half-truths, intentional obfuscation and outright deception (see Bonafede, 1998) – a machinery often engaging in subterfuges, the production of cover stories and leaking disinformation to the media, such as, the mix of real and illusionary events fed to the media to discredit Muammar Gaddafi (Bonafede, 1998: 108). This machinery can dupe journalists because:

- Most journalists are ill-equipped to read foreign contexts (Louw, 2001: chapter 9) and so can be easily led by both overseas spin-doctors and domestic foreign policy bureaucrats and experts;
- Domestic agendas take precedence over foreign agendas. Hence, as Fallows (1997: 197–8) notes: overseas contexts generally tend to be reported in ways that (mis-)read foreign events through domestic concerns;
- Journalists generally do not wish to see their own country's foreign policy fail. Especially in times of crisis, they are inclined to embrace their government's definition of events (Hackett, 1998: 142).

There is much evidence supporting the view that the media generally follow the lead of their own country's foreign affairs bureaucracies (and thereby help them to 'manufacture consent'). US reporting of Iran followed this pattern (see Malek, 1998). Grosswiler (1998: 209) notes that once the US foreign policy establishment lost interest in Africa, the US press dropped African coverage.

12.3.2 Media as lapdogs

A second view of the media's role within foreign relations is that the media are *tools of the ruling class*. This Marxist view was stated in the *German Ideology* as: 'the ideas of the ruling class are in every age, the ruling ideas', i.e. Marx argued an economically dominant class possesses the means to dominate the production and circulation of ideas in society, and a media system necessarily promotes its owner's interests. This thesis suggests that every context has a dominant class (or class alliance), and dominant classes always develop mechanisms – e.g. the culture industry – to ensure the ideas in circulation are appropriate to the reproduction of the existing social order. Hence, in any context and/or era a 'dominant ideology' can be identified (Abercrombie et al., 1980). In its most mechanistic form, Marxists contend, both the US foreign policy machinery and the US media would necessarily serve the interests of the dominant class/es within the USA. This view consequently overlaps with the 'manufacturing consent' thesis, except that the manufacturing consent thesis does not focus only upon class interests.

12.3.3 Media as watchdogs

A third view of the media's role within foreign relations is that media are *independent watchdogs*. This is the classic liberal view, which contends that journalists do not just passively accept the official line, but, rather, actively interrogate their environment and act as the (critical) eyes and ears of the masses. The watchdog view is the antithesis of the 'manufacturing consent' and 'dominant ideology' views. Liberal journalists are socialized to believe they can challenge the authority of ruling elites (and dominant classes), and in doing so, become actors within the policy process. Effectively, liberal journalists believe that one of their roles is placing the mass public's views onto the policy agenda, and that journalists have the power to make politicians/policy makers pay attention to public opinion. In many ways, the CNN effect thesis is an outgrowth of the watchdog view. A core feature of CNN organizational culture is the belief that CNN is a global player, independent of all vested interests. CNN sees itself as a kind of global watchdog. So CNN journalists believed, by providing a liberal platform available to all sides, and by exposing the plight of Kurds and Somalis that they impacted upon US foreign policy. Interestingly, in an attempt to demonstrate its globalness, CNN has deliberately recruited non-American staffers. However, the foreigners recruited come from a very narrow demographic – they are middle class, Westernized, and interpellated into professional discourses and practices meshing comfortably with liberal-capitalist cosmopolitanism (and hence affirm the worldview of America's New York–Washington elite). Ultimately CNN's news content is pervaded with the spirit of the Pax Americana.

12.3.4 Media as 'diplomatic channels'

A fourth view of the media's role is that the *global media are replacing diplomats*. At the extreme end, the CNN effect thesis leads to the notion that the diplomatic profession is being undercut by the arrival of global television. In this regard, Mowlana suggests that diplomats are traditionally engaged in intelligence gathering, negotiation, reporting and representation. He argues that when diplomatic channels are closed during crises, the new global media can become alternative vehicles for exchanging information – i.e.

> With the possible breakdown of diplomatic communications, which often characterizes some of the most recent phenomenon in international relations, the media are burdened with

a crucial and delicate role in the confrontation amongst powers. They often become conduits for official exchanges, reluctant publicists for the actors, and valuable sources of information for governments. (Mowlana, 1998: 39)

This proposal – that policy elites can talk to each other via the global media, with CNN providing a sort of diplomatic back channel between them (Bennett, 1994: 168) – ignores the fact that diplomacy is extraordinarily difficult in the glare of publicity because diplomacy involves horse-trading and compromises. Negotiators necessarily find it difficult to concede points while their constituencies are watching. Closed-door negotiations make it possible to be frank and open, and to jointly find face-saving measures for the compromises made. By the time parties are engaging in media-ized 'megaphone diplomacy' they have usually moved beyond seeking compromise, and are actually engaged in (public) points scoring. Megaphone diplomacy is targeted at mass publics, not at policy elites – i.e. it is a form of propaganda/psy-ops geared towards mobilizing one's own supporters for battle, while weakening the resolve of the enemy's publics.

12.3.5 Media as 'morality play'

A fifth view of the media's role proposes that the media substantively *impact on foreign policy* formulation because (firstly) policy makers are personally influenced by emotive stories; and (secondly), the media are able to shift public opinion. The media are assumed to shift policy because mass publics are part of democratic policy making, e.g. Mowlana (1998: 40). America's withdrawal from Vietnam and Somalia, over the so-called 'body bag effect', is used to substantiate this view. When the media impact on public opinion, it is by way of mobilizing 'moral outcries' which lead to public demands for governments to 'do something'. This can happen when the media simplify complex foreign situations into 'morality plays' (Hawkins, 2002: 225). The mechanics of generating (foreign-focused) 'moral outcries' are similar to how the media can build (domestic-focused) 'moral panics' over crime waves (Hall et al., 1978). Robinson (2002: 23) contends that most commentators now agree that television coverage has some impact on foreign policy making; the dispute is over when, why, and to what degree.

The question is: does media coverage always have an impact on foreign policy? The answer appears to be that media coverage has 'an effect' only if policy makers 'allow' such stories to have an influence, which happens when the following conditions are met:

- When policy makers derive some benefit from 'using' such stories;
- When policy makers are seriously divided on an issue.

Robinson (2002: 31) suggests that if there are controversies within the elite but there is policy certainty within the executive, the media will carry stories critical of the government, but media influence on policy will be resisted. However, if there are simultaneously controversies within the elite and policy uncertainties (i.e. the executive has no firm position), then the media will not only carry stories critical of the government, but media coverage will begin to have policy outcomes (i.e. the CNN effect becomes possible). When policy elites are having difficulty formulating a coherent policy, emotive news stories may become useful for promoting one or other policy direction – i.e. news stories can be mobilized to:

- Advance the bargaining position of one of the competitors within the policy team;
- Undermine the bargaining position of alternative policy arguments;
- Mobilize publics as constituencies for one of the policy positions. This can dramatically strengthen the bargaining position of one of the policy camps;
- Justify moving a particular issue higher up the agenda for discussion. This has been called 'Hurd's law' after British Foreign Secretary Douglas Hurd said: 'like it or not, television images are what forces foreign policy makers to give one of the current 25 crises in the world greater priority' (Taylor, 1997: 92);
- Prove a convenient justification for adopting a policy that might otherwise have been too unpopular – e.g. images of starving people can be used to excuse military action even though military action is not normally popular. This is called the 'enabling effect' (Robinson, 2002: 40). Robinson (2002: 126) argues that the strength of the enabling effect is contingent upon the type of policy issue – i.e. emotive media stories can be used to trigger humanitarian aid or air strikes more easily than they can be used to send ground troops into battle.

For those wanting to mobilize foreign news as a trigger; an enabling tool; or negotiating tool, three kinds of stories are most useful. Firstly, emotional televisual images – e.g. starving children or civilian deaths during conflict. Secondly, stories that can be run as 'morality plays' in which events are simplified (usually inappropriately) down to binary oppositions – i.e. villains (e.g. Serbs and white South Africans) suppressing victims (e.g. Kosovars and black South Africans). Thirdly, foreign stories which can be linked (usually inappropriately) to domestic issues so as to make them comprehensible – e.g. equating South Africa's 1980s' anti-apartheid struggle with US civil rights struggles against white supremacy.

Smart PRs understand this, and so will try and jig stories to service these criteria.

12.3.6 Media as 'hype'

A sixth view of the media's role is that the media only *impacts on the hype dimension of foreign relations*. Taylor (1997: 98) notes how CNN constructed a new genre of foreign news which the masses find exciting. In the process CNN, and other stations like it, simulated popular interest in international events. Inventing 24-hour television news created enormous pressures to fill the airtime. It has been filled with (often) sensational and emotional images, mixed with a parade of pundits expounding their views on these images. This has awakened mass public interest in a popularist form of foreign affairs that has been journalese-ized – i.e. complex themes and contexts are de-complexized, sensationalized and reduced to glib sound bite explanations.

This has added a new dimension to the job of politicians, because foreign issues can sometime spill over into the domestic political arena – e.g. Israeli–Palestinian issues significantly influence US domestic politics in areas with large Jewish or Arab populations; and African-American concerns made apartheid a US domestic issue. Politicians (and their spin industry) now have to pay attention to this new dimension of popular concern and learn to manage it in the same way they manage and steer domestic concerns. Similarly, televised/popularized foreign news adds a new dimension to the job of foreign policy makers – they must now deal with semi-informed publics, often mobilized on an issue because the media have sensationalized and emotionalized it. For policy makers, a key objective is to keep the masses at arm's length – i.e. to manage mass public opinion as much as possible. Consequently, a whole industry of foreign affairs-related PR/psy-ops, and spin-doctoring was created to manage public opinion – e.g. the PR/psy-ops machinery developed to sell the war dimension of foreign relations.

The arrival of televised/popularized foreign news means that foreign policy makers/bureaucrats must now incorporate calculations about possible negative publicity into their policy calculations (Bennett, 1994: 171). Foreign affairs continue to have a strong 'behind-the-scenes dimension', but now also have a parallel 'public dimension', where issues have been media-ized. This necessitates building a more complex foreign relations machinery comprised of six (inter-connected) functions: a diplomatic contact and negotiations machinery; intelligence gathering; intelligence analysis; policy discussion and formulation; machinery to lobby legislators and domestic interests groups; and a hype machinery of PR/psy-ops and spin-doctors (geared both towards foreign and domestic audiences). One of the key functions of the PR machine is to monitor media outlets like CNN. This is not done because the media carries information/intelligence the policy makers need to make policy – it is done because PRs, spin-doctors and politicians need to minimize the potential impact that sensationalized and emotionalized news can have on their mass publics. The aim is to minimize the impact that an aroused mass public can have on policy making. This requires on-going news monitoring, so spin-doctors can immediately get to work on any negative news. Consequently, officials designated to monitor the environment may leave their office televisions turned on all day – tuned into CNN – as a kind of 'alert mechanism' (Rotberg and Weiss, 1996: 185). Not surprisingly, White House players report that they constantly monitor news services like CNN so the President can develop quick tactical responses to breaking stories (see Bonafede, 1998: 112–14; Taylor, 1997: 96). Some analysts made the error of assuming that this implies that CNN impacts on actual foreign policy – e.g. Taylor (1997: 93) says: 'George Stephanopoulis gave the game away when he admitted: in the White House ... we have 24 hour news cycles ... CNN assures that you are forced to react at any time'. In reality, Stephanopoulis was President Clinton's spin-doctor, not a foreign policy formulator – he would generate a PR (hype) reaction not a policy reaction. This is something many commentators, including Taylor have missed – it is important to distinguish between the policy dimension of governance and the hype dimension. CNN functions in the hype-sphere of foreign relations. And it is the hype-response officials who pay attention.

12.3.7 Media as powerless

A seventh view of the media's role is that the media have *no effect on foreign policy* formulation because foreign affairs officials take decisions based on information and considerations other than the 'moral outcries' generated by the media. After an examination of a range of humanitarian and foreign crises, some of which generated US intervention, and some of which did not, Rotberg and Weiss (1996: 187) concluded: 'the U.S. government responds to crises for reasons other than nonstop coverage on CNN'. Similarly, Mowlana (1998: 31) contends that 'it is generally agreed the American media do not play a direct role in the formulation of foreign policy but continue to have a growing influence in its implementation' – i.e. policy elites (especially professional officials within the foreign affairs and intelligence bureaucracies) drive policy making. Many instances can be cited where sensationalized and emotive media images provoked audience outcries to 'do something', where policy elites simply ignored these outcries (Taylor, 1997: 90). Some examples would be: Tienanmen Square where policy officials knew that US power was insufficient to compel compliance; Rwanda's massacre, where US officials saw no strategic reason to intervene; and Ethiopia's famine, where US officials blocked aid because of a policy not to assist Mengistu's Marxist government.

Ironically, policy makers contribute to beliefs that the media influences policy making when they try and excuse their failures – e.g. the media were blamed for losing the Vietnam War by destroying public support for the war; and blamed for generating pressure for involvement in the Somali disaster (Robinson, 2002: 130). Actually, poor policy making was responsible, not the media, but by using the media as convenient scapegoats, the media power and influence thesis was bolstered.

Generally, foreign policy makers appear successful in keeping mass publics at arm's length in most of their business, with both journalists (and their mass audiences) steered away from asking questions about those foreign issues policy makers would prefer remained only on the agenda of a select few.

12.3.8 Media enmeshed in power struggles

An eighth view of the media's role is that the media can be viewed as *part of a hegemonic power game* – i.e. the media become embroiled in struggles over policy and meaning being fought out between various factions of the governing elite. Each faction tries to bolster its own policy preferences, while undermining their opponent's positions. To achieve this they will deploy media releases, briefings, press conferences, cover stories and spin-doctoring (see 7.5 on p. 168). Journalists can also be fed 'leaks', 'leads' and 'plants' in an attempt to undermine opponents. In this regard, Rotberg and Weiss (1996: 188) note how the media can be used to set agendas, build constituencies, as well as project messages within the bureaucracy itself. A range of actors (and their PRs) use the media in this way, including bureaucrats (especially in foreign affairs and the security establishment), politicians, NGOs and humanitarian groups (e.g. Amnesty International), and special interest groups (e.g. the Jewish lobby, trade unions, business groups and so on). Sometimes PRs working for interest groups use the media as back channels to try and reach policy makers. On other occasions the aim is to produce a two-step effect – i.e. try and influence the 'general' public mood or the mood of specific interest groups, in the hope this will have an impact upon policy makers. Those inside the policy process itself will generally deploy their PR machinery to try and steer the public mood in their direction; try and prevent 'problematic' story-lines and images from reaching the public; and if problem stories do enter the public domain, try and recast (spin) them so they become less damaging.

From the above it is apparent that there is no consensus about the media's impact on foreign policy making. But it seems that the media are only one of many players in a complex game, and the actual role played depends upon whatever mix of variables exists in a particular context. But if there is no consensus about the media's role in policy making, there is less of a problem establishing the media's role in selling policies once they are developed.

12.4 The media-ized dimension of foreign relations

The CNN-effect thesis proposes two things. Firstly, that policy making has been media-ized. Secondly, that this is seen as positive because it enhances democracy. However, the CNN effect thesis has flaws. This does not mean that the entire media-ization thesis is flawed. Rather, what is flawed is the question upon which the CNN effect thesis was built – i.e. how much do the media impact upon policy? More appropriate questions would be: are policy makers concerned with selling their policy to the masses? What is the role of media/journalists/PRs in this selling function? Does the need to sell policy impact upon policy making itself? These questions are essentially focused on how policy elites seek to use the media to steer mass publics – one might call this a concern with how much the *steering effect* influences policy makers.

Analyzing the media-ization of foreign affairs requires foreign relations to be recognized as consisting of two functionally separate (yet related) dimensions – a policy and a hype dimension (see 2.2.1 on p. 20). The policy dimension takes place behind the scenes and is concerned with the designing policy, plus planning and designing communicative hype (i.e. strategies and tactics geared to influencing and steering mass publics).

In planning the hype dimension, policy makers consider what policies they will *not* be able to sell. In this sense, communication considerations do impact upon policy. When communication professionals tell policy makers that no communication technique, PR or spin will be able to influence the audience, they have to pull back and think again (i.e. reappraise their policy plans). Consequently, within democracies, the limits for communicatively steering the masses often sets the boundaries for what policies can realistically be adopted. Hence, whereas the CNN effect thesis sees media-ization as a 'positive' influence (i.e. 'more' democracy), the steering effect thesis focuses on the extent to which policy elites let their PRs/spin-doctors influence their decision making – i.e. the 'negative' influences of media-izing policy-making. Foreign affairs may be less media-ized than other policy areas because foreign issues are less salient in the lives of most people than domestic issues. The only time foreign relations become a salient issue for most people is when warfare and body bags impinge upon their lives. Not surprisingly therefore, warfare is a significantly media-ized area of foreign policy.

Ultimately, foreign relations are media-ized in two senses. Firstly, policy makers deploy PRs, spin-doctors, propagandists and psy-ops specialists to influence and steer mass publics as part of implementing foreign policy. Secondly, they allow the advice of communication professionals to influence their policy-making decisions. Effectively, considerations about the possibility, or otherwise, of communicatively steering mass publics is now built into foreign policy design and implementation in four ways:

1   Policy elites deploy communication to distract their own public(s). This often involves creating (often patriotic) hype and 'puffery' to focus public attention on issues helpful to foreign policy implementation. Communication for distraction is often geared towards agenda setting as a steering mechanism – i.e. keeping potentially 'problematic' issues out of the public view, e.g. PR-ized warfare tries to keep death and blood off television screens (see 10.3 on p. 221);

2   When 'problematic' themes become media issues, PRs/spin-doctors are deployed to try and manage these issues off the news agenda, and/or at least try and manage some 'negativity' out of such stories;

3   Psy-ops, propaganda and misinformation are deployed to confuse populations deemed 'hostile';

4   Campaigns will be run to stir the masses and interpellate them into 'appropriate' belief systems. Foreign relations generally requires citizens see the world in terms of 'good guys' and 'bad guys' (allies and enemies), hence government leaders demonize some states and peoples, and praise others. This generally sets the tone for the picture of the world the media propagates.

An important feature of the media's relationship to foreign policy agendas is the extent to which the media help policy elites to keep mass publics in broad agreement with government foreign policies. It is noteworthy how readily the media and mass publics shift their views to match their country's foreign relations agendas. In part this happens because foreign issues have little salience domestically, hence most people appear content to trust their governments and foreign affairs officials to take the lead in these matters. It also happens because governments invest energy in promoting their preferred us/them and good/evil binary oppositions. Much communicative energy is expended selling the idea of villains to be defeated; victims to be rescued; pariah groups to be scorned, and if necessary fought; scapegoats to be blamed; and friends to be embraced and helped. When policy elites successfully manage the issues agenda, media coverage will highlight issues they want brought to the public's attention and be silent about 'problematic' issues – e.g. while the mainstream Western media highlighted Iraq's repression of Kurds, they downplayed (Nato member) Turkey's repression of Kurds. In general, it is only when policy elites become seriously divided on an issue that governments battle to control the coverage of foreign news because, when this happens, spin-doctors working for disaffected factions start to leak negative news. An example of this was when, in 2004, divisions emerged within the Bush and Blair policy teams concerning the Iraq War. Those periods when factional disputes produce 'leaking' are wonderful for journalists, but – because they disrupt the smoke-and-mirrors show – such periods are a disaster for the back stage policy makers (see chapter 2, Table 2.1).

If governments are to maintain the broad support of their populations for foreign policy initiatives, they need the media coverage of foreign affairs to be broadly sympathetic. Fortunately for policy elites, communication professionals now have a large enough repertoire of PR, spin and smoke-and-mirrors techniques (see 7.4 and 7.5 on pp. 16 and 168) to keep the media filled with 'appropriately' entertaining stories so as to facilitate the policy elite getting on with their jobs unencumbered by too much journalistic or public scrutiny concerning the activities of foreign affairs and military officialdom. For as long as the policy elites remain united enough to ensure all their PR's spin roughly compatible stories, discourse closure can be secured and public opinion can be safely steered.

Summary

You should now be familiar with the following key concepts and themes:
the CNN effect; media as a 'diplomatic channel'; media coverage as a 'morality play'; elite decision-making thesis; journalistic influences on policy making; public opinion's influence on policy making; attentive publics; the media's relationship to policy elite power struggles; 'united' policy elites versus 'divided' policy elites; and how journalists can get used in policy struggles, and in foreign policy spin-doctoring.

For further consideration

1 To what extent is it more difficult for the media to 'correctly' report foreign news?

2 To what extent is the 'CNN effect thesis' the result of:

   (a) media determinist thinking?

   (b) Journalists wishing to believe they are powerful?

   (c) The disgruntled who seek to blame the media for certain policies?

3 The US media have handled some foreign stories like 'morality plays' (e.g. Kosovo in 1999 and South Africa in the 1980s). Does such 'morality play' reporting actually *impact* on foreign policy? Or did such media coverage simply *reflect* foreign policy?

4 Is it foolish for governments to use the media as a source of intelligence about foreign contexts?

5 Are journalists more likely to be manipulated by spin-doctors in foreign contexts? Or less likely to be manipulated? Or is there no difference between foreign and local spinning?

6 Can you find any evidence that suggests that reporting of foreign contexts is affected by policy elites being divided or united?

7 CNN sees itself as a global watchdog. Is this self-image a reasonable portrayal?

8 Why have some stories become 'big news' in the West while other stories get 'played down'? e.g. *big news* – Israeli–Palestinian conflict; 1980s' South African conflict; Bosnian civil war; Somali war; *played down* – Indonesian genocide (1965); Rwanda genocide (1990); Conflict in China's Sinkiang-Uighur province; Central African/Congo wars (mid-1990s onwards).

9 Does the White House monitor networks like CNN as part of its policy-making function or hype-making function?

10 How can spin-doctors use journalists to alter foreign policy? If this has been done so, can you find examples?

13 Conclusion: Searching for Answers (and Questions)

In chapter 1 I stated that this book would deploy critical theory and constructivism to construct an exploration of the symbiosis that has developed between spin-doctors, journalists and politicians. For this purpose, the book has assembled an array of themes geared towards unpacking the media-ization of contemporary politics. What has been presented is a *construction* – i.e. questions and answers which hopefully provoke more questions about today's highly media-ized political processes. This chapter now recaps and highlights a number of issues covered in the book with a view to stimulating the reader to reflect upon these themes and draw his/her own conclusions.

13.1 What is media-ization?

Although there is widespread agreement that politics has been media-ized during the twentieth century, there is no agreement on what media-ization means. Broadly, media-ization has been seen as:

- The deepening of mass democratic control over political processes because the media:

    (a) Give the public the information needed to understand policy processes;

    (b) Provide a conduit for the masses to influence political decision makers – i.e. the media are seen as having become an integral part of the political process by serving as a conduit for *facilitating mass* *public participation* in policy making. Media-ization is thus equivalent to enhancing the democratization of representative parliamentary systems;

- Enhancing the *importance of the media* (e.g. journalists) within the political process because the media help determine policy agendas. This view (deriving from the watchdog notion) appeals to journalists because it places journalism center stage within liberal democratic processes. This school has advocated the Vietnam (and Somali) syndrome (see 10.2 on p. 218), and the CNN effect (see 12.1 on p. 252);
- The *intrusion of public relations, spin-doctoring and hype* into the political process. Media-ization is associated with the need that policy elites have to 'manufacture consent' and communicatively 'steer' the masses.

The first two views see media-ization as enhancing democracy. But these 'democratization' models encode tensions and confusions – praising media-ization's expansion of mass political participation; but (often) simultaneously expressing concern that media-ization has 'lowered the tone' of the political process; generated cynicism and damaged policy making (see Jamieson, 1992). Further, some writers encode the assumption that the media influence of mass publics is automatically equivalent to the media influencing policy makers. The assumption is only valid if policy makers are influenced by mass citizenries, which is not always the case.

This book advocates a third view – i.e. media-ization as the intrusion of managed, spin-doctored hype into a two-tiered political process. This proposal may help overcome an oft seen conceptual confusion of praising media-ized democratization, while simultaneously bemoaning its actual impacts on the political process. Could it be that this conceptual confusion has arisen because the policy and hype dimensions are run together?

This book has proposed that media-ization is the work of a policy elite that, although factionalized, shares a common interest in a PR-ized system that tries to steer mass publics. Hence, elites deliberately and systematically:

- Try and use the media to create consent and build mass legitimacy;
- Try and manage the masses communicatively and try and keep them at arm's length from the policy machinery. This involves trying to distract mass publics through spin-doctoring; impression management; deploying celebrity politicians; and selling policies through 'showmanship';
- Attempt to use PR techniques to steer journalists – i.e. try and integrate the media into a 'distraction machinery'.

Although never 100 percent successful, political PRs have grown increasingly skilled at using the media for the above purposes. From the point of view of students of politics and the media, the extent to which political PRs do and don't succeed is certainly worthy of systematic study. In this regard, Gramsci's notion of hegemony can be helpful. Gramsci (1971) developed the idea of legitimacy building as a system of defensive trenches. This notion is helpful for conceptualizing the PR/hype machine (and the media) as a set of trenches used by policy elites to keep their inner 'policy citadel' as free as possible from mass pressure. They will not always succeed in securing these defensive lines. But it is worth exploring:

- The extent to which policy elites try to build such trenches, and why?
- What techniques political PRs use;
- Their successes and failures.

13.2 The routines and practices of media-ized politics

For students of politics and the media, a central issue for examination would be: is political spin a marginal add-on to contemporary governance or not? Is what needs to be examined the extent which today's hype machines build professionalized communication into the very heart of Western governance? Further, is it correct to say that the spin industry (that grew up to advise how the media can be used to further the designs of policy makers) now actually steers mass public opinion? Any examination of what media-ized politics has become would do well to start with unpacking the following sorts of media impacts on political machinations:

- Policy making involves policy elites negotiating with a range of interest groups; financial backers; and other politicians (both inside their own political parties and in other parties). During these negotiations, the media can often be used to help to build leverage by mobilizing interest groups or public opinion in ways that undermine one's opponents' position, and/or boost one's own position. Many techniques can be used to generate beneficial media coverage, ranging from conventional PR to leaking stories to journalists;
- Communication experts are now routinely consulted to advise policy elites on what is politically possible – i.e. to what extent the public can be managed/steered. If communication experts inform politicians that they cannot deliver public approval, or acquiescence, or passivity on a proposed policy, policy elites appear to often pull back – i.e. it appears that communication experts now often set the limits on what is regarded as 'politically possible' – limits set by how far communicative steering is deemed feasible;

- After policy is formulated, the media can be enlisted to help secure public approval/acquiescence. Various PR tools are available to help to sell policies to mass (and niche) publics. Deploying such tools leads to the PR-ization of politics. It seems that politicians originally turned to PRs as a result of the massification of liberal democracy between 1820 and 1920 – i.e. as ever more people were enfranchised, policy elites needed to find ways to try and (communicatively) manage their mass publics. Could it be argued that the result has been the empowerment of the spin industry rather than politicians? Or has politics become so Machiavellianized that such a distinction between contemporary politicians and the spin industry is no longer meaningful?

13.3 Creating hype politics

Hype politics is about attempting to 'manufacture consent' through:

- Trying to sell policies and belief systems;
- Trying to popularize and naturalize discourses (and associated practices);
- Attempting to successfully stage-manage (or more correctly 'televisually manage') events and pseudo-events so as to try and steer news agendas;
- Manufacturing celebrities (pseudo-people), and attempting to interpellate mass publics into relationships with political celebrities.

It is for students of politics and the media to examine the extent to which hype politics achieves the above outcomes.

Those scripting hype politics are concerned with *agenda setting* – i.e. trying to direct the gaze of the public away from issues that might prove problematic for policy makers, and directing their gaze towards (scripted and managed) issues deemed helpful for steering society in the direction desired by the policy elites. However, audiences are not simply passive recipients of media messages. Indeed, they can (and do) resist the messages being propagated (Louw, 2001: chapter 10). This makes the need to employ PRs/spin-doctors more crucial for politicians because there is no single straightforward recipe guaranteeing success in steering (mass or niche) public opinion. Trying to steer the masses and manufacture consent involves a never-ending communicative struggle to find the right recipe for that particular issue, moment and context. Demagoguery is a highly contextual and imprecise art – its practitioners cannot guarantee success; but demagogues with a strong record of success are in high demand.

Journalists are necessarily implicated in hype politics because they process and re-package the information, events, pseudo-events and pseudo-people (celebrities) PRs have manufactured. Journalists routinely oppose the notion they are part of hype politics – i.e. deny they are steered by PRs/spin-doctors. Although it is true that not all journalists are 'steered' by PR/spin, many are. In part, this has happened because, as many newsrooms have been downsized and de-skilled, news production has effectively been 'outsourced'. Consequently, PRs have become the main source of information for the media and a de facto symbiotic relationship has emerged between PRs and journalists. In any case, PRs/spin-doctors are at their most successful when journalists are unaware that they have been manipulated. Such manipulations (e.g. leaks, plants and cover stories) can have significant political repercussions, such as bringing down politicians and/or factions, and thereby reallocating political power. For example, reformers in apartheid South Africa used leaks to undermine the government's far-right ruling faction, thereby transforming the political landscape. Reformers within the ruling party leaked a story to the (anti-apartheid) press about a SA Information Ministry covert operation to establish pro-apartheid newspapers and magazines, and attempts to buy overseas media (like the *Washington Post*). This produced the 'Information Scandal' (or 'Muldergate') which forced SA Prime Minister Vorster to resign and sidelined the ruling party's conservative Mulder faction (Rees and Day, 1980). Journalists took the credit for what was PR-ized politics.

Journalists do not like to think that they are implicated in demagoguery. The reality is that without journalists, PRs/spin-doctors would be unable to function. Both Lord Northcliffe's and William Randolph Hearst's careers were testaments to the role of the popular media and popular journalism in circulating discourses functional to liberal capitalism. The Northcliffe/Hearst model of popular journalism remains alive and well and, significantly, is a model affording PRs multiple opportunities for placing (hyped and scripted) stories. From this has emerged hype politics as a political genre born from the way celebrity politicians, the spin industry, public opinion analysts, journalists, anchors and pundits need each other, and feed off each other, in a game of smoke and mirrors and impression management geared towards trying to build mass consent. What is worthy of consideration is:

- Is hype politics necessarily bad, or is it functional? And if it is functional, for whom is it functional?
- Is hype politics simply a contemporary (televised) version of the sort of demagoguery that has always characterized politics?
- Is there really a realistic alternative to hype politics?
- What is the relationship between J.S. Mill's vision for liberal journalism and the Northcliffe/Hearst model of popular journalism?
- Has the relationship between Mill's vision and popular journalism changed over the last century?

- Under what conditions is J.S. Mill's vision for liberal journalism relevant?
- Who gains and who loses from hype politics?

13.4 When things go wrong for spin-doctors

Spin-doctoring is, at heart, about agenda setting, i.e. trying to:

- 'Distract' mass publics;
- 'Steer' mass publics and the media.

In this regard, the political hype machine (see chapter 2, Table 2.1) is geared towards performing entertaining smoke-and-mirror shows that, as far as possible, keep attention away from back stage policy making, while simultaneously legitimating the decisions made. But things go wrong, i.e.:

- Performances fail;
- Journalists write disruptive stories;
- Policy making is so bad that no amount of spin-doctoring can deflect attention away from what has gone wrong;
- Opposition spin-doctors plant 'disruptive' stories.

As Thompson (2000: 262–3) says: the communicative process is so complex that spin-doctors can never absolutely control the process of manufacturing political visibility – i.e. the media's power to disrupt political performances is greater than the ability of the spin machine to control these performances. Steering and agenda setting are at best imperfect arts.

However, the most common reason the hype machine's steering-function fails is that that policy elites become so seriously divided on an issue that they stop working together to maintain a consistent theme. When this happens, spin-doctors working for disaffected factions start leaking negative news that effectively disrupts the smoke-and-mirrors façade, and thereby provides some glimpses into the back stage work and policy mistakes which are normally concealed. Such periods are a disaster for back stage policy makers, and generate huge crises for the spin machines which then have to go into overdrive to: try and repair the damage done; prepare rhetorical defenses against future potential leaks; and attack or discredit the negative sources, e.g. running 'smears'.

During such crisis periods, the first instinct of spin-doctors is to try and 'bury the problem' by:

- Creating distractions and diversions – e.g. pseudo-events, pseudo-controversy, stage-managed conflicts, spectacular celebrity performances and so on;

- Creating plausible deniability;
- Scapegoating somebody;
- Scripting a new performance or a new celebrity face.

However, there will be occasions when the issue cannot be buried. On such occasions, spin-teams may need to actually make the story bigger and focus more attention on the problematic issue. This often involves constructing an enemy to be aggressively attacked and/or demonized. An example of this was when Blair's credibility was threatened by accusations that the Iraq weapons of mass destruction (WMD) story was a spin-doctored construct. Since the WMD story could not be buried, it was actually highlighted so as to cleverly refocus the issue (as much as possible) away from Blair and his spin-doctors and onto journalists and the BBC (see 7.3.6 on p. 159). The result was a high-profile aggressive performance that sufficiently obfuscated the issue so as to distract attention away from the fact that the WMD story was spin-doctored and that the mass media had for months been complicit in promoting it.

But spin-doctoring also goes wrong because audiences do not always react as anticipated. This is because meaning making involves a process of sharing and engagement between a communicator(s) and someone who has to receive, read and use the meaning being imparted. Because an active human subjectivity has to engage with any message before any meaning is actually made – i.e. the receiver of a message is as much part of the meaning-making process as the person(s) encoding the message – this leaves open the possibility that the meaning intended by the encoder may never be realized because of how the message can be interpreted, ignored, mis-read, deliberately reconstructed or even resisted. Stuart Hall provided a useful perspective on the role interpretation played within the overall process of constructing meaning. Hall (1980b) pointed out that encoding a message was merely the first step in the process of creating meaning, and the process was not completed until the message was *decoded*. He argued that all messages had encoded into them a 'preferred' meaning (i.e. the meaning that the hegemonically dominant would prefer the decoders of the message to accept), but he suggested the preferred meaning would not always be successfully conveyed. Instead, Hall proposed that three potential decodings were possible:

1 The first occurred when decoders simply unproblematically accepted and internalized the 'preferred' meaning(s) as intended by the encoder;
2 A second possibility was that decoders, operating within 'an oppositional code' rejected the message;
3 A third possibility was that a 'negotiated' meaning was achieved by decoders who accepted some elements of the 'preferred' meaning, but rejected other aspects.

Spin-doctors obviously hope that journalists and media audiences accept their 'preferred' meanings. And it does often happen that journalists (who are lazy or pressed for time) simply accept the line spun by PRs and spin-doctors. Similarly, many members of mass publics simply accept the political performances and agendas crafted by the spin industry. However, it also happens that some journalists and some citizens either completely reject the messages and performances or actively engage with these performances to produce 'negotiated' meanings. At such times spin-doctors do not achieve their intended results. However, such failures do not constitute the defeat of the spin process. Instead such failures simply lead to the need for a reengagement with the communicative problem at hand. In essence when spin-doctoring goes wrong, it generally leads to more spin-doctoring.

13.5 Hype politics: a system in trouble?
Or a system re-inventing itself?

Hype politics emerged from the evolution of liberal democracy, i.e.:

- Liberal democracies have always been concerned with building political processes maximizing the conditions required for capital accumulation;
- Mass unrest was dysfunctional for capitalism. This led to reforms leading to mass enfranchisement;
- Mass democracy produced potential new dysfunctions associated with the masses making (consumption and participation) demands undermining capitalism. This led to the building of PR/spin mechanisms for agenda setting and steering (geared towards trying and communicatively managing public opinion, building legitimacy and manufacturing consent). From this grew media-ized politics.

By the turn of the century, liberal democracy was experiencing steering problems – e.g. declining voter turnouts; a growing cynicism towards the political process; plus the growth of sizeable constituencies clearly alienated from the mainstream political process (associated with an increase in 'oppositional' decoding of political performances). Media-ized politics contributed to these phenomena in two ways.

Firstly, many political journalists began to feel uncomfortable with the symbiotic relationship between themselves and PRs/spin-doctors. This symbiosis generated dissonance between the reality of being semi-insiders within a political process driven by spinned hype, and a belief in watchdog journalism. One means to resolve this was to turn towards cynical journalism – i.e. journalists started 'exposing' the spin-doctored political 'game' to their audiences. But exposing this demagoguery proved highly dysfunctional for liberal democracies because it bred cynicism and voter apathy (especially among the media audiences most attentive to political issues). It also fed into a general distrust of mainstream politics, so contributing to the growth of alienated voters some of whom abandoned mainstream parties to support the 'politics of disaffection' – e.g. Jean-Marie Le Pen (France); Jorge Heider (Austria); Pim Fortyn (Netherlands); and Pauline Hanson (Australia). In this regard, an interesting phenomenon that students of politics and the media need to consider is the reason why, when cynical journalists perceived the middle-ground 'consensus' to be threatened by alienation, they generally fell back into line and (together with mainstream political parties) worked to try and counter the 'politics of disaffection'.

A second phenomenon for students of politics and the media to examine is, to what extent has the media-ization of politics been associated with the bland-izing of mainstream politics and a narrowing of policy options? What needs to be examined, and unpacked, are the following developments in political behavior. As politics became (overly?) communicatively managed, advisors seemingly steered politicians towards the uncontroversial center of the political spectrum. Political leaders mutated into scripted celebrities. Politicians became rewarded for their abilities to be Machiavellian 'performers' (with appropriate scripted 'personalities') rather than statesmen. Party machines, previously staffed by people committed to policies, were replaced by machines staffed by spin-doctors and impression managers. In the place of 'position statements' came (televisually) staged political 'faces', and pseudo-events, scripted to appeal to as broad a cross-section of the masses as possible. Appealing broadly, meant avoiding 'controversy' – i.e. avoiding saying things that might offend potential voters. Many things became simply 'unsayable' – with politicians and journalists learning to function within ever-narrowing, and increasingly bland discourses. (In its extreme form this bland-izing of discourse fed into a wider intellectual phenomenon of 'political correctness'/ PC-speak.) It could be argued that over time, the political process (as a scripted and communicatively managed affair) became bland and boring; which no amount of hyped celebrity nor hyped pseudo-events could disguise.

During the 1990s this scripted political show coincided with the triumph of neo-liberalism and 'globalization'. It is for students of politics and the media to unravel the relationships between the triumph of 'neo-liberal' and 'globalization' discourses and the emergence of a global networkers elite asserting its hegemony over the OECD, and attempting to assert its hegemony over the rest of the world. In Western democracies the 1990s witnessed the scripting of 'the great consensus' – a middle-ground position adhered to by all mainstream political parties which included the following dimensions:

- Political performance was measured in terms of competence at economic management, rather than implementing 'political principles';
- Economic management was geared towards successfully implementing 'neo-liberalism'. This became a virtually uncontested ideological 'given';
- A range of discourses were promoted which serviced the economic interests of the global networking elite. In this regard students of politics and the media can consider: 'globalization' (facilitating freer capital and trade flows; and the utilization of cheaper labor in places like Asia); 'feminism' (facilitating the expansion of the labor pool, and hence the reduction in labor costs); 'multiculturalism' (facilitating the expansion of the labor pool and markets); and the inter-related nexus of 'cosmopolitanism', 'human rights' and 'the information superhighway' (which facilitated 'universalizing' the values of the Anglo-dominated global networkers elite). It is worth considering: who has gained from these discourses?

By the turn of the century, Western political processes had become so contrived, spin-doctored and steered that it became difficult to distinguish between some Western political parties claiming to be opposed to each other – e.g. Conservatives and Labour in the UK; Republicans and Democrats (USA); and Liberals and Labor (Australia).

They all effectively subscribed to the same 'middle-ground consensus'. The mainstream media contented itself with circulating news, information and opinion confirming this consensus, creating a significant degree of 'discursive closure' in the 1990s.

People whose interests were served by, or compatible with, the emergent hegemony, failed to recognize this creeping discursive closure. However, people whose interests were not served by the hegemony of the global networkers grew increasingly uncomfortable with this 'consensus' and those scripting bland middle-ground positions. This generated a number of responses including:

- A growing cynicism towards hype politics. Politicians, spin-doctors and journalists were seen by many as part of the same 'untrustworthy' group of 'insiders';
- A growing apathy and voter withdrawal from participation in liberal democracy;
- A backlash inside the OECD from those unhappy with the new hegemonic order. This led to some stridently non-middle-ground positions – e.g. Le Pen, Heider, Fortyn, Hanson, the 'Patriot Movement', 'Nation of Islam', and the anti-globalization movement;
- A religious revival, often associated with orthodox interpretations (of Christianity, Hinduism, Judaism and Islam).

The above phenomena perhaps suggest that Western democracies may have become managed and contrived to the point that steering mechanisms became dysfunctional? Hyped politics appears to work best when spin-doctors have available material lending itself to the building of:

- A 'sense of excitement';
- Entertaining political 'shows';
- Collectivities for people to identify with (because people appear to derive emotional fulfillment from supporting 'a team'). When teams clash, levels of excitement, entertainment and identity are enhanced.

At the turn of the century, liberal democracy's teams (tweedle-dum and tweedle-dee political parties) had become too obviously stage-managed. The resultant curious mix of 'hyped' yet 'bland' politics was not proving a uniformly successful recipe for trying to manage mass public opinion and trying to manufacture consent.

Then came al-Qaeda's 9/11 attacks, leading to 'the war on terrorism'. This produced the following effects in the West:

- The middle-ground 'consensus' was destabilized, with issues previously considered 'settled' (e.g. migration, multiculturalism and law and order) once again in dispute. Post 9/11 politics is just as hyped, but is less bland;
- A post-9/11 'sense of threat' lent itself to politicians, PRs and psy-ops mobilizing 'us-them' binary oppositions. These have been deployed to sell policy options;
- Hype, spinning and impression management are still deployed to manage public opinion, but now politicians, PRs and psy-ops personnel have a whole new repertoire of themes to mobilize for demagogic purposes;
- 9/11 crystallized (for both sides) 'identifiable enemies', 'causes' and new 'collective identities' into which individuals could be interpellated. This has provided a wealth of material for the hype professionals;
- New leadership scripts and performances have emerged as politicians and their impression managers have learned to exploit (and exacerbate) the sense of threat and identity realignments generated by 9/11;
- Continued refinement of the demagoguery techniques associated with PR-izing much warfare.

It seems that 9/11 may have generated a plethora of new possibilities for re-inventing hype politics – i.e. it provided spin-doctors with the material from which to build a 'sense of excitement'; entertaining 'shows';

'us–them' binary oppositions; 'passions' and 'beliefs'. The post-9/11 environment seems to facilitate the building of new 'teams' to identify with, and/or oppose (e.g. nations, 'ways of life', anti-war groups, heroes and villains). Are these new teams both more exciting and (seemingly) less contrived than the old pre-9/11 teams? Hype politics has always manufactured teams and inter-team conflict. But liberal democracy's pre-9/11 teams had become stale because they revolved around increasingly unexciting horse-race politics based upon political parties that had become contrived and so little differentiated from one another that they no longer serviced the 'conflict needs' of hype politics. Could it be that 9/11 and its aftermath have created a plethora of new opportunities (e.g. war, conflict, polarization, patriotism, new collective identities) for liberal democracies to re-direct and re-energize their hype machines? For politicians, PRs, spin-doctors and psy-op personnel, a whole new range of communicative possibilities appears to have emerged for those attempting to 'steer' mass publics and build hegemony. Of course, simultaneously, whole new ranges of communicative possibilities have been created for counter-hegemonic hype. Has 9/11 therefore enhanced and deepened the role of hype merchants by providing them with the material needed to inject new energy and passion into their hype? And if 9/11 has re-energized the hype machine, what will its long-term effects be on hype politics?

13.6 Is media-ization bad?

It is now widely accepted that Western politics has been media-ized. Open to debate is whether this is necessarily a bad thing. As each of us ponders the question: 'is media-ization a bad thing?' it may be worth considering the role the media have played in constructing your own knowledge of and understanding of political issues and the political process. Have the media been fundamental in constructing your view of the political landscape over a long period of time (i.e. the 'drip-drip' of the cultivation theory) by putting pictures in your head? Alternately, are the media only one part of the process? Do you think you have been 'steered'? Is Plato's cave a reasonable analogy for today's televisualized world? Without the mass media how might mass democracies function? Without the mass media would there be less demagoguery? Or simply a different type of demagoguery?

Having thought through the above questions ask yourself, is media-ized politics:

- A bad thing?
- Inevitable?

- Functional in mass democracies?
- Necessarily associated with PR-ization?
- An intellectual construct that is an exaggeration and an example of media-centric thinking?

For further consideration

1 Identify arguments against the notion of a two-tier political process;

2 Identify arguments against the notion of policy elites who use PR to 'steer' journalists;

3 Identify arguments against the notion of passive publics;

4 Identify instances of liberal watchdog journalism that undermine the notion that spin-doctors now steer the political process;

5 Identify instances where PRs have used the very notion of watchdog journalism to successfully 'spin' a line;

6 Identify instances of where spin-doctoring backfired. Examine what the spin-doctors did in these instances to try and rectify the situation;

7 Do active audiences always undermine the effectiveness of spin-doctoring?

8 Can spin-doctors 'use' an active audience to make 'spin' and agenda setting more effective?

9 Can you identify politicians who are not scripted 'faces'?

10 Examine the relationship(s) between the 'war on terror' and spin-doctored hype politics.

Glossary

Agenda setting   refers to the way the media guide public opinion. The notion derives from the way committees structure their business through agendas – i.e. a list of topics to be discussed. The committee only discusses what is on the agenda. It is argued that the media act (often unintentionally) as such an agenda – issues not reported by the media do not become part of the public debate. Bernard Cohen's (1963) notion of agenda setting argued that the media may not be successful much of the time in telling people what to think, but they are stunningly successful in telling people what to think about. Spin-doctors (qv) try and use this media agenda-setting capacity as a devise for steering (qv) media audiences.

Alienation   describes how an individual can feel estranged from his/her own existence or from society. Marx ascribed alienation to the structures of society which placed people into 'alienating' circumstances (where people felt they had lost control over their own lives).

Anglo   refers to a (global) culture – i.e. a 'pool' or 'cluster' of meanings, practices and discourses. This Anglo 'pool' incorporates various sub-pools, including England, the USA, Canada, Australia, Ireland and New Zealand. Anglos dispersed themselves globally through two waves of colonization (British and American). Significantly, Anglo-American culture is assimilationist. Consequently, membership of contemporary Anglo culture is not exclusively derived from having roots in an Anglo 'ethnicity'; rather it is derived from having adopted (or having been assimilated into) Anglo meanings, practices and discourses. On-going assimilation processes are continually modifying Anglo cultural forms. Los Angeles has become one of the key sites for the production of contemporary Anglo-assimilationist culture, which is then disseminated throughout a global culture industry. From this has derived a view that global culture is being 'Americanized'. However, although global mass culture has strong geographical roots in southern California, it is simplistic to call it 'American'. Rather, this 'Los-Angeles-derivative' global culture is circulating meanings that are emerging from a process of cultural hybridization grounded upon a solidly Anglo foundation.

Anomie   refers to a situation in which people experience a 'loss' of social norms to guide them. Durkheim saw anomie as resulting from a break-down of social regulation. Anomie is often associated with the process of urbanization.

Assimilation   is the process by which individuals or groups belonging to different ethnic groups are absorbed into other groups. Anglo society has been assimilationist – i.e. it has systematically absorbed others in this way.

Bourgeoisie/Burghers   this urbanized class arose in northwestern Europe during the sixteenth century as an intermediary or *middle class* between the peasants and the feudal nobility. They were the middle-class *freemen* of burghs (free cities). These bourgeois/burgher freemen established European trading networks and built the trans-Atlantic trading system (which led to the colonization of the Americas). Their enterprise produced the growth of prosperous European cities which gradually grew into the core centers of power and influence in Europe and the world. A core feature of burgher enterprise was thrift and capital accumulation. From this grew capitalism. Eventually, bourgeois/burgher frustrations with the remnants of feudal power (monarchies and aristocratic privilege) produced revolutions, e.g. the Dutch Republic, Cromwell's Republic, England's 'Glorious Revolution', the French Revolution and the American Revolution. This set the stage for the establishment of middle-class liberal-capitalist hegemony across Western Europe and North America.

CNN effect   refers to the argument that the arrival of global television altered the nature of foreign relations because the conduct of foreign policy decision making was media-ized (qv). This was based on the observation that during the 1990 Gulf War, CNN provided: all players with round-the-clock information which appeared to provide real-time visual intelligence for both sides; a vehicle for delivering mis-information; a vehicle for 'back channel' negotiations (i.e. a potential short-circuiting of the role for professional diplomats); and a means for delivering PR/psy-ops messages directly to the other side's population.

Comprador   elites are associated with the notion of *neo-imperialism* (qv). Compradors are seen to act as '*deputies*' (or 'agents') for powerful foreign interests, i.e. 'comprador' ruling elites are deemed to be foreign impositions (by a range of socialist theorists; theorists opposed to 'neo-colonialism'; and more recently by Muslim fundamentalist theorists). The West is deemed responsible for local minorities of *Westernized* people becoming 'comprador' ruling elites in many Third World countries. These elites are deemed to be in power (despite often being corrupt, incompetent and brutal) because the West keeps them in power because they serve the economic interests of the West, and because having become Westernized, they are culturally proximate to those in power in the Western heartland.

Constructivist thinking argues that as human beings we *construct* our knowledge of the world in our minds by reflecting on our experiences. So knowledge is *not* 'out there' in a 'real world' to be discovered; rather it is made internally by a *mental process* which frames the questions we ask about the world, and frames the 'rules' by which we process/interpret the incoming data. Constructivism is a theory of knowledge that stands in contradistinction to empiricism (qv).

Cultural imperialism refers to the idea that economically powerful Western nations dominate smaller nations by cultural means. Culturally dominant nations (e.g. the USA and UK) are seen to export their *cultural products* (e.g. television programs, films, fashion) to weaker nations (especially underdeveloped Third World states). These products carry *cultural values* which then change the cultures of the weaker states. The notion of cultural imperialism is often associated with the view that the world is being Americanized.

Culture industry refers to a notion developed by the Frankfurt School (qv) that cultural production has been institutionalized and industrialized. Culture is now produced by small groups of professionals employed by the mass media and mass education organizations. The result is top-down 'mass culture' (qv). The culture industry inherently limits the range of opinions able to be expressed and is seen to manipulate and 'steer' the masses.

Dark arts refers to the term often disparagingly used by journalists to refer to public relations and spin-doctoring. PRs/spin-doctors are seen to be demagogues who use trickery and smoke-and-mirror shows to 'hide the truth' and obstruct journalists from doing their job.

Decoding refers to the way meaning is extracted from a language system. It is suggested that communicators *encode* meanings in the hope that the recipients of their messages extract the meaning they intended (i.e. decode the text as intended). When this does not take place *'aberrant decoding'* is said to have occurred (i.e. the meaning extracted is not the one intended by the author/encoder).

Demagoguery is the work of a demagogue. Demagoguery involves mobilizing the masses through the unprincipled use of populist language that incites passions and prejudice.

Digitization of communication refers to the way in which all types of communication can now be encoded in a form that enables them to be computerized. All human communication can now be (digitally) stored in computers; easily altered (through digital manipulation); and globally distributed via the (digitally based) internet system. Digitization has produced 'media convergence' – i.e. previously discrete media forms (print, visual, music and so on) are now merging.

Discourse refers to the way meaning is *socially produced*. We are born into existing societies and hence born into pre-existing 'discursive formations' (existing 'networks of meaning'). Individuals construct themselves out of these available discourses as meanings are internalized and used. Foucault argued that discourses (identifiable 'patterns of meaning') are produced (plus reproduced and altered) within *institutional* frameworks that are tied to specific contexts. Social relations, power relations and ideologies (qv) shape the making and circulation of these discourses. Meaning making is thus socially, historically and institutionally bound – media discourses, for example, are the constructed outcomes of institutionalized *practices* learned by those working within the media industry. Within the media industry people learn certain 'meanings' and 'practices' which thereafter 'guide' their perception and how they do their jobs – in this way media discourses are reproduced.

Elite refers to a minority group in society (often regarded as socially superior) which exercises some form of control over everyone else. When this control is political a ruling elite is said to exist. In pre-modern societies (e.g. feudalism) elites members achieved their status through hereditary means. Hence pre-modern elites clone themselves by having children. In modern liberal democracies, elite membership is not closed or ascribed by birth, i.e. 'elite churn' occurs because successful children of the non-elite can gain entry to modern elites. In modern societies elites are large and complex – they are not homogeneous, closed or static; in fact, elite divisions and disagreements result in competition between different sections of the elite.

Empiricism is a theory of knowledge which contends that a real objective world exists 'out there', independently of thinking subjects. Humans get access to this real world through their senses. Senses connect the 'inner' subjective world (of thinking) to the 'outer' objective world of empirical reality. Knowledge of the world is achieved by carefully recording empirical regularities. Subjectivism (i.e. ideas constructed within individual minds) must be eliminated from knowledge. 'Good' empirical knowledge results from ensuring there is correspondence between what is described and the world 'out there'.

Feudal system refers to the way European society was ordered after the collapse of the Roman Empire. Following the collapse of this empire local strongmen took control. From this grew the European aristocracy. Feudalism was a hierarchal system of institutions which imposed obligations of obedience and service. This grew out of the way aristocratic Lords had undertaken to protect local populations (*vassals*) during the chaos following the collapse of the Roman Empire. This Lord–vassal (protection–obligation) relationship became entrenched within a dense network of contractual relationships which tied people into 'their place' in society, reaching from the King at the top to the lowest serf at the bottom. The basic unit of social control was the manorial estate, where a local Lord governed his vassals.

Fourth Estate refers to the idea, developed by John Locke, that the best guarantee of good governance was that elected legislators should be scrutinized by an independent media – i.e. the media should be regarded as an autonomous 'fourth estate' within the political system whose job it was to continually monitor the other three estates so that bad policy making and corruption would be immediately exposed. The media therefore needed to be granted the right to access all the necessary information to make their monitoring task possible. Locke saw independent media and the right to an unhindered (uncensored) free flow of information as central to a functioning liberal democracy.

Frankfurt School of 'critical theory' consisted of a group of neo-Marxist intellectuals which included Adorno, Horkheimer, Fromm, Marcuse, Benjamin and Habermas. Their work on US mass media and mass culture resulted in the notion of a 'culture industry' (qv) and mass society (qv). The Frankfurt School developed a pessimistic view of society in which they argued that the mass media would permanently manipulate the masses. Marxists criticized the Frankfurt School's pessimism and argued that the mass society theory was wrong because the masses were 'active' not 'passive'.

Hegemony is a concept developed by Gramsci to describe the way ruling groups get those whom they rule to accept the fact that they are being ruled. Hegemony is achieved by a mixture of using coercion, legitimacy and alliance building (politicking). Ruling groups which achieve this are 'hegemonic'. An important feature of becoming hegemonic is *'winning consent'* from the ruled, so that they accept the ruling groups' dominance, their 'definitions of reality' and their systems of governance and laws. Ruling groups use the media and education systems to *naturalize* their discourses (qv), ideologies (qv), institutions and governance.

Hype   is a colloquialism widely used within the media industry. Hype involves stimulating an atmosphere of excitement or enthusiasm. This activity is carried out by politicians (trying to whip up support for themselves); sports coaches (trying to activate teams); choreographers of mass entertainment (scripting mass sports events, pop concerts and so on); and publicists/advertisers (trying to make some product fashionable/popular). Hype encodes the notion that hype makers are aware that they are creating publicity that is somehow 'false', a 'bluff', or a 'con job'. Hence, professional hype makers (e.g. spin-doctors) are regarded as 'confidence tricksters' engaged in deliberately deceiving audiences to advantage themselves or their employers. The end result is seen as some sort of 'false' belief. In politics, such 'false belief' might be myth, ideology, celebrity, or distraction.

Ideology   has been used commonsensically by non-Marxists to refer to a set of attitudes or emotions towards the world. These thoughts or emotions are often emotional belief systems. These beliefs guide the way the world is seen and how the believers behave. Ideology as an academic concept has its roots in Marxist theory. For Marxists, an ideology is a system of ideas used by a ruling group to *control subordinate classes*. Ideology is thus a system of thought designed to service the vested interests of a particular social group. For Marxists, ideology *disguises* the real state of affairs, making it impossible for the subordinated groups to see that they are being subordinated. Marx argued that the ideas of the ruling class would always be the *'ruling ideas'* in any epoch – i.e. at any point in time a ruling group will make sure the ideas (ideology) that serve their interests are dominant in that society. These ideas will be naturalized (qv).

Information rich/Information poor   is a dichotomy that emerged during the growth of information economies. The information rich are those with: (a) easy access to the information technologies underpinning information economies (e.g. computers, the Internet, niche media, and the growing pool of information); plus (b) adequate knowledge for using these technologies and information. The information poor are those who have little or no access to this 'information-ized' and digitized world. The citizens of some regions – e.g. the OECD (qv) – have high levels of access to these information technologies/information while other regions (e.g. most of Africa) do not.

Interpellate refers to the way in which personalities on television (or film) grab our attention. Interpellation means 'hailing' (or 'calling') – an analogy being the way we always respond when our names are called out. Althusser argues that each of us 'knows' who we 'are' *within relationships* because each of us is 'interpellated' as we speak. Other people around us are similarly 'interpellated' as we speak to each other. Effectively, our identity (who we think we are) and our status are embedded within representational systems – i.e. we are positioned within a system of language. When we respond to someone 'hailing' us, we (unconsciously) accept our social position, and the position of the person calling us. The point is, these positions are socially constructed – they are 'meanings' made in, and through, the language we share. Celebrities (including celebrity politicians) are deliberately constructed to interpellate 'ordinary' people into a fantasy world. Televised celebrity-ness helps people to make sense of the world, and becomes a device for the scriptwriters to steer the masses.

Keynesian economics emerged as a result of the Great Depression. J.M. Keynes proposed that governments abandon liberal *laissez faire* policies and instead argued they should directly intervene in the economy to manage economic recessions/unemployment out of the system. Until the 1970s, Keynesianism resulted in major government interventionism in Western economies.

Legitimacy refers to the process by which those who have power and influence in society seek to have their power seen as legitimate – i.e. legitimacy is achieved when those over whom they exercise power believe this exercise of power to be justified and morally defensible. All societies are held together by ideas and rules. Ruling elites (qv) work hard to bring about a legitimation of those 'rules of the game' and ideas which serve their interests. The media and education systems are centrally implicated in creating legitimacy for these rules and ideas. A failure to achieve legitimacy creates steering (qv) problems.

Machiavellian refers to an unscrupulous manipulator. Machiavellian politicians see the end as justifying the means and so they routinely practice duplicity to achieve their ends. The notion emerged from the ideas of Niccoló Machiavelli (1469–1527), an Italian statesman who developed a theory of unscrupulous statecraft. Machiavelli (1975) argued that in politics the end justifies the means. His advice to politicians was:

'one must know how to colour one's actions and to be a great liar and deceiver. Men are so simple, and so much creatures of circumstance, that the deceiver will always find someone ready to be deceived' (1975: 100).

Mass culture   is the form of culture produced by the mass media (qv). It is the cultural form associated with mass societies (qv). Mass culture is manufactured by the culture industry (qv). It is consequently a top-down form of culture because it is made by a small number of professional communicators and then communicated to mass audiences. The opposite of mass culture is 'popular culture', which is culture produced organically by people themselves, rather than culture manufactured for them. An example of the difference between mass and popular culture would be: commercialized sport (organized as a spectator sport of hyped-up competition by professionals, and then marketed to 'fans' to make a profit) versus a local community organizing its own sports team in which they participate. Mass culture is seen to be driven by commercialized fads and fashions driven by marketers who are specialists in creating 'followers' of what is 'cool' or status symbols and so on.

Mass democracy   emerged as a result of liberal oligarchies reforming themselves during the nineteenth and twentieth centuries. These reforms expanded the number of voters until universal franchise (where everyone had the vote) was achieved.

Mass media   first emerged in the late nineteenth century when new technologies and distribution systems made it possible to reproduce hundreds of thousands of copies of a newspaper. Newspapers developed by Northcliffe and Pulitzer (qv) became the first mass media to reach enormous audiences. Contemporary mass media now reach multi-million strong audiences. The mass media are newspapers, magazines, radio, television, film, and the World Wide Web.

Mass society   theory was developed by, among others, the Frankfurt School (qv). Industrialized urbanized society was seen as having produced workforces of isolated individuals who suffered from alienation (qv) and anomie (qv). These isolated individuals were 'gathered together' by the mass media (qv). Significantly, they never actually interacted with each other (and so never actually constituted a community of people engaged with each other). Instead, the media placed them into a set of imaginary relationships with each other – i.e. they 'met' through media portrayals. These portrayals created 'mass societies' in which huge numbers of people ('the masses') believed themselves to be part of mass collectivities (e.g. nations, 'the people', citizens and so on), while in reality they lived isolated lives effectively cut off from each other in suburbia or apartment blocks. Because their identities and 'interaction' were mediated (i.e. created via the media), the masses were effectively steered and manipulated by those who created media content and mass culture (qv). In mass societies 'the masses' were 'passive' – being led by media representations which turned them into passive publics, fans and audiences. Advocates of the 'active audience' thesis dispute the 'mass society' theory because they argue audiences are 'active' not 'passive'.

Media-ized   politics refers to the way in which professional communicators now script the performances and appearance of politicians. A significant amount of the time and energy of politicians and their professional support staff is now focused on impression management and public relations. Contemporary politics in Western democracies is increasingly about using public relations to create 'a public' – i.e. professional 'public builders' now use the mass media (qv) to assemble publics out of isolated individuals. The result is that politics has become a secondhand mediated reality for most people because they do not encounter politics in a direct (firsthand) manner that involves active participation. Instead, passive mass audiences now encounter *mediated* politics via the media. Politics in mass societies (qv) is thus increasingly confined to encountering scripted politicians as a set of secondhand (manipulated and distorted) media images.

Modern   culture first emerged during the eighteenth century as part of the Euro-American Enlightenment phenomenon. The modernization process became strongly associated with the growth of objectivist science and nineteenth- and twentieth-century industrialization. Modernism was strongly associated with the printed word. Underpinning this modernization process was the discourse of 'modernism', which emphasizes rationalism and materialist secularism (qv). Following the Enlightenment, modernization and modernity became the unquestioned teleological end goals of Western 'progress'. Thereafter, as modernization spread across the globe from its Western European epicenter, pre-modern cultures and societies have been systematically effaced. Modernists have always sought to build a better future; indeed they have been convinced they had a clear vision of a better future and a rational plan to get there. A characteristic of modernism (whether in its capitalist or Marxist forms) has been its refusal to accept any limits to modernity's teleological (qv) vision of 'progress'. However, in the early 1970s an anti-modern 'counter-culture' emerged which matured into a postmodern (qv) critique of modernism.

Montage   refers to the piecing together of different visual shots in a film. This editing technique, developed by Eisenstein, uses the tendency of the human mind to fill in blanks and to construct a single narrative from disparate and unrelated shots. Montage can therefore create visual effects that were not actually present in reality and can get viewers to actively link together elements of a story that are not really connected.

Myth   refers to narratives/stories which help a particular cultural group make sense of their world. These tend to take the form of 'traditional stories' (which none the less mutate over time). Unlike ideologies (which are organized belief systems), myths are 'commonsensical' beliefs that circulate organically within a community. Myths are culture-specific constructs that serve to naturalize a belief and/or value systems within the particular linguistic community the myth circulates within.

Naturalized   ideas are made to seem 'just the way things are'. Naturalized ideas become so 'normal' that they are simply taken for granted in a particular society. Everybody simply knows that is the way the world is. To question naturalized ideas becomes difficult, if not impossible, because it involves the questioner stepping so far outside the worldview 'acceptable' in that society that the questioner appears aberrant (even 'insane').

Narrowcasting   refers to the distribution of radio/TV signals to a targeted *niche* audience or geographical area – i.e. the signal is 'cast' narrowly. This is as opposed to broadcasting where signals are distributed to a widespread, scattered and diverse *mass* audience.

Neo-imperialism   refers to a form of foreign control. Imperialism involves foreign empires directly ruling countries which they annex into their empires (e.g. the British Empire). Neo-imperialism is associated with the way the USA has established a trading 'empire' which it does not directly rule. Instead, nominally independent states are integrated into trade relationships as subservient players such that they are effectively dependencies of the dominant state. The rulers of these dependent states are described as compradors (qv).

New World Order   (NWO) refers to the emergence of a changed global balance of power after the collapse of the Soviet Union in 1991. This made the USA economically and militarily dominant across the globe. The global dominance of a single superpower was referred to as a New World Order.

Northcliffe/Pulitzer press model   emerged in the late nineteenth century. From this early attempt to appeal to the newly enfranchised masses grew a new genre of hype-oriented mass media. Pulitzer in the USA and Northcliffe in the UK invented a genre of profitable mass journalism. Their *mass circulation* newspapers became financially successful by running easy to read short hype stories with jazzy headlines, which appealed to the (newly enfranchised) lower middle classes with enough disposable income to interest advertisers. This popular press pioneered a new way of reporting politics – focusing on personalities and gossip rather than principles, and on trivia rather than policy issues. Journalists were taught to seek out news that ordinary people would want to talk about on buses, trains and in their offices.

Objectivity   refers to the attempt made by empirical science and by liberal journalists to avoid subjectivism/bias. Objective knowledge and objective journalism – which are informed by empiricism (qv) – are geared towards ensuring a correspondence between what is described and the world 'out there'.

OECD   (Organization for Economic Cooperation and Development) consists of the USA, Canada, UK, France, Germany, Italy, Switzerland, Austria, Netherlands, Belgium, Luxemburg, Denmark, Sweden, Norway, Finland, Iceland, Spain, Portugal, Greece, Ireland, Japan, Australia and New Zealand. Although seemingly disparate and geographically scattered across the globe, the OECD is an important political-economic category because this collection of countries effectively constitutes the world's economic heartland; as well as representing those countries most thoroughly colonized by the Anglo-American liberal model of governance.

Oligarchy   refers to a form of government where a sub group in society (e.g. a dominant class) exercises power. This dominant group may organize decision making democratically.

Pan-human universalism   refers to the way the Anglo-American form of governance and social organization has come to be seen as universally valid within the Anglo-American world – i.e. a model that should become the basis of how all human societies organize themselves. The USA has become a powerful agent of this 'pan-human universalism'. Greenfeld argues that the model can be traced back to how the English notion of 'national' political participation was exported to the USA ready-made. Because Americans did not have to build ('struggle for') this national identity, it simply became a 'given'. Transplanted Anglo notions of governance became taken-for-granted 'givens' that were necessarily opaque to Americans. Because they were effectively de-contextualized ideals within the USA, and new migrants were simply assimilated into these given ideals, it became possible to believe 'national' political participation was a 'universal'. This (Anglo) ideal has been systematized into a teleological (qv) model of political modernization.

Patronage   refers to a situation where a person/s with power or wealth, gives support, favors, or protection to another person/s. A patron–client power relationship is thereby established. Feudalism was one form of political patronage, where powerful nobles protected peasants in return for loyalty and service. A contemporary form of patronage can be found in place like Malaysia, Indonesia and South Africa where political elites encourage favored individuals or groups to become 'crony capitalists' by granting them special favours or dispensations. These favored groups reciprocate by becoming loyal allies.

Pax Americana   (American Peace) refers to the USA's military and economic global dominance since 1991 within a New World Order (qv). The USA exercises its dominance not by means of direct imperial control, but through (a) a network of trade relations; (b) a capacity to project its military might globally; (c) a network of multilateral and bilateral agreements; and (d) through cultural imperialism (qv). The extent of US dominance varies from country to country, and the construction of a Pax Americana is still a work in progress.

Polysemic   refers to the capacity for encoding multiple meanings. A televised personality scripted to be polysemic will encode multiple personality traits in order to appeal to as many different kinds of audiences as possible.

Postfordism   describes the way production is organized in post-industrial capitalism. Postfordism involves a departure from 'fordist' factory methods of (modernist) mass production and mass consumption. The growth of postfordism saw a shift towards a service and information economy, plus the integration of computers into the production process; the growth of niche production and marketing; and a shrinking working class in OECD countries.

Postmodern   culture emerged towards the end of the twentieth century, accompanying the growth of postindustrial capitalism and postfordism (qv). Postmodern culture is more visual than modern (qv) culture – the postmodern experience is increasingly 'lived through' media-ized electronic-media representations (television, videos, DVDs, CDs,

Walkmans, and the Internet). Postmodern discourses problematize and question modernist 'truths'; with postmodernists seemingly wallowing in the chaotic, fragmentary rapidly changing experiences associated with experiencing media-ized lives.

Psy-ops (psychological operations) is a specialist branch of propaganda wherein psychologists are used to help design messages. Because 'propaganda' has acquired negative connotations, Anglo democracies no longer officially run propaganda operations – they have been re-badged as psy-ops. Psy-ops were given a major boost by the cold war, with the establishment of the USA's Psychological Warfare Center at Fort Bragg.

Public opinion is commonly used to refer to what voters think in mass democracies. Public opinion has become a shorthand term for describing what all citizens are thinking. Lippmann saw public opinion as the outcome of the deliberate self-conscious art of persuasion. For Lippmann, the notion that public opinion emanated spontaneously within democracies was false. Instead, public opinion was the outcome of leaders cultivating symbols and stereotypes, designed to organize, lead and steer (qv) the masses, i.e. public opinion is manufactured into existence by a communicatively skilled elite. So 'publics' are assembled by professional 'public builders' from the isolated individuals of mass societies (qv). They use the mass media (qv) to assemble these publics – the media acting as a form of social glue, constructing and holding together public opinion. Hence, 'publics' and 'public opinion' are artificial constructs. 'Publics' have no real 'presence' because they are assembled in the ether of media representations. One cannot find 'a public', because it does not 'exist'. But one can find 'public opinion' by constructing it as an intellectual exercise (i.e. conducting public opinion surveys). Like Lippmann (1965), Hartley (1992) saw 'the public' as a mediated phenomenon (i.e. born of media representations). However, Hartley disagreed that elites created publics. Instead Hartley argued that ordinary people also participated in the creation of 'publics' through being the active audiences of media representations.

Pundits arose when journalists tried to lessen their dependence on sources with clear vested interests by turning to another kind of source, namely, the ('non-involved') expert–observer or commentator, e.g. academics (in universities, think-tanks and the policy sector). This practice grew to also include other 'non-involved' sources, e.g. pollsters, other journalists, campaign/communication consultants, and retired politicians and officials. Using these people as sources gives them profile and status, and transforms them into something of a 'priestly caste' of 'experts', 'sages' and 'oracles'. Effectively, by selecting them as sources, the media transforms them into 'professional commentators' or 'pundits'. An especially worrying element of 'punditocracy' is the way in which the media now use other journalists as 'expert commentators', i.e. journalists effectively promote other journalists into the role of 'experts'.

Secularism　refers to the way in which the influence of religious belief has declined in modern (qv) societies. Secularization has been a major feature of modernizing societies as religious and supernatural beliefs have been replaced with new sets of beliefs, associated with materialism, rationalism and 'science'. As societies are secularized, religious institutions lose status and authority. A backlash to secularization has emerged in the form of the fundamentalist religions.

Semiosis　refers to the way signs are actively constructed within the semiotic process. Semiotics (as the study of signs, codes and culture) sees meaning as socially produced at the (micro) level of sign systems. Meaning is structured by the way a 'signifier' (the physical form received by our senses) is attached to a 'signified' (the mental concept being conveyed). Saussure argued that 'signification' (qv) happens when the relationship between these two is achieved, such that meaning is constructed and transferred.

Signification　refers to the relationship between a 'signifier' and 'signified' within the semiotic process. These relationships are arbitrary, but come to be seen as 'natural' givens. Barthes argued that there were two levels of signification, namely denotation and connotation. Higher level (connotative) meaning making generates the various myths (qv), ideologies (qv) and discourses (qv) associated with different cultural formations.

Spin-doctor　is a term first used with reference to Ronald Reagan's media team in a 21 October 1984 *New York Times* editorial. Spin-doctors are professional *impression managers* who have become the interface between politicians and journalists. Journalists see spin-doctors as practitioners of the dark arts (qv) and demagoguery (qv). Spin-doctors are experts in 'hype' (qv) and the arts of televisualized politics, i.e. they craft the 'faces' of politicians and script and stage manage political performances. To be successful, requires that spin-doctors know how to use the media to their own advantage. This involves being familiar with journalistic practices and discourses. Ultimately spin-doctors are involved in trying to (a) get journalists to see the world from an angle that suits the spin-doctor's agenda; (b) deflect attention away from issues and stories they want to 'bury'; and (c) plant and leak stories. Spin-doctors are experts in using the media to 'steer' (qv) public opinion (qv).

Spin industry refers to the way in which spin-doctoring has been routinized in contemporary western politics through the widespread employment of a range of specialists who are expert in crafting televisual performances with a view to steering both mass and niche publics. These specialists include spin-doctors, public relations consultants, minders, advertising consultants, public opinion pollsters, make up artists, and speechwriters. The spin industry is not a coherent, homogeneous block geared to a single goal. Rather spin-doctors (qv) work for different employers who are often in competition with each other – hence, spin-doctors compete with each other, i.e. a success for one spin-team may be a loss for another. Consequently, the spin industry does not have a single effect; rather it has multiple (sometimes contradictory) effects.

Steering refers to the notion that public opinion (qv) does not arise spontaneously, but is the outcome of how the media is used in mass societies (qv) to create imaginary relationships between individuals; to propagate belief systems; and to create celebrities. These devices are used to influence or 'steer' the behavior of media audiences. Politicians and the spin industries they employ are experts in using the media to construct and steer publics. In effect, spin-doctors attempt to use the media agenda setting (qv) capacity to steer audiences. A major tool for managing mass publics is the building of legitimacy (qv). Failure to achieve legitimacy results in ruling elites (qv) experiencing 'steering problems', i.e. the masses (qv) are non-compliant or rebel (cease to be passive).

Symbolic interactionism is an empirical approach to understanding how human beings construct their meanings through social encounters. Meanings are seen to be ever shifting – emerging from 'negotiations' and 'interactions' between individuals functioning within groups. Mead argued that individuals staged performances. Through these performances they constructed the faces they wanted to present to the world. Everybody within a group needed to collaborate in the sharing of symbols in order to make the 'staged performances' work. Successful sharing of symbols within rule-governed interactions is what effectively held society together as a functional unit.

Teleology refers to a belief that an end goal or 'purpose' is pre-encoded into a phenomenon's evolutionary path, thereby making the end pre-ordained. Certain phenomena are therefore seen to be inherently superior because they are the end goal of a 'necessary' progress. This idea of (teleological) 'natural progress' can be seen in the Marxist view that communism is the highest stage of social organization, and in the modernist view that Western political modernization is necessarily 'progressive'.

Westminster Parliamentary system   is regarded as the mother of Anglo democratic governance. The Westminster model originally emerged as a compromise between England's feudal nobility and the rising bourgeois/ burgher 'middle class'. In terms of this compromise, legislation is formulated by an elected lower house of Parliament (which originally represented the middle classes; but later came to include representatives of all social classes). A non-elected upper house (which originally represented the nobility) reviews this legislation. The executive function of government is carried out by a Cabinet made up of members of the political party winning the majority of seats in the lower house. As a system of constitutional monarchy, the Westminster model relocated power away from a hereditary monarch towards an elected parliament; with the monarchy being reduced to a ceremonial role. The Westminster model functions in the UK, Canada, Australia and New Zealand. The USA's republican model of governance remains grounded in the Westminster tradition.

References

Abercrombie, N., Hill, S. and Turner, B.S. (1980) *The Dominant Ideology Thesis*. London: Allen and Unwin.

Abrahamson, J.B., Arterton, F.C. and Orren, G.R. (1990) *The Electronic Commonwealth. The Impact of New Media Technologies on Democratic Politics*. New York: Basic Books.

Adatto, K. (1993) *Picture Perfect. The Art and Artifice of Public Image Making*. New York: Basic Books.

Adorno, T. and Horkheimer, M. (1979) 'The culture industry: enlightenment as mass deception', 120–67 in T. Adorno and M. Horkheimer, *Dialectic of Enlightenment*. London: Verso.

Almond, G. (1965) 'A developmental approach to political systems', *World Politics*, 17 (2): 183–214.

Althusser, L. (1971) *Lenin, Philosophy and Other Essays*. London: New Left Books.

Anderson, B. (1991) *Imagined Communities. Reflections on the Origin and Spread of Nationalism*. London: Verso.

Anon (1941) *The Atlantic Charter. A full Text of the Joint Declaration of the President of the United States of America and the Prime Minister of Great Britain* (12 August). London: Whitcombe & Tombs Ltd.

Arterton, F.C. (1987) *Teledemocracy*. Newbury Park, CA: Sage.

Bahro, R. (1981) *The Alternative in Eastern Europe*. London: Verso.

Barrington-Moore, J.R. (1973) *Social Origins of Dictatorship and Democracy*. Harmondsworth: Penguin.

Bartle, J. and Griffiths, D. (2001) *Political Communication Transformed: From Morrison to Mandelson*. Basingstoke: Palgrave.

Bassiouni, M.C. (1979) 'Prolegomenon to terror violence', *Creighton Law Review*, 12 (3) Spring: 752.

Beaufre, A. (1965) *An Introduction to Strategy*. London: Faber.

Becker, T. (1981) 'Teledemocracy', *The Futurist*, December: 6–9.

Becker, T. (1993) 'Teledemocracy: gathering momentum in state and local governance', *Spectrum*, 66 (2): 14–19.

Bell, D. (1973) *The Coming of Post-Industrial Society. A Venture in Social Forecasting*. New York: Basic Books.

Bennett, W.L. (1990) 'Towards a theory of press state relations in the United States', *Journal of Communication*, 40 (2): 103–25.

Bennett, W.L. (1994) 'The media and the foreign policy process', in D.A. Deese, *The New Politics of American Foreign Policy*. New York: St Martin's Press.

Bennett, W.L. (1995) 'The clueless public: Bill Clinton meets the new American voter in Campaign '92', in S.A. Renshon (ed.), *The Clinton Presidency*. Boulder, CO: Westview Press.

Bennett, W.L. and Entman, R.L. (2001) *Mediated Politics. Communication in the Future of Democracy*. Cambridge: Cambridge University Press.

Bennett, W.L. and Manheim, J.B. (2001) 'The big spin: strategic communication and the transformation of pluralist democracy', 279–98 in W.L. Bennett and R.L. Entman, *Mediated Politics. Communication in the Future of Democracy*. Cambridge: Cambridge University Press.

Berger, P.L. (1977) *Pyramids of Sacrifice*. Penguin Books.

Berger, P. and Luckman, T. (1979) *The Social Construction of Reality*. Harmondsworth: Penguin.

Birn, R. (1977) *Crisis, Absolutism, Revolution: Europe, 1648–1789/91*. Hinsdale, IL: Dryden Press.

Blumler, J.G. and Gurevitch, M. (2001) 'Americanization reconsidered: UK–US campaign communication comparisons across time', 380–406 in W.L. Bennett and R.L. Entman, *Mediated Politics. Communication in the Future of Democracy*. Cambridge: Cambridge University Press.

Blumler, J.G., Kavannagh, D. and Nossiter, T.J. (1996) 'Modern communications versus traditional politics in Britain: unstable marriage of convenience', 49–72 in D.L. Swanson and P. Mancini (eds), *Politics, Media, and Modern Democracy. An International Study of Innovations in Electoral Campaigning and Their Consequences*. Westport, CT: Praeger.

Bonafede, D. (1998) 'The President, Congress, and the media in global affairs', 95–120 in A. Malek (ed.), *News Media and Foreign Relations. A Multifaceted Perspective*. Norwood, NJ: Ablex.

Boorstin, D.J. (1971) *The Image. A Guide to Pseudo-Events in America*. New York: Atheneum.

Boulding, K. (1956) *The Image*. Ann Arbour, MI: University of Michigan Press.

Bourdieu, P. (1998) *On Television and Journalism*. London: Pluto Press.

Bramsted, E.K. (1965) *Goebbels and National Socialist Propaganda 1925–1945*. East Lansing, MI: Cresset Press.

Bridgland, F. (1990) *The War for Africa*. Johannesburg: Ashanti.

Brivio, E. (1999) 'Soundbites and irony: Nato information is made in London', 515–22 in P. Goff and B. Trionfi (eds), *The Kosovo News and Propaganda War*. Vienna: International Press Institute.

Cannon, L. (1991) *President Reagan. The Role of a Lifetime*. New York: Simon & Schuster.

Caprini, M. and Williams, B. (2001) 'Let us infotain you: politics in the new media environment', 160–81 in W.L. Bennett and R.L. Entman, *Mediated Politics. Communication in the Future of Democracy*. Cambridge: Cambridge University Press.

Cappella, J.N. and Jamieson, K.H. (1997) *Spiral of Cynicism. The Press and the Public Good*. Oxford: Oxford University Press.

Castells, M. (1997) *The Power of Identity*. Oxford: Blackwell.

Clutterbuck, R. (1981) *The Media and Political Violence*. London: Macmillan.

Cockerell, M., Hennessy, P. and Walker, D. (1984) *Sources Close to the Prime Minister. Inside the Hidden World of the News Manipulators*. London: Macmillan.

Cohen, B.C. (1963) *The Press and Foreign Policy*. Princeton, NJ: Princeton University Press.

Cohen, S.S. and Zysman, J. (1987) *Manufacturing Matters: The Myth of the Post-Industrial Economy*. New York: Basic Books.

Crenshaw, M. (1981) 'The causes of terrorism', *Comparative Politics*, July: 379–99.

Crenshaw Hutchinson, M. (1978) *Revolutionary Terrorism. The FLN in Algeria, 1945–1962*. Stanford, CA: Hoover Institution.

Cunningham, B. (2003) 'Re-thinking objectivity', *Columbia Journalism Review*, July/August: 24–32.

Dahl, R.A. (1967) *Pluralist Democracy in the United States: Conflict and Consent*. Chicago: Rand McNally.

Denton, R.E. Jr. (1988) *The Primetime Presidency of Ronald Reagan*. New York: Praeger.

Diamond, E. and Bates, S. (1992) *The Spot. The Rise of Political Advertising on Television* (3rd edition). Cambridge, MA: MIT Press.

Downs, A. (1957) *An Economic Theory of Democracy*. New York: Harper & Row.

Dye, T.R. (1998) *Understanding Public Policy*. Englewood Cliffs, NJ: Prentice-Hall.

Edelman, M. (1964) *The Symbolic Uses of Politics*. Urbana, IL: University of Illinois Press.

Elgin, D. (1993) 'Revitalizing democracy through electronic town meetings', *Spectrum: the Journal of State Government*, 18 (2): 6–13.

Emery, E. (1962) *The Press and America*. Englewood Cliffs, NJ: Prentice-Hall.

Engelhardt, T. (1994) 'The Gulf War as total television', 81–95 in S. Jeffords and L. Rabinovitz (eds), *Seeing Through the Media*. New Brunswick, NJ: Rutgers University Press.

Entman, R. (1991) 'Framing US coverage of international news: contrasts in narratives of the KAL and Iran Air incidents', *Journal of Communication*, 41 (4): 6–27.

Entman, R.M. (1989) *Democracy without Citizens. Media and the Decay of American Politics.* Oxford: Oxford University Press.

Entman, R.M. and Bennett, W.L. (2001) 'Communication in the future of democracy', 468–480 in W.L. Bennett and R.M. Entman, *Mediated Politics. Communication in the Future of Democracy.* Cambridge: Cambridge University Press.

Etzioni, A. (1972) 'Minerva: an electronic town hall', *Policy Sciences*, 3: 457–74.

Ewen, S. (1996) *PR! A Social History of Spin.* New York: Basic Books.

Fairbairn, G. (1974) *Revolutionary Guerilla Warfare: The Countryside Version.* Harmondsworth: Penguin.

Fallows, J. (1997) *Breaking the News. How the Media Undermine American Democracy.* New York: Vintage Books.

Fanon, F. (1965) *The Wretched of the Earth.* London: MacGibbon & Kee.

Featherstone, M. (1991) *Consumer Culture and Postmodernism.* London: Sage.

Fiedler, M.R. (2000) *United Nations Peace Operations: Conditions for Success.* Ann Arbour, MI: UMI Dissertation Services.

Flower, K. (1987) *Serving Secretly: Rhodesia's CIO Chief on the Record.* Johannesburg: Galago.

Foucault, M. (1972) *The Archaeology of Knowledge.* London: Tavistock Publications.

Frankel, P.H. (1984) *Pretoria's Praetorians. Civil–Military Relations in South Africa.* Cambridge: Cambridge University Press.

Franklin, B. (1994) *Packaging Politics. Political Communications in Britain's Media Democracy.* London: Edward Arnold.

Franklin, H.B. (1994) 'From realism to virtual reality: images of America's wars', 25–43 in S. Jeffords and L. Rabinovitz (eds), *Seeing Through the Media.* New Brunswick, NJ: Rutgers University Press.

Freedman, L. (2000) 'Victims and victors: reflections on the Kosovo war', *Review of International Studies*, 26 (3): 335–58.

Fukuyama, F. (1989) 'The end of history?', *The National Interest*, Summer: 3–18.

Ganley, G.D. (1992) *The Exploding Political Power of Personal Media.* Norwood, NJ: Ablex.

Gans, C. (1993) 'Television: political participation's enemy #1', *Spectrum*, 66 (2): 26–30.

Garrow, D.J. (1986) *Bearing the Cross. Martin Luther King Jr. and the Southern Christian Leadership Conference.* New York: William Morrow & Co.

Gellner, E. (1983) *Nations and Nationalism.* Oxford: Blackwell.

George, A. (1969) 'The "operational code": a neglected approach to the study of political leaders and decision-making', *International Studies Quarterly*, 13: 190–222.

Gerbner, G., Gross, L., Morgan, M. and Signorelli, N. (1984) 'Charting the mainstream: television's contribution to political orientations', 118–30 in D.A. Graber, *Media Power in Politics.* Washington, DC: CQ Press.

Giliomee, H. and Simkins, C. (1999) *The Awkward Embrace: One-Party Dominance and Democracy.* Amsterdam: Harwood Academic Publishers.

Goffman, E. (1971) *The Presentation of Self in Everyday Life.* Harmondsworth: Penguin.

Goldstein, M.C. (1999) *The Snow Lion and the Dragon. China, Tibet, and the Dalai Lama.* Berkeley, CA: University of California Press.

Graber, D.A. (2001) 'Adapting political news to the needs of twenty-first century Americans', 433–52 in W.L. Bennett and R.L. Entman, *Mediated Politics. Communication in the Future of Democracy.* Cambridge: Cambridge University Press.

Graham, T.W. (1994) 'Public opinion and U.S. foreign policy decision making', in D.A. Deese, *The New Politics of American Foreign Policy.* New York: St Martin's Press.

Gramsci, A. (1971) *Selections from the Prison Notebooks.* London: Lawrence & Wishart.

Grant, M. (1994) *Propaganda and the Role of the State in Inter-War Britain.* Oxford: Clarendon Press.

Greenfeld, L. (1993) *Nationalism. Five Roads to Modernity.* Cambridge, MA: Harvard University Press.

Grossman, L.K. (1995) *The Electronic Republic.* New York: Penguin Books.

Grosswiler, P. (1998) 'The impact of media and images on foreign policy: elite U.S. newspapers editorial coverage of surviving communist countries in the post-cold war era', 195–210 in A. Malek (ed.), *News Media and Foreign Relations. A Multifaceted Perspective*. Norwood, NJ: Ablex.

Grotius, H. de (1922) *De jure belli ac pacis, libri tres*. London: Sweet & Maxwell.

Habermas, J. (1976) *Legitimation Crisis*. London: Heinemann.

Hackett, R.A. (1998) 'The press and foreign policy dissent: the case of the gulf war', 141–60 in A. Malek (ed.), *News Media and Foreign Relations. A Multifaceted Perspective*. Norwood, NJ: Ablex.

Hall, J. (2001) *Online Journalism*. London: Pluto Press.

Hall, S. (1977) 'Culture, the media and the "ideological effect"', 315–48 in J. Curran, M. Gurevitch and J. Woollacott, *Mass Communication and Society*. London: Edward Arnold.

Hall, S. (1980a) 'Recent developments in theories of language and ideology: a critical note', 157–62 in S. Hall, D. Hobson, A. Lowe and P. Willis (eds), *Culture, Media, Language*. London: Hutchinson.

Hall, S. (1980b) 'Encoding/decoding', 128–138 in S. Hall, D. Hobson, A. Lowe and P. Willis (eds), *Culture, Media, Language*. London: Hutchinson.

Hall, S. (1996) 'Who needs identity?', in S. Hall and P. du Gay (eds), *Questions of Cultural Identity*. London: Sage.

Hall, S., Critcher, C., Jefferson, T., Clarke, J. and Roberts, B. (1978) *Policing the Crisis: Mugging, the State, and Law and Order*. London: Macmillan.

Hallin, Daniel C. (1986) *The Uncensored War. The Media and Vietnam*. Oxford: Oxford University Press.

Hallin, D.C. (1994) 'Images of the Vietnam and Persian Gulf wars in US television', in S. Jeffords and L. Rabinovitz (eds), *Seeing Through the Media*. New Brunswick, NJ: Rutgers University Press.

Hartley, J. (1982) *Understanding News*. London: Methuen.

Hartley, J. (1992) *The Politics of Pictures*. London: Routledge.

Haste, C. (1995) 'The Machine of propaganda', 105–36 in R. Jackall (ed.), *Propaganda*. New York: New York University Press.

Hawes, W. (1991) *Television Performing. News and Information*. Boston: Focal Press.

Hawkins, V. (2002) 'The other side of the CNN factor: the media and conflict', *Journalism Studies*, 3 (2): 225–34.

Heck, M.C. (1980) 'The ideological dimension of media messages', 122–27 in S. Hall, D. Hobson, A. Lowe and P. Willis (eds), *Culture, Media, Language*. London: Hutchinson.

Henningham, J. (1988) *Looking at Television News*. Melbourne: Longman Cheshire.

Herman, E. and Chomsky, N. (1988) *Manufacturing Consent*. New York: Pantheon.

Hickey, N. (2002) 'Access denied', *Columbia Journalism Review*, January/February: 26–31.

Hill, K.A. and Hughes, J.E. (1998) *Cyberpolitics: Citizen Activism in the Age of the Internet*. New York: Rowman & Littlefield.

Hoge, J. (1994) 'Media pervasiveness', *Foreign Affairs*, 73: 136–44.

Hollander, R. (1985) *Video Democracy*. Mt Airy, MD: Lomond Publications.

Hoogvelt, A. (1997) *Globalization and the Postcolonial World*. London: Macmillan.

Horowitz, D. (1985) *Ethnic Groups in Conflict*. Berkeley, CA: University of California Press.

Huntington, S.P. (1997) *The Clash of Civilizations and the Remaking of World Order*. New York: Touchstone.

Ingham, B. (1991) *Kill the Messenger*. London: HarperCollins.

Jackall, R. and Hirota, J.M. (1995) 'America's first propaganda ministry: the committee on public information during the Great War', 137–73 in R. Jackall (ed.), *Propaganda*. New York: New York University Press.

Jacobs, S. and Calland, R. (2002) *Thabo Mbeki's World*. Pietermaritzburg: University of Natal Press.

Jamieson, K.H. (1984) *Packaging the Presidency. A History and Criticism of Presidential Campaign Advertising*. Oxford: Oxford University Press.

Jamieson, K.H. (1992) *Dirty Politics. Deception, Distraction, and Democracy*. Oxford: Oxford University Press.

Jenkins, B.M. (1978) 'The study of terrorism: definitional problems', 4–5 in Y. Alexander and J.M. Gleason (eds), *Behavioral and Quantitative Perspectives on Terrorism*. New York: Pergamon Press.

Keane, J. (1991) *The Media and Democracy*. Cambridge: Polity Press.

Kelly, M.J. and Mitchell, T.H. (1981) 'Transnational terrorism and the western elite press', *Political Communication and Persuasion*, 1 (3): 269–96.

Knightley, P. (1982) *The First Casualty*. London: Quartet Books.

Knightley, P. (2002) 'Journalism, conflict and war: an introduction', *Journalism Studies*, 3 (2): 167–74.

Kuhn, T.S. (1970) The *Structure of Scientific Revolutions*. Chicago: University of Chicago Press.

Kuhne, W. (2001) 'From peacekeeping to postconflict peacebuilding', in L. Reychler and T. Paffenholz, *Peacebuilding. A Field Guide*. Boulder, CO: Lynne Rienner.

Laffin, J. (1985) *The War of Desperation: Lebanon 1982–85*. London: Osprey.

Laqueur, W. (1977) *Terrorism*. London: Weidenfeld & Nicolson.

Larsson, L. (2002) 'Journalist and politicians: a relationship requiring a manoeuvring space', *Journalism Studies*, 3 (1): 21–33.

Lash, S. and Urry, J. (1994) *Economies of Signs and Space*. London: Sage.

Le Bon, G. (1922) *The Crowd. A Study of the Popular Mind*. London: T. Fisher Unwin.

Lenin, V.I. (1969) *The State and Revolution. Collected Works*. Moscow: Progress Publishers.

Lerner, D. (1958) *The Passing of Traditional Society*. New York: Free Press.

Lippmann, W. (1965) *Public Opinion*. New York: Free Press.

Lippmann, W. (1985) *Drift and Mastery: An Attempt to Diagnose the Current Unrest*. Madison, WI: University of Wisconsin Press.

Lloyd, C.J. (1988) *Parliament and the Press*. Melbourne: Melbourne University Press.

Locke, J. (1966) *The Second Treatise of Government*. Oxford: Basil Blackwell.

Louw, P.E. (2001) *The Media and Cultural Production*. London: Sage.

Louw, P.E. (2004) *The Rise, Fall and Legacy of Apartheid*. Westport, CT: Praeger.

Louw, P.E. (2005) *New Voices Over the Air. The Transformation of the South African Broadcasting Corporation in a Changing South Africa*. Cresskill, NJ: Hampton Press.

Louw, P.E. and Chitty, N. (2000) 'South Africa's miracle cure: a stage-managed TV spectacular?', 277–96 in A. Malek and A.P. Kavoori (eds), *The Global Dynamics of News Coverage and News Agendas*. Stamford, CA: Ablex.

Louw, P.E. and Tomaselli, K.G. (1991) 'Semiotics of apartheid: the struggle for the sign', *European Journal for Semiotic Studies*, 3 (1–2): 99–110.

Lukes, S. (1974) *Power: A Radical View*. London: Macmillan.

Maarek, P.J. (1995) *Political Marketing and Communication*. London: John Libbey.

MacArthur, J.R. (1992) *Second Front. Censorship and Propaganda in the Gulf War*. New York: Hill & Wang.

MacArthur, J.R. (2003) 'The lies we bought', *Columbia Journalism Review*, May–June: 62–3.

McCuen, J.L. (1966) *Counter Revolutionary Warfare – The Strategy of Counter-insurgency*. London: Faber.

Machiavelli, N. (1975) *The Prince*. Harmondsworth: Penguin.

McNair, B. (1999) *An Introduction to Political Communication* (2nd edition). London: Routledge.

McQuail, D. and Windahl, S. (1981) *Communication Models for the Study of Mass Communication*. New York: Longman.

Malbin, M. (1982) 'Teledemocracy and its discontents', *Public Opinion*, June/July: 58–9.

Malek, A. (1998) '*New York Times*' editorial position and U.S. foreign policy: the case of Iran revisited', 225–46 in A. Malek (ed.), *News Media and Foreign Relations. A Multifaceted Perspective*. Norwood, NJ: Ablex.

Maltese, J.A. (1994) *Spin Control. The White House Office of Communications and the Management of Presidential News* (2nd edition). Chapel Hill, NC: University of North Carolina Press.

Maltese, J.A. (2003) 'The presidency and the new media', in M.J. Rozell, *Media Power. Media Politics*. Lanham, MD: Rowman & Littlefield.

Marcuse, H. (1964) *One-Dimensional Man*. London: RKP.

Marshall, P.D. (1997) *Celebrity and Power*. Minneapolis: University of Minnesota Press.

Masmoudi, M. (1979) 'The new world information order', *Journal of Communication*, 29 (2).

Masuda, Y. (1980) *The Information Society as Post-Industrial Society*. Bethesda, MD: World Future Society.

Mickelson, S. (1989) *From Whistle Stop to Sound Bite*. New York: Praeger.

Mill, J.S. (1986) *On Liberty*. Buffalo, NY: Promethius Books.

Miller, M. (2003) 'A tyranny of symbols', *Columbia Journalism Review*, November/December: 26–33.

Mills, C.W. (1959) *The Power Elite*. Oxford: Oxford University Press.

Mooney, C. (2004) 'The editorial pages and the case for war', *Columbia Journalism Review*, March/April: 28–34.

Mosca, G. (1939) *The Ruling Class*. New York: McGraw Hill.

Mowlana, H. (1998) 'The media and foreign policy: a framework of analysis', 29–42 in A. Malek (ed.), *News Media and Foreign Relations. A Multifaceted Perspective*. Norwood, NJ: Ablex.

Negrine, R. (1994) *Politics and the Mass Media in Britain*. London: Routledge.

Negrine, R. (1996) *The Communication of Politics*. London: Sage.

Nelson, J.S. and Boynton, G.R. (1997) *Video Rhetorics. Televised Advertising in American Politics*. Urbana, IL: University of Illinois Press.

Neuman, W.R. (1991) *The Future of the Mass Audience*. Cambridge: Cambridge University Press.

Newman, B.I. (1994) *The Marketing of the President*. Thousand Oaks, CA: Sage.

Nieburg, H.L. (1969) *Political Violence. The Behavioural Process*. New York: St Martin's Press.

Nimmo, D. and Combs, J.E. (1990) *Mediated Political Realities*. New York: Longman.

Nimmo, D. and Combs, J.E. (1992) *The Political Pundits*. New York: Praeger.

Noelle-Neumann, E. (1991) 'The theory of public opinion: the concept of the spiral of silence', in J.A. Anderson (ed.), *Communication Yearbook 14*. Newbury Park, CA: Sage.

Nordlinger, E. (1981) *On the Anatomy of the Democratic State*. Cambridge, MA: Harvard University Press.

Paletz, D.L. and Entman, R.M. (1982) *Media. Power. Politics*. New York: Free Press.

Pareto, V. (1968) *The Rise and Fall of Elites*. Totowa, NJ: Bedminster Press.

Parker, D. (1990) *The Courtesans. The Press Gallery in the Hawke Era*. Sydney: Allen & Unwin.

Patterson, B. (1997) 'Confessions of a spin doctor', *Public Relations Tactics*, 4/7: 27.

Pessen, E. (1978) *Jacksonian America. Society, Personality and Politics*. Homewood, IL: The Dorsey Press.

Pickering, M. (2001) *Stereotyping. The Politics of Representation*. Basingstoke: Palgrave.

Pinsdorf, M.K. (1994) 'Image makers of desert storm: Bush, Powell and Schwarzkopf', 37–52 in T.A. McCain and L. Shyles, *The 1000 Hour War. Communication in the Gulf*. Westport, CT: Greenwood Press.

Pool, I. (1983) *Technologies of Freedom*. Cambridge, MA: Belknap.

Postman, N. (1985) *Amusing Ourselves to Death. Public Discourse in the Age of Show Business*. New York: Viking Penguin.

Preston, I. (1994) *The Tangled Web They Weave: Truth, Falsity and Advertisers*. Madison, WI: University of Wisconsin Press.

Preston, P.W. (1997) *Political/Cultural Identity. Citizens and Nations in a Global Era*. London: Sage.

Reep, D.C. and Dambrot, F.H. (1989) 'Effects of frequent television viewing on stereotypes: "drip, drip" or "drench"?', *Journalism Quarterly*, 66 (3): 542–50.

Rees, M. and Day C. (1980) *Muldergate. The Story of the Info Scandal*. Johannesburg: Macmillan.

Riddell, P. (1998) 'Members and Millbank: the media and Parliament', 8–17 in J. Seaton (ed.), *Politics and the Media*. Oxford: Blackwell.

Risse-Kappen, T. (1994) 'Masses and leaders: public opinion, domestic structures, and foreign policy', in D.A. Deese, *The New Politics of American Foreign Policy*. New York: St Martin's Press.

Robinson, P. (2002) *The CNN Effect. The Myth of News, Foreign Policy and Intervention*. London: Routledge.

Rock, P. (1981) 'News as eternal recurrence', 64–70 in S. Cohen and J. Young (eds), *The Manufacture of News*. London: Constable.

Rokeach, M. (1960) *The Open and Closed Mind*. New York: Basic Books.

Roshco, B. (1984) 'The evolution of news content in the American press', 7–22 in D.A. Graber, *Media Power in Politics*. Washington, DC: CQ Press.

Rotberg, R.I. and Weiss T.G. (1996) *From Massacres to Genocide. The Media, Public Policy, and Humanitarian Crises*. Cambridge, MA: The World Peace Foundation/Brookings Institute.

Sabato, L.J. (1981) *The Rise of Political Consultants*. New York: Basic Books.

Sabato, L.J. (1989) *Campaigns and Elections. A Reader in Modern American Politics*. Glenview, IL: Scott, Foresman & Co.

Sabato, L.J. (1991) *Feeding Frenzy. How Attack Journalism has Transformed American Politics*. New York: Free Press.

Sabato, L.J., Stencel, M. and Lichter, S.R. (2001) *Peep Show. Media and Politics in an Age of Scandal*. Lanham, MA: Rowman & Littlefield.

Sadkovich, J.J. (1998) *The U.S. Media and Yugoslavia, 1991–1995*. Westport, CT: Praeger.

Sarkesian, S.C. (1975) *Revolutionary Guerilla Warfare*. Chicago: Precedent Publishing.

Scalmer, S. (2002) *Dissent Events. Protest, the Media and the Political Gimmick in Australia*. Sydney: University of New South Wales Press.

Scammell, M. (1995) *Designer Politics. How Elections are Won*. London: Macmillan.

Schlesinger, P., Murdock, G. and Elliot, P. (1983) *Televising 'Terrorism'*. London: Comedia.

Schmid, A.P. and de Graaf, J. (1982) *Violence as Communication. Insurgent Terrorism and the Western News Media*. London: Sage.

Schultz, J. (1998) *Reviving the Fourth Estate*. Cambridge: Cambridge University Press.

Seaton, J. (1998) 'A fresh look at freedom of speech', 117–29 in J. Seaton (ed.), *Politics and the Media*. Oxford: Blackwell.

Seekings, J. (2000) *The UDF*. Athens, OH: Ohio University Press.

Selnow, G.W. (1994) *High-Tech Campaigns. Computer Technology in Political Campaigns*. Westport, CT: Praeger.

Severin, W.J. and Tankard, J.W. (1988) *Communication Theories. Origins, Methods, Uses*. New York: Longman.

Shari'ati, Ali (1980) *Marxism and Other Western Fallacies: An Islamic Critique*. Berkeley, CA: Mizan Press.

Shaw, M. (1996) *Civil Society and Media in Global Crisis. Representing Distant Violence*. London: Pinter.

Simons, M. (1999) *Fit to Print. Inside the Canberra Press Gallery*. Sydney: University of New South Wales Press.

Smith, A.D. (1991) *National Identity*. Reno, NE: University of Nevada Press.

Smith, A.D. (1998) *Nationalism and Modernity*. London: Routledge.

Street, J. (1997) *Politics and Popular Culture*. Cambridge: Polity Press.

Street, J. (2001) *Mass Media, Politics and Democracy*. Basingstoke: Palgrave.

Stuckey, M. (2003) 'Presidential election and the media', in M.J. Rozell, *Media Power. Media Politics*. Lanham, MD: Rowman & Littlefield.

Swanson, D.L. and Mancini, P. (1996) *Politics, Media, and Modern Democracy. An International Study of Innovations in Electoral Campaigning and Their Consequences*. Westport, CT: Praeger.

Tarde, G. (1969) *On Communication and Social Influence: Selected Papers*. Chicago: Chicago University Press.

Taylor, P.M. (1992) *War and the Media. Propaganda and Persuasion in the Gulf War*. Manchester: Manchester University Press.

Taylor, P.M. (1997) *Global Communications, International Affairs and the Media Since 1945*. London: Routledge.

Thompson, J.B. (2000) *Political Scandal. Power and Visibility in the Media Age*. Cambridge: Polity.

Thornton, T.P. (1964) 'Terror as a weapon of political agitation', 71–99 in Harry Eckstein (ed.), *Internal War: Problems and Approaches*. New York: Free Press.

Toffler, A. (1990) *Powershift*. New York: Bantam Books.

Tomaselli, K.G. and Louw, P.E. (1991) *The Alternative Press in South Africa*. Bellville: Anthropos.

Tonnies, F. (1988) *Community and Society*. New Brunswick, NJ: Transaction Books.

Tuchman, G. (1978) *Making News*. New York: Free Press.

Turner, G., Bonner, F. and Marshall, P.D. (2000) *Fame Games. The Production of Celebrity in Australia*. Cambridge: Cambridge University Press.

Underwood, D. (2001) 'Reporting and the push for market-oriented journalism', 99–116 in W.L. Bennett and R.L. Entman, *Mediated Politics. Communication in the Future of Democracy*. Cambridge: Cambridge University Press.

Van den Berghe, P. (1978) 'Race and ethnicity: a sociological perspective', *Ethnic and Racial Studies*, 1 (4): 401–11.

Van Kessel, I. (2000) *Beyond Our Wildest Dreams*. Charlottesville, VA: University Press of Virginia.

Varn, R.J. (1993) 'Electronic democracy: Jeffersonian boom or teraflop?', *Spectrum: the Journal of State Government*, 66 (2): 21–5.

Volkmer, I. (1999) *News in the Global Sphere. A Study of CNN and Its Impact on Global Communication*. Luton: University of Luton Press.

Volosinov, V.N. (1973) *Marxism and the Philosophy of Language*. New York: Seminar Press.

Von Glaserfeld, E. (1995) *Radical Constructivism: A Way of Knowing and Learning*. London: Falmer Press.

Von Klarwill, V. (1924) *The Fugger News-Letter*. S. Edinburgh: T & A Constable.

Vygotsky, L.S. (1978) *Mind in Society*. Cambridge, MA: Harvard University Press.

Watson, D. (2003) *Death Sentence. The Decay of Public Language*. Sydney: Knopf.

Weber, M. (1978) *Economy and Society: An Outline of Interpretive Sociology*. Berkeley, CA: University of California Press.

Westmoreland, W.C. (1980) *A Soldier Reports*. New York: Dell Books.

Wheeler, M. (1997) *Politics and the Mass Media*. Oxford: Blackwell.

Wheeler, N. (2000) *Saving Strangers: Humanitarian Intervention in International Society*. Oxford: Oxford University Press.

White, D. (1950) 'The "gatekeeper": a case study in the selection of news', *Journalism Quarterly*, 41.

Williams, F. (1984) *Dangerous Estate. The Anatomy of Newspapers*. Cambridge: Patrick Stephens.

Williams, P. (1997) *The Victory*. Sydney: Allen & Unwin.

Wood, J.R.T. (1983) *The Welensky Papers. A History of the Federation of Rhodesia and Nyasaland*. Durban: Graham Publishing.

Young, P. and Jesser, P. (1997) *The Media and the Military*. Melbourne: Macmillan.

Index